Service Computing

Service Computing
Concepts, Methods and Technology

Zhaohui Wu
Shuiguang Deng
Jian Wu

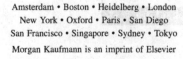

Amsterdam • Boston • Heidelberg • London
New York • Oxford • Paris • San Diego
San Francisco • Singapore • Sydney • Tokyo

Morgan Kaufmann is an imprint of Elsevier

Morgan Kaufmann is an imprint of Elsevier
225 Wyman Street, Waltham, MA 02451, USA

Notices
Knowledge and best practice in this field are constantly changing. As new research and experience broaden
our understanding, changes in research methods, professional practices, or medical treatment may become
necessary.

Practitioners and researchers must always rely on their own experience and knowledge in evaluating and using
any information, methods, compounds, or experiments described herein. In using such information or methods
they should be mindful of their own safety and the safety of others, including parties for whom they have
a professional responsibility.

To the fullest extent of the law, neither the Publisher nor the authors, contributors, or editors, assume any
liability for any injury and/or damage to persons or property as a matter of products liability, negligence or
otherwise, or from any use or operation of any methods, products, instructions, or ideas contained in the
material herein.

ISBN: 978-0-12-802330-3

British Library Cataloguing-in-Publication Data
A catalogue record for this book is available from the British Library

Library of Congress Cataloging-in-Publication Data
A catalog record for this book is available from the Library of Congress

For Information on all MK publications
visit our website at http://mkp.com

Typeset by TNQ Books and Journals
www.tnq.co.in

Printed and bound in the USA

Contents

Preface

Service computing is a cross-discipline that covers the science and technology and represents the promising direction of distributed computing and software development methodology. It aims to bridge the gap between business services and information technology services by supporting the whole life cycle of services innovation. The last 10 years has witness the progress and success from both academic research and industry application.

This book compiles some recent work from the E-service research group of the CCNT (advanCed Computing aNd sysTem) laboratory at Zhejiang University, China. It presents the concept of service computing and proposed a multilayered technical framework for service computing, which divided the main issues of service computing research into four layers from bottom to up: service resource layer, service convergence layer, service application layer, and service system layer. And then it briefly introduces two underneath technologies, i.e., Web services and service-oriented architecture. After that, it presents the research group's latest research findings in the hot topics such as Web service QoS prediction, Web service discovery, service selection, service recommendation, composition, and verification. Some new models and methods are proposed including collaborative filtering-based QoS prediction, behavior-based service discovery, skyline-based service discovery, Bayes-based service recommendation, top-k service composition, type theory-based service formalization and verification, and so on. And also, it discussed three challenging issues of complex service computing, i.e., service computing with big data, with complex mobile environment, and with service pattern model. At last, this book introduces JTang, an underneath platform supporting service computing, which has been widely used in more than seven different areas such as e-business, e-government, public services, and financial industry. This book presents the architecture and components of JTang and gives the details on its core systems such as distributed storage system for big data and distributed service enterprise bus for service integration.

This book would not have been possible without many contributors whose names did not make it to the cover. We would like to give our special thanks to Prof. Jianwei Yin and Prof. Ying Li in our research group, Prof. Li Kuang and Prof. Yuyu Yin who had been affiliated to the CCNT laboratory of Zhejiang University, as well as some Ph.D. candidates in our group including Mr Liang Chen, Mr Longtao Huang, Mr Yuesheng Xu, Mr Wei Luo, Mr Zhiling Luo, and Mr Hongyue Wu. For a long time already, it has been our pleasure to do research with them in service computing. They have devoted their energy and enthusiasm to this area and relevant research projects.

The work in this book was mainly supported by the Natural Science Foundation of China (No. 61170033, No. 61173176, and No. 61272129), the National Key Basic Research Program of China (No. 2013CB329504), the National Technology Support Program (No. 2013BAD19B10 and

No. 2013BAH10F02), the National 863 High-Tech Program (No. 2013AA01A604), and the Zhejiang Provincial Natural Science Foundation of China (LR13F020002).

Zhaohui Wu, Shuiguang Deng, and Jian Wu
Hangzhou, China
October 2014

Introduction

Chapter Outline

Throughout the history of the software industry, each birth of new software development technology and design ideas has triggered a major revolution in the software industry. In the 1960s, the emergence of object-oriented technology was a substantive revolution for structured programming design and analysis. It greatly reduced the complexity and improved the efficiency of software development. In the 1980s, the flourish of software component technology initiated the transformation of the software production mode from workshop production to industrial production. It fundamentally changed the traditional software production mode and brought the software industry into an unprecedented rapid developmental track. Today, with services as the basic elements, service-oriented architecture (SOA) as the guiding principle, and service reuse and service composition as the software design methods, service-oriented computing has become the latest developmental direction in current distributed computing. It is undeniable that service computing is leading the new round wave in software industry development. This chapter mainly focuses on the concept and research framework of service computing, as well as state-of-the-art of service computing both from the industrial and academic perspective.

1.1 Overview

With the development of computer and network technology, modern enterprise is entering an era when enterprise forms are continuously changing, enterprise extensions are being

Service Computing: Concepts, Methods and Technology. http://dx.doi.org/10.1016/B978-0-12-802330-3.00001-1

continuously expanded, enterprise environments are continuously changing, and enterprise businesses are being continuously adjusted. The traditional software development concepts and methods, characterized by "once development" and "continuous usage," are becoming increasingly stale and outdated. How to solve the problem of "on-demand" for enterprise application systems has become an increasing critical issue for the modern software industry. Moreover, it has been the stumbling block that hinders the rapid development of the software industry. Under such circumstances, service computing technology is proposed, as a new kind of computing schema, to resolve this problem.

1.1.1 The Origin of Service Computing

From the time service computing was first proposed, it took only three years' time for service computing to be established as an independent computing discipline. The concept of service computing can be traced back to the International Conference on Internet Computing held in June 2002. In the web service computing track of this conference, service and computing were combined for the first time. The important role that web service played in distributed computing and dynamic business integration was emphasized and widely approved by all experts and scholars at the conference, which laid the foundation for the future promotion of service computing. From that time, service computing has continuously attracted the interests of researchers and industrial giants and has become regarded as the latest development direction of distributed computing. In November 2003, the Technical Community for Service Computing was established by the Institute of Electrical and Electronics Engineers (IEEE). In May 2004, it was renamed the Technical Steering Committee for Service Computing, dedicated to promoting the development of service computing disciplines and creating related standards. This marked the point at which service computing became an independent computing discipline. In September 2004, the first session of the IEEE International Conference on Service Computing was held by the Technical Steering Committee for Service Computing in Shanghai. It was the first global event on service computing. A large number of scholars and experts were attracted, and a large number of research results emerged from this conference. The successful holding of this conference drew wide attention from both academia and industry, greatly promoted the development of service computing discipline, and made service computing become a popular computing discipline.

The reason service computing could rapidly grow and develop in only three years lies in the continuously evolving computing environments. The computing environment consists of a group of computers, software platforms, protocols, and interconnected networks. In this environment, computers and software platforms can exchange data and process information through the network according to the established protocols. The computing environment has transformed from an early centralization mode to a current distribution mode. In this process, it has gone through four stages: mainframe computing environment, client/server computing environment, multilayer distributed computing environment, and service computing environment.

The mainframe computing environment in the 1960s was a completely centralized computing environment, in which the majority of the computing devices and resources were concentrated on the expensive and bulky mainframe. Users could use it only through their dumb terminals, which contained only a display and a keyboard.

In the early 1980s, with the development of hardware technology, especially the large-scale integrated circuit technology, small personal computers began to enter households. Computing devices and resources had been transferred from the central machine rooms with mainframes to households, while the computing environment was still limited to the signal-machine environment. In the middle and late 1980s, with the development of computer networks and the growing popularization of personal computers, the computing environment entered the distributed era. Interoperability and sharing were achieved in this distributed but interconnected computing environment. During this period, the client/server computing environment emerged, in which client computers and server computers were separated. The former are always personal computers or workstations, while the latter are always mainframes, minicomputers, personal computers, and workstations, which provide clients with functions including large-scale data storage, file sharing, printing, key business processing, etc.

In the 1990s, to provide better performance, flexibility, and scalability, a multilayer distributed computing environment was derived from the client/server environment. It realized the separation of the presentation layer, business layer, data layer, etc. However, the computing environments were still built on relatively closed protocols, so they lacked general standardization support. Owing to the more open Internet, especially the continuous application and development of XML and web services technology, the computing environment had evolved into an Internet-oriented service computing environment, which is based on open standards and protocols. In the service computing environment, computing devices and software resources also evolved by showing necessary trends, including both standardization and transparency. This new computing environment needed a new computing technology to support, which led to the environmental foundation for service computing.

The formation of the service computing environment brought new requirements for software architecture and software-development methods. Software architecture refers to the software elements that constitute the software system, the external visible properties of these software elements, and the relationships between these software elements [1]. The ever-changing computing environment that made up the centralized software architecture in the early era of mainframe computing gradually developed into service-oriented software architecture. In the service computing environment, all kinds of computing devices and software resources are highly distributed and autonomous. Variation becomes the essential innate characteristic of this environment. Software systems are facing unprecedented challenges brought about by dynamic elements, the changing environment, and complexity. Service-oriented software architecture is a loose, flexible, scalable, distributed software architecture scheme that is formed to be adapted to the dynamic, distributed, autonomous, and transparent service-computing environment. The formation of service-oriented software architecture lays the most important technical foundation for the formation of a service computing discipline.

Meanwhile, with the variations in the service computing environment and software architecture, the concepts, principles, and methods of a service-oriented software system design and development emerge as required. Every variation in software development methodology had brought significant changes to the software industry. As we know, the birth of component-oriented software development technology initiated the transformation of the software production mode from traditional workshop production to industrial production. Service-oriented software system design and the development approach is the real source power to further promote this transformation and the critical theory and method to complete this transformation. Therefore, the concepts, principles, and methods for service-oriented software system design and development, continuously developed and improved with service-oriented software architecture, provide the basis for the most important methodology foundation for the formation of service computing discipline.

In conclusion, the birth of service computing is the result of the continuously evolving computing environment, software system architecture, and software development methods. It is the inevitable result of further enhanced and accelerated development of the software industry.

1.1.2 The Concept of Service Computing

Although service computing has become a new research hotspot both in current academia and industry, it has not a unified concept. Besides, as it is in a continuously developing process, its definition and connotation are also constantly changing. Experts and scholars have different understandings from different perspectives.

Mike P. Papazoglou, who is from the software system design and development perspective, thinks that "Service computing is a way of developing application systems with services as the basic elements" [2].

Munindar P. Singh and Michael N. Huhns, who are from the application of service technology, think that "Service computing is the set of technologies that combine service concept, service system architecture, service technology and service infrastructure together to guide how to use these services" [3].

Maria E. Orlowska and Sanjiva Weerawarana, who are from the distributed computing perspective, think that "Service computing is a kind of distributed computing paradigm evolved from object-oriented and component-oriented computing. It makes different commercial application systems that are distributed within the enterprises or across the border of enterprises achieving rapid, flexible seamless integration and cooperation" [4].

Liangjie Zhang, who is from the discipline perspective, thinks that "Service computing is a basic discipline that crosses computers, information technology, commercial management and consultation services. Its objective is to use service science and service technology to eliminate the gap between commercial services and information technology services" [5].

The definitions above were formed in different developmental periods of service computing. They focus on different perspectives and do not conflict with each other. To sum up, we think service computing is put forward in terms of the dynamic, versatile, and complex Internet environment. It is a new computing discipline with web service and service-oriented system architecture as the basic supporting technology, service composition as the main software development approach, and service-oriented software analysis and design principles as the basic ideas. Service is the most important core concept in the technical framework of service computing. Note that service here refers to the software entity that is based on the network environment and characterized by adaptive ability, self-description, modularity, and good interoperability, while web service is a specific representative form and function carrier that is in accordance with these requirements.

1.2 Technical Framework of Service Computing

As an independent computing discipline, service computing is established on a series of key technologies, which together form the technical framework of service computing. This framework offers solutions for service computing system design, software development, application integration, and business integration under the dynamic, versatile, and complex Internet environment. It covers technologies including service modeling, service description, service development, service implementation, service management, service discovery, service selection, service recommendation, service composition, service adaptation, service coordination, service validation, service execution, service monitoring, enterprise service bus, etc. These technologies are divided into four layers from bottom to top: service resource layer, service convergence layer, service application layer, and service system layer, shown in Figure 1.1.

Figure 1.1
Technical framework of service computing.

1.2.1 Service Resource Layer

As the bottom layer of the framework, the service resource layer mainly provides the basic standards, techniques, and methods necessary to transform data and software resources to services. This layer mainly solves two problems. The first is to understand the essence of service; namely, what does the service model include? What language should we use to describe service? What are the basic protocols of service? The second is how to implement and use service; namely, how to develop, encapsulate, test, deploy, publish service, etc.? With web service technology and its related standards becoming mature and improved, the industry community has almost reached a common understanding on the essence of service. Web service has become the technical standards of service implementation in the industry community. The corresponding software and systems for service development, testing, deployment, operation, and publication are emerging in an endless stream, which provides solid support for data and software resources to be used as services. However, the discussion about service essence and connotation has never stopped in academia. To enable services to be automatically understood by machines and intelligent agents, so as to realize the automatic service invocation, discovery, and composition, the semantic web service is put forward in academia, which has become a hotspot of current service computing research.

1.2.2 Service Convergence Layer

The service resource layer achieves the service standardization of various heterogeneous software resources. Based on the service resource layer, the service convergence layer further realizes the transformation from fine-grained service to large-grained service. In other words, the service convergence layer offers a series of standards, technologies, and methods for the collaboration of different services and the management of service flows that consist of several services. It covers service integration, service collaboration, service composition, service orchestration and service choreography, service process management, etc.

Service integration and coordination is the technology needed to achieve seamless integration and business collaboration for the remaining business systems within the enterprise or across enterprise boundaries under service computing environments. This technology requires flexibility and scalability. Therefore, compared with traditional point-to-point system integration and message agent-based system integration technology, it can be better adapted to the dynamic versatile business environment.

When a single service cannot meet users' requests, service composition can be used to compose several services to a large-grained composite service with Internal process logic. Service composition is not only an important way to achieve value-added services, but also a basic software development method in the service computing environment. There are two main kinds of service composition schemas, service orchestration and service choreography. The former requires a control center to control the participating services and coordinate the implementation of these services. The services involved do not know that they are parts of the collaborative process, and only the central control center knows how to conduct the collaborative work. In contrast, the service choreographer does not rely on the service control center, and each involved service knows when to perform its operations and with whom to interact [6].

Service flow is the process generated by performing message exchange and logic composition to the related services according to their business processes. It is a new representation form of workflow technology after its combination with service technology [7]. The management of service flow is similar to the traditional workflow, which is also divided into a management in modeling stage and an implementation stage. The former mainly achieves the theoretical modeling and formal definition of service flow, while the latter mainly manages the operation, monitoring, optimization, and analysis of service flow.

1.2.3 Service Application Layer

Through the service resource layer and service convergence layer, various heterogeneous data and software resources are transformed to standard services with different granularity, ensuring services are invoked in a convenient, rapid, and transparent way. The service application layer mainly offers the basic technical and methodology support in the service invocation process. Specifically, it consists of technologies including service invocation, service discovery, service matching, service validation, service adaptation, service monitoring, etc. In the following, we give a brief introduction for several of the key techniques.

Service discovery is an important prerequisite to apply service technologies. It uses service discovery algorithms to search services from the service registry according to the users' functional and nonfunctional needs and constraints. Service recommendation is a proactive service-discovery technique, which proactively recommends services to users according to users' preferences.

Service matching and service discovery are closely related, and the latter is always based on the former. In particular, service discovery matches user's' specific requirements with the description of the services in the registry, and then selects the matched service. Therefore, service matching can be viewed as an important step for service discovery.

Service verification aims to examine whether the semantic, function, and behavior of the service is in accordance with the requirements of the user, intelligent agent, or system before invoking the service. Its objective is to reduce the possibility of service misuse and ensure that only appropriate services are invoked. Service verification also includes testing the correctness of the composite flow of the component services.

Service adaptation is used when the service cannot fully satisfy the requirements of the user. It establishes corresponding adapters between target services and customer services, intelligent agents, or systems to solve problems including interface mismatch, parameter mismatch, or behavior mismatch, thus resolving the problems that the service cannot successfully invoke.

Service trust aims to comprehensively evaluate services, including service function, service quality, service ability, service security, etc., thus comprehensively evaluating the availability and reliability of the services.

The service application layer links the service resource layer and service convergence layer. It offers important technical support for the service resource layer to realize integrity and collaboration. The technologies involved in this layer are the most popular technologies in current service computing research and development.

1.2.4 Service System Layer

Based on the technology of the service application layer, the service system layer is a set of standards, techniques, and methods to guide the design, development, operation, and management of service-oriented software systems under the service-oriented computing environment. It includes the SOA, enterprise service bus, and service system engineering.

SOA is a loosely coupled framework, which is used to guide the design of service-oriented software systems [8]. It ends the 40-year dominance of the current centralized software architecture and becomes the most fashionable and popular distributed system architecture. It has already been sought after by the industry enterprise giants. A series of related reference implementation, standards, tools, and platform software are emerging in an endless stream. Gartner, a globally famous IT research and analysis organization, predicts that by 2010, more than 80% of the enterprises will adopt SOA. Furthermore, some scholars and experts believe that the previous 10 years witnessed the achievements of the giants including Microsoft, IBM, Oracle, etc.; while looking toward the future, SOA is undoubtedly the most competitive technique that will become the software overlord. From that, we can see how immensely SOA influences the future of the software industry. Just because of that, the continuous maturity of SOA makes service computing, as a computing discipline, gradually acknowledged.

Service system dynamic configuration is a kind of management and maintenance technique that has been built based on service in application systems. With users' requests or system environment changes, it can use a series of configuration policies and methods to ensure that the service system can continue to provide services. When a service with higher quality is required, or some component services of the system are not accessible, the service system dynamic configuration can dynamically replace it by seeking a better service or the candidate's service without a machine halt. Therefore, this technology is an important way to improve the reliability and robustness of service systems.

Enterprise service bus (ESB) is an important message transmission technology that supports and realizes SOA. It is the product of the combination of traditional middleware technology and technologies including XML and web service, etc. ESB supports interaction between services, messages, and events in heterogeneous environments. Therefore, it can achieve an accurate, efficient, and safe transmission of different messages and information between enterprise applications and services. Therefore, it plays a backbone role in the integration of enterprise information systems [9].

Currently, ESB receives significant attention from the enterprise giants in the service computing technology system. These giants have launched their own implementation standards and software platforms. For example, Sun proposes JBI (Java Business

Integration) [10], which provides an ESB implementation reference scheme based on Java technology. For another example, IBM proposes the WebSphere Enterprise Service Bus [11], which is an ESB product executed under the J2EE environment.

A service system project is a set of methods that guide service-oriented software system planning, design, development, implementation, deployment, operation, and management. It covers a full life-cycle service system process including requirement analysis, theoretical modeling, system design, development testing, operation management, implementation, and maintenance. Currently, the research and practice on service system engineering is still in its infancy, and the relevant theories and methods are still being continuously developed and improved.

1.3 The State-of-the-Art of Service Computing

The rapid development of service computing is the result of the joint efforts of industry and academia. Industry mainly focuses on setting relevant technical standards and developing various supporting software tools and platforms, while academia focuses on service computing discipline construction, theoretical innovation, and methodology research.

1.3.1 The State-of-the-Art in Industry

The industry is the source power that promotes the generation and development of service computing. It is the strong demand for "on-demand" software systems that creates the most important supporting technologies in the web service system, such as web service technology and SOA. We can view the current development of service computing in industry from the standardization organizations and enterprise giants.

In terms of standardization organizations, the World Wide Web Consortium (W3C) and Organization for the Advancement of Structured Information Standards (OASIS) are active in the specification and standardization construction of a service computing technology system.

W3C is a non-profit organization founded by Tim Berners-Lee, the father of the world wide web, in October 1994 at the computer science laboratory of Massachusetts Institute of Technology. It is dedicated to creating web-related technical standards and promoting the development of web technology [12]. Focusing on basic technology of service computing, especially web service technology, this organization has founded several work groups, covering web service description, web services architecture, web services strategy, web services choreography, web services semantic annotation, etc. Through its efforts, several important service computing technology standards were developed, such as Web Services Description Language (WSDL), Simple Object Access Protocol (SOAP), and Web Services Choreography Description Language (WS-CDL).

OASIS, founded is 1993, is dedicated to promoting the development, integration, popularization, and application of e-business standards. It is the organization that has developed the most standards in the current service computing technology area [13]. It has founded several technical committees for service computing technology, covering service safety, reliability, quality, transaction, trust and flow, etc. Moreover, it has developed a series of important standards, such as Universal Description, Discovery, and Integration standard (UDDI), Business Process Execution Language (WS-BPEL), Service Component Architecture (SCA), and Service Data Object (SDO).

The continuous efforts of these two major standardization organizations have developed a series of basic specifications and standards in the past several years, which laid the foundation for the application of service computing-related technologies. However, with the further promotion and application of service computing, the standardization requirements, such as service coordination, service security, service transactions, and service trust, become particularly critical. Therefore, the standardization work will be continued in the future.

The continuous improvement of specifications and standards of service computing technology makes it popular for enterprise giants to develop service computing middleware. Many famous software giants, such as IBM, Microsoft, BEA, and SAP, turned to service computing technologies represented by web services technology and SOA. They developed corresponding supporting tools, software, and system platforms, such as WebSphere at IBM, BizTalk at Microsoft, AquaLogic at BEA, and NetWeaver at SAP, which all helped with supporting the rapid application and implementation of service computing technology. These middleware products became important weapons for software giants to attract users and partition the software market.

Meanwhile, some Chinese middleware manufacturers have gradually realized the important influence of service computing technology to the future software industry. They began to invest in service computing-related software technology platforms and started to apply and implement service computing technologies in industries including e-government, telecommunication, tobacco, etc. Among them, some influential technology platforms and solutions include the SOA application platform EOS and SOA process platform BPS of Shanghai Puyuan, SOA solution Apusic of Kingdee that integrates Portal, ESB, integrated components, and development tools, and service-oriented middleware management product UFIDA of U9. Among them, it is worth mentioning that Shanghai Puyuan, a burgeoning middleware technology manufacturer, is the only Chinese enterprise that is involved in the development of international service computing technology standards. It successfully held "SOA China Technology Forum" several times in several Chinese cities and played a positive role in the application and promotion of service computing technology in China.

1.3.2 The State-of-the-Art in Academia

Service computing as an independent computing discipline has received high attention from academia and become a popular research topic for various experts and scholars. In recent years, major academic organizations and research institutes have founded multiple service computing and technology-themed academic journals, such as *IEEE Transactions on Service Computing*, *International Journal of Web Services Research*, *Service Oriented Computing and Applications*, and *International Journal of Web Services Practices*. Meanwhile, some important international conferences focusing on service computing also emerged, such as the International Conference on Service-Oriented Computing (ICSOC), IEEE International Conference on Web Services (ICWS), and IEEE International Conference on Service Computing (SCC). In China, the China Computer Federation (CCF) established the Technical Committee of Service Computing in 2010, which holds a national conference on service computing every year to promote the development of Chinese service computing science and industry and strengthen international exchanges and cooperation in this field. The two leading computer journals, *Chinese Journal of Computers* and *Journal of Software*, have several times organized special issues on service computing, which have drawn wide attention from Chinese researchers. In the journals and conferences mentioned above, a large number of research results are produced every year. These results cover theories, methods and techniques in the service model, service language, service technology, service method, service engineering, etc., and they have greatly promoted the development of the service computing discipline. In the following, the academic institutions and research organizations active in service computing research will be briefly introduced.

The Information Laboratory at Netherland University (Infolab) [14] is one of the earliest research organizations that advocated service computing. Researchers, represented by Mike P. Papazoglou, extended the standard SOA and presented an xSOA system. Based on the xSOA system, they proposed an SOC Research Road Map and defined the research scope, research content, and research direction of service computing. This research roadmap has received very good acknowledgments from various researchers. It is one of the research results that has been cited most often in the service computing field.

The Intelligent Software Agent Lab at Carnegie Mellon University in the United States [15] proposed the concept of semantic web service and introduced it into service computing technology. It is the major power for developing and promoting the first semantic web service description language, DAML-S (the predecessor of OWL-S). This lab proposed the first DAML-S-based semantic web service matching algorithm and matching tools in 2002, and hence set off a research boom of semantic-based service discovery technology.

The Large Scale Distributed Information Systems Laboratory at the University of Georgiain the United States [16] focuses on applying semantic technology to service annotation, Quality of Service (QoS) description, service discovery, service composition, and service process management in its under development project, METEOR-S. They proposed the concept of a semantic web process and realized a semantic-based service discovery architecture and service composition framework. In addition, the WSDL-based lightweight semantic web service description language WSDL-S, developed by this laboratory and IBM, has greatly promoted the development and application of semantic web service.

The Service Oriented Computing Group at the University of New South Wales, Australia [17], is committed to the research of rapid service composition and execution in its early SELF-SERV project. Researchers represented by Boualem Benatallah proposed a service flow implementation scheme based on Peer-to-Peer. After that, this group produced many influential research results in the QoS of service and service composition, service coordination adaptation, service trust management, and service computing in the mobile environment, etc. Due to these contributions, it has become an influential research group in the current service computing area.

The Grid and Service Computing Research Center at the Institute of Computing Technology, Chinese Academy of Sciences [18], is the first team that worked on the research of grid and service computing in China. The service grid platform VINCA, developed by this center, can support on-demand and real-time service integration and business systems construction. It has been applied in e-government and enterprise information management. This platform proposes an integration methodology system CAFISE, which can support dynamic integration of service resources, and on-demand construction of business applications. In addition, it can provide a corresponding development tool set and business side programming language under a service computing-oriented open environment VINCA and realize rapid and real-time business application construction for business users.

The Middleware Technology and Engineering Research Center at the College of Computer Science and Technology, Zhejiang University [19], is dedicated to the research of basic middleware technology. The JTang middleware platform, produced by this center, provides a series of methodology and tool support for the application and implementation of service computing technology, including basic methods such as semantic-based service discovery methods, backward tree-based automatic service composition methods, and pi calculus-based service verification methods. It also provides basic tools, including the service component development environment, visualized service community, distributed enterprise service bus, etc. These methods and tools can help users quickly design, develop, operate, maintain, and manage large-scale distributed service systems.

1.4 Organization

This book comprehensively introduces the concept of service computing and the related technologies, methods, and platforms. It is divided into 10 chapters. The contents of each chapter are briefly introduced as follows:

Chapter 1 discusses the origins, concepts, and technical framework of service computing. It also introduces the current development of service computing in the fields of industry and academia, both at home and aboard.

Chapter 2 presents the fundamental technologies of service computing: web service and SOA. The relevant standards of web service and semantic web service are particularly introduced. As for SOA, the reference models and two important supporting standards, service component architecture and service data object, are presented.

In Chapters 3–9, the key technologies of service QoS prediction, service discovery, service selection, service recommendation, service composition, service verification, and complex service computing issues are introduced.

Chapter 10 introduces the JTang middleware platform, which was developed by the authors' research group to support service computing.

References

[1] L. Bass, P. Clements, R. Kazman, Software Architecture in Practice, second ed., Addison-Wesley Professional, Boston, 2003.
[2] M.P. Papazoglou, D. Georgakopoulos, Introduction to a special issue on service-oriented computing, Commun. ACM 46 (10) (2003) 24–28.
[3] Munindar P. Singh, Michael N. Huhns, Service-Oriented Computing: Semantics, Processes, Agents, John Wiley & Sons, Ltd, 2005.
[4] Maria E. Orlowska, Sanjiva Weerawarana, et al. (Eds.), Proceeding of First International Conference on Service-Oriented Computing, Springer, 2003.
[5] Liangjie Zhang, Jia Zhang, Hong Cai, Service Computing, Springer, 2007.
[6] C. Peltz, Web services orchestration and choreography, Computer 36 (10) (2003) 46–52.
[7] S.G. Deng, Z.H. Wu, K. Li, C. Lin, Y.P. Jin, Z.W. Chen, Management of serviceflow in a flexible way, Int. Conf. Web Info. Syst. Eng. (2004) 428–438.
[8] Dirk Krafzig, Karl Banke, Dirk Slama, Enterprise SOA: Service-Oriented Architecture Best Practices, Prentice Hall, 2004.
[9] M.T. Schmidt, B. Hutchison, P. Lambros, R. Phippen, The enterprise service bus: making service-oriented architecture real, IBM Syst. J. 44 (4) (2005) 781–797.
[10] Ron Ten-Hove, Peter Walker, Java™ Business Integration (JBI) 1.0, Sun Microsystems, 2005.
[11] http://www-01.ibm.com/software/integration/wsesb/.
[12] http://www.w3.org/.

[13] http://www.oasis-open.org/.

[14] http://infolab.uvt.nl/.

[15] http://www.cs.cmu.edu/∼softagents/.

[16] http://lsdis.cs.uga.edu/.

[17] http://selfserv.web.cse.unsw.edu.au/.

[18] http://vega.ict.ac.cn/.

[19] http://middleware.zju.edu.cn.

CHAPTER 2

Service-Oriented Architecture and Web Services

Chapter Outline

Service Computing: Concepts, Methods and Technology. http://dx.doi.org/10.1016/B978-0-12-802330-3.00002-3

2.1 Web Services

2.1.1 Overview of Web Services

A web service is a software system designed to support interoperable machine-to-machine interaction over a network. It has an interface described in a machine-processable format (specifically WSDL). Other systems interact with the web service in a manner prescribed by its description using SOAP messages, typically conveyed using HTTP with an XML serialization in conjunction with other web-related standards. [1]

A web service is a concrete manifestation and function carrier of the concept of service computing. It is a kind of application, based on a web environment, that is adaptive, self-describing, and modular and has good interoperability. However, different organizations for the web service concept and its connotation may create different understanding and awareness.

IBM believes that a web service should use XML to describe a group of messaging through XML for its operation, but these operations can be accessed via the network and still meet the target task. The description of the service provides all the details of what is necessary to interact with the service, including message formats, transport protocols, and location.

Microsoft thinks that a web service is an application logic unit providing data and services to other applications. The application accesses the web service by the ubiquitous web service protocols and data formats, such as HTTP, XML, and Simple Object Access Protocol (SOAP), and it does not need to care about how to implement each web service.

SUN thinks that a web service is a software component that has the features of being discoverable, reusable, and re-combinable, solving the problems or requirements of users.

W3C thinks that a web service is a system supporting interoperability interaction through the network. It uses the Web Services Description Language (WSDL) to describe the service interface and uses the SOAP message based on HTTP protocol to implement the implementation between the service and the service and customer communication.

Each view above emphasizes some parts of a web service, and there are no conflicts. By combining the above views, we think that the biggest characteristics of a web service lies in its interoperability and reusability. The interoperability makes the web service become a kind of attractive adhesive, used for seamless integration of heterogeneous applications and systems; and the feature of reuse makes the web service a good carrier to convert a software to service. Compared with other software entities, a web service has the following features:

- Can be described: A web service can be described by a service description language.
- Can be released: A web service can be registered in the registering center and released.
- Can be found: The user can send a search request to a registering center to find the service and the access information.
- Can be bound: The web service description information can be bound with a runable service instance or service proxy.
- Can be called: A web service can be called by remote code with the description information.
- Can be composited: The web services can be composited together to a large granularity service.

In recent years, web service technology went through a long development period and formed the web service protocol stack as shown in Figure 2.1, with service communication, service description, service quality, and service processes. We can divide the development process into two parts: the web service foundation protocol developing

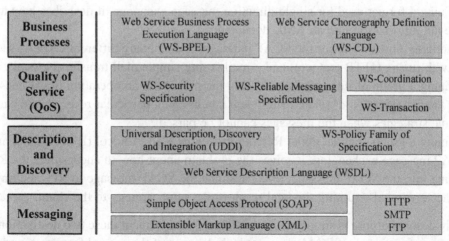

Figure 2.1
Web service protocol stack.

period and the web service high-level protocol developing period. The first period completed the foundation protocols, such as SOAP [2], Web Service Description Language (WSDL) [3], and Universal Description, Discovery and Integration (UDDI) [4]. In this period, the majority of the research in technology was about service developing, testing, calling, and other basic problems. The second period completed the high-level protocols, such as Business Process Execution Language (BPEL) [5], Web Service Choreography Language (WS-CDL) [6], and Web Service Choreography Interface (WSCI) [7]. The technologies were about service interaction and cooperation. Now we are in the second period, and the service composition, service process management, service interaction, and service adoption are the hot topics. The concept of web service totally satisfies the definitions in service-oriented computing (SOC) and service-oriented architecture (SOA). Web service technology is thought to be the best for supporting SOC and SOA.

2.1.2 Basic Standards of Web Services

With the development of standards and protocols, web service computing has stepped into the mature period. The basic standards include SOAP, WSDL, and UDDI.

2.1.2.1 Simple Object Access Protocol

SOAP is a light protocol used in the distribution environment to exchange information, which was published by W3C in 1999. SOAP 1.0 is based totally on the HTTP protocol, while SOAP 1.1 published in May 2000 supports several different transport protocols. The latest version is SOAP 1.2, which was published in July 2001 by W3C.

SOAP is a no-state single-direction message exchange protocol, containing the following four aspects:

1. Defining a format used for single-direction message exchange, it describes how to organize the information into an XML document.
2. Describing how to transfer the SOAP message, it uses many different carriers, such as the web (using HTTP protocol) and e-mail (using simple mail transfer protocol).
3. Defining a group of rules compiled within the process of an operating SOAP message and the classification of related entities; it can assign a particular receiver and can handle strategies when the messages cannot be parsed.
4. Defining a group contract about Remote Procedure Call Protocol (RPC) calling and SOAP message exchanging, it solves the problem about how to encapsulate the RPC calling into the SOAP message, re-encapsulate the SOAP message to RPC, calling back to the server and returning the final result in the same strategy to the client.

The main design purpose is simple and extendable. To implement these two destinations, the core message framework of SOAP does not include some of the normal features found in other distribute systems, e.g., reliability, security, and Message Exchange Patterns (MEPs).

A SOAP message consists of a SOAP envelope, encoding rules, RPC representation, and a SOAP binding.

1. SOAP envelope: SOAP protocol is based on message exchange. Each message can be thought of as an envelope with some data information inside. A SOAP envelope contains two parts, the header and the body. Each part can also be divided into low levels. The header is optional, while the body is necessary. In most situations, some information that is not related to an application, such as cooperation information, signal, and a security certificate, is put in the head. We can also assign the particular operator and detailed operation. A SOAP message body contains the data related to the application. The errors that happen in message parsing are also reported in the message body.
2. SOAP encoding rules: The rules define a data coding mechanism to declare the data type used in the application. It follows the XML structure and data-type definition, including simple types (e.g., integer and string) and some complex types (e.g., structure and array).
3. SOAP RPC representation: It defines how to express the calling and replying of the remote process. In most situations, a SOAP RPC contains following information:
    a. The node address of the SOAP destination
    b. The name of the called method
    c. The parameters and returned information
    d. The web resource identification of the real destination of the RPC calling
    e. Message exchanging pattern
    f. The information included in the SOAP head (optional).
4. SOAP binding: It defines which low-level transmission protocol is used to imply the SOAP message exchange.

The following is an example using SOAP to represent a notification message:

```
<env:Envelope xmlns:env=http://www.w3.org/2003/05/soap-envelope>
<env:Header>

    <n:notification xmlns:n="http://www.jtang.org/notification">
      <n:priority>1</n:priority>
      <n:expires>2008-12-11T15:30:00</n:expires>
    </n:notification>
</env:Header>
<env:Body>

  <m:meetingnotify xmlns:m="http://www.jtang.org/meetingnotify">
      <m:msg>We have a meeting at 4pm.</m:msg>
  </m:meetingnotify>
</env:Body>
</env:Envelope>
```

This message is used to express a simple meeting notification. The SOAP head describes the priority and expiration time of this message. The SOAP body describes the detailed message content, which is to notify each participant that the meeting will be held at 4 pm.

There are four request methods in an HTTP protocol: GET, POST, DELETE, and PUT. SOAP can use the first two methods. When using the GET method, the request from the client is not a SOAP message, but the server returns a SOAP message. When using a POST method, both the request and response are a SOAP message. For a SOAP message using HTTP, the Multi-Purpose Internet Mail Extensions (MIME) type of the HTTP head should be set as text/xml to indicate that this HTTP content is an XML document.

The following is an example of an HTTP response message:

```
HTTP/1.1 200 OK
Content-Type: text/xml; charset="utf-8"
Content-Length: nnnn
<env:Envelope xmlns:env=http://www.w3.org/2003/05/soap-envelope>
<env:Body>
        <m:meetingresponse xmlns:m="http://www.jtang.org/meetingresonse">
        <m:delay>20</m:delay>
        <m:persion>Joe</m:person>
        </m:meetingresponse>
</env:Body>
</env:Envelope>
```

This message is a response for the meeting notification, expressing that the participant Joe will be late by 20 min.

2.1.2.2 Web Service Description Language

WSDL is language used to describe web service and explain how to communicate with the web service. It was introduced in common by Ariba, Intel, and Microsoft. WSDL 2.0, the latest version, has been promoted as a recommended standard by W3C.

WSDL describes a web service from two different levels, abstract level and concrete level.

In the abstract level, WSDL describes a web service by describing sending/receiving messages. The messages are described by an XML schema. The operation composites the messages by a message exchange pattern. The message exchange pattern points out the sequence of send/receive messages and the send and receive logic. The interface organizes the operation independently with protocol and formats.

In a concrete level, the binding points out the protocol and formats for the interface. The endpoint associates the network address with the binding. The service organizes the endpoints related to the same interface.

A WSDL 2.0 document contains the following elements:

- Type: <types> element defines the data type used in the web service. To keep the standard independent with the platform, the XML schema grammar is used to define the data type and data structure.
- Message: The message reference component includes the message reference, direction, and message. The message reference points out the message pattern. The message data is defined by <types>. When using a SOAP binding, a WSDL document element is corresponding to the body of a SOAP message, and this process is automatic.
- Operation: <operation> defines the set of messages. The message exchange pattern determines the order of the message process. The optional message exchange patterns include: IN-ONLY, ROBUST IN ONLY, IN-OUT, IN-MULTI-OUT, OUT-ONLY, ROBUST OUT-ONLY, OUT-IN, ASYNCHRONOUS OUT-IN, and OUT-MULTI-IN.
- Interface: <interface> is the abstract description of the web service, which contains neither the detailed address nor the transmission protocol. The interface, which is an inheritance, can reuse the operations of the existing interfaces. It replaces the <portType> in WSDL 1.1.
- Binding: <binding> element describes the detailed message format and transmission protocol. The binding is either general or used for a particular interface. It is possible to define a binding for the interface or a detailed operation in the interface. WSDL 2.0 defined the binding for HTTP, SOAP, and MIME.
- Endpoint: <endpoint> element associates the network address with a detailed binding. It replaces <port> in WSDL 1.1.
- Service: <service> element groups the endpoint related to a particular interface.

The relation between elements is shown in Figure 2.2. The following is an example of a WSDL segment of a web service:

```
<interface name="PriceInterface">
 <operation name="getPrice" pattern="http://www.w3.org/ns/wsdl/in-out">
  <input messageLabel="getPriceRequest" element="tns:request"/>
  <output messageLabel="getPriceResponse" element="tns:response"/>
 </operation>
</interface>
<binding name="PriceInterfaceHttpBinding" interface="tns:PriceInterface"
type="http://www.w3.org/ns/wsdl/http">
</binding>
<service name="PriceService" interface="tns:PriceInterface">
 <endpoint name="PriceServiceHttpEndpoint" Binding="tns:PriceInterfaceHttpBinding"
Address="http://www.jtang.org/price/">
</service>
```

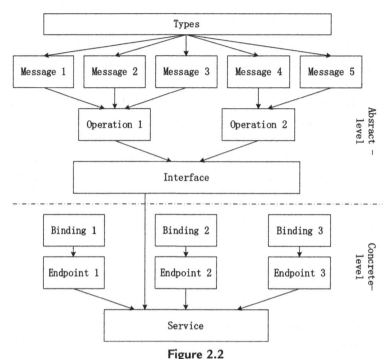

Figure 2.2
The Web Service Description Language document elements.

In this example, interface "PriceInterface" is defined. It contains an operation "getPrice."
"getPrice" owns an input message named "getPriceRequest" and an output message named
"getPriceResponse." The message exchange pattern is IN-OUT. "PriceInterface" is bound
on "PriceInterfaceHttpBinding." Endpoint "PriceServiceHttpEndpoint" associates
"PriceInterfaceHttpBinding" with the service address http://www.jtang.org/price.

2.1.2.3 Universal Description, Discovery and Integration

For a web service provider, it does not make sense if a service cannot be easily found and
used by the user. UDDI standard provides an agency for building the bridge between
service providers and service users to make it easy to find and discover the web service.
UDDI was created by 33 companies, including Ariba, IBM, and Microsoft, and the latest
version is UDDI 3.0.2.

UDDI standard aims in providing an implication of foundation architecture, including
service providers (companies and organizations) releasing service in this platform
and service users searching and getting complete information about the services.
UDDI is built on a series of existing standards, including HTTP, XML, XML Schema, and
SOAP.

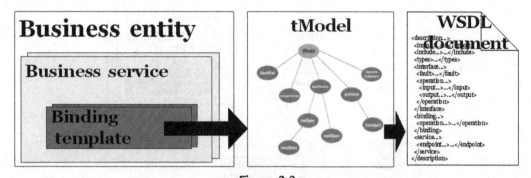

Figure 2.3
Universal Description, Discovery and Interface data types relationship.

- Business entity: the companies and organizations providing services.
- Business service: the service list.
- Binding template: tech-information describing particular service.
- tModel: used to store the reuse elements, including web service type and protocols.

The core component of UDDI is the UDDI business registration. It uses an XML document to describe the company and its web services. The UDDI registering center has four main data types. Figure 2.3 presents the relationship between these data types.

Based on the abovementioned data types, UDDI has the ability to describe companies and services. Generally, the registration information can be divided into three classes:

- White page information: the basic company information including company name, description of business scope, contact information, and contactors.
- Yellow page information: the classification information based on UNSPSC (universal standard products and services classification) or ISO 3166 state codes.
- Green page information: the technology information about how to use a web service, including how to refer to the WSDL description file and other technical standards. The information is not stored in the UDDI registration center.

Generally, a business entity has stored the white and yellow page information. Each business entity has a unique identification code, businessKey, which is pointed to when the business entity was created in the UDDI registration center. A business Key is a point to a particular business entity, and this index relationship is available in the context of the registration center. As shown in Figure 2.3, a business entity can own many business services. UDDI permits a service register to belong to other service providers.

A business service represents a web service or a group of related web services (these web services should be provided by the same business entity). A business service contains many binding templates.

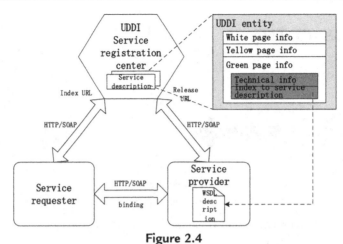

Figure 2.4

Universal Description, Discovery and Interface (UDDI) working diagram.

The binding template is used to bind the description of the web service in a logic level to the concrete solution. A business service can have many binding templates.

The binding template describes the concrete implementation of the web service, including the web service network address and technologies. It also contains a group of tModels.

The tModel is a general container to express information, which can envelope technical information within it, such as interface implementations.

Figure 2.4 presents the detailed role and its interaction with other models of UDDI in the web service architecture. UDDI uses HTTP protocol and SOAP protocol to communicate with the service requester and service provider. At first, the service provider should create a business entity representing itself and provide some basic information. Then, the service provider releases and registers its service in the UDDI service registration center. This service description should be placed so it belongs to the provider's business entity. When a service requester uses UDDI searching, it is using this service description that helps to understand how to locate and call this service. So far, UDDI has finished its work. With the help of UDDI, a binding relationship is built between the service provider and the service requester. After that, the service requester can begin calling information from the description.

2.1.3 Web Services Security

More and more companies are beginning to use web service to provide functions through their network to their customers and partners. This is because the message exchanged when calling a service usually contains some business data, and it is secure. Therefore, the message should not be illegally cut out or modified in the process of network transmission.

OASIS organizes a series of standards, including WS-Security [8], WS-Policy [9], WS-Trust [10], etc. These standards construct a web service security protocol clan to solve the problem of service security.

2.1.3.1 WS-Security

WS-Security, an extension on the SOAP protocol, aims at adding a security token in the SOAP head to strengthen the message integrity and security [8]. This standard helps to ensure the security of the message source and the integrity of the message. Besides, it can ensure that the security message will not be cut out of the third party. WS-Security, which is quite flexible, can be used in SOAP 1.1 and SOAP 1.2. It supports many security tokens and encryption techniques.

The structure of a SOAP message head with WS-Security is shown as follows:

```
<?xml version="1.0" encoding="utf-8"?>
  <soapenv:Envelope>
  <soapenv:Header>
    ......
    <wsse:Security>
    ......
    </wsse:Security>
    ......
  </soapenv:Header>
  <soapenv:Body>
    ......
    <xenc:EncryptedData>
    ......
    </xenc:EncryptedData >
    ......
  </soapenv:Body>
  </soapenv:Envelope>
```

- <soapenv:Envelope>: the start and end signal of a SOAP message.
- <wsse:Security>: contains three parts, the security token for identification, the signature information, and key information.

WS-Security standards define four optional types for a security token: user/password, binary, XML, and token reference. The simplest way is to use the user/password token. In WS-Security, <UsernameToken> is used to verify the user name and password.

```
<wsse:UsernameToken>
<wsse:Username>JTang</wsse:Username>
<wsse:Password>mY5ecRet</wsse:Password>
</wsse:UsernameToken>
```

In message integrity, WS-Security ensures that the message will only be modified by using the XML signature and the security token. This mechanism supports many kinds of signatures and even the extensions to more signatures. Besides, the signature can also prove the availability of the token.

In security, WS-Security uses XML encryption and a security token to ensure its safety.

2.1.3.2 WS-Policy

WS-Policy describes how to extend the WSDL language to create a policy that describes the needs, preference, and performance. This standard contains a policy assertion, policy alternative, and policy.

- Policy assertion is the atomic unit of the policy, which defines a behavior describing the need, function, and other properties of the policy.
- Policy alternative is a set (can be empty) consisting of policy assertions. It can contain 0, 1, or more policy assertions.
- Policy is a set consisting of policy alternatives. It can contain 0, 1, or more policy alternatives.

The policy based on XML in WS-Policy has the following structure:

```
<wsp:Policy...>
  <wsp:ExactlyOne>
    <wsp:All>
      ...
    </wsp:All>
    <wsp:All>
      ...
    </wsp:All>
  </wsp:ExactlyOne>
</wsp:Policy>
```

Policy assertion is included in the policy operators (wsp:Policy, wsp:ExactlyOne, wsp:All). The following example describes a policy expression:

```
<wsp:Policy xmlns:sp=http://docs.oasis-open.org/ws-sx/ws-securitypolicy/200702
xmlns:wsp="http://www.w3.org/ns/ws-policy">
  <wsp:ExactlyOne>
   <wsp:All>
    <sp:SignedParts>
     <sp:Body/>
    </sp:SignedParts>
   </wsp:All>
   <wsp:All>
    <sp:EncryptedParts>
     <sp:Body/>
    </sp:EncryptedParts>
   </wsp:All>
  </wsp:ExactlyOne>
</wsp:Policy>
```

2.1.3.3 WS-Trust

WS-Trust is a web service security standard used for handling role and token identification. This standard is based on the security message exchange of WS-Security and extends the token exchange to implement the password and the digital token of different trusty domains.

WS-Trust defines a web service security model, in which the service can ask for a security token from the service requester to prove that the requester satisfies the conditions (safety, priority) set by the service provider. This security token can be described by a WS-Policy or WS-Policy attachment. If the requester cannot provide this security token, the service can ignore or reject this request. The following is an example of a request of X.509 v3:

```xml
<?xml version="1.0" encoding="utf-8"?>
<soapenv:Envelope xmlns:soapenv="..." xmlns:wsse="..." xmlns:wsu="...">
   <soapenv:Header>
    <wsse:Security>
     <wsse:UsernameToken wsu:Id="x509cert">
      <wsse:Username>JTang</wsse:Username>
      <wsse:Password>mY5ecRet</wsse:Password>
     </wsse:UsernameToken>
    </wsse:Security>
   </soapenv:Header>
  <soapenv:Body>
   <wsse:RequestSecurityToken>
    <wsse:TokenType>wsse:X509v3</wsse:TokenType>
    <wsse:RequestType>wsse:ReqIssue</wsse:RequestType>
    <wsse:Base>
     <wsse:Reference URI="# x509cert"/>
    </wsse:Base>
   </wsse:RequestSecurityToken>
  </soapenv:Body>
</soapenv:Envelope>
```

If the request is a success, the following SOAP message should be returned:

```xml
<soapenv:Body>
  <wsse:RequestSecurityTokenResponse>
   <wsse:RequestedSecurityToken>
    <wsse:BinarySecurityToken
     ValueType="wsse:X509v3"
     EncodingType="wsse:Base64Binary">
    </wsse:BinarySecurityToken>
   </wsse:RequestedSecurityToken>
  </wsse: RequestSecurityTokenResponse>
</soapenv:Body>
```

2.1.4 Web Services Transaction

A reliable web service transaction [11] ensures that the many different web services cooperate together and complete the function. Therefore, it is the main foundation of the distribution system based on the web service. WS-Transactions are proposed by BEA, IBM, and Microsoft. The earliest version, proposed in August 2002, consisted of three basic standards: WS-Coordination [12], WS-AtomicTransaction [13], and WS-BusinessActivity [14].

2.1.4.1 WS-Coordination

WS-Coordination provides a coordinate framework of web services in a distribute system. A remarkable feature of this framework is its openness and expandability.

In this framework, the coordination protocol, coordination protocol service, and coordination service are the three most important concepts. The coordination protocol is a process of message exchange between the service requester and the coordinator. The coordination protocol service builds the coordination service and coordinates the message. The coordination service contains activate service, registration service, and some coordination protocol services. The following is an example of an activate service:

```
<wscoor:CreateCoordinationContextResponse>
<CoordinationContext>
<Identifier>
        http://www.jtang.org/transactions/context1211
</Identifier>
<CoordinationType>
http://docs.oasis-open.org/ws-tx/wast/2006/06
</CoordinationType>
        <RegistrationService>
        <wsa:Address>
        http://www.jtang.org/transactions/registration
        <wsa:Address>
        </RegistrationService>
        </CoordinationContext >
</wscoor:CreateCoordinationContextResponse>
```

The activate service contains: <CoordinationType> element, which points out the type of coordination of the service requester.

2.1.4.2 WS-AtomicTransaction

WS-AtomicTransction defines the atomic service coordinate type. This standard defines two coordinate protocols, completion protocol and two-phase commit (2 PC) protocol. The former is used to submit or re-roll the transaction. The latter defines how to commit when two or more participants exist.

2.1.4.3 WS-BusinessActivity

WS-BusinessActivity defines the function coordinate protocol type. It is used with the WS-Coordination standard. This standard defines two coordinate protocols: BusinessAgreementWithParicipantCompletion and Business AgreementWithCoordinatorCompletion. These two coordinate protocols support long-time processes. The participants using the former should know when to complete all the tasks, while the participants using the latter rely on the coordinator to tell them when to start.

2.1.5 Semantic Web Services

Since the standard web service lacks semantic information, the function of the service cannot be clearly described. It impacts service selection, discovery, and composition. A semantic web service is used to solve the challenges from these problems. It is a combination of web service and semantic web [15].

Semantic web is the concept proposed by Tim Berners Lee and James Hendler in 1998. It is defined as the extension of the existing web helping process interacting between humans and machines [16]. These important works include Web Ontology Language for Service (OWL-S) [17], WSMO/WSML (Web Service Modeling Ontology) [18], SWSO/SWSL [19], and WSDL-S [20].

2.1.5.1 OWL-S

The predecessor of OWL-S is DARPA agent markup language for services (DAML-S), which is a service ontology based on OWL. It is the most influential work on semantic service. OWL-S divides the ontology into three levels: service profile, service model, and service grounding.

- Service profile is used to describe the basic service information, including information about the service provider and service function.
- Service model describes the inner process of the service. It describes both the atomic process and composite process. In addition, it includes an abstract process that can be executed by binding to the concrete process.
- Service grounding describes the service calling details, including protocol, message format, and address.

2.1.5.2 Web Service Modeling Ontology

WSMO is a service ontology based on WSMF (Web Service Modeling Framework) through a European Semantic Systems initiative. WSML is a language describing WSMO. WSMO/WSML describes the web service from four aspects: ontology, web service, goal, and mediator.

- Ontology provides the concepts used for description including relation, function, and theorem.
- Web service is the functional part.
- Goal describes the nonfunctional request from the user.
- Mediator, the core element of WSMO, is used to solve the problem of incompatibility. There are four kinds of mediators: GG mediator, OO mediator, WG mediator, and WW mediator.

2.1.5.3 Semantic Web Service Ontology

Semantic Web Service Ontology (SWSO)/SWSL is a web service ontology description language proposed by the Semantic Web Initiative based on OWL-S and WSMO/WSML.

- SWSL includes two sublanguages, SWSL-FOL and SWSL-Rules. The former, based on first-order logic, proposes the ability to operate with other process model and service ontology. The latter is a language based on rules. These two languages are both hierarchical languages.
- SWSO provides a group of concept models describing the web service. It has two web ontologies: FLOWS (First-Order Logic Ontology for Web Service) and ROWS (Rules Ontology for Web Service).

2.1.5.4 WSDL-S

WSDL-S is an ontology-based Web Service Description Language proposed by the University of Georgia and IBM. It extends the WSDL service model and adds semantic information in the operation, interface, and message. Differing from OWL-S, WSMO/WSML, and SWSO/SWSL, WSDL-S is independent from the ontology language. Both OWL and Unified Modeling Language (UML) can be used in WSDL-S.

2.2 Service-Oriented Architecture

2.2.1 Overview of SOA

Since SOA was proposed by Gartner Inc. in the 1990s, it has been in development for nearly 20 years. The detailed explanation of the latest version of SOA can be found in [21]. This section presents a brief introduction on SOA.

The concept of SOA is also in the process of changing and developing. Although there is not a widely acceptable definition for SOA, generally it is defined as a component model facing service. It associates the application units by well-defined interfaces and protocols.

Basically, SOA is a business-IT-aligned approach in which applications rely on available services to facilitate business processes. A service is a self-contained reusable software component provided by a service provider and consumed by service requestors. SOA creates a vision of IT flexibility that enables business agility. Implementing an SOA mainly involves componentizing the enterprise and/or developing applications that use services, making applications available as services for other applications to use, etc.

2.2.2 Model of SOA

Although the implementation of SOA is closely related to a user request, the implementations are all referred to some basic rules. This section mainly discusses the Reference Model for Service-Oriented Architecture 1.0 proposed by OASIS.

The referenced model is an abstract model that helps understand the relationship between the entities in a particular environment. It provides a unified standard and explanation. A referenced model usually contains the unified concepts, theorems, and relationships. It does not rely on particular techniques, implementations, and details.

A Reference Model for Service-Oriented Architecture provides the high-level elements being adopted for all SOA implementations. Figure 2.5 presents the relationship with the SOA referenced model and other distribute systems.

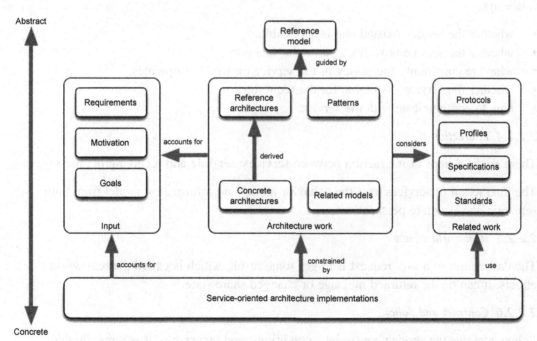

Figure 2.5
Service-oriented architecture referenced model [21].

There are seven basic elements (service, visibility, service description, interaction, real-world effect, contract and policy, and execution context) of a SOA referenced model, and these elements will be discussed in detail in the following sections.

2.2.2.1 Service

Service is a mechanism ensuring that the service requester can access the functions provided by the service provider. It hides the detailed implementation of the functions and provides some needed information for the requestor.

2.2.2.2 Visibility

SOA most ensure that the service provider is visible to the service requestor and vice versa. The elements of the visible node and interactive node are as follows:

- Sensible: Each service participants should be aware of the existence of others.
- Willing: A participant can reject all the operations once it is willing to in this process.
- Accessible: The participants can communicate with each other.

2.2.2.3 Service description

An important feature of SOA is containing lots of descriptive documents, including the following:

- whether the service existed and is accessible,
- whether the service provides a particular function,
- what are constraints and policy of the service on which it operates,
- whether the service is suitable for the requestor,
- how to communicate with the service.

2.2.2.4 Interaction

There are two steps of interaction between services: sending and receiving the message.

The interaction of services uses the behavior model and information model from both semantic and structure perspectives.

2.2.2.5 Real-world effects

The destination of a user request is to get some result, which is called the real-world effects. It can be the returned message or changed share state.

2.2.2.6 Contract and policy

Policy contains the service constraints, conditions, and ownership. It is a measurable assertion and is used for managing requests and expectations.

2.2.2.7 Execution context

Service context contains some basic foundation elements, process entities, policy assertion, and protocols. It is a path connecting the service requestor and service provider.

Service context does not belong to any part of the service, and it only cares about the procedure of interactive.

2.3 Service Component Architecture

Currently, the development of SOA has stepped into the standard phase. Service component architecture (SCA) [22] is being proposed by IBM, Oracle, IONA, and SAP to help refer to the implementation of SOA.

2.3.1 Concepts of SCA

SCA defines a simple service-based design model for constructing an SOA system. The main idea of SCA is composing a series of services to satisfy the new request. SCA provides a high-level entensive, and independent programming language model. It supports Java, C++, BPEL, and PHP. Both Java Message Service (JMS) and Enterprise JavaBeans (EJB) are supported as the bottom interactive mechanism. In constructing a SOA system, the different size of the service granularity is one of the most difficult problems being considered. However, in SCA, different granularity services can be defined by a recursive definition, which provides a good situation for SOA. On the other hand, SCA allows for a different binding (Web Service, JMS, and EJB) in solving the problem of service communications in distribute systems.

2.3.2 Model of SCA

The SCA assembly model consists of a series of composites and defines a profit for the SCA domain. The composites include component, service, reference, properties, and wiring. Among them, composite is the atomic unit of the SCA application, which consists of an implementation of a profit. Service is the way of using this function. Reference describes the relay relationship between an implementation with the other service. Property is the data in operation. Wiring describes the relationship between all these elements.

An SCA composite, as shown in Figure 2.6 [23], is a set containing components, service, reference, and their wires. A special property setting is also a part of the SCA composite. The SCA composite consists of 0 or more properties, services, components, references, and wires.

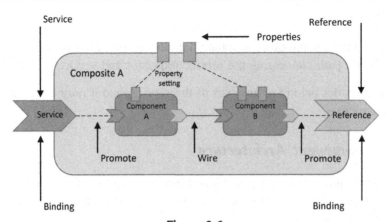

Figure 2.6
Service component architecture composites [23].

2.3.2.1 Property

A property has a type, which can be a simple type or a complex one. A property defined in a composite adopts the following format:

```
<?xml version="1.0" encoding="ASCII"?>
<composite xmlns="http://www.osoa.org/xmlns/sca/1.0"
        name="xs:QCName"...>
...
    <property name="xs:NCName" (type="xs:QName" | element="xs:QName")
      many="xs:boolean"? mustSupply="xs:boolean"?>*
      default-property-value?
    </property>
...
</composite>
```

2.3.2.2 Reference

The reference is expressed under the composite element. A composite can have 0 or more reference elements. The following code segment presents the definition of the reference elements:

```
<?xml version="1.0" encoding="ASCII"?>
  <!--Reference schema snippet-->
  <composite xmlns="http://www.osoa.org/xmlns/sca/1.0"
      targetNamespace="xs:anyURI"
      name="xs:NCName" local="xs:boolean"? autowire="xs:boolean"?
      constrainingType="QName"?
      requires="list of xs:QName"? policySets="list of xs:QName"?>
      ...
    <reference name="xs:NCName" target="list of xs:anyURI"?
          promote="list of xs:anyURI" wiredByImpl="xs:boolean"?
```

```
            multiplicity="0..1 or 1..1 or 0..n or 1..n"?
            requires="list of xs:QName"? policySets="list of xs:QName"?>*
        <interface/>?
        <binding uri="xs:anyURI"? name="xs:QName"?
            requires="list of xs:QName" policySets="list of xs:QName"?/>*
        <callback>?
            <binding uri="xs:anyURI"? name="xs:QName"?
                    requires="list of xs:QName"?
                    policySets="list of xs:QName"?/>+
        </callback>
    </reference>
    ...
</composite>
```

2.3.2.3 Service

A composite can have 0 or more service elements. The following code segment presents the definition of a service element in its composite description file:

```
<?xml version="1.0" encoding="ASCII"?>
<!--Servicee schema snippet-->

<composite xmlns="http://www.osoa.org/xmlns/sca/1.0"
targetNamespace="xs:anyURI"
name="xs:NCName" local="xs:boolean"? autowire="xs:boolean"?
constrainingType="QName"?
requires="list of xs:QName"? policySets="list of xs:QName"?>
...
<service name="xs:NCName" promote="xs:anyURI"
        requires="list of xs:QName"? policySets="list of xs:QName"?>*
        <interface/>?
        <binding uri="xs:anyURI"? name="xs:QName"?
            requires="list of xs:QName" policySets="list of xs:QName"?/>*
        <callback>?
            <binding uri="xs:anyURI"? name="xs:QName"?
                requires="list of xs:QName"?
                policySets="list of xs:QName"?/>+
        </callback>
</service>
...
</composite>
```

2.3.2.4 Wire

The way of defining a wire is to set a composite reference by the target property. When the multiplicity is 0..n or 1..n, multiple services can be defined as targets. The following code segment presents the wire definition in a composite description file:

```
<?xml version="1.0" encoding="ASCII"?>
<!--Wires schema snippet-->
```

```
<composite xmlns="http://www.osoa.org/xmlns/sca/1.0"
    targetNamespace="xs:anyURI"
    name="xs:NCName" local="xs:boolean"? autowire="xs:boolean"?
    constrainingType="QName"?
    requires="list of xs:QName"? policySets="list of xs:QName"?>
    ...
<wire source="xs:anyURI" target="xs:anyURI"/>*
</composite>
```

2.3.3 Strategy Framework

Strategy framework defines the ability and constraints used in a service composite and the interaction between composites. The strategies can be divided into two classes: interactive strategy and implementation strategy. In SCA, the service and reference can both use some strategies, the interactive strategies, which affect the way of the interaction. The composite can use other strategies, the implementation strategies, which affect the way the composite is able to execute in the container.

In SCA, the strategies are collected in a strategy set. A strategy contains one or more strategies that are able to exist by a concrete type, such as a WS-Policy. Each strategy points to a concrete binding type and concrete implementation type.

2.4 Service Data Objects

As we know, the data in different program languages have different formats. To be able to use the data conveniently in the SOA environment, a service data object (SDO) [24] is proposed.

2.4.1 Concepts of Service Data Object

SDO is the standard addressing data programming architecture and application programming interface. It supports many programming languages, including Java, C++, COBOL, and C. SDO simplifies programming by the following methods: (1) using data source type to unify programming; (2) supporting a general application pattern; and (3) using tools and frameworks for helping data query, exploration, binding, updating, and searching.

An SDO framework contains three important concepts: data object, data graph, and data access service. A data object contains a series of properties, each of which includes a simple value or a reference to another data object. A data graph is the envelope of the data object. It is the standard transmission unit. A data graph can be used to trace the change of data (including data inserting, deleting, and changing of property). In general, a data graph can be constructed by a data source (e.g., XML document, EJB, database) and service (web service, JMS message). A data access service is the component constructing the data graph by its original data and restoring the data graph back to its original data.

2.4.2 Framework of Service Data Object

In an SDO framework, the data object represents the more general format of the data. A data graph uses graphs to describe the relationship between data objects, such as those shown in Figure 2.7. The user can get access to a data graph by a data access service, which usually adopts a distribute architecture as shown in Figure 2.8. A typical data accessing procedure includes the following steps:

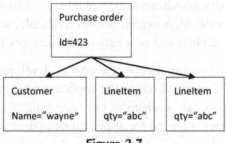

Figure 2.7
Data graph and data object.

1. User sends the request to a data access service.
2. Data access service starts a transaction, gets data from the data persistence, creates a data graph, and terminates the transaction.
3. Data access service sends the data graph to the user.
4. User operates the data graph.
5. User informs the data access service to change data.
6. Data access service starts a new transaction, writes the new data to the data persistence, and terminates the transaction.

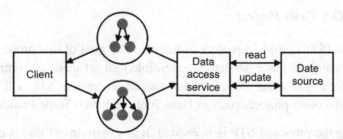

Figure 2.8
Distribute data architecture [24].

2.5 Open-Source Platforms for SOA

SCA is a complete standard system based on the idea of SOA. There are many developing tools supporting SCA. The open-source tool includes Apache Tuscany, Eclipse STP, PECL, SOA for PHP, CodeCauldron Newton, etc. The business tool includes IBM WPS/WAS, AquaLogic Data Services Platform, TIBCO ActiveMatrix, Rogue Wave HydraSCA, Covansys SCA Framework for SOA, Infinitflow DSF, etc.

2.5.1 Apache Tuscany

Apache Tuscany [25] provides an SOA and the infrastructure for easily developing and running applications using a service-oriented approach. This lightweight runtime is designed to be embedded in, or provisioned to, a number of different host environments. Apache Tuscany implements the SCA, which defines a flexible, service-based model for construction, assembly, and deployment of a network of services (existing and new ones).

With SCA as its foundation, Tuscany reduces the cost of developing SOA-based solutions, because it pushes handling of protocol out of the application business logic into pluggable bindings. As a result, protocols can be changed only one time, with minimal configuration changes. Tuscany also removes the need for applications to deal with infrastructure concerns such as security and transaction and handles this declaratively. This enables SOA solutions to be flexible and adaptable to change with minimal configuration changes.

Tuscany provides support for SCA 1.0 specification in Java. It also provides a wide range of bindings (web services, web20 bindings, etc.), implementation types (Spring, BPEL, Java, etc.), as well as integration with technologies such as web2.0 and OSGi. Tuscany is working on implementing SCA 1.1 that is being standardized at OASIS.

Apache Tuscany also implements SDOs, which provides a uniform interface for handling different forms of data, including XML documents that can exist in a network of services, and provides the mechanism for tracking changes. Tuscany supports the SCO and the SDO (2.01 for C++/2.1 for Java) specifications.

2.5.2 Eclipse SOA Tools Project

SOA Tools Project (STP) [26] is a project of Eclipse. The goal of this proposed project is to put the fundamentals in place, so that an extensible tool set made of components and exemplary tools for constructing SOA applications can be created. STP will leverage the existing work of the other projects such as Data Tools and Web Tools Platform projects.

A developer using the proposed STP is interested in an environment that is easy to use—one in which the challenges of application development are due to the problem domain, not the complexity of the tools used. To this end, the developer will strive to create a highly usable and consistent environment that works well with associated technologies, whether being used by a developer working/creating a service, an administrator maintaining or monitoring a production system, or someone constructing a larger SOA network. Such an environment starts with key frameworks designed both for use and extensibility. Examples include the location or creation of a service consumer or provider, the consumption of these services, the configuration of the physical attributes (transport, message format), and the policies required to access or consume the like (security policy, access control, transactional, availability). Further, the ability to locate and add services to the SOA interactions like transformation, routing, for process orchestration to a broker, or endpoint needs to be addressed.

Finally, there is a need for the creation of artifacts that can be used to deploy, enforce, or manage in an extensible way.

The proposed project will try not to attempt to define every type of service in a SOA, but to define the contracts to unify them into an SOA through an extensible framework. Then we can model the policies and interactions with an abstraction so that multiple specific vendor implementations can be supported from the vendor independent models of WSDL and other web service standards.

2.6 Summary

Web service, as the supporting technology in service computing, is widely used in many domains. This section introduces the basic concept of web service, developing procedures, and standards. Then the basic concept of SOA and its basic elements proposed by OASIS are discussed. At the same time, SCA and SDO are also introduced as the important supporting systems in SOA. Finally, two open-source platforms for SOA are discussed.

References

[1] H. Haas, A. Brown, Web Services Glossary, W3C Working Group Note, February 11, 2004.
[2] SOAP, http://www.w3.org/TR/soap.
[3] WSDL, http://www.w3.org/TR/wsdl20.
[4] UDDI, http://www.uddi.org/pubs/uddi_v3.htm.
[5] BPEL, http://www.oasis-open.org/committees/tc_home.php?wg_abbrev=wsbpel.
[6] WS-CDL, http://www.w3.org/TR/2004/WD-ws-cdl-10-20041217/.
[7] WSCI, http://www.w3.org/TR/wsci/.
[8] WS-Security, http://www.oasis-open.org/committees/download.php/16790/wss-v1.1-spec-os-SOAPMessage Security.pdf.
[9] WS-Policy, http://www.w3.org/TR/ws-policy/.
[10] WS-Trust, http://docs.oasis-open.org/ws-sx/ws-trust/200512/ws-trust-1.3-os.html.
[11] WS-Transactions, http://www.oasis-open.org/committees/ws-tx.

[12] WS-Coordination, http://docs.oasis-open.org/ws-tx/wstx-wscoor-1.1-spec-errata-os.pdf.

[13] WS-AtomicTransaction, http://docs.oasis-open.org/ws-tx/wstx-wsat-1.1-spec-errata-os.pdf.

[14] WS-BusinessActivity, http://docs.oasis-open.org/ws-tx/wstx-wsba-1.1-spec-errata-os.pdf.

[15] S.A. McIlraith, T.C. Son, H. Zeng, Semantic web services, IEEE Intell. Syst. 16 (2) (2001) 46−53.

[16] T. Berners-Lee, J. Hendler, O. Lassila, The semantic web, Sci. Am. 284 (5) (2001) 28−37.

[17] OWL-S, http://www.daml.org/services/owl-s/.

[18] WSMO, http://www.wsmo.org.

[19] SWSL, http://www.daml.org/services/swsl/.

[20] WSDL-S, http://www.w3.org/Submission/WSDL-S/.

[21] SOA, http://docs.oasis-open.org/soa-rm/v1.0/soa-rm.pdf.

[22] M. Beisiegel, H. Blohm, D. Booz, J. Dubray, A. Colyer, M. Edwards, et al., Service component architecture: building systems using a service oriented architecture, Whitepaper [online] (2005) 1−31.

[23] SCA, http://docs.oasis-open.org/opencsa/sca-assembly/sca-assembly-1.1-spec-cd03.html.

[24] SDO, http://devzone.zend.com/330/introducing-service-data-objects-for-php/.

[25] A. Tuscany, Apache Tuscany SCA Java Architecture Guide.

[26] Eclipse STP, http://wiki.eclipse.org/STP, 2009.

CHAPTER 3

Web Service Quality of Service and Its Prediction

Chapter Outline

3.1 Introduction

With the exponential growth of web services deployed on the Internet, numerous users enjoy high-quality services to get connected, and this causes the World Wide Web to be more flourishing. Quality-of-service (QoS) is used to describe the nonfunctional aspects of web services. At present, companies and organizations place unprecedented demands for web services, and studies done on QoS have raised concerns of service-oriented computing researchers.

QoS covers a whole range of techniques that match the needs of service requestors with those of the service providers based on the network resources available. QoS is referred to as the nonfunctional properties of web services such as performance, reliability, availability, and security [1,2].

Service Computing: Concepts, Methods and Technology. http://dx.doi.org/10.1016/B978-0-12-802330-3.00003-5

A number of QoS-based paradigms have been applied to the area of service selection [3–5], service discovery [6,7], service recommendations [8,9], service composition [10,11], service trust [12,13], service routing [14,15], etc. The common hypothesis of the above research areas is that QoS values for all of the web services are available. However, this premise is sometimes challenged in various real-world cases for the following reasons: (1) The web services hierarchy becomes more complex in different situations. As a result, it is time-consuming for an end user to explore massive QoS records. (2) Most web services are operated by commercial companies. Gathering QoS information by execution can be too costly for an end user. (3) The Internet environment becomes more dynamic yet vulnerable. It turns out that it is impractical and impossible to collect QoS records all the time. To satisfy the basic requirements from service-oriented research domains mentioned above, a necessary preprocess is to predict the missing QoS values.

QoS prediction is critical to many key problems in the web service domain, such as web service selection [3], discovery [16], composition [10], and recommendations [17]. Currently, collaborative filtering (CF) is the most widely adopted algorithm to predict QoS values in the web service community due to its simplicity and maturity. Shao et al. [18] used the user-based CF algorithm for QoS prediction, which was modified through a combination of positive and negative correlations. Zheng et al. [19] proposed a hybrid CF model fusing together user-based and item-based CF algorithms, in which confidence weights were used to balance the respective weights of the two models. Although CF-based methods are easy to implement and relatively effective, they suffer from declining accuracy in that QoS values are sparse and can hardly be integrated with any other factors in the model, for instance, the geographical information used in this chapter. The contribution of geographical information to the improvement of QoS prediction accuracy has recently been studied. Chen et al. [20] developed a hierarchical clustering algorithm to identify users' neighbors with a similar historical web service invocation experience, and then these people were supposed to be in the same region. This approach is unreasonable because, for example, although users in Seoul and in Tokyo may have similar QoS values in a certain period of time, changes of infrastructure in Seoul cannot make any difference on users' experiences of web service invocation in Tokyo. Lo et al. [21] took the influence of users' neighbors into consideration from the real geographical sense, which appended a third regularization term at the end of the objective function of singular value decomposition (SVD)-like matrix factorization (MF) [22]. Since the main purpose of this kind of usage is to prevent overfitting in the learning process, it is hard to give a persuasive interpretation from the perspective of neighbors' contributions to QoS values.

3.2 Collaborative Filtering-Based Quality of Service Prediction

CF techniques are widely used to fulfill this task and are inspired by the idea of user-collaboration in the era of Web 2.0. The core idea behind this is to identify a set of similar neighbors and to collect "the wisdom of the crowds." In this process, the measurement of similarity becomes vital. Previous CF approaches on QoS prediction mainly used a Pearson correlation coefficient (PCC) [23] to build up user-similarity neighborhoods [17,19].

3.2.1 Neighborhood-Based Collaborative Filtering

Two kinds of memory-based CF algorithms have been primarily used, i.e., user-based and item-based models, both of which use similar users or items sharing similar historical records [24]. The core process of CF is the similarity calculation between two users or items, which usually uses a PCC as the similarity measurement.

3.2.1.1 User neighborhood-based collaborative filtering

Given a data set consisting of M service users and N web services, the invocation records between users and services can be denoted by an $M \times N$ matrix, which is called a user–service matrix (see Figure 3.1; Table 3.1). An entry in this matrix r_{mn} represents a record of invocation (QoS values, e.g., response time and availability). Existing work [9,18,24] about QoS prediction uses PCC to compute the similarity of users or services. In a user-based CF approach, PCC is used to define the similarity between two users, u_1 and u_2, based on the services they have commonly invoked using the following:

$$\psi(u_1, u_2) = \frac{\sum_{s \in S}(r_{u1,s} - \bar{r}_{u1})^T (r_{u2,s} - \bar{r}_{u2})}{\sqrt{\sum_{s \in S}(r_{u1,s} - \bar{r}_{u1})^2} \sqrt{\sum_{s \in S}(r_{u2,s} - \bar{r}_{u2})^2}} \tag{3.1}$$

in which $S = S_1 \cap S_2$ is the set of services that are both invoked by users u_1 and u_2, $r_{u1,s}$ is the vector of the QoS values of service s invoked by user u_1, and $\bar{r}_{u1}$ stands for the vector of average QoS values of the services invoked by user u_1. While using the PCC equation,

Table 3.1: User-service matrix

	Service 1	Service 2	Service 3	Service 4
User 1	q_{11}			
User 2		q_{22}		q_{24}
User 3				
User 4	q_{41}			q_{44}
User 5			q_{53}	

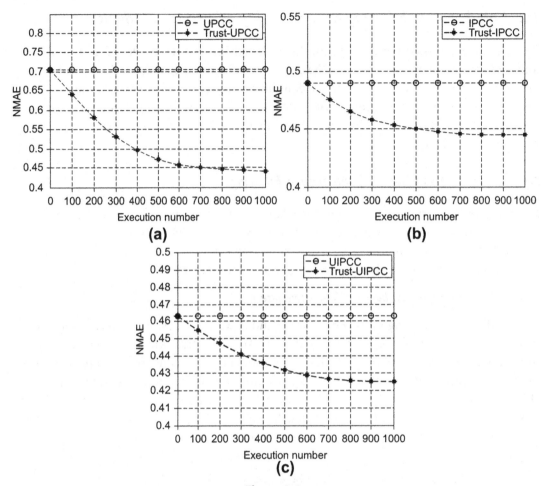

Figure 3.1
Impact of trust model.

the similarity between users is in the range of $[-1, 1]$, with a larger value indicating that u_1 and u_2 are more similar.

User-based prediction uses the data of similar users to predict the unknown value of target service s to target user u as follows:

$$p_u = \bar{r}_u + \frac{\sum_{u_1 \in S(u)} \psi(u_1, u)\left(r_{u1,s} - \bar{r}_{u1}\right)}{\sum_{u_1 \in S(u)} \psi(u_1, u)} \tag{3.2}$$

in which $\bar{r}_u$ is the vector of average QoS values of services invoked by u, $S(u)$ is the set of u's similar users, and $\bar{r}_{u1}$ is the vector of average QoS values of services invoked by u_1.

3.2.1.2 Service neighborhood-based collaborative filtering

Similarly, the detailed PCC equation for the similarity computation of services is as follows:

$$\psi(s_1, s_2) = \frac{\sum_{u \in U}\left(r_{u,s1} - \overline{r}_{s1}\right)^{T}\left(r_{u,s2} - \overline{r}_{s2}\right)}{\sqrt{\sum_{u \in U}\left(r_{u,s1} - \overline{r}_{s1}\right)^{2}}\sqrt{\sum_{u \in U}\left(r_{u,s2} - \overline{r}_{s2}\right)^{2}}} \tag{3.3}$$

Further, the analysis of real-world web service QoS values finds that the QoS scale of different users is quite different. For example, due to the security or gateway being used, the response time of all services to user A is greater than 3000 ms, whereas that to user B is less than 200 ms because of a faster network. In such situations, the similarity between two services is impacted by other irrelevant issues, instead of the service itself, when using PCC. Considering the differences in the QoS scale between different users, the A-cosine equation [25] used to compute the similarity between services is as follows:

$$\psi(s_1, s_2) = \frac{\sum_{u \in U}\left(r_{u,s1} - \overline{r}_{u}\right)^{T}\left(r_{u,s2} - \overline{r}_{u}\right)}{\sqrt{\sum_{u \in U}\left(r_{u,s1} - \overline{r}_{u}\right)^{2}}\sqrt{\sum_{u \in U}\left(r_{u,s2} - \overline{r}_{u}\right)^{2}}} \tag{3.4}$$

in which $U = U_{s_1} \cap U_{s_2}$ is the set of users who both have invoked services s_1 and s_2. $r_{u,s1}$ is the vector of QoS values of service s_1 invoked by u, and $\overline{r}_u$ is the vector of average QoS values of services invoked by u. In this A-cosine equation, the impact of different QoS scales are removed by using $(r_{u,s1} - \overline{r}_u)$.

3.2.2 Trust-Based Collaborative Filtering

In a user-based CF QoS prediction approach, the unknown QoS value of user u_i to service s_j is calculated based on the QoS values of u_i's similar neighbors to s_j. Thus, u_i's feedback to the prediction result is only related to his similar neighbors. Given this scenario, assuming u_j is one of u_i's similar neighbors, some statistical parameters are set to explore the user feedback, as the following shows (Table 3.2):

A user may not give feedback to every prediction result, $C^*(u_i, u_j) \geq C^+(u_i, u_j) + C^-(u_i, u_j)$. As for the definition of user satisfaction, it is flexible and dependent on the scenario and dataset. Inspired by the Bayes average voting algorithm, our paper [26] proposes a trust-based CF model, in which a feedback-based trust model is built to evaluate u_i's trust to u_j as the following shows:

$$T(u_i, u_j) = \frac{C^+\left(u_i, u_j\right) + 0.5 \times C^?\left(u_i, u_j\right) + v}{C^*\left(u_i, u_j\right) + v} \tag{3.5}$$

Table 3.2: Statistical parameters for user trust model

Parameters	Description
$C^*(u_i,u_j)$	The times of QoS prediction for u_i based on u_j
$C^+(u_i,u_j)$	The times that u_i is satisfied with the result
$C^-(u_i,u_j)$	The times that u_i is not satisfied with the result

That is, $C^*(u_i,u_j)$ is the number of times that u_i does not give feedback. Parameter v is used to solve the cold-start problem, and the value of v is empirically set as five times the user number. To use the trust model in the process of QoS prediction, the user trust $T(u_i,u_j)$ with user similarity $Sim(u_i,u_j)$ is combined to generate the trust-based similarity, annotated as $ST(u_i,u_j)$.

$$ST(u_i, u_j) = \frac{2 \times Sim(u_i, u_j) \times T(u_i, u_j)}{|Sim(u_i, u_j)| + T(u_i, u_j)} \tag{3.6}$$

Similarly, in a service-based CF QoS prediction approach, the service trust $T(s_i,s_j)$ and the trust-based similarity $ST(u_i,u_j)$ can be obtained in the same way.

User-based prediction uses the data of similar users to predict the unknown QoS value of the target service s to target user u as follows:

$$UP_{u,s} = \bar{r}_u + \frac{\sum_{u_1 \in S(u)} ST(u_1, u)(r_{u1,s} - \bar{r}_{u1})}{\sum_{u_1 \in S(u)} ST(u_1, u)} \tag{3.7}$$

in which $\bar{r}_u$ is the vector of average QoS values of services invoked by u, $S(u)$ is the set of u's trust-based similar users, and $\bar{r}_{u_1}$ is the vector of average QoS values of services invoked by u_1. Service-based prediction is given as follows:

$$SP_{u,s} = \bar{r}_s + \frac{\sum_{s_1 \in S(s)} ST(s_1, s)(r_{u,s1} - \bar{r}_{s1})}{\sum_{s_1 \in S(s)} ST(s_1, s)} \tag{3.8}$$

in which $\bar{r}_s$ is the vector of average QoS values of s invoked by different users, $S(s)$ is the set of s's trust-based similar services, and $\bar{r}_{s_1}$ is the vector of average QoS values of s_1 invoked by different users.

However, due to the sparseness of the user-service matrix, predicting missing values only using user-based methods or service-based methods will potentially ignore valuable information that can make the prediction more accurate. To predict the missing value as accurately as possible, the user-based and service-based methods are systematically combined to fully use the information of the user-service matrix. Since these two prediction methods may have difference prediction accuracy, two confidence weights, con_u and con_s, are used to balance the two predicted values. con_u is defined as follows:

$$con_u = \sum_{u_1 \in S(u)} \frac{ST(u_1, u)}{\sum_{u_1 \in S(u)} ST(u_1, u)} \times ST(u_1, u) \tag{3.9}$$

The confidence weight of the service-based prediction con_s is defined as follows:

$$con_s = \sum_{s_1 \in S(s)} \frac{ST(s_1, s)}{\sum_{s_1 \in S(s)} ST(s_1, s)} \times ST(s_1, s) \tag{3.10}$$

The value of the confidence weight is in the range of [0,1], with a larger value indicating that the corresponding result is more preferable. Because the final prediction result is the aggregation of two predicted values, a parameter $\lambda \in [0,1]$ is set to determine how it relies on each individual prediction. When $S(u) \neq \varnothing$ and $S(s) \neq \varnothing$, the final equation for the QoS prediction is:

$$p_{u,s} = w_u \times UP_{u,s} + w_s \times SP_{u,s} \tag{3.11}$$

in which w_u and w_s stand for the participation that each predicted result takes in the final prediction, and $w_u + w_s = 1$. They are computed as follows:

$$w_u = \frac{\lambda \times con_u}{\lambda \times con_u + (1 - \lambda) \times con_s}$$
$$w_s = \frac{(1 - \lambda) \times con_s}{\lambda \times con_u + (1 - \lambda) \times con_s} \tag{3.12}$$

The parameter λ means that the participation that the user-based prediction result takes is the final result. If $0 < \lambda < 1$, the final result is generated from user-based and service-based approaches. If $\lambda = 0$, the final predicted result is totally generated from the service-based prediction. Similarly, if $\lambda = 1$, the user-based prediction approach generates the final result.

These experiments are conducted on a public real-world web service QoS dataset, which was collected by Zibin Zheng et al. [27]. It contains the records of 1,974,675 web-service invocations executed by 339 distributed service users on 5825 web services. The record of each invocation contains two parameters: response time and throughput. More details about this dataset can be found in [27]. In addition, 150 users and 100 web services are selected randomly as the experimental data.

The experiments are implemented with JDK1.6 0.0 21, Eclipse 3.6.0, and Mysql 5.0. They are conducted on a Dell Inspire 13R machine with 2.27 GHz Intel Core I5 CPU and 2GB RAM, running Windows 7 OS.

In the experiments, NMAE is used to evaluate the accuracy of the prediction. Mean absolute error (MAE) is as follows:

$$mMAE = \frac{\sum |r_{u,s} - \hat{r}_{u,s}|}{N}$$

in which $r_{u,s}$ is the predicted QoS value of services observed by user u, $\hat{r}_{u,s}$ stands for the expected or real QoS value, and N is the total number of predictions. The QoS value range may differ so tremendously that the use of only MAE is not objective enough. As an adjustment, NMAE normalizes the difference range of MAE by computing:

$$NMAE = \frac{MAE}{\sum_{U,S} \frac{r_{u,s}}{N}}$$

The smaller NMAE, the more accurate will be the QoS prediction.

The following approaches are proposed with the following state-of-the-art prediction methods:

1. UPCC: It is a user-based CF prediction approach, in which PCC is used to compute the similarities between users.
2. IPCC: It is a service-based CF prediction approach, in which PCC is used to compute the similarities between services.
3. UIPCC: This method [19] is a combination of UPCC and IPCC.
4. MF: In this method, MF is used to predict QoS values [22].
5. SVD: This method is proposed by Y. Korean [28] in the area of CF. It captures the latent structure of the original data distribution.
6. Trust-UPCC: This method is a combination of UPCC and the trust model.
7. Trust-IPCC: This method is a combination of IPCC and the trust model.
8. Trust-UIPCC: This method is a combination of UIPCC and the trust model.

The dataset used is for an experimental set of invocation records between 150 users and 100 web services, a 150 × 100 user-service matrix is created, in which each entry in it is a vector including two QoS values: response time and throughput. During the experiment, the 150 × 100 matrix is divided into two parts, N rows as the training matrix and the other (150-N) rows as the testing matrix. The users in the testing matrix are called target users. Then, the training matrix density is thinned randomly to $m\%$ to simulate the situation in which one user in a training matrix has used only $m\%$ of all services. This step is used to make the condition of experiments similar to that of a real scenario. In addition, the number of invocation records is varied so that target users can provide, for example, the number of web services that they have invoked, annotated as g10, g5 in Table 3.3. To minimize error, each experiment is looped 50 times, and the average value is reported.

Table 3.3: Comparison of prediction accuracy (a smaller value means a better performance)

Density	Methods	T = 100						T = 140					
		Response Time			Throughput			Response Time			Throughput		
		g5	g10	g20	g5	g10	g20	g5	g10	g20	g5	g10	g20
10%	UPCC	0.747	0.729	0.707	0.722	0668	0.626	0.699	0.657	0.633	0.656	0.620	0.604
	IPCC	0.592	0.559	0.529	0.560	0539	0.476	0.541	0.502	0.460	0.526	0.482	0.466
	UIPCC	0.548	0.498	0.473	0.532	0.511	0.470	0.492	0.462	0.457	0.515	0.471	0.451
	SVD	0.536	0.483	0.454	0.527	0.502	0.456	0.481	0.454	0.439	0.509	0.459	0.443
	MF	0.532	0.480	0.456	0521	0.504	0.456	0.483	0.454	0.440	0.510	0.456	0.445
	Trust-UPCC	0.565	0.532	0512	0.553	0.541	0.528	0.512	0.502	0.487	0.515	0.497	0.472
	Trust-IPCC	0.534	0.483	0.462	0.519	0.502	0.459	0.478	0.451	0.443	0.508	0.461	0.443
	Trust-UIPCC	0.511	0.465	0.434	0.504	0.487	0.443	0.461	0.440	0.432	0.490	0.451	0.429
30%	UPCC	0.721	0.707	0.680	0.682	0.630	0.595	0.676	0.637	0.625	0.629	0.609	0.567
	IPCC	0.557	0.490	0.462	0.518	0.476	0.458	0.518	0.445	0.422	0.498	0.448	0.428
	UIPCC	0.485	0.463	0.441	0.509	0.469	0.446	0.471	0.430	0.412	0.483	0.440	0.419
	SVD	0.473	0.450	0.428	0.497	0.447	0.432	0.454	0.427	0.401	0.462	0.428	0.403
	MF	0.468	0.451	0.430	0.483	0.452	0.430	0.451	0.432	0.408	0.457	0.431	0.405
	Trust-UPCC	0.491	0.472	0.448	0.503	0.487	0.454	0.461	0.434	0.413	0.478	0.445	0.419
	Trust-IPCC	0.465	0.450	0.428	0.489	0.450	0.428	0.448	0.437	0.410	0.458	0.436	0.408
	Trust-UIPCC	0.451	0.432	0.417	0.476	0.441	0.415	0.437	0.412	0.397	0.430	0.409	0.394

Table 3.3 shows the prediction performance of the above eight approaches on response time and throughput using 10%, and 30% density of the training matrix, respectively. For the users in the testing matrix (target users), the number of invoked web services is varied as 5, 10, and 20 by randomly sampling (named as g5, g10, g20 in Table 3.3). In addition, the influence of the size of the training matrix is considered, as is varying the number of training users, i.e., $T = 100$ or 140. Empirically, $\lambda = 0.1$, $\Psi = 0.25$, and $K = 10$ (the number of similar neighbors in algorithm 1). As for the prediction approach with a trust model, the execution number of the prediction is set as 500. Assuming u_1 is the target user, u_2 is the similar neighbor, Pre(ru1,s) is the predicted QoS value based on u_2 and other similar neighbors, Exp(ru1,s) is the expected QoS value (ground truth), then the satisfaction definition discussed in Section 3.2 is given as follows:

$$|\text{Exp}(ru1, s - \text{Pre}(rr1, s))| \, \text{Exp}(ru1, s) \leq 20\%$$

From Table 3.3, it is can be seen that Trust-UIPCC obtains the smallest NMAE values, which means the highest prediction accuracy in all cases. This demonstrates that the use of a feedback-based trust model improves the prediction accuracy. Further, if we observe that the prediction approach with a trust model outperforms the one without a trust model, e.g., Trust-UPCC outperforms UPCC, Trust-IPCC outperforms IPCC, and Trust-UIPCC outperforms UIPCC. Comparing the prediction results for cases of $T = 100$ and 140, the latter's NMAE values are smaller, which indicates that the increase of T improves the prediction accuracy. Similarly, the increase of the density of a training matrix improves prediction accuracy as well, because higher density means more training data. Furthermore, the increase of the number of invoked services (g5, g10, and g20) also improves the performance of QoS.

1.   Impact of trust model

In this subsection, the impact of the trust model to the performance of the QoS prediction is evaluated by evaluating the performance comparison between UPCC and Trust-UPCC, IPCC and Trust-IPCC, and UIPCC and Trust-UIPCC. The comparison results are found in Figure 3.1(a)−(c), respectively. From Figure 3.1, it is observed that the use of a feedback-based trust model largely improves the performance of QoS prediction.

In addition, it should be noted that the proposed trust model could be utilized in all types of CF-based QoS prediction approaches. Further, we found that the benefit brought by the trust model decreases when the execution number of the QoS prediction is large.

2.   Impact of λ

When $\lambda = 0$, the weight of user-based prediction is zero, then the predicted result is generated by a service-based prediction. Similarly, when $\lambda = 1$, the predicted result is obtained by a user-based prediction. Figure 3.2 shows the impact of λ to two datasets, i.e.,

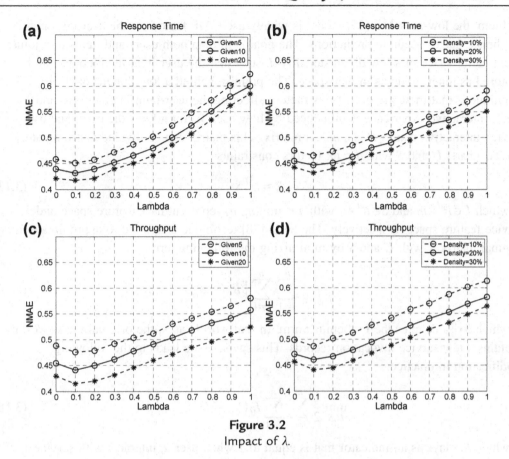

Figure 3.2
Impact of λ.

response time and throughput, with the variation of G and the matrix density. From Figure 3.2, it can be observed that a service-based prediction outperforms a user-based prediction, because the NMAE value in $\lambda = 0$ is smaller than the NMAE value in $\lambda = 1$ for all cases. Further, from the trends of the four figures in Figure 3.2(2), we found that the prediction accuracy first increases and then decreases with the increase of the λ value. It should be noted that the prediction performance reaches the highest point when $\lambda = 0.1$ for all cases. Thus, in this scenario, 0.1 should be the optimal value for λ.

3.3 Matrix Factorization-Based Quality of Service Prediction

3.3.1 Basic Matrix Factorization Model

In the real-world case, there are m users and n web services. They contribute to an $m \times n$ user-service matrix R, and each entry r_{u_i} represents a QoS value recording the specific usage information of the web service i executed by the user u. Usually, R is very sparse, and thus it contains a lot of missing QoS values. The problem is how to predict the missing QoS values of the user-service matrix R effectively and efficiently. To address this problem, the low-rank MF [29] model is widely used. MF factorizes the user-item matrix and hence makes accurate predictions. The goal is to map both users and items to a joint latent factor space of a low dimensionality d, such that the user-item interactions can be captured as inner products in that space. The premise behind a low-dimensional MF technique is that there are only a few factors affecting the user-item interactions, and a user's interactive experience is influenced by how each factor affects the user. The user-service interactive matrix R is a $m \times n$ matrix. This matrix can be divided approximately into two parts U and S with d-rank factors constraints:

$$R \approx U^T S \tag{3.13}$$

in which $U \in R^d \times m$ and $S \in R^d \times n$ with $d < \min(m, n)$ represent user feature space and service feature space, respectively. The SVD [28] technique is applied to approximate the original matrix R with U and S by minimizing the following term:

$$\min_{U,S} \frac{1}{2} \sum_{i=1}^{m} \sum_{j=1}^{n} \left\| R_{ij} U^T S \right\|_F^2 \tag{3.14}$$

in which $\| \cdot \|_F$ denotes the Frobenius norm. In real-world cases, the original matrix R only contains a few service invocation records. This sparse issue leads to the following modification in practice:

$$\min_{U,S} \frac{1}{2} \sum_{i=1}^{m} \sum_{j=1}^{n} I_{ij} \left(R_{ij} - U^T S \right)^2 \tag{3.15}$$

in which I_{ij} plays as an indicator that is equal to 1 when user u_i interacts with service s_j and is otherwise equal to zero. To avoid the issue of model overfitting, two regularization terms related to U and S are involved as follows:

$$\min_{U,S} \frac{1}{2} \sum_{i=1}^{m} \sum_{j=1}^{n} I_{ij} \left(R_{ij} - U^T S \right)^2 + \frac{\lambda_1}{2} \|U\|_F^2 + \frac{\lambda_2}{2} \|S\|_F^2 \tag{3.16}$$

in which λ_1 and λ_2 are the learning rates. The optimization problem in Eqn (3.16) minimizes the sum-of-squared-errors objective function with quadratic regularization terms. The above form is widely used in the domain of recommender systems.

3.3.2 Neighborhood-Based Matrix Factorization Model

Paper [30] builds a neighborhood-based MF model to incorporate the relational regularization terms to revamp the traditional MF model. Section 3.3.2.1 first focuses on using a user's relationship for the regularization part. Then Section 3.3.2.2 discusses how to extend this idea to the service side. Section 3.3.2.3 introduces the fusion of users and service relationships into a unified MF model.

3.3.2.1 User neighborhood-based matrix factorization model

The core idea of user-collaboration is to find a set of neighbors that behave very similarly to the current user. Similarity computation plays a vital role in the first step of the prediction process. (1) Generating a user neighborhood: Existing works on QoS value predictions use the PCC to compute the similarity relationship between users. This elegant algorithm is applied between user u_i and u_j as follows:

$$U\_Sim(i,j) = \frac{\sum_{s \in S}(r_{is} - \bar{r}_{u_i})(r_{js} - \bar{r}_{u_j})}{\sqrt{\sum_{s \in S}(r_{is} - \bar{r}_{u_i})^2}\sqrt{\sum_{s \in S}(r_{u_{js}} - \bar{r}_{u_j})^2}} \tag{3.17}$$

in which $S = S_{u_i} \cap S_{u_j}$ is the set of services both invoked by different users u_i and u_j, and $\bar{r}_{u_i}$ represents the average QoS values of different services invoked by user u_i. The $U\_Sim(i,j)$ is in the range of $[-1,1]$, in which a higher value indicates a higher user similarity. After calculating the similarity relationship between users, a set of TOP_K users are chosen as the neighborhood for the target user. The process of identifying the size of the neighborhood is crucial to the prediction accuracy, since dissimilar neighbors contribute useless information to make predictions and thus potentially harm the prediction accuracy. To choose an appropriate size, a traditional TOP_K algorithm is revamped to remove the dissimilar users in the neighborhood as follows:

$$TU(i) = \{k|k \in TOP\_K\_U(i), U\_Sim(i,k) > 0\}$$

in which *TOP_K_U(i)* represents a set of the TOP-K similar users ranking by similarity to user u_i, and *U_Sim(i,k)* is defined in Eqn (3.17).

This modification reduces the number of dissimilar users, and it generates an appropriate size for the neighborhood. (2) Capturing a user relationship: In practice, the interactive experience inside a neighborhood should be somehow similar. This captures the intuition because neighbors are very likely using a similar network infrastructure (network workloads, routers, etc.). As a result, they contribute similar patterns of web services usage information and thus are defined as neighbors. Based on this intuition, the following user relational regularization term is proposed as:

$$\min \left\| U_i - \frac{1}{\|TU(i)\|} \sum_{f \in TU(i)} U_f \right\|_F^2 \tag{3.18}$$

in which U_i is the feature vector of user u_i. The meaning of this term is used to minimize the interactive experience between a user u_i and its neighbors *TU(i)*. Given the neighborhood for user u_i, the assumption is built that u_i's feature vector is similar to the average feature vector of all its neighbors in this pool. The above constraint term holds the premise that every user's experience is close to the average level of neighborhood. However, this process treats every neighbor with equal importance, which may not be true in real-world cases. For example, there are thousands of neighbors inside a neighborhood. Apparently, those neighbors with higher relevance should be treated more seriously than the others. To re-weight the importance inside a neighborhood, the user constraint in Eqn (3.19) is changed as follows:

$$\min \left\| U_i - \sum_{f \in TU(i)} PU_{if} \cdot U_f \right\|_F^2 \tag{3.19}$$

This term combines different weights into the average feature vector of all neighbors. And PU_{if} is a normalized weight defined as follows:

$$PU_{if} = \frac{U\_Sim(i,f)}{\sum_{g \in TU(i)} U\_Sim(i,g)} \tag{3.20}$$

This user regularization term is incorporated to revamp the traditional MF model as follows:

$$\min_{U,S} L_1 = \frac{1}{2} \sum_{i=1}^{m} \sum_{j=1}^{n} I_{ij}(R_{ij} - U^T S)^2 + \frac{\lambda_1}{2}\|U\|_F^2 + \frac{\lambda_2}{2}\|S\|_F^2 + \frac{\alpha_1}{2} \sum_{i=1}^{m} \left\| U_i - \sum PU_{if} \cdot U_f \right\|_F^2 \tag{3.21}$$

in which $\alpha_1 > 0$ is controlling the importance of this term in the Extended Matrix Factorization (EMF) model. This objective function takes all the users into consideration and thus is aiming at minimizing the global differences within different neighborhoods. Although the objective function L_1 in Eqn (3.21) is convex in U only or S only, it is not convex in both matrixes [28]. Therefore, it is unrealistic to expect an algorithm to find the global minimum of L_1. The gradient descent method is used to find the local minimum as follows:

$$\frac{\partial L_1}{\partial U_i} = \sum_{j=1}^{n} I_{ij}(R_{ij} - U^T S)(-S_j) + \lambda_1 U_i + \alpha_1 \left(U_i - \sum PU_{if} \cdot U_f \right)$$

$$\frac{\partial L_1}{\partial S_j} = \sum_{i=1}^{m} I_{ij}(R_{ij} - U^T S)(-U_i) + \lambda_2 S_j \tag{3.22}$$

3.3.2.2 Service neighborhood-based matrix factorization model

The idea of using the wisdom of crowds can also be applied to the service side. However, the measurement of services similarity is different from that of the user ones. The reason is that the QoS information of each service is greatly affected by the network situation of those users. For example, because of network security and bandwidth constraints, the response time of all services invoked by user Jeremy is higher than the average level of other users. Meanwhile user Wade enjoys a higher speed of network bandwidth without constraints. Thus, the response time of all services is lower than others. This example shows that the QoS values contain diverse knowledge in each service. To precisely calculate the similarity relationship among services, the PCC algorithm is slightly modified to fit in the service side as follows:

$$S\_Sim(i,j) = \frac{\sum_{u \in U}(r_{u_i} - \bar{r}_u)(r_{u_j} - \bar{r}_u)}{\sqrt{\sum_{u \in U}(r_{u_i} - \bar{r}_u)^2}\sqrt{\sum_{u \in U}(r_u - \bar{r}_u)^2}} \qquad (3.23)$$

in which $U = U_1 \cap U_2$ is the set of users who both have invoked service s_i and s_j. $\bar{r}_u$ means the average QoS values of service invoked by u. In Eqn (3.23), the impact of different QoS scales is removed by using $(r_{u_i} - \bar{r}_u)$. After understanding the similarity relationship among services, those dissimilar service neighbors are filtered by using the *TOP_K_S* strategy as follows:

$$TS(i) = \{k | k \in TOP\_K\_S(i), S\_Sim(i,k) > 0\}$$

Similarly, the difference in latent features of each service inside a neighborhood is assumed to be minor. This assumption is transferred into a service regularization term and evolves to revamp the traditional MF model as follows:

$$\min_{U,S} L_2 = \frac{1}{2}\sum_{i=1}^{m}\sum_{j=1}^{n} I_{ij}(R_{ij} - U^T S)^2 + \frac{\lambda_1}{2}\|U\|_F^2 + \frac{\lambda_2}{2}\|S\|_F^2 + \frac{\alpha_2}{2}\sum_{j=1}^{n}\left\|S_j - \sum_{h \in TS(j)} PS_{jh} \cdot S_h\right\|_F^2 \qquad (3.24)$$

in which $\alpha_2 > 0$ and PS_{jh} is a normalized weight defined as follows:

$$PS_{jh} = \frac{S\_Sim(j,h)}{\sum_{l \in TS(j)} S\_Sim(j,l)} \qquad (3.25)$$

A local minimum of L_2 can be calculated by performing the gradient descent method as follows:

$$\frac{\partial L_1}{\partial U_i} = \sum_{j=1}^{n} I_{ij}(R_{ij} - U^T S)(-S_j) + \lambda_1 U_i$$

$$\frac{\partial L_1}{\partial S_j} = \sum_{i=1}^{m} I_{ij}(R_{ij} - U^T S)(-U_i) + \lambda_2 S_j + \alpha_2\left(S_j - \sum_{h \in TS(j)} PS_{jh} \cdot S_h\right) \qquad (3.26)$$

3.3.2.3 User and service neighborhood-based matrix factorization model

In previous research, most studies are performed on only one side to make predictions [20,31]. There are two reasons to explain this phenomenon: (1) these works do not treat the user side and service side symmetrically, and both sides thus could not be combined into a unified model and (2) the complexities of the previous algorithms lower the possibility of a combination. From the previous sections, each step in the proposed EMF framework is symmetrically: similarity calculation, neighborhood generation, regularization combination. Taking the different natures between both sides into consideration, two algorithms are used to measure the similarity. Also, different TOP_K values on both sides are chosen due to the varied population. The EMF framework is very efficient because the computation time is linear with respect to the matrix density. To sum up, a unified framework is constructed by fusing user side and service-side regularization terms as follows:

$$
\min_{U,S} L_3 = \frac{1}{2} \sum_{i=1}^{m} \sum_{j=1}^{n} I_{ij} \left(R_{ij} - U^T S \right)^2 + \frac{\lambda_1}{2} \|U\|_F^2 + \frac{\lambda_2}{2} \|S\|_F^2 + \frac{\alpha_1}{2} \sum_{i=1}^{m} \left\| U_i - \sum PU_{if} \cdot U_f \right\|_F^2
$$

$$
+ \frac{\alpha_2}{2} \sum_{j=1}^{n} \left\| S_j - \sum_{h \in TS(j)} PS_{jh} \cdot S_h \right\|_F^2
$$

$$(3.27)$$

A local minimum of L_3 is calculated by performing the gradient descent method as follows:

$$
\frac{\partial L_1}{\partial U_i} = \sum_{j=1}^{n} I_{ij} \left(R_{ij} - U^T S \right) \left(-S_j \right) + \lambda_1 U_i + \alpha_1 \left(U_i - \sum PU_{if} \cdot U_f \right)
$$

$$
\frac{\partial L_1}{\partial S_j} = \sum_{i=1}^{m} I_{ij} \left(R_{ij} - U^T S \right) \left(-U_i \right) + \lambda_2 S_j + \alpha_2 \left(S_j - \sum_{h \in TS(j)} PS_{jh} \cdot S_h \right)
$$

$$(3.28)$$

α is set to equal to α_1 and α_2 for simplicity.

3.3.2.4 Experiments for neighborhood-based matrix factorization models

The main computation of the EMF framework is evaluating the object function with their gradient parts. In this part, the EMF_F approach is evaluated because it is a combination between other methods. For EMF_F, the computational complexities for gradients $\partial L/\partial U$ and $\partial L/\partial S$ are both $O(\rho d + |u|kd)$ and $O(\rho d + |s|kd)$, in which ρ is the number of nonzero entries in matrix R, $|u|$ and $|s|$ are the population of both sides, k is the average population in each neighborhood and d is the dimensionality. In practice, the number of neighbors is far less than the total population of users and services. And it is also reasonable to assume that both populations are less than the total density of matrix R. Therefore, the total computational complexity in one iteration can be relaxed to $O(\rho d)$, which indicates that the computational time of *EMF_F* is linear with respect to the number of observations in the user-service QoS matrix. This complexity analysis shows that our proposed framework is very efficient and can be increased to a large-scale dataset.

The process of our proposed EMF approaches are general. It only requires the information from the QoS matrix, but not other heterogeneous data sources. As a result, they can be extended to other QoS invocation scenarios without any modification.

The experiments are conducted based on measuring the prediction accuracy of our EMF approaches. Our experiments are aimed at answering the following questions: (1) What is the measurement criterion? (2) How does our proposed EMF framework compare with other state-of-the art methods? (3) What is the impact of *TOP_K* thresholds on both sides? (4) What is the impact of the matrix density and dimensionality to our approaches?

The experiments are conducted on a public real-world web service QoS dataset, which was collected by Zibin Zheng et al. It contains 1,974,675 web service response time records. These results were collected from 339 distributed service users on 5825 web services. More details about this dataset can be found in [9].

The popular MAE is used as the measurement criterion of prediction accuracy. MAE is defined as:

$$\text{MAE} = \frac{1}{N}\sum_{i,j}\left|R_{ij} - \hat{R}_{ij}\right|$$

in which R_{ij} denotes the response time of the web service j observed by user i, $\hat{R}_{ij}$ is the predicted response time, and N is the number of predicted values. The MAE places equal weight on each individual difference.

The proposed approaches are compared with the following state-of-the-art methods.

1. UserMean (UMEAN): This method uses the mean QoS value of each user to predict the missing values.
2. ItemMean (IMEAN): This method uses the mean QoS value of every service to predict the missing values.
3. UPCC: This method is a classical one that involves similar user behavior to make predictions.
4. IPCC: This method is widely used in e-commerce scenarios. It captures similar service attributes to make predictions.
5. UIPCC: This method [19] is a combination between UPCC and IPCC.
6. SVD: This method is proposed by [22] in the CF area. It captures the latent structure of the original data distribution.

To make our experiments more realistic, QoS values are removed randomly to sparse the matrix. The matrix density is conducted from 5% to 20% with the ascending rate set as 5%. Matrix density equals 5% means that 5% of the entries are left for training and the rest, 95%, become test cases. In this part, the above six methods are compared with our proposed EMFs given the same training and test cases. The parameter settings of our proposed approaches are $TOP\_K\_U = 60$, $TOP\_K\_S = 300$, $\alpha = 0.001$, dimensionality $= 10$.

From Table 3.4, it is can be seen that our proposed EMF approaches obtain smaller MAE values than the others, which implies a higher prediction accuracy. Meanwhile, the MAE values slightly get smaller with the increase of the matrix density. This can be explained as more information can contribute to a better prediction performance. Besides, *EMF_F* consistently performs better than *EMF_U* and *EMF_S*, which means a combination of both sides can generate a better prediction result. MAE values of *EMF_S* are lower than *EMF_U* in general cases. The reason is that the number of services is approximately six times to the users, and hence more useful information is collected on the service side. Among all the prediction methods, the proposed approaches generally achieve lower prediction errors, which indicates that by incorporating relational constraints in the MF, we can generate better prediction accuracy.

1.　Impact of neighborhood size

In the EMF approach, the parameter *TOP_K_U* and *TOP_K_S* directly control the size of the neighborhood respectively. In the extreme case, if these values are set too small, EMF only listens to the advice from a few neighbors. If these values are set too high, EMF generates a large size of neighborhoods that contains varied noises. Figure 3.3 shows the impact of *TOP_K* values on the prediction accuracy. On the user side, as *TOP_K_U* increases, the MAE values at first decrease. But when *TOP_K_U* passes over a threshold, the MAE values soar again. This similar phenomena happens with respect to the service side. This observation can be explained when the *TOP_K* is smaller than a certain

Table 3.4: Comparison of prediction accuracy (a smaller value means a better performance)

Method	Density = 5% MAE	Density = 10% MAE	Density = 15% MAE	Density = 20% MAE	Density = 25% MAE	Density = 30% MAE
UMEAN	0.8813	0.8794	0.8787	0.8784	0.8753	0.8749
IMEAN	0.7888	0.7334	0.6810	0.6255	0.6078	0.5910
UPCC	0.8129	0.7412	0.7060	0.6834	0.6697	0.6504
IPCC	0.7916	0.7311	0.6910	0.6310	0.5937	0.5563
UIPCC	0.7632	0.6806	0.6337	0.6120	0.5736	0.5486
SVD	0.5691	0.5587	0.5437	0.5302	0.5222	0.5205
EMF_U	0.5571	0.5432	0.5391	0.5176	0.5070	0.4858
EMF_S	0.5409	0.5329	0.5192	0.5091	0.4976	0.4831
EMF_F	0.5189	0.5103	0.5022	0.4981	0.4718	0.4632

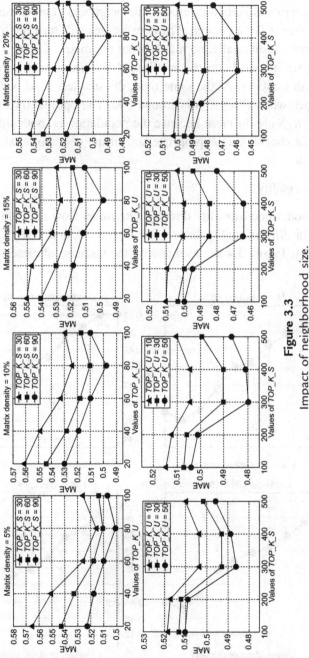

Figure 3.3

Impact of neighborhood size.

threshold, there are few neighbors contributing to the missing QoS value predictions, which prevents the users from fully absorbing the wisdom of the crowds.

When *TOP_K* is larger than a certain threshold, the neighbors contain much noise although the sample size is large enough. These two cases will turn out to lower the prediction performance. Additionally, no matter what the matrix density is, when *TOP_K_U* is around 80, it contributes the smallest MAE values, which means *TOP_K_U* meets a threshold in this dataset. At the same time, the smallest MAE values in all matrix density settings happen when *TOP_K_S* is around 300. The optimal thresholds of *TOP_K_U* and *TOP_K_S* are different because the population on both sides is varied. This observation shows that choosing an appropriate size of the neighborhood can achieve a better prediction result.

2.   Impact of dimensionality

In our proposed method, dimensionality directly determines how many factors involve MF. To study the impact of dimensionality, have *TOP_K_U* = 10, and *TOP_K_S* = 100 and tune the matrix density. Figure 3.4 shows that with the increase of dimensionality, the

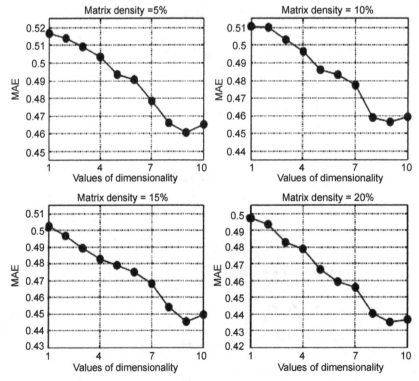

Figure 3.4
Impact of dimensionality.

values of MAE at first dramatically decrease. Then the values of MAE increase when dimensionality goes above a certain threshold (around 90 for MAE). These phenomena can be explained by the following two reasons: (1) the improvement of prediction accuracy confirms the intuition that a relatively larger dimension generates better results and (2) when the dimensionality surpasses a certain threshold, it may cause the issue of over fitting, which turns out to degrade the prediction performance.

3. Impact of matrix density

To study the impact of the matrix density on MAE, have $TOP\_K\_S = 100$ and dimensionality $= 10$, and TOP_K_U set as 5, 10, and 15.

Figure 3.5 shows that when the matrix density increases from 5% to 15%, the MAE values consistently decrease, which means the prediction accuracy has improved significantly. With the further increase in matrix density, MAE values slowly decrease. It shows that with more entries contributing to the training phase, EMF performs much better. Another observation is that if $TOP\_K\_U = 5$, the MAE values decrease sharply when the density is low. However, the MAE values decrease slowly when the density surpasses 20. This can be explained by the fact that in this configuration, when the training sample is small, our framework is sensitive to global information. Nevertheless, when the global information is abundant, the main power of improving prediction accuracy is the inner structure of our framework.

3.3.3 Location-Based Matrix Factorization Model

Previous CF approaches on web service studies used PCC [28] calculations to find a set of similar users. However, this type of similarity measurement is inappropriate to make

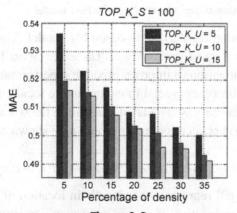

Figure 3.5

Impact of matrix density.

predictions on QoS values for the following reasons: (1) The QoS values in history records are not always accurate due to the complex nature of Internet environments. PCC relies heavily on accurate QoS values to identify similar user groups. (2) Classic CF methods are applied to the recommender systems that contain a lot of missing user ratings. Each rate represents a user's preference towards a specific item. However in web service scenarios, each QoS value is determined by the actual physical environment, and not by subjective judgment. This difference directly lowers the accuracy of the PCC similarity calculation.

It is natural to suppose that users in the same/near area tend to enjoy a similar web service invocation experience [20]. This idea captures the intuition since local users share the same IT infrastructures (network workloads, routers, etc.), and they thus tend to receive similar objective web service usage information. Although the neighborhood might choose different network configurations, and hence contribute diverse QoS information, these fluctuations exert far less influence than the geographical factor. Another advantage of using geographical information is that it can contribute to the framework and be more sensitive to the recent changes in QoS values. As a result, local information can be used to minimize the future errors with a higher confidence in the prediction process based on the above intuition, creating a novel collaborative QoS prediction framework built with a location-based regularization (LBR). First, the MFmodel [29] is expanded for missing values predictions. Then by understanding the local connectivity between web services users, the LBR incorporates geographical information to identify the neighborhood rather than classic PCC manners. Based on the assumption that users in the same neighborhood tend to receive similar objective information, two LBR terms are used to revamp the classic MF framework. More specifically, to capture the diverse experience inside the neighborhood, local users are treated differently in the above LBR terms. The computational complexity of the proposed framework is linear in practice, and thus LBR can be scaled to very large datasets.

3.3.3.1 Location regularization-based matrix factorization model

Paper [21] proposes a location regularization-based MF model. The core idea of user-collaboration is to identify a set of similar users. These neighbors living in a neighborhood contribute meaningful information to improve prediction performance. How to define the term, "neighborhood" becomes crucial in capturing the local connectivity. First, the Euclidean distance between users is calculated. Assuming the world is a sphere, the Euclidean distance $dist(i, j)$ between two users u_i and u_j is shown as the following:

$$dist(i,j) = \sqrt{(alt(i) - alt(j))^2 + (alt(i) - alt(j))^2} \tag{3.29}$$

in which $alt(i) \in (-180, 180]$ represents the altitude in location of u_i and $lat(i) \in (-180, 180]$ indicates the latitude in location of u_j. c is a constant converting the unit of degree to meter. In this case, $c = 111, 261$. After measuring the distance between users, the size of the neighborhood needs to be identified. In practice, the neighborhood size cannot be too large because it may contain a lot of noises and thus degrade the prediction performance. For a service user i, a set of neighborhood users $G(i)$ can be defined as follows:

$$G(i) = \{j | dist(i,j) \le \theta, \quad i \ne j\}$$

in which θ is a geographical threshold to control the neighborhood size. This definition implies that the neighbor relationships are symmetric because the local relationships are bidirectional. With the help of neighborhood information, two LBR approaches are built for the QoS prediction.

As mentioned above, it is natural to suppose that users in the same/near area tend to share a similar web service invocation experience. This intuition indicates that the differences of user feature vectors in the neighborhood should be minor. This idea is converted into the following mathematical form:

$$\min \left\| U_i - \frac{1}{|G(i)|} \sum_{g \in G(i)} U_g \right\|_F^2 \tag{3.30}$$

The above constraint term is used to minimize the invocation experience between a user u_i and its neighborhood to an average level. More specifically, if the neighborhood of user u_i is $G(i)$, then u_i's invocation experience (feature vector U_i) should be close to the general experience of all neighbors in $G(i)$, which is $^1/_{|G(i)|} \sum_{g \in G(i)} U_g$. This representation is consistent with this intuition. This regularization term is added in the first proposed approach to revamp the MF model as follows:

$$\min_{U,S} L_1 = \frac{1}{2} \sum_{i=1}^{m} \sum_{j=1}^{n} I_{ij} \left(R_{ij} - U^T S \right)^2 + \frac{\lambda_1}{2} \|U\|_F^2 + \frac{\lambda_2}{2} \|S\|_F^2 + \frac{\alpha_1}{2} \sum_{i=1}^{m} \left\| U_i - \frac{1}{|G(i)|} \sum_{g \in G(i)} U_g \right\|_F^2 \tag{3.31}$$

in which $\alpha_1 > 0$ is controlling the importance of this term. This objective function takes all of the users into consideration, and thus it is aiming at minimizing the global differences within different neighborhoods. Similar to the traditional MF model, the global minimum of L_1 cannot be achievable due to the nature of its inner structure [32]. The gradient descent method is proposed to calculate its local minimum as follows:

$$\frac{\partial L_1}{\partial U_i} = \sum_{j=1}^{n} I_{ij} \left(R_{ij} - U^T S \right) (-S_j) + \lambda_1 U_i + \alpha_1 \left(U_i - \frac{1}{|G(i)|} \sum_{g \in G(i)} U_g \right)$$

$$\frac{\partial L_1}{\partial S_j} = \sum_{i=1}^{m} I_{ij} \left(R_{ij} - U^T S \right) (-U_i) + \lambda_2 S_j \tag{3.32}$$

In the following, the proposed approaches are compared with the following state-of-the-art methods:

1. UserMean: This method uses the mean QoS value of each user to predict the missing values.
2. ItemMean: This method uses the mean QoS value of every service to predict the missing values.
3. UPCC: This method is a classical one that involves similar user behavior to make predictions.
4. IPCC: This method is widely used in e-commerce scenarios. It captures similar service attributes to make predictions.
5. UIPCC: This method [19] is a combination between UPCC and IPCC.
6. RegionKNN: This method is proposed by Chen et al. in [20]. It incorporates the geographical information to a hybrid memory-based CF method.
7. SVD: This method is proposed by Koren et al. in [22]. It captures the latent structure of the original data distribution.

In this section, to make our experiments more realistic, QoS values are randomly removed to sparse the matrix. The matrix density is conducted as 5%, 10%, 15%, and 20%. For example, the matrix density equals 5% means that 5% of the entries are left for training and the rest, 95%, become the test cases. In this part, the above seven methods are compared with our proposed approaches given the same training and test cases. The parameter settings of our proposed approaches are $\theta = 100$, $\alpha = 0.001$, dimensionality = 10, and $\lambda_U = \lambda_S = 0.001$.

Table 3.5 shows that the comparison results and detailed analysis on parameter tunings will be provided as follows. From Table 3.5, it is can be found that our proposed LBR1 and LBR2 approaches obtain smaller MAE and RMSE values than others, which implies a

Table 3.5: Comparison of prediction accuracy (a smaller value means a better performance)

Method	Matrix Density = 5%		Matrix Density = 10%		Matrix Density = 15%		Matrix Density = 20%	
	MAE	RMSE	MAE	RMSE	MAE	RMSE	MAE	RMSE
UMEAN	0.8813	1.8601	0.8794	1.8588	0.8787	1.8586	0.8784	1.8588
IMEAN	0.7888	1.6450	0.7334	1.6198	0.6810	1.6962	0.6255	1.6078
UPCC	0.8129	1.7204	0.7412	1.6578	0.7060	1.5753	0.6834	1.5497
IPCC	0.7916	1.5563	0.7311	1.4892	0.6910	1.3843	0.6310	1.3755
UIPCC	0.7632	1.5360	0.6806	1.4442	0.6337	1.4047	0.6120	1.3864
RegionKNN	0.6782	1.5319	0.6429	1.4031	0.6021	1.3784	0.5722	1.3810
SVD	0.5691	1.5022	0.5587	1.3849	0.5437	1.3615	0.5302	1.3495
LBR1	0.5673	1.4529	0.5532	1.3911	0.5376	1.3701	0.5058	1.3396
LBR2	0.5389	1.4130	0.5292	1.3481	0.5180	1.3260	0.4941	1.3147

higher prediction accuracy. Meanwhile, with the increase of matrix density, the MAE and RMSE values get slightly smaller. This can be explained as more information can contribute to better prediction performance. The MAE and RMSE values of LBR1 are consistently higher than LBR2, which means assigning different weights to neighbors improves the prediction performance. Among all the prediction methods, our proposed approaches improves by 23.7% the MAE prediction accuracy for general cases, which indicates incorporating geographical information in the MF model can generate better prediction performance.

1.   Impact of θ

In our proposed methods, the geographical threshold θ controls the size of the neighborhood. If the value of θ is small, only those neighbors living in a short distance can be identified. If the value of θ is large, neighbors, to a large extent, can be incorporated.

Figure 3.6 shows the impact of a geographical threshold θ on the prediction accuracy. As θ increases, the MAE and RMSE values at first decrease. When θ passes over a threshold, the MAE and RMSE values soar again. This observation can be explained as follows: When θ is smaller than a certain threshold, there are few neighbors contributing to the missing QoS values predictions, which prevents a user to fully absorb the wisdom of the crowds. When θ is larger than a certain threshold, the neighbors contain much noise even though the sample size is large enough. These two cases will turn out to lower the prediction performance. No matter what the matrix density is, θ around 100 contributes to the smallest MAE values, which means θ meets a threshold in this dataset. At the same time, the smallest RMSE values in all matrix density settings happen when θ is around 60. The optimal thresholds of MAE and RMSE are different because they are different criteria focusing on different aspects. The observation shows that choosing an appropriate size for a neighborhood can achieve a better result.

2.   Impact of α

In the LBR approaches, the parameter α controls how much the regularization terms influence the objective functions. In the extreme case, if α is set too small, the LBRs mainly focus on the general MF model and underestimate the importance of the LBR terms. Meanwhile if α is set too large, the geographical information dominates the prediction process, which would potentially harm the prediction performance. In other cases, α can be tuned to appropriately combine the MF and LBR. In the following section, we will mainly analyze how the changes of α can affect the prediction accuracy. Dimensionality is set to 10. Meanwhile the parameter θ is tuned from 80 to 120 and the density from 10% to 15%.

Figure 3.7 shows that as α increases, the MAE and RMSE values at first decrease (the prediction accuracy increases). When α goes above a certain threshold, the MAE and

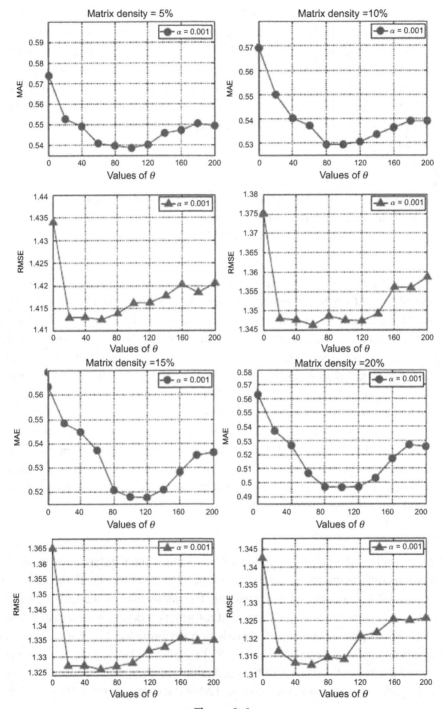

Figure 3.6
Impact of θ.

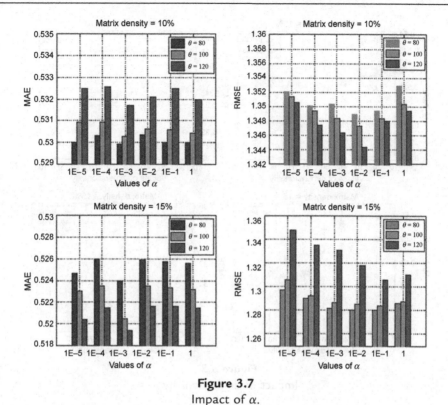

Figure 3.7

Impact of α.

RMSE values increase slightly. The threshold in MAE is around $\alpha = 10-3$ in all cases. Meanwhile, α around $10-2$ is the threshold in the RMSE criterion. The existence of a turning point confirms our intuition that solely using MF and geographical connectivity cannot contribute to a better prediction accuracy, rather than an appropriate combination. Moreover, the framework is steady because it remains the same for similar trends in all configurations with respect to different criteria.

3. Impact of dimensionality

In our proposed methods, dimensionality determines how many factors are involved in the MF. To study the impact of dimensionality, α is set to 0.001. We also tune the parameter θ as 100 and 160, and the density from 10% to 15%.

Figure 3.8 shows that with the increase of the dimensionality, the values of MAE and RMSE at first dramatically decrease. However, the values of MAE and RMSE increase when dimensionality goes above a certain threshold (90 for MAE and 80 for RMSE). These phenomena can be explained by the following two reasons: (1) the improvement of the prediction accuracy confirms the intuition that a relatively larger dimension generates better results and (2) when the dimensionality surpasses a certain threshold, it

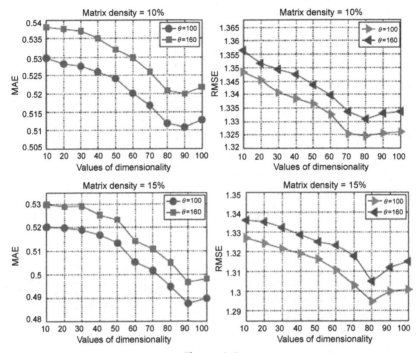

Figure 3.8
Impact of dimensionality.

may cause the issue of over fitting, which turns out to degrade the prediction performance.

4.   Impact of matrix density

To study the impact of the matrix density on MAE and RMSE, we set $\theta = 100$ and $\theta = 150$ respectively, and vary the density percentage from 2 to 20. Also, we set $\alpha = 0.001$.

Figure 3.9 shows that when the matrix density increases from 2% to 8%, both MAE and RMSE decrease sharply, which means the prediction accuracy is significantly improved. With the further increase in the matrix density, both MAE and RMSE slowly decrease. It shows that with more entries contributing to the training phase, our proposed approaches perform much better.

3.3.3.2 Location ensemble-based matrix factorization model

In the LBR model, the contributions of all neighbors are treated equally, which does not correspond well with the real scenario of web service invocation. In reality, the infrastructure of the neighbors who are nearer is more similar with that of the user, so the QoS values of the same web service invoked by them are closer, which is shown in Figure 3.10.

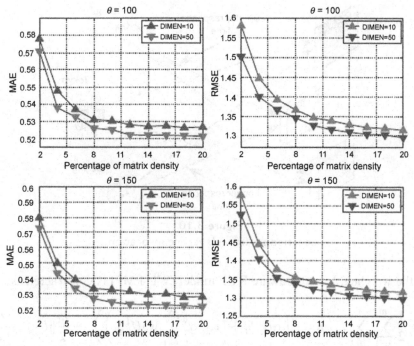

Figure 3.9
Impact of matrix density.

Taking this fact into account, this paper [33] builds a location ensemble-based MF model. First, the similarity is defined between two users as:

$$Sim_{il} = \exp(-d_{il}) \tag{3.33}$$

in which d_{il} is the distance between user i and user l, and $Sim_{il} \in (0,1]$. $Sim_{il} = 1$ means that d_{il} is equal to 0, namely that user i and user l live in the exact same place, and $Sim \rightarrow 0$ means that the two users live extremely far apart; for instance, user i lives in Tokyo, while user l lives in Kabul. Note that the form of the similarity calculation formula is not exclusive, because any similarity formula satisfying the properties that $exp(-d_{il})$ possesses can be a candidate. Further, the normalized similarity as the measurement of the individual importance of each neighbor is calculated as:

$$w_{il} = \frac{Sim_{il}}{\sum_{g \in L} Sim_{ig}} \tag{3.34}$$

Finally, the final QoS value of web service j invoked by user i is shown more properly as:

$$r_{ij} \approx \alpha U_i^T S_j + (1 - \alpha) \sum_{l=1}^{k} w_{il} U_l^T S_j \tag{3.35}$$

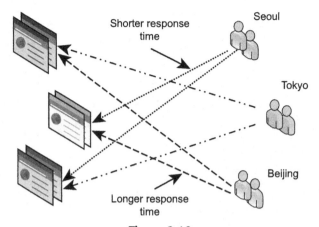

Figure 3.10
Location-aware web service invocation.

Therefore, the weighted location-aware PMF model (WL-PMF) is constructed as:

$$\min_{U,S} L = \frac{1}{2} \sum_{i=1}^{m} \sum_{j=1}^{n} I_{ij} \left(R_{ij} - \left(\alpha U_i^T S_j + (1-\alpha) \sum_{l=1}^{k} w_{il} U_l^T S_j \right) \right)^2 + \frac{\lambda_1}{2} \|U\|_F^2 + \frac{\lambda_2}{2} \|S\|_F^2$$

$$(3.36)$$

in which $\|\cdot\|_F^2$ denotes the Frobenius norm. The gradient descent can be used over matrix U and S to find a local minimum of the objective function in Eqn (3.36). So for the "cold-start" user or service, even if the result obtained from their own corresponding feature vectors is not very satisfying, the accuracy of the predicted value can be further improved by the rectification of the learning results of the neighbors' feature vectors. The partial derivatives of the objective function over latent user and service feature vectors are as follows:

$$\frac{\partial L_1}{\partial U_i} = \sum_{j=1}^{n} I_{ij} \left(R_{ij} - \left(\alpha U_i^T S_j + (1-\alpha) \sum_{l=1}^{k} w_{il} U_l^T S_j \right) \right)(-S_j)$$

$$+\lambda_1 U_i + (1-\alpha) \sum_{g \in G(i)} \sum_{j=1}^{n} I_{gi} w_{gi} S_j \left(\alpha U_g^T S_j + (1-\alpha) \sum_{l=1}^{k} w_{gl} U_l^T S_j - R_{gj} \right)$$

$$(3.37)$$

$$\times \frac{\partial L_1}{\partial S_j} = \sum_{i=1}^{m} I_{ij} \left(R_{ij} - R_{ij} - \left(\alpha U_i^T S_j + (1-\alpha) \sum_{l=1}^{k} w_{il} U_l^T S_j \right) \right)(-U_i)$$

$$\times \left(\alpha U_i^T + (1-\alpha) \sum_{l=1}^{k} w_{il} U_l^T \right) + \lambda_2 S_j$$

in which $G(i)$ contains all the users whose neighbors include user i.

Several other state-of-the-art approaches are chosen to compare with our two models, including:

1. UPCC: This approach is much similar with user-based CF, which first calculates the similarity between users based on PCC and then gains the predicted value as the weighted average of the known values of the similar users [18].
2. IPCC: This approach is similar with UPCC, except that the key procedure is the similarity calculation between items [25].
3. UIPCC: This approach combines the advantage of UPCC and IPCC by balancing the proportions of them in the final result [19].
4. RegionKNN: This approach classifies services and users into different regions, and modifies UPCC by the similarity computation between regions and the identification of similar services and users in the same regions [34].
5. Basic-PMF: This approach is proposed by [22], and has been verified to be effective in recommender systems. A detailed explanation has been given to show how the basic PMF model can be used for QoS prediction.
6. LBR2: This approach first calculates the differences of the latent feature vectors between the user and the neighbors, and then appends the Frobenius norm of the differences to the objective function of the MF model [21].

The whole dataset is divided into training data and testing data by randomly removing a large number of QoS values in the user–service invocation matrix. For instance, 95% of the values are randomly removed as testing data, and the 5% left in the matrix is trained to predict those removed ones. More specifically, four types of data sparsity are used to conduct the experiments, which are 95%, 90%, 85%, and 80%. In our experiments, the default parameter settings are $k = 40$, $\alpha = 0.6$, and $d = 10$, in which d represents the dimensionality of the latent feature vector. Moreover, λ_U and λ_S are set to 0.001 equally in all of the following experiments.

Table 3.6 shows that Basic-PMF gets better prediction accuracy than RegionKNN and UIPCC, which verifies its effectiveness. Meanwhile, our two models achieve smaller RMSE and MAE under all situations of data sparsity. In addition, WL-PMF achieves better performance than L-PMF in most cases, which is consistent with the fact that the neighbors who are nearer share more similar invocation experience with the user. Further, WL-PMF on average, gains 5.68% and 3.80% performance improvement in RMSE, as well as 10.27% and 6.61% improvement in MAE, in comparison with Basic-PMF and LBR2, respectively. Moreover, prediction accuracy increases with the increasing of the data density, which is a natural phenomenon showing that more historical records can depict user features more accurately.

Table 3.6: Comparison of prediction accuracy (a smaller value means a better performance)

| | Matrix Density (MD) | | | | | | | |
| | MD = 5% | | MD = 10% | | MD = 15% | | MD = 20% | |
Approach	RMSE	MAE	RMSE	MAE	RMSE	MAE	RMSE	MAE
UPCC	1.6670	0.7839	1.6012	0.7445	1.4745	0.6824	1.4179	0.6418
IPCC	1.5231	0.7838	1.4585	0.7296	1.4184	0.6839	1.3430	0.6111
UIPCC	1.5059	0.7639	1.4349	0.6862	1.4065	0.6698	1.3341	0.5919
RegionKNN	1.4932	0.7620	1.4047	0.6659	1.3564	0.6483	1.3134	0.5911
Basic-PMF	1.4995	0.7450	1.3790	0.6183	1.3326	0.6020	1.2730	0.5649
LBR2	1.4671	0.7132	1.3286	0.6130	1.3196	0.5726	1.2608	0.5332
L-PMF	1.4347	0.6635	1.2955	0.5667	1.2411	0.5292	1.2106	0.5095
WL-PMF	1.4345	0.6702	1.2908	0.5656	1.2389	0.5275	1.2099	0.5077

1. Impact of α

The parameter α regulates the respective proportions of latent feature vectors of the user and his or her neighbors in the learning process of the missing QoS values. We investigate the impact of α from the range of 0.1−0.9 in the experiment settings of $k = 40$ and $d = 10$, under the scenario of the matrix density being equal to 10% and 15%, respectively.

As shown in Figure 3.11, RMSE and MAE both reach the minimum in the range of 0.5−0.7 and get acceptable and relatively small values when α continues increasing. They suffer from drastic fluctuations and achieve large values below 0.5. This changing trend indicates that although the contributions of the feature vectors of the neighbors take on important roles, the significance of the user's own feature vectors are always dominant. Finally, we can draw such a conclusion that if the neighbor's feature vectors account for a too large proportion, it will lead to the deviation of the predicted value from the real QoS

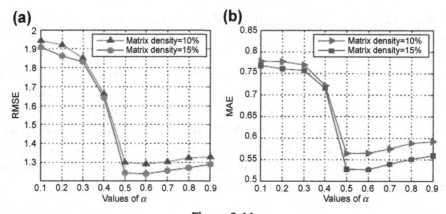

Figure 3.11
Impact of α.

value, so α must be not less than 0.5. In addition, if α is equal to one, then the WL−PMF model is degenerated into the basic PMF model, the performance of which is comparatively lower.

2. Impact of k

The parameter k determines the number of neighbors whose latent feature vectors are integrated into the targeted QoS value. In ideal conditions, only those neighbors who are near enough to ensure that they really share similar infrastructure with the user should be involved. We investigate the impact of k in the experiment settings of $\alpha = 0.6$ and $d = 10$.

Figure 3.12 shows that, from the perspective of both RMSE and MAE, WL−PMF achieves the highest prediction accuracy when $k = 40$, and suffers from performance degradation when k is much smaller or bigger. This phenomenon demonstrates that on the one hand, those neighbors relatively farther away may introduce noise into the predicted value, and, on the other hand, too small a number of neighbors cannot provide enough valuable auxiliary information for the learning process. Meanwhile, because the extent of the variation of RMSE and MAE is relatively small from $k = 10$ to $k = 190$, it shows that WL−PMF has a high scalability and flexibility to the number of neighbors.

3. Impact of d

The parameter d controls the number of latent features of a user, which cannot be directly observed. We investigate the impact of d in the value range of 5 to 30 in the experiment settings of $k = 40$ and $\alpha = 0.6$. As shown in Figure 3.13, as d increases, both RMSE and MAE at first decrease, and reach the minima at $d = 10$, and then begin to increase again.

Figure 3.13 also shows that WL-PMF gains satisfactory accuracy among values from 5 to 20, but does not perform as well from the value 25, which indicates that the actual number

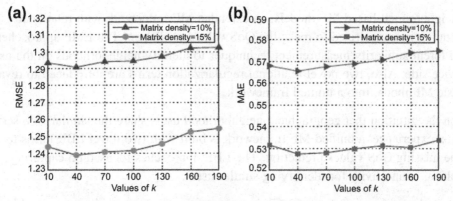

Figure 3.12

Impact of k.

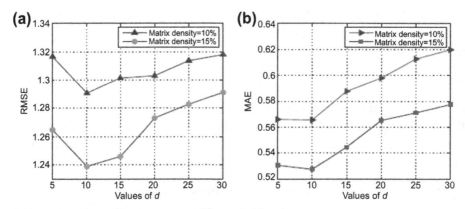

Figure 3.13
Impact of dimensionality.

of features dominating the experience of a user in web service invocation is limited. Meanwhile, because the threshold with the smallest RMSE is 10, it is inferred that the factors influencing the process of the web service invocation varies relatively in the real world. This result does not mean that in every practical scenario, the optimal value of d is always 10 due to the variety and complexity of the factors influencing the QoS values.

3.4 Summary

In this chapter, we primarily reviewed the two types of methods for QoS prediction, which are the CF-based model and MF-based model. In the neighborhood-based CF approach, the A-cosine equation is used to compute the service-based similarity. This method adds a data smoothing process to improve the prediction accuracy, and extract information from the QoS of similar services to similar users to handle the data sparsity problem.

In the neighborhood-based MF models, an extended MF framework with relational regularization is summarized to make the QoS values prediction. The EMF approaches adopt different similarity measurement techniques to identify neighborhoods on the user and service side. Also, two novel relational regularization terms are introduced to revamp the classic MF model into a unified framework.

Based on the intuition that geographical neighborhood users share the similar web services invocation experience, a unified MF framework is built with two novel LBR terms to make the missing QoS values prediction. The LBR approaches focused on capturing geographical connectivity for identifying similar users.

In future studies, other directions for CF-based service-selection architecture should be explored, e.g., pruning. Moreover, more QoS data from web services should be collected to perform larger-scale experiments. Finally, tags, which are annotated to web services by users, will be used to improve the performance of the CF-based service selection. In addition, more relational regularization terms should be applied to solve the problem of QoS prediction. The other parts in the EMF service selection framework will be explored extensively. Moreover, the geographical information of web services should also be used to further improve the prediction accuracy.

References

[1] L.-J. Zhang, J. Zhang, H. Cai, Services Computing, Springer, 2007.

[2] M.P. Papazoglou, Service-oriented computing: concepts, characteristics and directions, in: International Conference on Web Information System Engineering, Springer, 2003, pp. 3−12.

[3] Y. Liu, A.H. Ngu, L.Z. Zeng, QoS computation and policing in dynamic web service selection, in: Proceedings of the 13th International World Wide Web Conference, ACM, 2004, pp. 66−73.

[4] A.F. Huang, C.-W. Lan, S.J. Yang, An optimal QoS-based web service selection scheme, J. Inform. Sci. 179 (19) (2009) 3309−3322.

[5] M. Alrifai, T. Risse, Combining global optimization with local selection for efficient QoS-aware service composition, in: Proceedings of World Wide Web Conference, ACM, 2009.

[6] D. Grigori, J.C. Corrales, M. Bouzeghoub, A. Gater, Ranking BPEL processes for service discovery, IEEE Trans. Serv. Comput. 3 (3) (2010) 178−192.

[7] G. Meditskos, N. Bassiliades, Structural and role-oriented web service discovery with taxonomies in OWL-S, IEEE. Trans. Knowl. Data Eng. 22 (2) (2010) 278−290.

[8] M.-H. Kuo, L.-C. Chen, C.-W. Liang, Building and evaluating a location-based service recommendation system with a preference adjustment mechanism, Expert Syst. Appl. 36 (2) (2009) 3543−3554.

[9] Z. Zheng, H. Ma, M.R. Lyu, I. King, QoS-aware web service recommendation by collaborative filtering, IEEE Trans. Serv. Comput. 4 (2) (2011) 140−152.

[10] S.X. Sun, J. Zhao, A decomposition-based approach for service composition with global QoS guarantees, Inform. Sci. 199 (15) (2012) 138−153.

[11] P. Xiong, M. Zhou, A petri net approach to analysis and composition of web services, IEEE Trans. Syst. Man Cybern. A Syst. Humans 40 (2) (2010) 376−387.

[12] Y. Lu, W. Wang, B. Bhargava, D. Xu, Trust-based privacy preservation for peer-to-peer data sharing, IEEE Trans. Syst. Man Cybern. A Syst. Humans 36 (3) (2006) 498−502.

[13] H. Skogsrud, B. Benatallah, F. Casati, Model-driven trust negotiation for web services, Internet Computing, IEEE 7 (6) (2003) 45−52.

[14] M. Kim, H. Choo, M.W. Mutka, H.-J. Lim, K. Park, On QoS multicast routing algorithms using k-minimum steiner trees, Inform. Sci. 238 (20) (2013) 190−204.

[15] L. Layuan, L. Chunlin, A QoS multicast routing protocol for dynamic group topology, Inform. Sci. 169 (1) (2005) 113−130.

[16] S. Ran, A model for web services discovery with QoS, ACM SIGecom Exchanges 4 (1) (2003) 1−10.

[17] Z. Zheng, M. Lyu, I. King, WSRec: a collaborative filtering based web service recommender system, in: Int'l Conf. on Web Services (ICWS '09), IEEE, 2009, pp. 437−444.

[18] L. Shao, J. Zhang, Y. Wei, J. Zhao, B. Xie, H. Mei, Personalized QoS prediction for web services via collaborative filtering, in: Proc. Int. Conf. Web Serv., Salt Lake City, UT, 2007, pp. 439−446.

[19] Z. Zheng, H. Ma, M.R. Lyu, I. King, QoS-aware web service recommendation by collaborative filtering, IEEE Trans. Serv. Comput. (2011) 140−152.

[20] X. Chen, Z. Zheng, X. Liu, Z. Huang, H. Sun, Personalized QoS aware web service recommendation and visualization, IEEE Trans. Serv. Comput., IEEE.

[21] W. Lo, J. Yin, S. Deng, Y. Li, Z. Wu, Collaborative web service QoS prediction with location-based regularization, in: Proc. of ICWS, IEEE, 2012, pp. 464–471.

[22] Y. Koren, R.M. Bell, C. Volinsky, Matrix factorization techniques for recommender systems, IEEE Comp. 42 (8) (2009) 30–37.

[23] D. Goldberg, D. Nichols, B. Oki, D. Terry, Using collaborative filtering to weave an information tapestry, Commun. ACM 35 (12) (1992) 61–70.

[24] X. Su, T.M. Khoshgoftaar, A survey of collaborative filtering techniques, in: Advances in Artificial Intellegence Hindawi Publishing Corp, 2009, Volume, 2009, pp. 1–20.

[25] B. Sarwar, G. Karypic, J. Konstan, J. Riedl, Item-based collaborative filtering recommendation algorithms, in: Proc. Int. World Wide Web Conf., Hong Kong, China, 2001, pp. 285–295.

[26] L. Chen, Y. Feng, J. Wu, Collaborative QoS prediction via feedback-based trust model, in: Proc. of IEEE SOCA, IEEE, 2013, pp. 206–213.

[27] Z. Zheng, Y. Zhang, M.R. Lyu, Distributed QoS evaluation for real-world web services, in: Proc. of International Conference on Web Services (ICWS), IEEE, 2010, pp. 83–90.

[28] Y. Koren, Factor in the neighbors: scalable and accurate collaborative filtering, ACM Trans. Knowl. Discov. Data (2010).

[29] Y. Koren, R. Bell, Advances in collaborative filtering, in: Recommender Systems Handbook, Springer, 2011.

[30] W. Lo, J. Yin, S. Deng, Y. Li, Z. Wu, An extended matrix factorization approach for QoS prediction in service selection, in: Proc. of IEEE SCC, IEEE, 2012, pp. 162–169.

[31] L. Shao, J. Zhang, Y. Wei, J. Zhao, B. Xie, H. Mei, Personalized QoS prediction for web services via collaborative filtering, in: IEEE International Conference on Web Services (ICWS), IEEE, 2007.

[32] Y. Koren, Collaborative filtering with temporal dynamics, Commun. ACM (2010).

[33] Y. Xu, J. Yin, W. Lo, Z. Wu, Personalized location-aware QoS prediction for web services using probabilistic matrix factorization, in: Proc. of WISE, Springer, 2013, pp. 229–242.

[34] X. Chen, X. Liu, Z. Huang, H. Sun, RegionKNN: a scalable hybrid collaborative filtering algorithm for personalized web service recommendation, in: Proc. of ICWS, 2010, pp. 9–16.

CHAPTER 4

Service Discovery

Chapter Outline

4.1 Introduction

Web services are self-contained, self-describing, modular applications that can be published, located, and invoked across the web. The emergence of technologies and standards for web services has promoted the wide application of web service in many different areas, such as business, finance, and tourism. As a result, published services have mushroomed over the Internet, bringing about a pressing challenge to locate target services in a quick, accurate, and efficient way.

Service Computing: Concepts, Methods and Technology. http://dx.doi.org/10.1016/B978-0-12-802330-3.00004-7

Web service discovery is aimed at finding and selecting the target services that satisfy users' needs and constraints in the functional interface, interactive behavior, and nonfunctional attributes, through appropriate service-matching criteria and methods, from one or more service registries over a distributed network. In this process, a primary step is to analyze and compare service descriptions and service requests based on certain matching criteria, checking whether it meets and matches the needs of users. This step is also called service matchmaking. Web service discovery and service matching are closely related; the former is often built on the basis of the latter. Early web service description documents are based on natural language, and the description of service functionality is ambiguous in semantics, while the corresponding service discovery method is based on keyword matchmaking, which seriously affects the discovery recall rate and necessary precision.

The integration of semantic technology and web services technology is an effective solution to accurate and automatic service discovery. By adding machine-understandable semantic information to service descriptions and service requests, the interfaces, functionality interactions, etc. of a service can be exactly expressed, and the intrinsic relationship among messages, interface, and services can be reasoned, so an automatic, intelligent, accurate semantic web service discovery can be achieved. Among them, the semantic description models and languages of web services and service requests are the modeling basis of semantic web service discovery; various levels of service-matching criteria and methods, which are critical processes of semantic web service discovery, and services ranking and selection represent further optimization approaches for semantic web service discovery results. In addition, there are many important research issues in service discovery, e.g., how to store, organize, and manage vast amounts of web services in centralized, distributed, and hybrid registries to improve the performance of the service discovery, help to define the degree of matchmaking between service descriptions and service requests, and help to design appropriate ranking and selection mechanisms.

A service can be viewed as a primitive, in decomposable process, which is referred to as the "black-box" view. In this perspective, a service exposes its input and output interfaces to the outside (such as the service description languages WSDL [1] and OWL-S [2]). The service discovery for atomic services is always called "interface-level service discovery," and its criteria is that a service advertisement matches a request when all the outputs of the request are matched by the outputs of the advertisement, and all the inputs of the advertisement are matched by the inputs of the request. The criteria guarantees that the matched service satisfies the needs of the requester and that the requester provides to the matched service all the inputs that are needed to operate correctly. A forward approach is that by sequentially scanning all the services in the registry, each service is matched against the request. Each matching between the service and the request can be divided into matching on inputs and matching on outputs. We may foresee that much time may be wasted on matching many irrelevant services when there are millions of services kept in the registry.

A service can also be viewed as a process flow composed of a set of operations linked with control constructs, which is what we call the transparent view. In this perspective, services expose not only the interfaces, but also the behavior rules, such as the message exchanges and the state transitions (service model of OWL-S). The service discovery strategies for composite services are always called "behavioral-level service discovery," and its criteria is that a service matches a request on behavior, when the requested operations are included by the operations of the service, and the invoking order between the operations within the service is compliant with the requested behavior.

In the following sections, we will first review the related work on service discovery, including interface-level and behavioral-level service discovery in Section 4.2, and then introduce our work on interface-level and behavioral-level service discovery in Sections 4.3 and 4.4, respectively. For our work on interface-level service discovery, we propose to use web service clustering and tag recommendation to improve the effectiveness of web service discovery. Specifically, both WSDL documents and tags of web services are used for clustering, while tag recommendation is adopted to handle some inherent problems of tagging data, e.g., uneven tag distribution and noise tags. For our work on behavioral-level service discovery, we propose to formalize the behavior of a web service by π-calculus. Based on the formalization, we introduce two notions of behavioral substitution of web services, strong and weak simulation. Furthermore, we propose a derivative approach to analyzing the behavioral substitution of services according to the given notions, which is implemented based on an existing tool of π-calculus. The proposed approach takes advantage of the formalization and theory of π-calculus, so that the formalized services can be naturally analyzed and the behavioral substitution of them can be easily determined. Finally, a conclusion is given in Section 4.5.

4.2 Related Work

4.2.1 Interface-Level Service Discovery

Much of the work done in service discovery concentrates on the matchmaking of service interfaces [3–6]. This includes the lexical and semantic match of input/output messages and operations. The most representative work is the solution proposed by Paolucci and Sycara, which is able to represent functionalities of web services [3]. In their matchmaking algorithm, they differentiate among four degrees of matching: exact, plug in, subsume, and fail. The matchmaking of a service advertisement is separated into two parts: outputs of the request are matched by that of the advertisement, and inputs of the advertisement are matched by that of the request. Complex structures of services are not considered in these discovery approaches.

Since 2006, a lot of efforts have been made in describing the internal structures of services, evidenced by the emergence of Web Services Conversation Language (WSCL) [7] and Web Services Choreography Description Language (WS-CDL) [8]. WSCL allows the abstract interfaces of web services, i.e., the business-level conversations or public processes supported by a web service. WS-CDL describes collaborations of web services participants by defining, from a global viewpoint, their common and complementary observable behavior, by which ordered message exchanges result in accomplishing a common business goal. However, the capabilities of formalizations are only used for defining the languages itself, rather than exploring them to draw conclusions over the semantic of descriptions.

Recently, web service clustering has proved to be an effective solution to boost the performance of the web service discovery. The most widely used approach for it is similarity based, including (1) semantic based and (2) nonsemantic based. For the calculation of nonsemantic similarity between web services, WSDL-based approaches are the most representative type [9–11]. Content, context, host name, and service name are extracted as four main features from the WSDL document for web services clustering. Although WSDL-based techniques are widely adopted, the performance is rather limited because only WSDL documents are used. With the development of the web service community, more and more tags are annotated to web services by users. These tags can be used to enhance the accuracy of service discovery. However, limited work has exploited tagging data for service discovery. Thus, we propose to use both tagging data and WSDL documents to improve the performance of web service clustering. Moreover, we propose tag recommendation strategies to handle another performance limitation caused by the web services with few tags.

4.2.2 Behavioral-Level Service Discovery

During the past decade, various efforts have been devoted to explore the equivalence between web services at the behavioral-level. We briefly mention some of these proposals, focusing on those which use formal methods for the analysis of the behavioral equivalence of web services.

The most popular formal theories used for the formalization of web services include automata, Petri nets, and π-calculus. Automata is an effective model to describe a system with state transitions enabled by actions, while Petri nets and π-calculus are better at describing the control constructs of a process; hence the latter two are more suited to formalize composite services. Petri nets provide a series of property detections of a process such as deadlock and reachability detections, while π-calculus provides a bisimulation theory, which can be directly used for behavioral comparison between two processes. Hence we adopt π-calculus to formalize services in this chapter.

Sudhir Agarwal and Rudi Studer [12] combined the power of description logics and π-calculus to model static (schema and data) and dynamic (behavior) aspects of a web service. Their formalization can express the functionality of a service clearly, but it is relatively weak in expressing the working process of a service, only with the support of sequence and conditional choice. Frank Puhlmann and Mathias Weske [13] modeled a web service originally in BPMN with π-calculus. They focused on the representation of choreography of multiple activities by using link passing mobility. Gero Decker et al. [14] proposed to use π-calculus for formally representing service interaction patterns, which is summarized by Barros et al. [15]. Roberto Lucchi and Manuel Mazzara [16] proposed to model a web service in WS-BPEL 2.0 with a lightweight extension of π-calculus. They focused on the modeling of long-running transactions and compensations for coping with error handling in web services with the added transactional construct. Antonio Brogi et al. [17] proposed to model a web service in WSCI with π-calculus. They further modeled all the control constructs in WSCI, including all, sequence, loop, timeout, exception, switch, and choice. Compared with their work, we focus on modeling control constructs of a service process, and we use the idea of creating private channels as triggers to model all control constructs, which makes all control flows within a service process as internal actions, being invisible from the outside.

There have been many notions of substitutability/replaceability/equivalence for web services.

A. Wombacher et al. [18] proposed to formalize a service with automata extended by logical expressions associated to states and the formalization that explicates a message sequence that allows for more precise matchmaking than current approaches, which are limited to matching only individual messages. However, it turns out to be a trace-based equivalence, which is too weak.

Lucas Bordeaux et al. [19] proposed two types of substitutability: context-dependent and context-independent substitutability, in which the former requires service N′, which is compatible with a particular M that is compatible with N; and the latter requires N′, which is compatible with any M that is compatible with N. Benatallah et al. [20] proposed four classes of replaceability between protocols, namely protocols equivalence, protocol subsumption, protocol replaceability with respect to a client protocol, and protocol replaceability with respect to an interaction role. Martens [21] defined the notion of equivalence, which is based on the usability of a module: a module N′ simulates a module N if for each M that the composition of N and M is a weak sound, the composition of N′ and M is also a weak sound; N′ and N are equivalent if N′ and N simulate each other. Bonchi et al. [22] proposed to model a web service by consume-produce-read nets and defined the notion of a saturated bisimilarity between two CPR nets, checking their similarity on the interactions with one's CPR context, which represents a possible environment in which a service can be embedded. However it turns out to be quite hard to automatically analyze equivalence between web services according to these notions, because it is difficult to exhaustively enumerate M.

Researchers continue in-depth discussions on a clear and decidable notion of equivalence for web services. Jyotishman Pathak et al. [23] determined substitutability of a service by reducing it to the satisfaction of the quotient mu-calculus formulas. Christian Stahl et al. [24] proposed three notions of substitutability for services and further presented a decision algorithm for substitutability based on the concept of an operating guideline, which is an abstract representation of all environments with which a given service can cooperate. In [25], they further extended the notion of compatibility that requires that a certain set of activities is not dead and correspondingly extended the notion of operating guidelines with a global constraint.

Compared to their work, we take advantage of the formalization and theory of π-calculus, and the behavioral substitution between formalized services, which can be automatically analyzed by the modified bisimulation theory of π-calculus.

4.3 Interface-Level Service Discovery

A web service discovery can be achieved by two main approaches: Universal Description Discovery and Integration (UDDI) and web service search engines. Recently, the availability of web services in UDDI has decreased rapidly as many web service providers decided to publish their web services through their own website instead of using public registries. Al-Masri et al. showed that more than 53% of the UDDI business registry registered services are invalid, while 92% of web services cached by web service search engines are valid and active. Compared with UDDI, using search engine to search and discover web services becomes more common and effective.

Searching for web services using web service search engines is typically limited to keyword matching on names, locations, businesses, and buildings defined in the web service description file. If the query term does not contain at least one exact word, such as the service name, the service is not returned. It is difficult for users to be aware of the concise and correct keywords to retrieve the satisfied services. The keyword-based search mode suffers from low recall, in which results containing synonyms or concepts at a higher (or lower) level of abstraction describing the same service are not returned.

To handle the drawbacks of traditional web service search engines, some approaches are proposed. Elgazzar and Liu et al. [9,10] proposed to handle the drawbacks of traditional search engines by clustering web services based on WSDL documents. In their opinion, if web services with similar functionality are placed into the same cluster, more relevant web services could be included in the search result. In this chapter, we propose to improve the performance of web service clustering for the purpose of more accurate web service discovery.

In recent years, tagging, the act of adding keywords (tags) to objects, has become a popular way to annotate various web resources, e.g., web page bookmarks, online documents, and multimedia objects. Tags provide meaningful descriptions of objects and allow users to organize and index their contents. Tagging data was proved to be very useful in many domains, such as multimedia, information retrieval, data mining, and so on. Recently, a real-world web services search engine Seekda allowed users to manually annotate web services using tags. In our study, we use both WSDL documents and tags and cluster web services according to a composite similarity generated by integrating tag-level similarity and feature-level (features extracted from WSDL documents) similarity between web services.

4.3.1 Framework of Web Services Discovery

Figure 4.1 shows our proposed framework for web service discovery. This framework consists of two parts: (1) data preprocess and (2) service discovery. In the first part, WSDL documents and tags of web services are slowly taken from the Internet and used for clustering. Similar to Elgazzar's work [9], we extract five important features from WSDL documents, i.e., content, type, message, port, and service name. After obtaining these five features and tags of web services, we use our proposed WTCluster approach

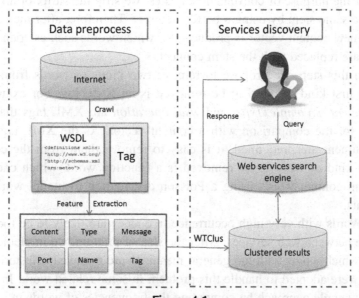

Figure 4.1
Framework for web service discovery.

to cluster web services. Since the data preprocess and clustering process is done offline, the efficiency is not a big concern, whereas the accuracy is more important. In the process of service discovery, the user first sends a query term to the web service search engine, and then the search engine returns an expanded search result by retrieving the clustered results.

4.3.2 Web Services Clustering based on WSDL and Tags

As discussed above, we extract five features (i.e., content, type, message, port, and service name) from the web service's WSDL document and use these five features and tags to cluster web services. In this section, we describe the detailed process of feature extraction, feature-level similarity computation, and tag-level similarity computation.

4.3.2.1 Content

The WSDL document, which describes the function of the web service, is actually an XML style document. Therefore, we can use some Information Retrieval approaches to extract a vector of meaningful content words that can be used as a feature for similarity computation. Our approach for building the content vector consists of four steps:

1. Building original vector—In this step, we split the WSDL content according to the white space to produce the original content vector.
2. Suffix stripping—Words with a common stem will usually have the same meaning, e.g., *connect, connected, connecting, connection,* and *connections* all have the same stem, *connect*. For the purpose of convenient statistics, we strip the suffix of all these words that have the same stem by using a porter stemmer. Therefore, after the step of suffix stripping, a new content vector is produced, in which words such as connected and connecting are replaced with the stem connect.
3. Pruning—In this step, we propose to remove two kinds of words from the content vector. The first kind of word to be removed is an XML tag. For example, the words *s:element, s:complexType,* and *wsdl:operation* are XML tags that are not meaningful for the comparison with a content vector. As the XML tags used in a WSDL document are predefined, it is easy to remove them from the content vector. The second kind of word to be removed is a function word, which can be distinguished from content words using a Poisson distribution to model word occurrence in documents.
4. Refining—Words with very high occurrence frequency are likely to be too general to discriminate between web services. After the step of pruning, we implement a step of refining, in which words with too general meanings are removed. Clustering-based approaches were adopted to handle this problem in some related work. In our work, we choose a simple approach by computing the frequencies of words in all WSDL documents and setting a threshold to decide whether a word has to be removed.

After the above four steps, we can obtain the final content vector. In this chapter, we use Normalized Google Distance (NGD) to compute the content-level similarity between two web services. Given web services s_1, s_2, and their content vector $content_{s1}$, $content_{s2}$, the detailed equation for content-level similarity computation is as follows:

$$Sim_{content}(s_1, s_2) = \frac{\sum_{w_i \in content_{s_1}} \sum_{w_j \in content_{s_2}} sim(w_i, w_j)}{|content_{s_1}||content_{s_2}|}$$

in which $|content_{s_1}|$ means the cardinality of $content_{s_1}$, w_i means the word in $content_{s_1}$, and the equation for computing the similarity between two words is as follows:

$$sim(w_i, w_j) = 1 - NGD(w_1, w_2)$$

In the above equation, we compute the similarity between two words using NGD based on the word co-existence in web pages. Due to space limitation, we don't introduce the detailed computation of NGD. Because the number of words left in the content vector is limited after the above four steps, the time cost for content-level similarity computation can be accepted.

4.3.2.2 Type

In a WSDL document, each input and output parameter contains a name attribute and a type attribute. Sometimes, parameters may be organized in a hierarchy by using complex types. Due to different naming conventions, the name of a parameter is not always a useful feature; whereas the type attribute, which can partially reflect the service function, is a good candidate feature.

As Figure 4.2 shows, the type of element *ProcessForm* (we name it *type*$_1$) is a complex type that has five parameters: *FormData* (string), *FormID* (int), *GroupID* (int),

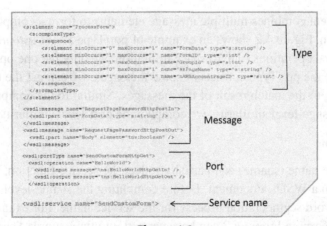

Figure 4.2
Types, message, port, service name in WSDL document.

szPageName (string), and *nAWSAccountPageID* (int). If another service s_2 has a complex-type *type$_2$* that also contains two string-type parameters and three int-type parameters, we say *type$_1$* and *type$_2$* are matched. Specifically, in the process of type matching, the order of parameters in the complex type is not considered. We therefore extract the defined types, count the number of different types in the complex type, and compute the type-level similarity between two services using the following equation:

$$Sim_{type}(s_1, s_2) = \frac{2 \times Match(type_{s_1}, type_{s_2})}{|type_{s_1}| + |type_{s_2}|}$$

in which *type$_1$* means the set of defined types in the s_1's WSDL document, $Match(type_{s_1}, type_{s_2})$ means the number of matched types between these two services, and $|type_{s_1}|$ means the cardinality of $type_{s_1}$.

4.3.2.3 Message

Message is used to deliver parameters between different operations. One message contains one or more parameters, and one parameter is associated with one type, as discussed above. Message definition is typically considered as an abstract definition of the message content, because the name and type of the parameter contained in the message are presented in the message definition. Figure 4.2 shows two simple message definitions. In the definition 1, the message named as *RequestPagePasswordHttpPostIn* contains one parameter *FormData*, which is a *string* type. In the definition 2, the message *RequestPagePasswordPostOut* contains one parameter *Body*, the type of which is a complex type named as *tns:boolean*. Similar to the computation of type-level similarity, we match the messages' structures to compute the message-level similarity between web services.

4.3.2.4 Port

The portType element combines multiple message elements to form a complete one-way or round-trip operation. Figure 4.2 shows an example of portType *SendCustomFormHttpGet*, which contains some operations (due to space limitation, we only list one operation in this portType). Because the portType consists of some messages, we can get the match result of portType according to the match result of the messages. Similar to the computation of type-level and message-level similarity, we compute the port-level similarity.

4.3.2.5 Service name

Because the service name (sname) can partially reflect the service function, it is an important feature in a WSDL document. Before computing the sname-level similarity, we first implement a word segmentation process for the service name. For example, the service name *SendCustomForm* in Figure 4.2 can be separated into three words *Send*, *Custom*, and *Form*. A simple version of word segmentation is splitting the service name according to the capital letters. However, the performance of this simple version is not satisfactory due to different naming conventions. In this chapter, we first use this simple version to split the service name and then manually adjust the final result. After the process of word segmentation, s_1s' name $SName_{s_1}$ can be presented as a set of words. Similar to content-level similarity, we compute the sname-level similarity between web services.

4.3.2.6 Tag

The tagging data of web services describes the function of web services or provides additional contextual and semantic information. In this chapter, we propose to improve the performance of traditional WSDL-based web service clustering by using the tagging data. Because a web service s_1 contains three tags t_1, t_2, t_3, we name the tag set of s_1 as $T_1 = \{t_1, t_2, t_3\}$. According to the Jaccard coefficient method, we can calculate the tag-level similarity between two web services s_1 and s_2 as follows:

$$Sim_{tag}(s_1, s_2) = \frac{|T_1 \cap T_2|}{|T_1 \cup T_2|}$$

in which $|T_1 \cap T_2|$ means the number of tags that are both annotated to s_1 and s_2, and $|T_1 \cup T_2|$ means the number of unique tags in set T_1 and T_2.

In the proposed approach, we use a K-Means clustering approach to cluster web services. K-Means is a widely adopted clustering algorithm, which is simple and fast. The drawback of this algorithm is that the number of clusters has to be predefined manually before clustering. According to the six similarities calculated above, the composite similarity $CSim(s_1,s_2)$ between web services s_1 and s_2 is as follows:

$$CSim(s_1, s_2) = (1 - \lambda)Sim_{wsdl}(s_1, s_2) + \lambda Sim_{tag}(s_1, s_2)$$

in which λ is the weight of the tag-level similarity, and the $Sim_{wsdl}(s_1,s_2)$ is the WSDL-level similarity that consists of five feature-level similarities between two services. The range of the value of λ is [0,1]. We measure the WSDL-level similarity between web services as follows:

$$\begin{aligned} Sim_{wsdl}(s_1, s_2) = {} & w_1 Sim_{content}(s_1, s_2) + w_2 Sim_{type}(s_1, s_2) + w_3 Sim_{message}(s_1, s_2) \\ & + w_4 Sim_{port}(s_1, s_2) + w_5 Sim_{sname}(s_1, s_2) \end{aligned}$$

in which w_1,w_2,w_3,w_4,w_5 are the user-defined weights of *Content*, *Type*, *Message*, *Port*, and *Service Name*, respectively. In particular, $w_1 + w_2 + w_3 + w_4 + w_5 = 1$.

4.3.3 Tag Recommendation

After examining the tagging data slowly taken from the Internet, we find that the distribution of tags is not uniform. Some web services have more than 10 tags, while some only have one or two tags. As we compute the tag-level similarity by matching the

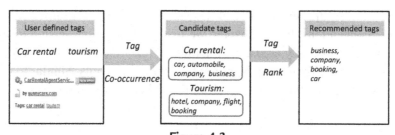

Figure 4.3

Example of the tag recommendation process.

common tags between two services, the web services with few tags reduces the value of tag-level similarity. In this section, we propose to handle this problem by recommending a set of relevant tags to the web services with fewer tags.

Figure 4.3 shows the overview of the tag recommendation process. From this figure, we find that the process of tag recommendation can be divided into two steps. Specifically, we collect all annotated tags before the process of tag recommendation. In the first step, we first compute the co-occurrence between the user-defined tags and any other tags, and then select the top-k co-occurrence tags of each user-defined tag as the candidate tags. In Figure 4.4, the number of k is set as 4, and the top-4 co-occurrence tags of *tourism* are *hotel, company, flight,* and *booking*. There are some approaches to compute the co-occurrence, and we propose to use the Jaccard coefficient method in this section. The detailed equation is as follows:

$$Co(t_i, t_j) = \frac{|t_i \cap t_j|}{|t_i \cup t_j|}$$

in which $|t_i \cap t_j|$ means the number of web services that have both t_i and t_j, and $|t_i \cup t_j|$ means the number of web services that have t_i or t_j. After the first step, for each user-defined tag $t \in T$ (T is the set of user-defined tags), we can get a list of candidate tags C_t.

In the second step, we rank the candidate tags and select the top-k tags as the recommended tags. In this chapter, we propose two strategies to rank candidate tags.

4.3.3.1 Vote

In the *vote* strategy, we use the idea of voting to compute a score for each candidate tag $c \in C$ (C is the set of all candidate tags). Given a candidate tag c, we first use the following equation to compute the value of *vote*(t, c) between tag c and each user-defined tag $t \in T$:

$$vote(t, c) = \begin{cases} 1 & if \ c \in C_u \\ 0 & otherwise \end{cases}$$

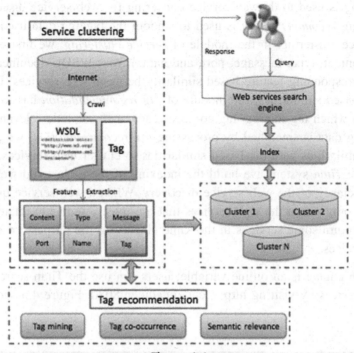

Figure 4.4
Architecture of Titan search engine.

After obtaining the voting result from each user-defined tag, we count the voting results to get the final score by using $score(c) = \sum_{t \in T} vote(t, c)$. After obtaining all final scores, we rank the candidate tags to get the top-k recommended tags.

4.3.3.2 Sum

In the *sum* strategy, we compute the score of the candidate tag c by summing the value of the co-occurrence between c and each user-defined tag t. The detailed equation is as follows:

$$score(c) = \sum_{t \in T} Co(t, c)$$

4.3.4 TiTan: A Search Engine for Web Services Discovery

Based on above studies about service clustering, we construct a real web service search engine, which consists of 15,000+ web services and 500,000+ mobile applications. Figure 4.4 shows the basic architecture of our proposed *Titan* system. The module of *service clustering* is used to do web service clustering for web service discovery, while the module of *tag recommendation* is used to smooth the tagging data used in the process of service clustering. In the module of *service clustering*, we first extract features (i.e., content, type, message, port, and name) from WSDL documents and compute the corresponding feature-based similarity between web services. Before computing tag-based similarities, the module of *tag recommendation* has to be implemented, in which tag mining, tag co-occurrence, and semantic relevance are used. After the tagging data is smoothed by processing *tag recommendation*, we combine feature-based similarities with tag-based similarities to cluster web services. In the realization of the *Titan* system, we build the indexing of these clustered web services to improve the efficiency of the web service discovery. When a web service query is coming, we not only return the web services that are mostly semantic related to the query, but also return some services in the same cluster for the purpose of retrieving more related services.

The *Titan* search engine is an online variable; users can use the Titan search engine to discover web services by visiting http://ccnt.zju.edu.cn:8080. Figure 4.5 shows the

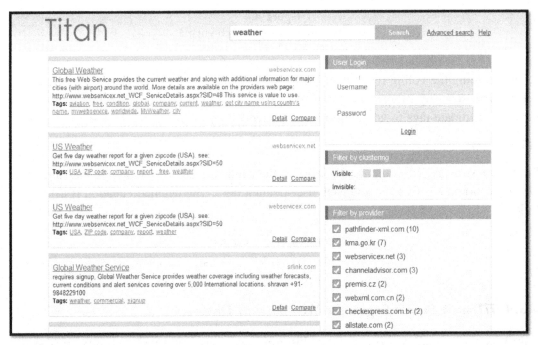

Figure 4.5
Search result page of Titan.

search result page when a user uses *weather* as a query term. From Figure 4.5, we can find that each search result entity contains four parts: (1) web service name; (2) service description; (3) tags given by users; and (4) service provider. The clustering result of the retrieved web services is shown in the division named *Filter by Clustering* in the right side of the search result page. Specifically, we use a unique color to represent one cluster. When users click one color block in the *Filter by Clustering* division, web services in the corresponding cluster will be removed from the search result. The service provider is also used as a metric to filter web services in the search result. In the division of *Filter by Provider*, there is a list of service providers. Once a user clicks the symbol of one service provider, web services provided by this provider will be removed from the search result.

4.4 Behavior Level Service Discovery

A web service can be any piece of software that is published, found, and universally invoked through the web according to a series of XML-based standard protocols, such as SOAP, UDDI, and WSDL.

Traditional service description languages such as WSDL are appropriate to describe simple services that are invoked by other services within once interaction. However, it cannot capture the ordering of message exchanges in multiple interactions between composite services and others. Various proposals have been put forward to feature such information, namely the behavior of web services. The representative ones include OWL-S and WS-CDL. Although they place different emphases on how to describe service behavior, they all try to provide the needed information for priori analysis of what will happen when a service is interacting with others to ensure successful interactions in the services invocation and composition.

A necessary behavioral analysis of web services is to identify whether a service can substitute another service not only in functionality but also in interacting behavior under some context of a composition. Such analysis can be applied when a service becomes unavailable so that the composition has to be updated. To achieve such analysis, many researchers model web services with formal theories, such as automata, Petri nets, and process calculus. Based on the formalization, different notions of substitution and corresponding analysis approaches have been used for reference and extended from these theories. However, most of them stay at a conceptual layer, in which the behavioral substitution of services is still hard to determine according to the given notions. In this chapter, we propose to take advantage of formalization and theory of π-calculus [26], so that the formalized services can be analyzed and their behavioral substitution can be automatically determined.

4.4.1 Behavioral Perspectives of Services

Suppose there is a French dictionary service[1] P as shown in Figure 4.6. It returns the meaning of a French word in French. It is a composite process using an English dictionary[2] and a BabelFish translator[3] service. The given word is first translated from French to English, then its meaning is obtained from the English dictionary, and the result is translated back to French.

According to different roles involved in a composite service, Figure 4.1 can be divided into three parts, *client*, *process*, and *implementation*, in which *client* is the potential consumer of the composite service, *process* is the working process of the service, and *implementation* is all atomic services to be invoked, including internal and third-party services.

There is another French dictionary service, P_1. It also returns the meaning of a French word in French. As Figure 4.7 shows, its realization is to invoke an actual French dictionary service R. Specifically speaking, it passes the French word received from client to R, waits until R finishes its work, and then passes back the response of R to the client.

P_1 is consistent with P in the interface with respect to the client; however, it cannot substitute P in behavior because it cannot interact with the atomic services that ought to be invoked by P in a specified order.

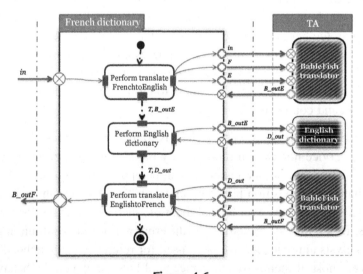

Figure 4.6
A French dictionary service, in which *F* stands for French and *E* stands for English.

---

[1] Its OWL-S description can be found at http://www.mindswap.org/2004/owls/1.1/FrenchDictionary.owl.
[2] Its OWL-S description can be found at http://www.mindswap.org/2004/owl-s/1.1/Dictionary.owl.
[3] Its OWL-S description can be found at http://www.mindswap.org/2004/owl-s/1.1/BabelFishTranslator.owl.

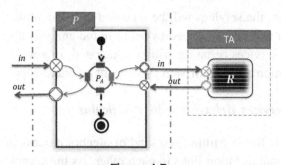

Figure 4.7
French dictionary service P_1.

Consider another more French dictionary service, P_2. It refers to three atomic services, including a translator, an English dictionary, and a Chinese dictionary service. As Figure 4.8 shows, its realization is translate the French word received from its client into English or Chinese randomly, and if it is translated into English, obtain its English meaning by invoking the English dictionary service; otherwise, get its Chinese meaning by invoking the Chinese dictionary service; and finally, translate the meaning of the word, either in English or Chinese, into French.

P_2 is consistent with P in the interface with respect to the client, and it can substitute P in behavior because it can interact with the atomic services that are invoked by P in a specified order when the input French word is translated into English.

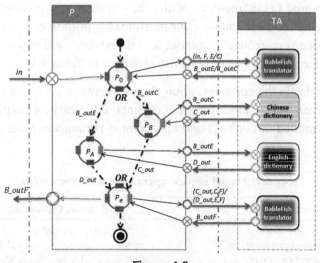

Figure 4.8
French dictionary service P_2.

In the following section, the services will be modeled in π-calculus, a clear definition of behavioral substitution will be introduced as being in the analysis above, and a formal approach to analyzing services behavior will be illustrated. In a word, we aim to automate the behavioral substitution analysis of web services in a formal approach.

4.4.2 Formalizing Services Behavior with π-Calculus

π-calculus, proposed by Robin Milner, is a kind of algebra process in which the processes interact by sending communication links to each other. As the complexity of web services increases, a web service can actually be deemed as a concurrent process composed by a set of operations, in which operations interact with each other by receiving and sending messages. It is natural for us to adopt π-calculus to express service behaviors. Also, there are a series of algebraic theories in π-calculus, such as bisimulation and congruence, which can help us analyze service behaviors. To introduce π-calculus is beyond the scope of this chapter; please refer to related literature for details.

Service behavior refers to the dynamic properties of a web service, which includes atomic operations involving message exchanges that can be performed by the service, and the constraints between operations of a service that define the allowed order of execution. Accordingly, we will illustrate how to express service behavior with π-calculus in two parts.

4.4.2.1 Atomic operation involving message exchanges

An operation in a service corresponds to a basic π-calculus process. To model a single operation involving message exchanges with π-calculus, we can map operation names to channels, which are used to communicate with other services, and inputs/outputs to messages transmitted through channels. Four transmission primitives of operations are defined in WSDL: one-way, request-response, solicit-response, and notification. For each transmission primitive, operations are modeled as shown in Table 4.1.

Here we use c_s to indicate the communication channel between service s and its partner services. More concretely, $c_s?$ stands for input channel, $c_s!$ stands for output channel, and the data values transmitted through $c_s?$ and $c_s!$ are input parameters I and output values O,

Table 4.1: Model service operations with π-calculus

Operation Type	Π-Calculus Expression
One-way	$c_s?(i_1, \ldots, i_n).\tau.0$
Request-response	$c_s?(i_1, \ldots, i_n).\tau.c_s!(o_1, \ldots, o_m).0$
Solicit-response	$c_s!(i_1, \ldots, i_n).c_s?(o_1, \ldots, o_m).0$
Notification	$c_s!(i_1, \ldots, i_n).0$

respectively. For operations of request-response and one-way, they are entities that realize some functions, so they are always waiting to be invoked by others, and whenever they receive invoking request with inputs, they will do some internal work and finally return corresponding outputs (or no outputs). For operations of solicit-response and notification, they are endpoints that invoke some function, so they first send invoking requests with necessary data to some serving operations and then wait for the returned answer (or no answer).

Take the following translator service as an example. It translates text from one language to another language. The service has three inputs: the text to be translated, its original language, and the target language. A segment of the service description is shown as follows, and we can translate it into Eqn (4.1) according to the formalizing rules stated above.

```
<process:AtomicProcess rdf:ID="BabelFishTranslator">
    <process:hasInput rdf:resource="#InputString"/>
    <process:hasInput rdf:resource="#InputLanguage"/>
    <process:hasInput rdf:resource="#OutputLanguage"/>
    <process:hasOutput rdf:resource="#OutputString"/>
    <process:hasPrecondition rdf:resource="#SupportedLanguagePair"/>
</process:AtomicProcess>
```

$$P_{S_B} \equiv c_{S_B}?\left(InputString, InputLanguage, OutputLanguage\right).$$
$$\left[SupportedLanguagePair = T\right]\tau.c_{S_B}!\left(OutputString\right): 0$$

(4.1)

4.4.2.2 Execution sequence among operations

In a composite service, operations interact with each other, and they constitute a process by sequence, parallel, choice, or other control constructs. In this chapter, we focus on basic control patterns to show how an execution sequence among operations can be formalized by π-calculus. The basic patterns include sequence, choice split, parallel split, choice merge, and parallel merge.

Sequence: If A and B are expressed as $P_A \equiv \alpha^*.0$ and P_B, to formalize that B can only be executed after A finishes, and A may pass data $(x_1, ..., x_n)$ to B, we create a private channel for A and B named sig_{AB} as a trigger to B, the dataflow $(x_1, ..., x_n)$ from A to B is represented as the data through channel sig_{AB}. Hence, it can be translated into Eqn (4.2):

$$\left(vsig_{AB}\right)\left(\alpha^*.sig_{AB}!\left(x_1, ..., x_n\right)0\middle|\middle|sig_{AB}?\left(x_1, ..., x_n\right).P_B\right)$$

(4.2)

Choice Split: If A, B, and C are expressed as $P_A \equiv \alpha^*.0$, P_B and P_C, to formalize a choice split from A to B or C, we create a private channel for A, B, and C named sig_{ABC} as a trigger from A to both B and C, and the received data $(x_1, ..., x_n)$ from A is used to calculate the preconditioned B and C to decide which operation will be executed. It can be translated into Eqn (4.3):

$$(vsig_{ABC})\,(\alpha^*.sig_{ABC}!(x_1,\ldots,x_n).\,0$$
$$||sig_{ABC}?(x_1,\ldots,x_n).\,([exp_1 = T]P_B + [exp_2 = T]P_C))$$

$$(4.3)$$

Parallel Split: If A, B, and C are expressed as $P_A \equiv \alpha^*.0$, P_B and P_C, to formalize a parallel split from A to B and C, we create a private channel for the two of A and B named sig_{AB}, acting as a trigger to B with data$(x_1, \ldots, x_n)$, and another one for the two of A and C named as sig_{AC}, acting as a trigger to C with data$(y_1, \ldots, y_m)$. It can be translated into Eqn (4.4):

$$(vsig_{AB}, vsig_{AC})\,((\alpha^*.(sig_{AB}!(x_1,\ldots,x_n)||sig_{AC}!(y_1,\ldots,y_m)).0)$$
$$||sig_{AB}?(x_1,\ldots,x_n).P_B$$
$$||sig_{AC}?(y_1,\ldots,y_m).P_C)$$

$$(4.4)$$

Choice Merge: If A, B, and C are expressed as $P_A \equiv \alpha^*.0$, $P_B \equiv \beta^*.0$, and P_C, to formalize a choice merge from A or B to C, we create a private channel for A, B, and C named sig_{ABC}, along which A passes out $(x_1, \ldots, x_n)$, B passes out $(y_1, \ldots, y_n)$, and C chooses internally which to receive. It can be translated into Eqn (4.5):

$$(vsig_{ABC})\,(\alpha^*.sig_{ABC}!(x_1,\ldots,x_n)0||\beta^*.sig_{ABC}!(y_1,\ldots,y_n).0$$
$$||sig_{ABC}?(z_1,\ldots,z_n).P_C)$$

$$(4.5)$$

Parallel Merge: If A, B, and C are expressed as $P_A \equiv \alpha^*.0$, $P_B \equiv \beta^*.0$, and P_C, to formalize a parallel merge from A and B to C, we create a private channel for the two of A and C named sig_{AC} along which A passes $(x_1, \ldots, x_n)$ to C, and another one for the two of B and C named sig_{BC} along which B passes $(y_1, \ldots, y_m)$ to C, and C receives both. It can be translated into Eqn (4.6):

$$(vsig_{AC}, vsig_{BC})\,(\alpha^*.sig_{AC}!(x_1,\ldots,x_n).0$$
$$||\beta^*.sig_{BC}!(y_1,\ldots,y_m).0$$
$$||sig_{AC}?(x_1,\ldots,x_n).sig_{BC}?(y_1,\ldots,y_m).P_C)$$

$$(4.6)$$

We will show how to formalize a composite service with π-calculus. Take the French dictionary service in Figure 4.1 as an example. It can be represented as follows:

$$P_{FD} \equiv c_{FD}?(in).P_A$$
$$P_A \equiv (vsig_{AB})\,(c_B!(in, F, E).c_B?(B_{outE}).sig_{AB}!(B_{outE}).0$$
$$||sig_{AB}?(B_{outE}).P_B)$$

$$P_B \equiv (\nu sig_{BC})(c_E!(B_{outE}).c_E?(D_{out}).sig_{BC}!(D_{out}).0$$

$$||sig_{BC}?(D\_out).P_C)$$

$$P_C \equiv c_B'!(D\_out, E, F).c_B'?(B\_outF).c_{FD}!(B\_outF).0$$

According to the PREFIX and COM rules of π-calculus, the behavioral derivation of P_{FD} can be represented as Eqn (4.7). It shows that, internal actions (denoted as τ) are triggering message exchanges among operations within the service process, and external actions are that with other services, including the ones it invokes and serves.

$$
\begin{aligned}
P_{FD} &\xrightarrow{c_{FD}?(in)} P_A \xrightarrow{c_B!(in,F,E)} (\nu sig_{AB})(c_B?(B_{outE}).sig_{AB}!(B_{outE}).0 \\
&||sig_{AB}?(B_{outE}).P_B) \xrightarrow{c_B?(B_{outE})} (\nu sig_{AB})(sig_{AB}!(B_{outE}).0 \\
&||sig_{AB}?(B_{outE}).P_B) \xrightarrow{\tau sig_{AB}} P_B \xrightarrow{c_E!(B_{outE})} (\nu sig_{BC})(c_E?(D_{out}). \\
&sig_{BC}!(D_{out}).0||sig_{BC}?(D_{out}).P_C) \\
&\xrightarrow{c_E?(D_{out})} (\nu sig_{BC})(sig_{BC}!(D_{out}).0||sig_{BC}?(D_{out}).P_C) \\
&\xrightarrow{\tau sig_{BC}} P_C \xrightarrow{c_B'!(D_{out},E,F)} c_B'?(B_{outF}).c_{FD}!(B_{outF}).0 \\
&\xrightarrow{c_B'?(B\_outF)} c_{FD}!(B\_outF).0 \xrightarrow{c_{FD}!(B\_outF)} 0.
\end{aligned}
\tag{4.7}
$$

4.4.3 Analyzing Behavioral Simulation of Services

Based on the formalization of web services, we use monodirectional simulation rather than bisimulation theory of π-calculus and apply it to analyze behavioral simulation of the services. Two kinds of simulation, strong and weak simulation, are introduced, which can adapt to different requirements on substitution.

Definition 1: Strong simulation on visible behavior

$P \doteq Q$, if and only if, for all $\alpha \in Q(\alpha \in \{\tau, a?(x), a!(x)\})$, whenever $Q \xrightarrow{\alpha} Q'$, then for some P', $P \xrightarrow{\alpha} P'$ and $P' \doteq Q'$.

Strong simulation requires a service N' that can simulate exactly the same actions of another service N from the initial state, including internal actions, so as to evolve to a next simulating state until N terminates.

Definition 2: Weak simulation on visible behavior

$P \cong Q$, if and only if, for all $\alpha \in Q(\alpha \in \{\tau, a?(x), a!(x)\})$, whenever $Q \xrightarrow{\alpha} Q'$, then for some P', $P(\xrightarrow{\tau})^* \xrightarrow{\alpha} (\xrightarrow{\tau})^* P'$ and $P' \cong Q'$.

Weak simulation just requires a service N' that can simulate actions of another service N in combination with the same actions and internal actions from the initial state, so as to evolve to a next simulating state until N terminates.

In the following, the derivation rules of a service process will be introduced, and the evolution of a service will be represented as a derivation tree. Formal definitions to the related concepts are given as follows:

Definition 3: Immediate derivations of P

1. if $P \equiv \alpha.P'(\alpha \in \{\tau, a?(x), a!(x)\})$, an immediate derivation of P is $P \xrightarrow{\alpha} P'$, i.e., a possible derivative is (α, P'), and we call α an action of P, and we call P' an α-derivative of P;

2. if $P \equiv (vb)\alpha.P'(\alpha \in \{\tau, a?(x), a!(x)\})$, for the case $b = a$, an immediate derivation of P is $P \xrightarrow{\tau} P'$; and if $b \neq a$, an immediate derivation of P is $P \xrightarrow{\alpha} P'$;

3. if $P \equiv \alpha_1.P_1 + \cdots + \alpha_n.P_n$ $(\alpha_i \in \{\tau, a?(x), a!(x)\}$, $i = 1, \ldots n)$, immediate derivations of P are $P \xrightarrow{\alpha_1} P_1 + \cdots + P \xrightarrow{\alpha_n} P_n$, i.e., possible derivatives are $(\alpha_1, P_1), \ldots$ and (α_n, P_n);

4. if $P \equiv \alpha_1.P_1 \| \cdots \| \alpha_n.P_n (\alpha_i \in \{\tau, a?(x), a!(x)\}, i = 1, \ldots n)$, immediate derivations of P
   are $\sum_{i=1}^{n}\{P \xrightarrow{\alpha_i} P_i\} + \sum\{P \xrightarrow{\tau} \alpha_1.P_1\| \cdots \|P_i\| \cdots \|P_j\| \cdots \|\alpha_n.P_n : \alpha_i.P_i \xrightarrow{a?(x)} P_i, \alpha_j.P_j \xrightarrow{a!(y)} P_j\}$.

Definition 4: Derivation tree of P

The derivation tree of P is the whole of the iterative derivations of P according to definition 3, in which the root is P, leafs are 0, and for each expression at a nonterminal node, all its immediate derivations are represented by outgoing arcs.

A general form of derivation tree is shown in Figure 4.9.

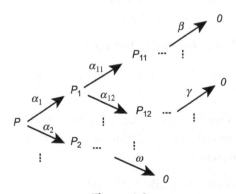

Figure 4.9
A general form of derivation tree of process P.

Next, we will show how to analyze behavioral simulation of services with π-calculus through some examples. We first formalize the other two French dictionary services in Figures 4.7 and 4.8, respectively, and then we track their behaviors with P_{FD} in Figure 4.6 to check whether they can strongly or weakly simulate P_{FD} according to definitions 1 and 2.

Example one. P_1 vs P_{FD}

P_1 can be formalized as:

$$P_1 \equiv c_P?(in).P_A$$
$$P_A \equiv c_R!(in).c_R?(out).c_P!(out).0$$

And the derivation process of P_1 is:

$$P_1 \xrightarrow{c_P?(in)} P_A \xrightarrow{c_R!(in)} c_R?(out).c_P!(out).0 \xrightarrow{c_R?(out)} c_P!(out).0 \xrightarrow{c_P!(out)} 0$$

P_1 can simulate the first action $c_P?(in)$ of P_{FD}; however, it cannot simulate the second action $c_B!(in,F,E)$ either in strong or weak simulation, and hence P_1 cannot substitute P_{FD} in behavior, which is consistent with our analysis in Section 4.2.

Example two. P_2 vs P_{FD}

P_2 can be formalized as:

$$P_2 \equiv (\nu sig_{PAB})(c_P?(in).sig_{PAB}!.0 || sig_{PAB}?.(P_A + P_B))$$
$$P_A \equiv (\nu sig_{AA'})(c_B!(in, F, E).c_B?(B_{outE}).sig_{AA'}!(B_{outE}).0$$
$$|| sig_{AA'}?(B\_outE).P_{A'})$$
$$P_{A'} \equiv (\nu sig_{A'A''})(c_E!(B_{outE}).c_E?(D_{out}).sig_{A'A''}!(D_{out}).0$$
$$|| sig_{A'A''}?(D\_out).P_{A''})$$
$$P_{A''} \equiv c_B'!(D\_out, E, F).c_B'?(B\_outF).c_P!(B\_outF).0$$
$$P_B \equiv (\nu sig_{BB'})(c_B!(in, F, C).c_B?(B_{outC}).sig_{BB'}!(B_{outC}).0$$
$$|| sig_{BB'}?(B\_outC).P_{B'})$$
$$P_{B'} \equiv (\nu sig_{B'B''})(c_C!(B_{outC}).c_C?(C_{out}).sig_{B'B''}!(C_{out}).0$$
$$|| sig_{B'B''}?(C\_out).P_{B''})$$
$$P_{B''} \equiv c_B'!(C\_out, C, F).c_B'?(B\_outF).c_P!(B\_outF).0$$

And the derivation process of P_2 is:

$$P \xrightarrow{c_P?(in)} (vsig_{PAB})(sig_{PAB}!.0||sig_{PAB}?.(P_A + P_B)) \xrightarrow{\tau_{sig_{PAB}}} P' \nearrow P_A \longrightarrow \cdots \\ \searrow P_B \longrightarrow \cdots$$

P_2 cannot strongly simulate P_{FD} because for the transition $P_{FD} \xrightarrow{c_{FD}?(in)} P'$, P_2 has a simulating transition $P_2 \xrightarrow{c_P?(in)} (vsig_{PAB})(sig_{PAB}!.0||sig_{PAB}?.(P_A + P_B))$; and then for P', there is a transition $P' \xrightarrow{c_B!(in,F,E)} P''$, while P_2 can just execute the τ action after the action of $c_P?(in)$, rather than an action simulating $c_B!(in,F,E)$. But we can deduce that P_2 can weakly simulate P_{FD} by analyzing their behavioral derivation. Hence, P_2 can substitute P_{FD} in behavior, which is consistent with our analysis in Section 4.2.

4.4.4 Implementation of Reasoning on Services Behavioral Equivalence

We can make use of an existing tool, the Mobility Workbench (MWB),[4] to automate the analysis of behavioral simulation of services. MWB is a tool for manipulating and analyzing mobile concurrent systems described in the π-calculus developed by Bjorn Victor, Faron Moller, Lars-Henrik Eriksson, and Mads Dam. A basic functionality of MWB we used is to define an agent with command *agent* and check whether an agent is a strong or weak simulation equivalent to another agent with command *eq/weq agent$_1$ agent$_2$*.

The agent definitions of three French dictionary services mentioned above are shown in Figure 4.10 according to the input syntax of MWB. Basically, it is consistent with

Figure 4.10
Agent definitions of P_{FD}, P_1, and P_2 in MWB.

---

[4] http://www.it.uu.se/research/group/mobility/mwb.

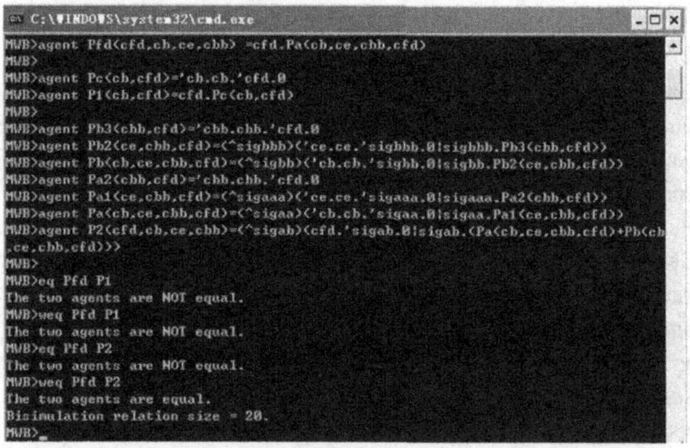

Figure 4.11
Strong and weak simulation analyses between P_{FD} and P_1 and that between P_{FD} and P_2 in MWB.

the formalization proposed in Section 4.3; however, we need to change it a little when feeding it to MWB, because in MWB each definition of a process should start with "agent," and an agent definition must be closed, i.e., its free names must be a subset of the argument list.

Based on the agent definitions, we can check whether an agent is a strong or weak simulation equivalent to another agent. The result is shown in Figure 4.11, which is consistent with the derivation and analysis shown in Section 4.4. Hence, the analysis of behavioral simulation between services can be automated with the help of MWB as long as the services are defined.

4.5 Summary

In this section, we introduced the work on service discovery, consisting of interface-level service discovery and behavioral-level service discovery. For our work on interface-level service discovery, we proposed using a web service clustering and tag recommendation to improve the effectiveness of web service discovery. Specifically, both WSDL documents and tags of web services are used for clustering, while a tag recommendation is adopted to handle some inherent problems of tagging data, e.g., uneven tag distribution and noise tags. For our work on behavioral-level service discovery, we proposed to formalize the behavior of a web service by π-calculus. Based on the formalization, we introduced two notions of behavioral substitution of web services namely strong and weak simulation. Furthermore, we proposed a derivative approach to analyzing the behavioral substitution of services according to the given notions, which is implemented based on an existing tool of π-calculus. The proposed approach takes advantage of formalization and theory of π-calculus, so that the formalized services can be naturally analyzed and the behavioral substitution of them can be easily determined.

References

[1] Web Services Description Language (WSDL). http://www.w3.org/TR/wsdl.

[2] OWL-S: semantic markup for web services. http://www.w3.org/Submission/OWL-S/.

[3] M. Paolucci, T. Kawamura, T.R. Payne, K. Sycara, Semantic matching of web services capabilities, in: Proc. of the 1st International Semantic Web Conference (ISWC), Springer, Berlin, Heidelberg, 2002.

[4] M.C. Jaeger, G. Rojec-Goldmann, G. Muhl, C. Liebetruth, Ranked matching for service descriptions using OWL-S, in: Proc. of Kommunikation in Verteilten System (KiVS), Springer, Berlin, Heidelberg, 2005.

[5] A. Patil, S. Oundhakar, A. Sheth, K. Verma, Meteor-s web service annotation framework, in: Proc. of the World Wide Web Conference (WWW), ACM, 2004.

[6] X. Dong, A.Y. Halevy, J. Madhavan, E. Nemes, J. Zhang, Similarity search for web services, in: Proc. of Very Large Date Bases (VLDB), VLDB Endowment, 2004.

[7] Web Services Conversation Language. http://www.w3.org/TR/wscl10/.

[8] Web Services Choreography Description Language. http://www.w3.org/TR/2004/WD-ws-cdl-10-20040427/.

[9] K. Elgazzar, A.E. Hassan, P. Martin, Clustering WSDL documents to bootstrap the discovery of web services, in: Proc. of International Conference on Web Services (ICWS), IEEE, 2009, pp. 147–154.

[10] W. Liu, W. Wong, Web service clustering using text mining techniques, Int. J. Agent-Oriented Softw. Eng. 3 (1) (2009) 6–26.

[11] W. Liu, W. Wong, Discovering homogeneous service communities through web service clustering, in: Service-Oriented Computing: Agents, Semantics, and Engineering, Springer, Berlin, Heidelberg, 2008, pp. 69–82.

[12] S. Agarwal, R. Studer, Automatic matchmaking of web services, in: Proceedings of IEEE International Conference on Web Services (ICWS), IEEE, 2006, pp. 45–54.

[13] F. Puhlmann, M. Weske, Interaction soundness for service orchestrations, in: Proceedings of International Conference on Service-oriented Computing (ICSOC), Springer, Berlin, Heidelberg, 2006, pp. 302–313.

[14] G. Decker, F. Puhlmann, M. Weske, Formalizing service interactions, Lect. Notes Comput. Sci. 4102 (2006) 414–419.

[15] A. Barros, M. Dumas, A.H.M. Hofstede, Service interaction patterns, Lect. Notes Comput. Sci. 3649 (2005) 302–318.

[16] R. Lucchi, M. Mazzara, A pi-calculus based semantics for WS-BPEL, J. Logic Algebr. Progr. 70 (1) (2007) 96–118.

[17] A. Brogi, C. Canal, E. Pimentel, A. Vallecillo, Formalizing web service choreographies, Electron. Notes Theor. Comput. Sci. 105 (10) (2004) 73–94.

[18] A. Wombacher, P. Fankhauser, B. Mahleko, E. Neuhold, Matchmaking for business processes based on choreographies, Int. J. Web Serv. Res. 1 (4) (2004) 14–32.

[19] L. Bordeaux, G. Salaun, D. Berardi, M. Mecella, When are two web services compatible? in: Proceeding of VLDB-TES, Springer, Berlin, Heidelberg, 2004, pp. 15–28.

[20] B. Benatallah, F. Casati, F. Toumani, Representing, analysing and managing web service protocols, I Data Knowl. Eng. 58 (3) (2006) 357–527.

[21] A. Martens, On compatibility of web services, Petri. Net. Newsletter 65 (2003) 12–20.

[22] F. Bonchi, A. Brogi, S. Corfini, F. Gadducci, A behavioural congruence for web services, in: Proceedings of International Symposium on Fundamentals of Software Engineering, Springer, Berlin, Heidelberg, 2007, pp. 240–256.

[23] J. Pathak, S. Basu, V. Honavar, On context-specific substitutability of web services, in: Proceedings of 5th IEEE International Conference on Web Services (ICWS), IEEE, 2007, pp. 192–199.

[24] C. Stahl, P. Massuthe, J. Bretschneider, Deciding substitutability of services with operating guidelines, in: Jensen, K., van der Aalst, W.M.P. (eds.). Transactions on Petri Nets and Other Models of Concurrency II, vol. 2, issue 5460, (2009), pp. 172–191, Springer, Heidelberg. Special Issue on Concurrency in Process-Aware Information Systems.

[25] C. Stahl, K. Wolf, Deciding service composition and substitutability using extended operating guidelines, Data Knowl. Eng. 68 (9) (2009) 819–833.

[26] R. Milner, A Calculus of Communicating Systems, LNCS 92, Springer, 1980.

Service Selection

Chapter Outline

Service selection is an important issue of service-oriented computing (SOC), which is a fundamental step in the composition of complex and large-grained services from single-function components. Since it is relatively easy to match services based on functional requirements, users always pay more attention to service selection based on the Quality of Service (QoS) of the candidate. The efficiency of traditional QoS-based service selection is vastly restricted by the number of alternative services. With the increase in the number of services, it is becoming a bigger challenge. In this section, we propose an efficient approach for QoS-based service selection, which decreases the range of choices without effectively pruning the potential candidates by taking advantage of the skyline method. The basic selection with QoS-based skyline is to compute all skyline services in a static environment and then recommend them to be selected, while the advanced selection deals with real cases in practical applications.

Service Computing: Concepts, Methods and Technology. http://dx.doi.org/10.1016/B978-0-12-802330-3.00005-9

5.1 Introduction

Web services are self-described software entities that can be located, used, and advertised through the Internet using a series of standard languages such as WSDL, UDDI, and SOAP [1,2]. SOC offers a powerful approach to the assembly of complex and large-grained services from single-function components. The increase in the number of services brings both opportunity and challenge to service composition. In addition, it was observed that there are many functionality-equivalent services with different QoS on the Internet [3]. It increases the level of difficulty to select appropriate services for composition, substitution, and so on. Therefore, an efficient and effective service selection approach is needed. Because function-based service selection has been addressed by many researchers [4–8], we focus on addressing QoS-based service selection in this chapter.

Some QoS-based selection approaches [6,9,10] have been proposed during the recent years. We feel each of these approaches is relevant but has an important restriction. All these previous studies have not seriously considered some important facts and requirements. The following is a discussion of these cases.

- Service environment is *dynamic*. An existing web service may be unavailable because of some elements, such as network traffic, machine problems, or may even be removed from the cloud computing platform. Meanwhile, a new functionality-equivalent service may appear in the list of candidate services for selection. The influence of the dynamic service environment should be considered in the process of service selection.
- QoS of service is *uncertain*. In the real world, services are impacted by some elements, e.g., net-traffic, data randomness, incompleteness, limitation of measuring method, which can make the performance of service uncertain. Further, due to the service level agreement, the service provider may periodically change the QoS of existing services. The uncertainty of service confuses the results of service comparisons, which is the foundation of service selection.
- *User's preference* should be considered. Traditional QoS-based service selection approaches use utility functions to compute the optimal solution without considering user's preferences. It should be noted that user's preferences have a great influence on the user's decision. Therefore, user's preferences should be carefully deliberated. Also, it is not a good idea to recommend too many candidate services to users.

Effectiveness is an important indicator to measure the performance of QoS-based service selection. Suppose one component service of a composite service is unavailable and we have to select one service from the set of concrete services with the corresponding abstract service. It should be mentioned that the substitutions of component service will have an impact on overall QoS (e.g., response time, throughput, availability) of the composite service. Therefore, we need a criterion to determine which service is the best one to replace the unavailable component. We believe that selected services should optimize the overall QoS as much as possible, while satisfying the functional requirements and QoS constraints.

In addition to the quality of selected services, the efficiency of service selection is also critical for the performance of service selection. Given three abstract services, each has m concrete services, and the number of QoS parameters to be considered is n. The goal is to select one concrete service from each set and compose the three services to be a composite service. For sake of simplicity, the process of composition is predefined. Then the time it costs to find the best combination will exceed the constraints for real-time execution (try m^n combinations). This problem becomes especially important and challenging as the number of functional equivalent concrete services available on the web increases. The statistics published by the web services search engine Seekda indicate an exponential increase in the number of web services over the last three years [11]. However, if we can reduce the value of m (the number of candidate concrete services) before the process of selection, the time cost of selection will decrease substantially.

In this section, we improve the efficiency of QoS-based service selection by using the skyline [12] method to reduce the number of candidate concrete services. In this approach, for each abstract service, the range of selection is limited to the services in QoS-based skyline. It has two features: (1) the number of services in skyline is vastly smaller than the number of concrete services for each abstract service and (2) each non-skyline service is dominated by one or more skyline services in respect to QoS. The first feature improves the efficiency of our approach, while the second feature guarantees the completeness of the selection result as the skyline service set includes all nondominated services which are potential candidates for the optimal completion.

Furthermore, we consider three cases that have not been considered in previous research and propose corresponding solutions. For the first case, we propose an algorithm called "DSCA" for the dynamic skyline computation by making use of our proposed "paper-tape" model. Second, we compute the dominance probability of each two uncertain services and prune the services that are not in the probability skyline. As for the case of user preference, we propose to recommend the representative services of each cluster of tradeoffs instead of recommending the services with high utility.

Because the skyline services are trade-offs among QoS parameters, we propose a ranking mechanism to evaluate the effectiveness of selection by computing the utility of service. We met some problems while applying this idea into a real scenario. For example, the number of services in skyline may still be too large. It has been shown in [13,14] that the expected number of skyline points is $\Theta(\ln^{d-1} n/(d-1)!)$ for a random dataset (n is the size of the dataset, d is the number of dimensions). To overcome this problem, we propose the notion of "similarity-based representative skyline" and present a corresponding algorithm, "similarity-based RSA." Meanwhile, we also propose the algorithms for the computation of skyline services in a dynamic environment.

5.2 QoS-Based Skyline Service Selection

5.2.1 Preliminaries

Given a set of points in an n-dimensional data space, point P_j is said to be dominated by P_i, if P_i is better than or equal to P_j at all dimensions, and further P_i is better than P_j in at least one dimension [12]. In this n-dimensional space, all points that are not dominated by other points combine to a set named skyline. According to the skyline query, we can find the candidate data that users require. Skyline queries are widely applicable to multicriteria decision-making applications. For the sake of clarity, we formulate the definitions of skyline and its dominance relationship as follows.

Definition 1: Dominance relationship && skyline. Given a set of points S in an n-dimension data space and two points $x, y \in S$. x dominates point y, denoted as $x \prec y$, iff $\forall i \in [1, n]: x_i \leq y_i$. Skyline, denoted as SK, is the set of points that are not dominated by any other points in S, i.e., $SK = \{x \in S | \nexists y \in S: y \prec x\}$.

Definition 2: Dominance region && only dominance region. The dominance region of a point x, denoted as x_{dr}, is the union of the point k, which is the arbitrary point in the data space and is dominated by x, i.e., $x_{dr} = \{\cup k | x \prec k\}$. The only dominance region of point x, denoted as x_{od}, is the union of the point k, which is only dominated by x, i.e., $x_{od} = \{\cup k | x \prec k, \nexists p \notin SK: p \neq x, p \prec k\}$.

For example, consider the classic scenario shown in Figure 5.1, in which a user wants to find a hotel both near to downtown and cheap in price among a set of hotels. In Figure 5.1, each hotel is described by two parameters, namely price and distance. Then these hotels are projected into a two-dimensional space, with the coordinates of each point corresponding to the values of the hotel in these two parameters. It is obvious that point A is in the skyline,

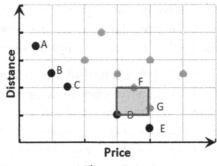

Figure 5.1
Skyline example.

because it is not dominated by any other point, i.e., there is no other hotel that has a lower price and shorter distance than hotel A. The same holds for points B, C, D, and E, which also belong to the skyline. However, the points F and G are not in the skyline points, because they are both dominated by point D. The result provided by skyline is a set of trade-offs among the parameters to be considered, which could be understood as an anticorrelated set. The blue region in Figure 5.1 is the only dominance region of point D, because the points in this blue region can only be dominated by point B. However, the points in the upper or right boundary of the only dominance region could be dominated by other skyline points.

From the above definition and example, we can determine that for each non-skyline point p, there exists at least one skyline point that dominates p. Therefore, the QoS-based service skyline guarantees the completeness of the selection result as it includes all potential candidates.

5.2.2 Basic Skyline Service Selection

Before calculating the skyline service, we should first project services into multidimensional data space according to their QoS values. Given a set of services $\check{s} = \{s_1, s_2,..., s_m\}$, each service contains n nonfunctional attributes, denoted as $Q_{si} = \{q_1, q_2,..., q_n\}$. In the n-dimension data space, each dimension corresponds to an attribute of service, and the coordinate of service in this dimension is equal to the value of the corresponding attribute.

After changing the QoS-based service selection into the traditional scenario of skyline computation, we could use a basic skyline computation algorithm to address this problem. Because the basic skyline computation algorithm is not the key point of our research, we will just give a brief introduction here. There have been many studies on the basic skyline computation algorithm, and some great algorithms have been proposed, i.e., BNL, NN, and BBS. Currently, BBS is the most efficient skyline computation algorithm, traversing an R-tree by using a best-first search paradigm, which has been shown to be optimal with respect to accessing an R-tree page.

The skyline services are not dominated by any other services in data space. As Figure 5.2 shows, there are 11 services in a two-dimension space with response time and cost as its coordinates. The set of skyline services, denoted as $SK(\check{s})$, contains $\{s_1, s_2, s_3, s_4, s_5, s_6, s_7\}$, because they are not dominated by any other services, i.e., s_8.

5.2.3 Representative Skyline Service Selection

To solve the problem of user preference, we propose to recommend the representative skyline services to users, and the number of representative skyline services should be

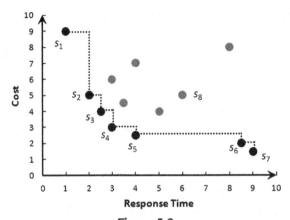

Figure 5.2
Example of skyline services.

small. In this way, our solution satisfies the two requirements in the case of user preference.

It should be recognized that comparability decreases with the increase in the dimension of data. For example, the QoS of service s_A is better than s_B in $(n-1)$ dimension (attribute), but worse than s_B in only one dimension. In the skyline definition, s_A and s_B cannot dominate each other. Therefore, the number of skyline services may still be too large, while the number of attributes to be considered is not small. To solve this problem, we propose a "similarity-based representative skyline" that contains some services that best describe the contour of the full skyline.

The process of calculating representative skyline services is divided into two steps:

1. Separate the skyline services into several clusters that contain "similar" services;
2. Select one representative service from each cluster. In the first step, we divide the skyline services into some clusters according to the similarity between each of the two services. The threshold of cluster-similarity is determined by the requested number of representative services. In the second step, we select the most representative from each cluster according to the covering circle approach. Specially, if the user is satisfied with the representative services, there is no need to consider the other skyline services.

We separate skyline services into some clusters according to their service similarities on QoS combined with user preferences. The specific formula of similarity computation is shown in Eqn (5.1). According to the equation of similarity computation, we can determine that two similar services have a small value of similarity.

$$sim(s_A, s_B) = \sqrt[2]{\sum_{i=1}^{n} \left(Q_{s_A}(i) - Q_{s_B}(i)\right)^2 w_i},$$
$$\sum_{i=1}^{n} w_i = 1 \tag{5.1}$$

Definition 3: λ-Similar service (λ-SS). Service s_A is the λ-SS of Service s_B if and only if the similarity between s_A and s_B is not more than λ, i.e., $\lambda - SS(s_A, s_B) =$ true, iff $sim(s_A, s_B) \le \lambda$.

As shown in Figure 5.3, if we define $\lambda = 2$, then (s_2, s_3), (s_3, s_4), (s_4, s_5), (s_6, s_7) are all 2-SS. However, as the value of λ increases from two to five, only s_1 and s_2 are similar services. After observation, we find (s_2, s_3), (s_3, s_4) are 2-SS; however, (s_2, s_4) are not 2-SS. There is no transitive theory in λ-SSs. To emphasize, there is a service s_3 that makes (s_2, s_3), (s_3, s_4) to both be 2-SS, we call (s_2, s_4) approximate 2-SS.

Definition 4: Approximate λ-similar service (λ-ASS). (s_i, s_j) are λ-ASS if and only if there are $(j - i - 1)$ services such as s_{i+1}, s_{i+2}, ..., s_{j-1} making (s_i, s_{i+1}), (s_{i+1}, s_{i+2}), ..., (s_{j-1}, s_j) are all λ-SS, i.e., λ-$ASS(s_i, s_j) =$ true, if and only if $\exists (s_{i+1}, s_{i+2}, ..., s_{j-1})$: $\forall k \in [i, j - 1], \lambda - SS(s_k, s_{k+1}) =$ true.

From the definition of approximate λ-SS, we can also determine that (s_2, s_5), (s_3, s_5) are approximate 2-SS.

Theory 1: The relation of approximate λ-SS is transitive. If (s_i, s_j), (s_j, s_k) are both λ-ASS, then (s_i, s_k) is also λ-ASS, i.e., if λ-$ASS(s_i, s_j) =$ true and λ-$ASS(s_j, s_k) =$ true, then λ-$ASS(s_i, s_k) =$ true.

Proof: Given (s_i, s_j), (s_j, s_k) are both λ-ASS, then the (s_{j-1}, s_j) and (s_j, s_{j+1}) are both λ-SS. According to definition 4, we could determine the fact that (s_{j-1}, s_{j+1}) are λ-ASS, so (s_i, s_k) are λ-ASS, too.

Definition 5: λ-Similar service cluster (λ-SSC). We call a set of services $\check{s} = (s_1, s_2, ..., s_n)$ a λ-SSC if and only if the arbitrary two services in $\check{s}$ are λ-ASS, i.e., $\lambda - SSC(\check{s}) =$ true, iff $\forall i, j \in [1, n], i \ne j, \lambda - ASS(s_i, s_j) =$ true.

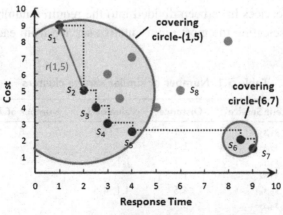

Figure 5.3

Covering circle.

Theory 2: If there are two λ-SSC, $\check{s}_1$ and $\check{s}_2$ that have the same service s_i, then the set $\check{s}_1 \cup \check{s}_2$ is also λ-SSC.

Proof: Since $\check{s}_1$ is λ-SSC, all services in $\check{s}_1$ are λ-ASS to s_i. Because they are the same, all services in $\check{s}_2$ are λ-ASS to s_i. According to the transitivity of λ-ASS, all services in $\check{s}_1 \cup \check{s}_2$ are λ-ASS to s_i. So we can get $\check{s}_1 \cup \check{s}_2$ is also λ-SSC.

The number of λ-SSC could be adjusted through changing the value of λ. For the sake of simplicity, we set the weight of each attribute as being equal. Then the similarity between each two services could be recognized as the distance between these two services in the n-dimension space. We use L_{max} to denote the longest distance of arbitrary adjacent services and L_{min} the shortest one. While the λ is larger than L_{max}, all the services are clustered in the same λ-SSC. Similarly, if λ is smaller than L_{min}, each service is a unique λ-SSC, so the range of λ to be considered is (L_{min}, L_{max}).

In Table 5.1, we record the similarity of each of the two adjacent skyline services in Figure 5.2. The trend of the number of λ-SSC is presented in the right part of Table 5.1. We order the distances in Table 5.1 from long to short and denote it D_i, while this distance is the i-th longest. Also, we use N_i to denote the number of distance that is equal to D_i. Then we can clearly explain the relationship between the value of λ and the number of λ-SSC.

Theory 3: When λ is in the range of (D_{i+1}, D_i), the number of λ-SCC is $N_1 + ... + N_i + 1$.

Take the data in Table 5.1 as an example, $D_1 = 4.5, N_1 = 1, D_2 = 4.1, N_2 = 1, D_3 = 1.1$, $N_3 = 3, D_4 = 0.7, N_4 = 1$. If we set λ as 2, then we can get $i = 2$, the number of 2-$SCC = N_1 + N_2 + 1 = 3$. When the value of λ is 1, then the value of i changes to be 3, the number of 1-$SCC = N_1 + N_2 + N_3 + 1 = 6$. According to theory 3, it is able to adjust the value of λ to get the required number of service clusters.

While all the skyline services have been divided into the required number of λ-SCC, the rest of the problem is selecting the most representative service from each λ-SCC. We

Table 5.1: Number of similar service clusters

Adjacent Service	Distance	Value of λ	Number of λ-SSC
s_1, s_2	4.1	0.7, 1.1	6
s_2, s_3	1.1		
s_3, s_4	1.1	1.1, 4.1	3
s_4, s_5	1.1		
s_5, s_6	4.5	4.1, 4.5	2
s_6, s_7	0.7		

propose the covering circle method [15] to select these services. For any $1 \leq i \leq j \leq n$, we use the covering circle (i,j) to denote the smallest circle that covers points $s_i, s_{i+1}, \ldots, s_j$ and has the center at one of these $j - i + 1$ points. We compute the smallest covering circle of the λ-*SCC* and choose the center of this covering circle as the representative point of the corresponding λ-*SCC*. As Figure 5.3 shows, the center of the covering circle is s_2, as the dis (s_1, s_2) is the smallest radius of the circles that could cover these five services. In particular, the center of the covering circle that covers two services could be the arbitrary one, i.e., (s_6, s_7). Because the dis (s_6, s_7) is the same as dis (s_7, s_6).

After the extraction of the service similarity and the definition of the covering circle, we could start the computation of the representative skyline services. The pseudo-code of "similarity-based RSA" is shown as Algorithm 1.

Algorithm 1 Similarity-based RSA

Input: $\mathcal{S}(s_1, s_2, \ldots, s_m)$, the number of requested representative services: N

Output: Representative skyline points

1: int $N_{cluster}$=1
2: for 0<i<n
3:      $d_i \leftarrow$ the distance between s_i and s_{i+1}
4: $N_i, D_i \leftarrow$ sort d_i
5: $\lambda \leftarrow$ compute D_i, N_i,N through *theory 3*
6: for 0<i<n
7:      If d_i<λ
8:          s_i, s_{i+1} belong to λ-SSC
9:      else
10:         $N_{cluster}$+=1
11: end
12: for 0<i<=$N_{cluster}$ do
13:     compute the covering circle of λ-SCC(i)
14:     return the center of the covering circle
15: end

We first initialize $N_{cluster}$ (the number of λ-*SCC*) (line 1), then record the distances between any two adjacent skyline services (lines 2, 3). To choose an appropriate value of λ, we sort all the distances that are recorded in lines 2, 3 and get N_i, D_i. Then we use theory 3 to compute the value of λ, which is constrained by the number of requested services (lines 4, 5); divide all the skyline points into λ-*SCC* (lines 6, 7, 8, 9, 10); for each λ-*SCC*, we compute the smallest covering circle, and return the center of this circle as the representative skyline point (lines 12, 13, 14).

In a similarity-based RSA algorithm, any other work should be delayed until all the services have been checked. After long-term training, the choice of the value of λ could be solved without traversing all services and it is easy for the system to choose an appropriate value of λ to extract representative services.

5.2.4 Dynamic Skyline Service Selection

With the development and promotion of service-oriented architecture, the number of web services increases quickly, which leads to a larger cost for computing skyline. Furthermore, the dynamic nature of the service environment increases the cost for computing skyline services. To solve this problem, we propose to maintain the skyline information instead of computing it over again because the cost of adjusting the skyline is less than the cost of computing it again.

Take Figure 5.4 as an example; there are three new services registered in the service registry. Service s_{11} has no impact on the skyline, while s_{10} should be added into the new skyline. The newly added s_9 causes a quite large change to the skyline, because it dominates the three original skyline services.

It could be directly observed that the impact of varying the service depends on its coordinates. An intuitive approach is to compare the location of the varying service with each skyline service to determine its influence on the skyline. However, the cost of this approach is large due to the number of times for pair-wise comparisons. To decide the influence of the varying service, we propose a paper-tape model to rapidly locate the coordinate of the varying service. A paper-tape could be treated as an array, as we record the skyline service's information of each nonfunctional attribute in the

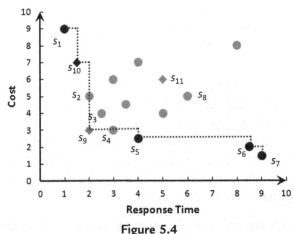

Figure 5.4
Dynamic skyline example.

corresponding paper-tape; i.e., we record the cost of each skyline service in the cost tape. Furthermore, we give each skyline service a tag, which means the order of service in each tape. For sake of simplicity, we just consider two attributes, including cost and response time, and name these two paper-tapes C-tape and R-tape, respectively.

Suppose the scenario is as shown in Figure 5.4, s_{10}, s_{11} first appears, and then another new service s_9 appears as shown in Figure 5.5. According to the definition of skyline, the original skyline before the appearance of service s_9 contains $\{s_1, s_{10}, s_2, s_3, s_4, s_5, s_6, s_7\}$. Our objective is to compute the new service skyline after the appearance of s_9 using our dynamic skyline approach. As the preprocess of computing the dynamic skyline, we order the values of each original skyline service's response time from small to large and rename the services; i.e., the response time of s_2 is the third smallest one in the original skyline, so we put s_2 into the third bucket in the R-tape. We then order the cost of the original skyline services from large to small in C-tape; i.e., the cost of s_2 is the third largest in original skyine services, so we put s_2 into the third bucket in C-tape. In particular, we can find that the order of the same service in two different tapes is the same, which is the fundamental point of our dynamic skyline computation approach.

When service s_9 appears as shown in Figure 5.4, we can find s_9 has its response time equal to s_2 and its cost equal to s_4. Thus, we can get its paper-tape model as shown in Figure 5.5.

The location (bucket) of the varying service s_i in R-tape is denoted as $L_R(i)$. For example, the location of service s_9 is $L_R(9) = 3$, $L_C(9) = 5$. In particular, if the value of s_i is between the value of s_k and s_{k+1} in R-tape, then $L_R(i) = k + 0.5$.

According to the skyline definition and proof, we get the following theory 4. Due to the limitation of space, we do not give the proof process here.

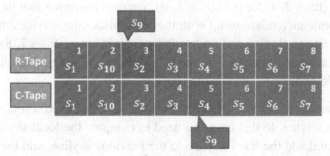

Figure 5.5
Paper-tape model.

Theory 4: Paper-tape dominance. If $L_R(i) < L_C(i)$, then s_i is a skyline service and dominates one or more original skyline services. If $L_R(i) = L_C(i)$, then s_i is skyline service and does not dominate the original skyline service. If $L_R(i) > L_C(i)$, then s_i is a dominated service.

There are three types of service changes to be considered: (1) new service appears; (2) old service disappears; and (3) value of QoS changes. In particular, the third case could be considered as the combination of the second and the first changes. The following algorithm is only for the scenario that a new service appears. In particular, the initiation of R-tape and C-tape are considered preprocesses.

Algorithm 2 DSCA_add
Input:R-Tape, C-Tape, $s_i(q_r, q_c)$
Output: R-Tape, C-Tape
1: $L_R(i) \leftarrow$ compare$q_r$with values in R-Tape
2: $L_c(i) \leftarrow$ compare$q_c$with values in R-Tape
3: if $L_R(i) < L_C(i)$
4:         Delete services belong to $[L_R(i), L_C(i)]$
5:             Insert $s_i(q_r, q_c)$ and Update R-Tape, C-Tape
6:   end if
7:   else if $L(i) = L_c(i)$
8:                 **Insert $s_i(q_r, q_c)$ and Update R −**
Tape, C − Tape
9:   end else if
10: else
11: end else

We first get the coordinates of the added service in R-tape and C-tape through comparing q_r and q_c with the corresponding tape (lines 1, 2); if $L_R(i) < L_C(i)$, according to Theory 4, we can know this service dominates one or more original skyline services. We delete those dominated services in the previous skyline, add the new service to the skyline, and update R-tape and C-tape (lines 3, 4, 5); if $L_R(i) = L_C(i)$, we can determine that the new service does not have a dominance relationship with the original skyline services; thus we can simply add the service to skyline and update R-tape, and C-tape (lines 7, 8); if $L_R(i) > L_C(i)$, we can determine that the new service is dominated by some original skyline services; thus we do nothing to the skyline (lines 10, 11).

As for the disappearance of service, two cases should be considered. First, the disappeared service is a skyline service. In this case, we need to compute the local skyline for its only dominance region and add the local skyline to the previous skyline, and then we get the full skyline. Second, the disappeared service is not the skyline service. In this case, nothing needs to be done.

Algorithm 3 DSCA_delete
Input: R-Tape, C-Tape, $s_i(q_r, q_c)$
Output: R-Tape, C-Tape
1:   $L_R(i)$ ←compare q_r with values in R-Tape
2:   $L_c(i)$ ←compare q_c with values in R-Tape
3:   if $L_R(i)=L_C(i)$
4:       š←compute the local skyline of s_i's only dominance region
5:          Delete $s_i(q_r, q_c)$ and insert š into previous skyline
6:       Update R-Tape, C-Tape
7:   **end if**
8:   **if** $L_R(i) \neq L_C(i)$
9:   **end if**

We also consider the representative skyline computation in the dynamic environment. The "similarity-based RSA" algorithm we mentioned is suitable for a static environment, but incapable for a dynamic case. For example, services A and B are in two different 2-*SSCs* (s_A belongs to $š_1$, s_B belongs to $š_2$); the similarity of s_A and s_B is 3. If a new service s_c is inserted into the service registry that also leads to the fact that (s_A,s_c) and (s_c,s_B) both change to be 2-*SS*, then we can determine that (s_A,s_c) is 2-*ASS* according to theories one and two. These two clusters ($š_1$ and $š_2$) are combined to be one 2-*SSC*, which is the union of $š_1$ and $š_2$. In the following section, we will show the solution to solve these three types of changes:

New service appears—In this case, we should take the set of services $š_{new}$ that are λ-*SS* to the new service into account, because two arbitrary services that belong to $š_{new}$. If s_A and s_B are not in the same λ-*SCC* before, then we should combine the clusters to which the two services previously belonged. If all the services are in the same service cluster, then we just insert this new service into this λ-*SCC* and compute the center of the covering circle that covers all services in λ-*SCC*.

Old service disappears—In this case, the λ-*SCC*$Ç_{old}$ that is the disappeared service that once belonged to the old service may be divided into several small clusters. Instead of analyzing the services that are related to disappeared service, we directly compute all the services that are in $Ç_{old}$, because we find that the time directly computing $Ç_{old}$ costs less than analyzing the relationship through experiments.

QoS value changes—The change of the QoS value should be considered as the original service disappears and a new service appears. Thus the solution of this case is the combination of the above two solutions.

5.2.5 Uncertain Skyline Service Selection

In the real world, services are impacted by different elements, i.e., net-traffic, data randomness, incompleteness, and limitation of measuring method, which makes the performance of the service uncertain. The uncertainty of the service also confuses the results of service comparison, which is the foundation of service selection. How to deal with uncertainty is becoming a big challenge to service selection. In this part, we propose to use the probability of dominance to address uncertainty. We compute the probability of dominance and determine the winner according to the predesigned threshold.

Considering the different performances of the same uncertain service, we use a probability density function f to describe its distribution in the data space D. Generally, $f(u) \geq 0$ for any service s in data space D, and obviously:

$$\int_{s \in D} f(s)ds = 1 \tag{5.2}$$

However, the probability density function of an uncertain service is practically unavailable. Actually, a set of performances are collected in the hope of approximating the probability density function. We model an uncertain service s_M, denoted by $s_M = \{m_1,..., m_{L1}\}$. The number of s_M's performances is written as $|s_M| = L1$. In this method, it can be regarded as the discrete case.

Given s_M and s_N are two uncertain services, and f and f′ are the corresponding probability density functions, then the probability that s_M dominates s_N is:

$$\begin{aligned} Prob[S_M \prec S_N] &= \int_{n \in D} f(n) \left(\int_{m \prec n} f'(m)dm \right) dn \\ &= \int_{n \in D} \int_{m \prec n} f(n)f'(m)dmdn \end{aligned} \tag{5.3}$$

For the sake of simplicity, we calculate the dominance probability through the discrete case. Let $s_M = \{m_1, ..., m_{L1}\}$ and $s_N = \{n_1, ..., n_{L2}\}$ be two uncertain services, L1, L2 are the number of service performances, and each performance information contains the values of nonfunctional attributes. Then the probability that s_M dominates s_N is as follows:

$$\begin{aligned} Prob\left[s_M \prec s_N\right] &= \sum_{i=1}^{L1} \frac{1}{L1} \cdot \frac{\left|\{m_j \in M | m_j \prec n_i\}\right|}{L2} \\ &= \frac{1}{L1L2} \sum_{i=1}^{L1} \left|\{m_j \in M | m_j \prec n_i\}\right| \end{aligned} \tag{5.4}$$

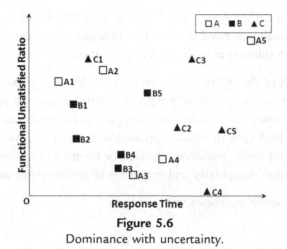

Figure 5.6
Dominance with uncertainty.

Case study. In Figure 5.6, there are three services s_A, s_B, and s_C. Each of these services has some different instances. The performance of s_B is stable, while the performance of s_C is precarious. To calculate $Prob[s_B \prec s_A]$, we have that $B_1 \prec A_2$, $B_2 \prec A_2$, $B_3 \prec A_4$, and A_5 is dominated by all the instances of B. According to Eqn (5.2), the probability that service B dominates A is:

$$Prob[S_B \prec S_A] = \frac{1}{5 * 5}\sum\nolimits_{i=1}^{5}\left|\left\{B_j \in B \middle| B_j \prec A_i\right\}\right| = \frac{8}{25}.$$

Identically, $Prob[S_A \prec S_B] = \dfrac{1}{25}$

$$Prob[S_A \prec S_C] = \frac{9}{25}, \ Prob[S_B \prec S_C] = \frac{13}{25} \text{ and } Prob[S_C \prec S_A] = \frac{1}{5}.$$

In this way, we can compute the dominance probability between each of the two services. Then we can compute the probability that service s_N is not dominated by any other service. The detail equation is as follows.

$$Prob[s_N] = \prod\nolimits_{s_M \in S}(1 - Prob[s_M \prec s_N]) \tag{5.5}$$

After computing the probability that each service is not dominated by any other service, we can set a threshold probability to get the probability skyline. Each service with the probability higher than the threshold is a member of the probability skyline.

5.3 MapReduce and Skyline Service Selection

The skyline method is especially attractive to achieve optimal or semioptimal service selection in a multiattribute decision-making process. The quality of composite web services or intercloud applications can be greatly enhanced by fast MapReduce skyline query processing. In our earlier work [16,17], we adopted the skyline method for solving the QoS problem. Basically, we need to solve two fundamental issues to yield QoS-guaranteed skyline solution in web service applications.

- Exponential growth of the skyline selection process: The complexity of the skyline selection process increases exponentially with the attributes and the cardinality of the data space. The skyline space may become too complex to be optimized in real-time.
- How to ensure the high QoS in cloud-supported web services? The QoS may degrade rapidly when Internet traffic becomes saturated or jammed. The situation becomes worse if both selection complexity and network traffic deteriorate at the same time.

In this section, we will solve the above two problems.

5.3.1 Architecture

Ever since 2001, the skyline operators [18] and their extensions have been advocated for QoS-based service selection by many authors [10,19–24]. The skyline method is especially attractive to achieve optimal or semioptimal service selection in a multiattribute decision-making process.

We apply MapReduce to upgrade the computing efficiency with scalable performance in a large-scale skyline query processing. We propose a variant of the MapReduce method by adding a process between *Map* and *Reduce*. The idea is illustrated in Figure 5.7 in three steps.

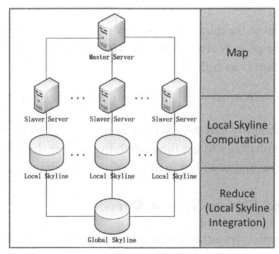

Figure 5.7
MapReduce model for selecting skyline services to achieve optimal QoS.

1. The map process: Service data points are partitioned by the master server (e.g., UDDI) into multiple data blocks based on the QoS demand. The data blocks are dispatched to slaver servers for parallel processing.
2. Local skyline computation: This process is used to generate the local skylines from service data points in subdivided data blocks.
3. The Reduce Process: In this process, local skylines generated by all slaver servers are merged and integrated into a global skyline, which applies to all services being evaluated.

Even DeWitt and Stonebraker [25] have assessed MapReduce as ineffective in handling relational database operations; we find that MapReduce is extremely attractive to speed up the skyline query processing process. We need to compare pair-wise services in parallel. With MapReduce, the new service is first mapped into a group and added into the local skyline computation. Then all local skylines are integrated into the global skyline at the reduce stage.

We have adopted the skyline method for solving the QoS problem in two earlier works. We evaluate three MapReduce versions of the block name label (BNL) skyline algorithm based on three different data space partitioning schemes. MapReduce for skyline services was also studied in [19,26].

5.3.1.1 Mapping of partitioned skyline tasks

The quality of the selected skyline services depends on the efficiency of the local skyline computation and the performance of the integration process. Thus, the efficiency and QoS of the MapReduce skyline process depends mainly on how to explore the distributed parallelism to accelerate the map stage.

The efficiency of the mapping depends on data space partitioning. The service data points are partitioned into divided regions. The goal is to achieve load balancing, to fit into the local memory, and to avoid repeated computations when old services are dropped and new services are dynamically added.

5.3.1.2 Merging in reduce computations

Before the process of reduce, we introduce a middle process (local skyline computation) at step two. The reason is that computing skyline services is expensive when the number of candidate services is extremely large. By introducing the middle process, only local skyline services are delivered to the reduce process at step three. This will largely decrease the number of services to be processed at the reduce stage.

5.3.2 MapReduce and Skyline Service Selection Algorithms

BNL, NN, Bitmap, and BBS are well-known skyline algorithms. We extend from these skyline algorithms by incorporating the MapReduce model to exploit distributed parallelism in server clusters or in a cloud platform. We evaluate three MapReduce skyline methods, denoted as MR-dim, MR-grid, and MR-angular in Table 5.1, in which MR stands for MapReduce in all figure labels and text bodies.

Consider two service data points, s_1 and s_2, in the QoS space Q. The service s_1 dominates service s_2, if s_1 is larger than or equal to s_2 in all attribute dimensions of Q. Furthermore, s_1 must be larger than s_2 in at least one attribute dimension. The subset S of services form the skyline in space Q, if all service points on the skyline are larger than or equal to other services along all attribute dimensions. In other words, all skyline services are not dominated by any other service in the space Q.

Three MapReduce skyline algorithms are specified below based on the three data partitioning schemes shown in Figure 5.8(a)–(c). The MR-dim algorithm is the simplest one to implement, based on one-dimensional partitioning (Figure 5.8(a)). The MR-grid algorithm is based on grid partitioning (Figure 5.8(b)).

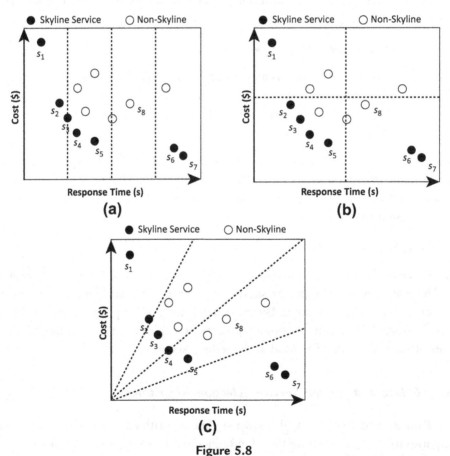

Figure 5.8
Three data partitioning methods for MapReduce-based skyline query processing.

The MR-angular algorithm is illustrated in Figure 5.8(c), based on the original work by Vlachou, Doulkeridis, and Kotidis (2008) and simply called the VDK method. There is no dominance relationship between any two angular sectors in the data space. Therefore, the execution time of the second step of the MR-angular algorithm is longer than that of MR-grid algorithm. However, the time at the third step is much shorter than that of the MR-grid algorithm. In the next section, we will prove these claims via experimental results.

5.3.2.1 MR-dim algorithm

The MR-dim algorithm contains two stages: (1) partitioning job, in which we divide the data space into some disjoint subspaces and compute the local skyline of each subspace; and (2) merging job, in which we merge all local skylines to compute the global skyline. Empirically, the number of partitions is set as (two times of *nodes*) in the MR-dim algorithm.

Specially, in the process of implementation, the range of each partition in dimension d is equal to V_{max}/N_p, in which V_{max} is the maximum value in dimension d, and N_p is the number of partitions. The local skyline of each partition is computed using the BNL algorithm. In the merging process, all local skyline services are given the same key in the map process. They are merged to generate the global skyline in the reduce process.

In MR-dim, only the QoS parameter values in one dimension are used to do the partitioning. For example, we separate the data space into four blocks according to the response time of each service in Figure 5.8(a). This method is easy to implement, while the redundant computations still exist in this case. In addition, this method needs to balance the load in the reduce process.

5.3.2.2 MR-grid algorithm

Different from MR-dim algorithm, there are dominance relationships between partitions in the MR-grid algorithm, as further illustrated in Figure 5.9. Any point in block A dominates any point in block D. Therefore, we need not compute the local skyline in partition D. Many redundant domination computations can be thus pruned.

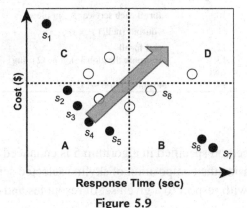

Figure 5.9

Dominance relationship in grid-based partitioning skyline methods.

In the MR-grid method as shown in algorithm 1, data space is partitioned into 2^d (d is the dimension number) blocks. To achieve load balance, the dividing point in each dimension is the median of the dimension. Lines (1—5) specify the process of grid partitioning, while lines (6—9) generate the local skylines in sections. The global skyline is generated with lines 10—14. We include algorithm 1 here as a baseline reference. The newly enhanced method is specified in algorithm 2.

In algorithm 4, we only compute the local skyline services which are not dominated by other blocks (lines 8—9). By doing so, step two saves 25% of the comparison time, and the complexity of the pair-wise comparison process increases exponentially with the dimensionality. The speed improvement of the MR-grid method in step two is rather limited when the number of dimensions becomes very large. When the number of dimensions reaches 10, the improvement is less than 11.08% based on our measurement.

Algorithm 4: MapReduce-grid method revisited

Input: The original data set S
Output: The skyline subset Ω

Generate the local skyline points in each partition

1:     Get the maximum value of each dimension and calculate the boundary of each partition

2:     **forall** service s_n in dataset S

3:     **compute** the partition P_i that service s_n belongs

4:     **output**(P_i, s_n)

5:     **end forall**

6:     **for** each partition P_i which are not dominated

7:     **compute** the local skyline LS_i using BNL

8:     **output** (P_i, LS_i) in file st

9:     **end for**

Merging local skyline subsets into the global skyline

10:     **forall each** service s_i in file st

11:     **output** (null, (P_i, s_i))

12:     **end forall**

13:     **compute** the global skyline Ω using BNL

14:     **output**(skyline set Ω)

5.3.2.3 MR-grid algorithm

The angular partitioning method specified in algorithm 5 is enhanced from the original VDK design. Overall, we emphasize the composition of skyline selected services, which aim at achieving optimized QoS with respect to a given set of resources and cost constraints.

5.3.2.3.1 Algorithmic enhancement

We modify the VDK method in two technical aspects. First, we apply an equi-volume partitioning strategy. Second, we do not transform the reduce part in a hyperspherical data space. These two distinctions make our scheme much faster and space-efficient to take advantage of the elastic resources and interplay between cloud mashups.

This enhanced angle-based partitioning reduces many redundant computations and balances the workload, because each subdivided data block involves both high- and low-quality data points. For instance, each partitioned block (an angular sector) involves some global skyline services: $\{s_1,s_2\},\{s_3\},\{s_4,s_5\}$, and $\{s_6,s_7\}$.

The angular partitioning process contains two steps: (1) mapping the Cartesian coordinate space into the service data space and (2) dividing the data space into an N sector according to the angular coordinates. We divide the data space into $(0, \pi/8)$, $(\pi/8, \pi/4)$, $(\pi/4, 3\pi/8)$, $(3\pi/8, \pi/2)$.

We check the sector to ensure that the angular $\tan(\emptyset) = y/x$ belongs to and delivers the service s to the corresponding slave server. The hyperspherical coordinate is used in the map process. The Cartesian coordinate is used in the local skyline computation and in the reduce process.

Algorithm 5: MapReduce-angular Skyline method
Input: the original data set S
Output: the skyline subset Ω
Generation of local skyline points
1:        **forall** service s_n in dataset S
2:        **compute** the coordinate of s_n using Eq.(1)
3:        **compute** the partition P_i that s_n belongs to based on the service s_n's coordinate value
4:        **output**(P_i, s_n)
5:        **end forall**
6:        **forall** partitioned sectors P_i
7:        **compute** local skyline LS_i using BNL
8:        **output** (P_i, LS_i) in file st
9:        **end forall**
Merging of Many Skyline subsets
10:        **forall** service s_i in file st
11:        **output** (null, s_i)
12:        **end forall**
13:        **compute** the global skyline Ω using BNL
14:        **output** Ω

5.3.2.3.2 Complexity analysis

In what follows, we analyze the complexities of the MR-grid and MR-angular algorithms presented above. As Figure 5.4 shows, service s_4 is the nearest one to the axes. It can be shown that the first nearest neighbor, i.e., s_4, is part of the skyline. On the other hand, all the points in the dominance region of s_4 can be pruned to save time.

The dominance ability of skyline services is critical to the efficiency of the skyline computation. For example, if the dominance ability of s_4 is stronger, more services will be pruned, which leads to higher efficiency. Therefore, dominance ability is selected as the evaluation metric of the algorithm complexity. The dominance ability of the skyline service s_i is defined by the ratio $D_{s_i} = \frac{Num_{s_i}}{Num_{all}}$, in which Num_{s_i} is the number of services dominated by s_i, and Num_{all} totals all services.

For simplicity, we assume uniform distribution of the data points in this dominance definition. Thus we can approximate the dominance ability of s_i by the area ratio $D_{s_i} = \frac{Area_{s_i}}{Area_{all}}$, in which $Area_{s_i}$ is the area dominated by service s_i in the partition containing s_i, as shown in the *D-gird* and *D-angular* regions of Figure 5.5. The $Area_{all}$ is the area of this partition.

In Figure 5.10, we compare the grid-based and angle-based method to divide the data space into four partitions, respectively. The data space is a square with *2L* long sides. The area of the overall data space is $4L^2$, while the area of each partition is L^2. Given a skyline service *s* with coordinate (x, y), it belongs to the partition closest to the axes in most of the cases.

Figure 5.10 clearly demonstrates that the D-angular region demands much fewer pair-wise dominance comparisons than that required in the D-grid region. The following three

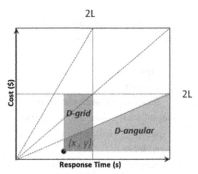

Figure 5.10

Comparison of the MR-grid and MR-angular partitioning methods in dominance coverage.

theorems give quantitative differences in dominance ability among three MapReduce skyline algorithms.

Theorem 1: To use the MR-grid method, the dominance ability of a given service s is specified by:

$$D_s^{grid} = \frac{(L-x)(L-y)}{L^2} \qquad (5.6)$$

Proof: As shown in Figure 5.10, the dominance region of s is the brown region using the MR-grid method, with an area of $(L-x)(L-y)$. The area of the partition is L^2, thus the dominance ability of s is $\frac{(L-x)(L-y)}{L^2}$. Q.E.D.

Similarly, we can compute the dominance ability if the MR-angular method is used.

Theorem 2: To apply the MR-angular method, the dominance ability of a given service s is specified by:

$$D_s^{angle} = \frac{L^2 - \frac{x^2}{4} - (2L-x)y}{L^2} \qquad (5.7)$$

Proof: The dominance region of service s is the gray region for MR-angular, $L^2 - \frac{x^2}{4} - (2L-x)y$. And the area of partition that s belongs to is still L^2 while using the MR-angular method. Therefore, the dominance ability is:

$$\frac{L^2 - \frac{x^2}{4} - (2L-x)y}{L^2} \qquad \text{Q.E.D.}$$

In the following Theorem 3, the dominance ability of the MR-grid method is found weaker than the MR-angular method. This result is also valid in high-dimensional cases. Therefore, we conjecture that the MR-angular method outperforms the MR-grid method in theory. We will validate this claim by the Hadoop experimental results.

Theorem 3: The dominance ability of the MR-angular method is higher than that of the MR-grid method by the following amount.

$$\Delta D = D_s^{angle} - D_s^{grid} \geq \frac{x}{2L^2}\left(L - \frac{x}{2}\right) \qquad (5.8)$$

Proof: To compare the dominance ability of the MR-grid and MR-angular, we compute the difference amount ΔD, which is equal to $D_s^{angle} - D_s^{grid}$ as computed below:

$$\Delta D = \frac{L^2 - \dfrac{x^2}{4} - (2L - x)y}{L^2} - \frac{(L - x)(L - y)}{L^2} = \frac{1}{L^2}\left(-\frac{x^2}{4} - yL + xL \right)$$

$$\geq \frac{1}{L^2}\left(-\frac{x^2}{4} - \frac{x}{2}L + xL \right) \left(\text{because } y \leq \frac{x}{2} \right)$$

$$= \frac{x}{2L^2}\left(L - \frac{x}{2} \right) \quad \text{Q.E.D.}$$

5.3.3 Experiments

5.3.3.1 Experiment setup

Our experiments apply to the QWS dataset (http://www.uoguelph.ca/~qmahmoud/qws/index.html). This dataset comprises measurements of nine QoS attributes over 10,000 real-life web services. The majority of web services are obtained from public sources, including UDDI, search engines, and service portals.

Considering the rapid development of web services, we extended the size of the QWS dataset by randomly generating QoS values that are limited to a narrow range following the distribution of the QWS dataset. The number of services was extended to 100,000 over 10 QoS attributes in our experiments.

All experiments are implemented in Java, and the MapReduce-related experiments are run on a Hadoop 0.20.2 framework. Our Hadoop experiments run on a server cluster built up to 64 server nodes at Zhejiang University. Each server node has an Intel Core Duo E7400 2.99 GHz CPU, 3.25 GB main memory, with Ubuntu 10.9 OS and 1 GB memory allocated to JVM.

5.3.3.2 Efficiency

To evaluate the efficiency of various MapReduce skyline selection methods, we use the basic metric of processing time, which consists of both reduce time and map time. Figure 5.7 shows the processing time used for selecting the optimal or suboptimal skyline services, because the service cardinality (the number of candidate services) becomes very large (100,000 data points for 10,000 composite service requests in extended QWS dataset). The attribute dimension increases from 2 to 10.

When the QoS dimension is low, say two, the total processing time is rather low, around 50 s. As the dimension increases in Figure 5.11, all three methods show hardly any change

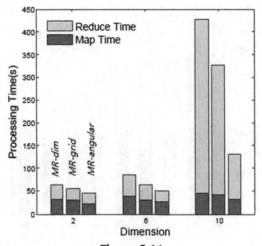

Figure 5.11
Performance effects of three MapReduce skyline methods over a very large dataset.

in the map time. The MR-angular method shows the lowest increase in reduce time as the attributes increase to 10. Even with 100,000 data points over 10 dimensions, the total processing time of the MR-angular method is about 130 s, compared with 430 and 320 s in the other two methods. The conclusion is that MR-angular performs much better than the other two methods in a large data space with more attribute dimensions.

The MR-angular method outperforms the MR-grid method with up to 320% reduction in processing time as the dimension increases to 10. The MR-dim method performs the worse, with up to 420% longer processing time than the MR-angular method. With 10 dimensions, the reduce time is seven, five, and three times longer than the map times in the three MapReduce skyline selection processes. It should be noted that 130 s processing time is obtained on a 64-node server cluster. If a 1000-server cluster is used, this processing time could be significantly reduced to just a few seconds.

In summary, with a very large service cardinality of 100,000 data points over 10 attributes, our MR-angular method outperforms the MR-grid and MR-dim methods by a factor of three and two, respectively. These results clearly demonstrate the advantages of the enhanced angular-partitioned MapReduce skyline method operating in a very large service data space.

5.3.3.3 Scalability

The number of servers used greatly affects the cluster performance. We consider a large data space of 100,000 service data points. There are 10 dimensions of performance attributes. The server cluster used increases from 4 to 8, 12,..., 32 and 64 servers. Figure 5.12 shows the processing time of the MR-angular method plotted against the number of servers used.

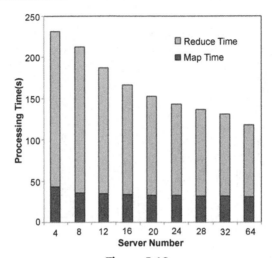

Figure 5.12

Scalability in the MapReduce cluster used in experiments.

The processing time decreases sublinearly with respect to more servers being used. When the number of servers exceeds 24, the speedup improvement becomes gradually saturated. The map time reduces almost flatly as more servers are used. The reduce time also is reduced by using more servers. In other words, the drop in reduce time contributes the most to the scalability.

Compared with four servers used, the processing time is reduced by only 10% when eight servers are used; the processing drops from 230 to 130 s with 70% improvement as the number of servers used increases from 4 to 32. The sectioned bar diagram in Figure 5.12 clearly shows the scalability of using the MR-angular method to accelerate the reduce process in skyline selection of optimal web services. The advantages increase with larger data space and more attribute dimensions adopted.

5.4 Summary

The efficiency of the traditional QoS-based service selection, such as integer programming and utility function approach, is vastly limited by the number of alternative services. With the increase in the number of services, it is becoming a big challenge. In this section, we propose an efficient approach for QoS-based service selection, which decreases the range of choices without pruning the potential candidates effectively by taking advantages of the skyline method. The basic selection with QoS-based skyline is to compute all skyline services in a static environment and recommend them to be selected. Meanwhile, we consider the different skyline service selection variations for real applications, such as representative skyline service selection, dynamic skyline service selection, and uncertain skyline service selection. Further, we use the MapReduce framework to handle the skyline service selection with big scalability and propose three different data space partitioning algorithms.

References

[1] F. Curbera, M. Duftler, R. Khalaf, W. Nagy, N. Mukhi, S. Weerawarana, Unraveling the web services web: an Instruction to SOAP, WSDL and UDDI, IEEE Internet Comput. 6 (2) (2002) 86−93.

[2] L. Zeng, B. Benatallah, A.H.N. Ngu, M. Dumas, J. Kalagnanam, H. Chang, QoS-aware Middleware for web services composition, IEEE Trans. Softw. Eng. 30 (5) (2004) 311−327.

[3] M. Alrifai, T. Risse, Combining global optimization with local selection for efficient QoS-aware service composition, in: Proc. of the 18th International Conference on World wide web, 2009, pp. 881−890.

[4] B. Benatallah, F. Casati, F. Toumani, Representing, analysing and managing web service protocols, Data Knowl. Eng. 58 (3) (2006) 327−357.

[5] L. Bordeaux, G. Salaun, D. Berardi, M. Mecella, When are two web services compatible? Lect. Notes Comput. Sci. 3324 (2005) 15−28.

[6] F. Liu, L. Zhang, Y. Shi, L. Lin, B. Shi, Formal analysis of compatibility of web services via ccs, in: Proc. of The International Conference on Next Generation Web Services Practices, IEEE Computer Society, 2005, p. 143.

[7] C. Bohm, H. Kriegel, Determining the convex hull in large multidimensional database, in: Data Warehousing and Knowledge Discovery (DaWaK), 2001, pp. 294−306.

[8] J. Pathak, S. Basu, V. Honavar, On context-specific substitutability of web services, in: Proc. of the International Conference on Web Services, IEEE Computer Society, 2007, pp. 192−199.

[9] D. Ardagna, B. Pernici, Adaptive service composition in flexible processes, IEEE Trans. Software Eng. 33 (6) (2007) 369−384.

[10] S. Ran, A model for web services discovery with QoS, ACM SIGecom Exch. (2003) 1−10.

[11] M. Alrifai, D. Skoutas, T. Risse, Selecting skyline services for QoS-based web service composition, in: WWW, 2010.

[12] S. Borzsonyi, D. Kossmann, K. Stocker, The skyline operator, IDCE, 2001.

[13] J.L. Bentley, et al., On the average number of maxima in a set of vectors and applications, JACM 25 (4) (1978) 536−543.

[14] P. Godfrey, R. Shipley, J. Gryz, Maximal vector computation in large data sets, in: Proc. of the 31st International Conference on Very Large Data Bases, 2005, pp. 229−240.

[15] D. Kossmann, F. Ramsak, S. Rost, Shooting stars in the sky: an online algorithm for skyline queries, in: Very Large Database (VLDB), 2002, pp. 275−286.

[16] L. Chen, J. Wu, S. Deng, Y. Li, Service recommendation: similarity-based representative skyline, in: IEEE World Congress on Services, 2010, pp. 360−366.

[17] D. Papadias, Y. Tao, G. Fu, B. Seeger, An optimal and progressive algorithm for skyline queries, in: Int'l Conf. on Management of Data (SIGMOD), 2003, pp. 467−478.

[18] S. Borzsonyi, D. Kossmann, K. Stocker, The skyline operator, in: Int'l Con. on Data Engineering, 2001, pp. 421−430.

[19] L. Pan, L. Chen, J. Wu, Skyline web service selection with MapReduce, in: International Conference on Computer Science and Service System, 2011.

[20] J. Sander, M. Ester, H. Kriegel, X. Xu, Density-based clustering in spatial databases: the algorithm GDBSCAN and its applications, Data Min. Knowl. Discov. 2 (2) (1998) 169−194.

[21] S. Wang, B.C. Ooi, A.K.H. Tung, L. Xu, Efficient skyline query processing on peer-to-peer networks, in: Int'l Conf. on Data Engineering, 2007, pp. 1126−1135.

[22] Q. Wu, A. Bouguettaya, Computing service skyline from uncertain QoWS, IEEE Trans. Serv. Comput. 3 (1) (2010) 16−29.

[23] T. Yu, Y. Zhang, K.J. Lin, Efficient algorithms for web services selection with end-to-end QoS constraints, ACM Trans. Web 1 (1) (2007) 1–26.

[24] L. Zeng, B. Benatallah, A.H. Ngu, M. Dumas, J. Kalagnanam, H. Chang, QoS-aware middleware for web services composition, IEEE Trans. Software Eng. 30 (5) (2004) 311–327.

[25] M. Ester, H. Kriegel, J. Sander, X. Xu, A density-based algorithm for discovering clusters in large spatial databases with noise, in: Proc. of ACM SIGKDD Conf. on Knowledge Discovery and Data Mining, 1996, pp. 226–231.

[26] H. Han, H. Jung, S. Kim, H. Yeom, A skyline method to the matchmaking web service, in: Int'l Symp. on Cluster Computing and the Grid (CCGrid), 2009.

CHAPTER 6

Service Recommendation

Chapter Outline

6.1 Overview of Service Recommendation

The service-oriented computing (SOC) paradigm and its realization through standardized web service technologies provides a promising solution for the seamless integration of single-function applications to create new large-grained and value-added services. In

Service Computing: Concepts, Methods and Technology. http://dx.doi.org/10.1016/B978-0-12-802330-3.00006-0

recent years, SOC, especially service composition, was applied in a lot of domains, e.g., workflow management, finances, e-business, e-science, etc.

The growing number of web services brings both opportunities and challenges to SOC. Similar to service composition and service discovery, service recommendation is also widely applied in industrial and academic circles. To the best of our knowledge, many solutions have been proposed to recommend services by using collaborative filtering-based approaches [1,2], context-aware approaches [3,4], the graph-based approaches [5], and so on. In the domain of service recommendation, identifying and composing a set of atomic services to recommend an optimized composite service that the user may be interested in based on the original composite services that the user has previously used, which we call composite service-oriented recommendation (CSOR), which has attracted a lot of attention and is becoming a hot research topic.

Figure 6.1 presents a conceptual overview of the CSOR. As shown in Figure 6.1, the composite service is composed of several atomic services that achieve part functionality within the composite service. With the development of SOC, more and more services with different types of functionalities appear in the service pool (e.g., service repository). Apparently, some services, which we call candidates, are similar or equal to the atomic services in the composite service. The goal of a CSOR is to compose and recommend an optimized composite service that outperforms the original one by using the services in the service pool.

Although CSOR has attracted a lot of attention in recent years, the current solutions to the CSOR problem are far from satisfactory. There are two main drawbacks with the current solutions:

1. Compatibility—Accurate service matchmaking is the most important fundament and guarantee of an atomic service replacement. Previous research makes use of the

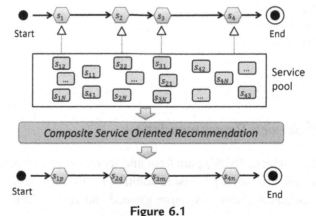

Figure 6.1
Overview of composite service-oriented recommendation.

input/output and interfaces of services and proposes some semantic-based or adapter-based approaches to handle this problem. Due to the limitation of semantic information, the output of these solutions is not ideal. In addition, the robustness of the recommended composite service cannot be guaranteed by existing solutions.

2. Quality—Current solutions about the CSOR problem mostly use quality of service (QoS) as the metric to evaluate the performance of composite services. QoS contains many attributes, e.g., cost, response time, and availability, and is presented as a set of numerical values. However there are some features (e.g., user preference) that cannot be presented by numerical values, which we call implicit quality, while QoS is an explicit quality. Existing solutions to CSOR problems have not taken implicit quality into consideration.

In this chapter, we model the problem of service recommendation and propose two approaches to improve the performance of service recommendation. In the following sections, we first propose a Bayes-based service recommendation approach in Section 6.2 and then introduce an instant service recommendation approach in Section 6.3. Finally, a conclusion is given in Section 6.4.

6.2 Bayes-Based Service Recommendation

This section proposes a novel CSOR approach by using service execution logs and a Bayesian approach. Further, we propose three recommendation algorithms based on this approach: (1) simple service recommendation (SSR) algorithm; (2) Bayes service recommendation (BSR) algorithm; and (3) Bayesian approach and K-medoids clustering (BKSR) algorithm. Experiments based on a large-scale service dataset show the efficiency and effectiveness of these three algorithms.

6.2.1 Preliminary

Bayes theorem is a theorem of probability theory originally stated by the Reverend Thomas Bayes. It can be seen as a way of understanding how the probability that a theory is true is affected by a new piece of evidence [6]. It has been used in a wide variety of contexts, ranging from marine biology to the development of "Bayesian" spam blockers for e-mail systems. In this section, we will give a simple introduction of the Bayes theory.

Begin by having a look at the theorem, displayed below. Then we will look at the notation and terminology involved.

$$P(T|E) = \frac{P(E|T) \times P(T)}{P(E)} \tag{6.1}$$

In this equation, T stands for a theory or hypothesis that we are interested in testing, and E represents a new piece of evidence that seems to confirm or disconfirm the theory. $P(T|E)$ stands for the probability that T is true given that E is true and is the posterior probability of T. In particular, $P(T)$ represents the best estimate of the probability of the theory we are considering, prior to consideration of the new piece of evidence. It is known as the prior probability of T. $P(E)$ stands for the probability that the evidence is true, while $P(E|T)$ is the likelihood probability that E can be calculated according to T.

In the scenario of CSOR, we want to find the recommended composite service based on the original composite service. By setting T as the recommend composite service and setting E as the original composite service, we can introduce Bayes theorem into the CSOR problem and transform the problem of finding the optimized composite service into the problem of finding the composite service, which can maximize the value of $P(T|E)$. Detailed analysis will be presented in the following sections.

Definition 1: Web service (WS). A web service WS is defined by a tuple (N, F, I, O, CI, CO, QoS), in which N is the name of the service, F is the function of the service, I is the input list, O is the output list, CI is the list of preconditions, CO is the list of post-conditions, and QoS is the explicit quality of the service.

Definition 2: Service composition. Service composition [7] can be defined as a directed acyclic graph $G = (V, E)$ of services, in which V is the set of vertices and E is the set of edges of the graph.

Each vertex in the graph represents a service involved in the composition. The following condition should be held on the vertices of the graph: Given WS_i is a service that has at least one incoming edge, and WS_{i1}, WS_{i2}, ..., WS_{in} are vertices from which there is a directed edge to WS_i, then $I_i \subseteq (O_{i1} \cup O_{i2} \cup ... \cup O_{in})$ and $CI_i \leftarrow (CO_{i1} \cap CO_{i2} \cap ... \cap CO_{in})$. Specifically, $\subseteq$ is the subsumption relation and $\leftarrow$ is the implication relation. In other words, a service at any stage of the composition has its inputs from the outputs of its predecessors, and the post-conditions of services at any stage of the composition should imply the preconditions of services in the next stage.

In a composite service, there are four kinds of relationships between any adjacent atomic services WS_i and WS_j, as Figure 6.2 shows: (1) order relation—If WS_j is executed after WS_i, the relationship between WS_i and WS_j is order; (2) branch relation—If only one of these two atomic services is selected to execute according to the post-condition of their predecessors, the relationship between WS_i and WS_j is branch; (3) parallel relation—If the execution of WS_i and WS_j does not depend on each other, the relationship between WS_i and WS_j is parallel; and (4) self-circulation relation—If WS_i is executed continuously for many times, WS_i is self-circular.

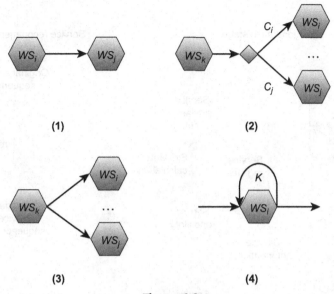

Figure 6.2
Structures in composite service.

Definition 3: Service sequence (S). A composite service is a service sequence if there is only order relation between any adjacent services in the composition. A service sequence is defined by a tuple (WS_1, WS_2, ..., WS_n), in which WS_i are the services composing the service sequence.

Service sequence is a simple and commonly used type of composite service in the real world. In this chapter, we focus on the recommendation of service sequence and leave other interesting variants for our future work.

Definition 4: QoS. QoS is the explicit quality of service, which can be measured, while the implicit quality cannot be measured. It consists of nonfunctional attributes of the service that can describe some features of the service, such as response time, availability, reliability, and so on [8].

In this chapter, QoS is presented as a vector, which consists of the values of QoS attributes.

6.2.2 Architecture

The process of Bayes-based service recommendation can be divided into two stages: a data generation stage and service recommendation stage, as shown in Figure 6.3.

The first stage is data generation. This stage mainly has two aspects. The first is calculating the similarity between services registered to a service repository to acquire the

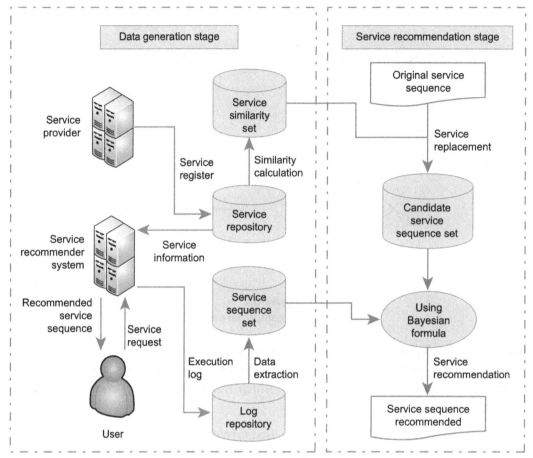

Figure 6.3
Architecture of Bayes-based service recommendation.

service similarity set. The second is extracting a service sequence set from the service execution logs, covered in Section 6.2.3 that describes details about this.

The second stage is service recommendation. This stage can also be divided into two steps: service replacement and Bayes-based recommendation. First, acquiring a candidate service sequence set by replacing one or more services in the original service sequence. With the service similarity set, services with similarity larger than a threshold are selected to replace the original ones. Specifically, this step is not essential as it is only used in a BSR algorithm to improve the efficiency. Second, determining the recommended service sequence by using the Bayes formula based on service sequences in the candidate service sequence set. This needs the execution times of each service sequence in the service sequence set. The next section will give a detailed description of this proposed recommendation approach.

6.2.3 Bayes Theorem for Service Recommendation

As described in Figure 6.3, the architecture of service recommendation consists of two components. In this section, we will introduce the details of data generation and service recommendation, respectively.

6.2.3.1 Data generation stage

Given two services s_1 and s_2, the similarity between these two services, which is defined as $Sim(s_1, s_2)$, consists of many aspects, such as functional similarity, interface similarity, QoS similarity, and so on [9−11]. Up to now, there were many existing solutions to the calculation of service similarity. In this chapter, we use a widely accepted method in [12] to calculate the similarity of four parameters (N, F, I, O) in definition 1. The similarity of these four parameters is calculated based on the concept hierarchy built by WordNet and HowNet.

Given a concept hierarchy built by WordNet and HowNet, word w_1 is in level l_1 and word w_2 is in level l_2. The level corresponds to the shortest path from the word to the imaginary root. Suppose $Dis(w_1, w_2)$ is the distance between two words, then the similarity between these two words is calculated as follows:

$$Sim(w_1, w_2) = \frac{\alpha \times (l_1 + l_2)}{(Dis(w_1, w_2) + \alpha) \times Max(|l_1 - l_2|, 1)}, \qquad (6.2)$$

in which α is a predefined constant, and $|l_1 - l_2|$ means the absolute value of $(l_1 - l_2)$. Given service $s_1 = (N_1, F_1, I_1, O_1, CI_1, CO_1, QoS_1)$ and $s_2 = (N_2, F_2, I_2, O_2, CI_2, CO_2, QoS_2)$, then similarity $Sim(N_1, N_2)$, $Sim(F_1, F_2)$, $Sim(I_1, I_2)$, and $Sim(O_1, O_2)$ can be calculated based on Eqn (6.2). Due to the limitation of space, we do not introduce the detailed calculating equations of these four parameters.

As for the parameters CI and CO, we use the number of matches to calculate the similarity, and the detailed equation is as follows:

$$Sim(CI_1, CI_2) = \frac{\cap(CI_1, CI_2)}{\cup(CI_1, CI_2)}, \qquad (6.3)$$

in which $\cap (CI_1, CI_2)$ means the number of precondition matches between CI_1 and CI_2, and $\cup (CI_1, CI_2)$ means the union set of CI_1 and CI_2.

As the QoS of service is described by a vector that consists of the values of each QoS attribute, we use the cosine similarity equation to calculate the QoS similarity:

$$Sim(QoS_1, QoS_2) = \frac{QoS_1 \cdot QoS_2}{||QoS_1|| \times ||QoS_2||} \qquad (6.4)$$

After calculating the similarity of these seven parameters, we combine these seven similarities to get the similarity between two services. In this chapter, we use a weighted average approach to calculate final service similarity, i.e., $Sim(s_1, s_2) = \frac{Sim(N_1,N_2)+\cdots+Sim(CI_1,CI_2)+Sim(CO_1,CO_2)+Sim(QoS_1,QoS_2)}{7}$. For simplicity, we normalize the similarity between services to a value in the range of [0,1]; the higher the value is, the more similar they are. $Sim(s_1, s_2) = 0$ means that services s_1 and s_2 are absolutely dissimilar to each other, while $Sim(s_1, s_2) = 1$ means that these two services are completely the same. It should be noted that service similarity $Sim(s_1, s_2)$ has the following properties:

1. Symmetry—Similarity between services s_1 and s_2 is equal to similarity between services s_2 and s_1; i.e., $Sim(s_1, s_2) = Sim(s_2, s_1)$.
2. Reflexivity—Similarity between service s_1 and itself is equal to 1; that is, $Sim(s_1, s_1) = 1$.
3. Nonstrict transitivity—If s_1 and s_2 are similar to each other, and s_2 and s_3 are similar to each other, then services s_1 and s_3 are more likely to be similar to each other.

Based on the service similarities, the similar services set can be calculated. The detailed definition of similar services set is as follows:

Definition 5: Similar services set. A set of services is the similar services set of service s_1 for threshold Sim_{min}, if similarity between each service in the set and s_1 is larger than Sim_{min}, i.e., $SS(s_1,Sim_{min}) = \{s|Sim(s_1,s) > Sim_{min}\}$.

In experiment and practice, the threshold Sim_{min} is usually a constant, so the similar services set can be calculated offline. Consequently, it does not affect the efficiency of the recommendation algorithm, although it is a time-consuming calculation.

As discussed above, we only use the service sequences that have been executed; therefore the service sequence set for recommendation can be acquired from the execution logs of service sequences. The definition of a service sequence set is as follows.

Definition 6: Service sequence set (R). The service sequence set R consists of all service sequences that have been executed before. The numbers of times of execution of each service sequences in the set are required, and it can be acquired from the execution log. The number of times of execution of service sequence S is defined by $T(S)$. For instance, if service sequence S_1 appears thrice in the execution logs, then $T(S_1) = 3$.

Similar to the service similarity set, acquiring a service sequence set can be completed offline in experiment and practices. Therefore it does not affect the efficiency of the recommendation algorithm either.

6.2.3.2 Service recommendation stage

The service recommendation stage is the second stage of the service recommendation process. It is also the major stage. It recommends services based on the information provided by the data-generation stage.

The target of composite service recommendation is, based on an original service sequence S_0 that is composed manually or automatically, to find a similar service sequence S, which has a higher quality (both explicit and implicit) and is more robust than S_0, from the service sequence set R.

Formally, the target is to maximize the probability $P(S|S_0)$. In other words, find a service sequence S that is more likely to be able to satisfy the user's requirement, that is, with a higher quality. According to the Bayesian formula, probability $P(S|S_0)$ can be transformed as follows:

$$P(S|S_0) = \frac{P(S_0|S) \times P(S)}{P(S_0)},$$ (6.5)

in which the probability $P(S_0)$, which means the execution probability of service sequence S_0, can be regarded as the execution times $T(S_0)$. As the value of $P(S_0)$ is a constant and is not influenced by service sequence S, thus the above equation can be transformed as:

$$P(S|S_0) \propto P(S_0|S) \times P(S),$$ (6.6)

in which the likelihood function $P(S_0|S)$ is regarded as the similarity between service sequence S_0 and S, and the prior probability $P(S)$, which means the execution probability of service sequence S, can be expressed by the execution times $T(S)$. The detailed definition of similarity between service sequences is as follows.

Definition 7: Service sequence similarity. Given S_i and S_j are two service sequences with the same length, and they are represented by $S_i = (S_{i1}, S_{i2}, \ldots, S_{in})$ and $S_j = (S_{j1}, S_{j2}, \ldots, S_{jn})$. The similarity between S_i and S_j is defined as:

$$SSim(S_i, S_j) = \prod_{k=1}^{n} Sim(S_{ik}, S_{jk})$$ (6.7)

Since the value of $Sim(S_{ik}, S_{jk})$ is in the range of [0,1], their produce $SSim(S_i, S_j)$ is also in the range of [0,1]. Similar to service similarity, service sequence similarity has three features: (1) symmetry; (2) reflexivity; and (3) nonstrict transitivity.

Because the probability $P(S_0|S)$ can be expressed by $SSim(S_0, S)$, and $P(S)$ can be expressed by $T(S)$, Eqn (6.6) can be transformed as:

$$P(S|S_0) \propto SSim(S_0, S) \times T(S)$$ (6.8)

By using the Bayesian approach, we transform the problem of composite service recommendation into a novel problem that finding a service sequence S in the *service sequence set* to maximize the value of $SSim(S_0, S) \times T(S)$, in which S_0 is the original service sequence. In the next section, we will present three algorithms based on this novel recommendation approach.

6.2.4 Recommendation Algorithms

In this section, we present three algorithms for composite service recommendation and give detailed performance analysis after the introduction of each algorithm.

6.2.4.1 SSR algorithm

In the previous section, we transformed the composite service recommendation problem into a new problem maximizing the value of $SSim(S_0, S) \times T(S)$. An intuitive approach is using the method of exhaustion, the SSR algorithm. In the SSR algorithm, for each service sequence S_i in the service sequence set R, we calculate the service sequence similarity $SSim(S_0, S_i)$, acquire the execution times $T(S_i)$, calculate the product $SSim(S_0, S_i) \times T(i)$, and then find the service sequence S with the maximum product value.

Algorithm SSR Algorithm

Input: S_0: original service sequence; R: service sequence set;

Output: S: recommended service sequence

1:   int ssim=1, $S = S_0$

2:   for all S_i in R do

3:      $ssim_i = Sim(S_0, S_i)$

4:      if $ssim_i \times T(S_i) > ssim \times T(S)$ then

5:         $S = S_i$, ssim = $ssim_i$

6:      end if

7:   end for

8:   Return S

According to the definition of service sequence similarity, the time complexity is $O(n)$ for calculating $Sim(S_0, S_i)$, with an n-length original service sequence S_0. Suppose there are m service sequences in R, then the time complexity of the BSR algorithm is $O(m \times n)$; that is, the time complexity is proportionate to the size of the service sequence set R. Obviously, this algorithm is slow when the service sequence set is huge.

6.2.4.2 BSR algorithm

The bottleneck of the BSR algorithm is traversing all service sequence in set R. We propose to attach this bottleneck by reducing the range of candidate service sequences.

Specifically, we replace one or more atomic services in S_0 to generate the set of candidate service sequences, as Figure 6.1 shows. Before introducing the BSR algorithm, we would like to give a definition of service sequence edit distance.

Definition 8: Service sequence edit distance. The edit distance between two service sequences is the number of operations required to transform one sequence into the other. The operations include replacing one service with another, inserting one service, and deleting one service. In this chapter, we only consider replacing one service with another.

The process of a BSR algorithm is composed of two steps: (1) finding all candidate sequences by replacing at most D (the maximum edit distance) atomic services of the original service sequence; the calculation of candidate sequences can be completed by using an iteration approach, in which we acquire the candidate sequences with d services replaced by replacing one more service of the candidate sequences with $(d-1)$ services replaced (lines 1−14) and (2) iterating all candidate service sequences to find out the service sequence with maximum value of $SSim(S_0, S) \times T(S)$ (line 15). It should be noted that the value of $T(S)$ is set as 0 if S has not appeared in the execution log. In this way, we guarantee the robustness of the recommended service sequence, because the recommended service sequence must have been executed before.

Algorithm BSR Algorithm

Input: S_0 : original service sequence ; Sim_{min}: service similarity threshold; D: maxi-mum edit distance

Output: S: recommended service sequence

1: $SS = SS_d = \{S_0\}$
2: for $d = 1$ to D do
3:   $SS_{d-1} = SS_d$, $SS_d = \{\}$
4:   for all S_i in SS_{d-1} do
5:     for all s_j in S_i do
6:       for all s_k in $SS(s_j, Sim_{min})$ do
7:         $S_t = S_i$
8:         replace s_j with s_k in S_t
9:         $SS_d = SS_d \cup \{S_t\}$
10:      end for
11:    end for
12:   end for
13:   $SS = SS \cup SS_d$
14: end for
15: Return $S = SSR(S_0, SS)$

As discussed previously, a BSR algorithm consists of two steps: (1) calculating the candidate sequences by replacing and (2) finding out the recommended service sequence. We first consider the case in which the edit distance is d; that is, replace and only replace d services. Assume that the length of the service sequence is n, and the average number of services that are similar (similarity between services is larger than the minimum similarity Sim_{min}) with one service is $\overline{L}$. In the first step, because there are C_n^d cases while choosing d services from n service, and average $\overline{L}$ replaceable services for one service, the time complexity of calculation candidate sequences is $O(C_n^d \times \overline{L}^d)$. In the second step, we have to evaluate the similarity $SSim(S_0, S_1)$ between original service sequence and every candidate service sequence. Because the time complexity of evaluating the similarity between two n-length service sequences is $O(n)$, the time complexity of the second step is $O(C_n^d \times \overline{L}^d \times n)$. Therefore, the time complexity of BSR algorithm is $O(C_n^d \times \overline{L}^d + C_n^d \times \overline{L}^d \times n)$, which could be reduced to $O(C_n^d \times \overline{L}^d \times n)$.

Further, we consider the case in which the maximum edit distance is D. The time complexity should be the sum of those with edit distance from one to D; that is, $O(C_n^D \times \overline{L}^D \times n + C_n^{D-1} \times \overline{L}^{D-1} \times n + \cdots + C_n^1 \times \overline{L}^1 \times n)$, which could also be reduced to $O(C_n^D \times \overline{L}^D \times n)$. Specifically, $C_n^D \times \overline{L}^D$ could be expressed as $C_n^D \times \overline{L}^D = \frac{n \times (n-1) \times \cdots \times (n-D+1)}{D!} \times \overline{L}^D$. Because the value of D is usually small in practice (usually two or three), $D!$ can be regarded as a constant. Therefore, the time complexity of BSR algorithm is $O(C_n^D \times \overline{L}^D \times n) = O(n^{D+1} \times \overline{L}^D)$. Compared with the time complexity of SSR algorithm ($m \times n$), the time complexity of BSR algorithm is less than that of SSR algorithm when $n^D \times \overline{L}^D < m$. Because D is usually a small value, as mentioned above, and the value of $\overline{L}$ can be controlled via the minimum similarity Sim_{min}, BSR outperforms SSR in terms of efficiency most of the time.

6.2.4.3 BKSR algorithm

The bottleneck of the BSR algorithm is that replacing services of the original service sequence produces a lot of candidate service sequences, while the bottleneck of the SSR algorithm is that it needs to calculate the product of each service sequence with the original one. K-medoids clustering can be used to improve the service recommendation algorithms. That is the service recommendation algorithm based on the BKSR.

The BKSR algorithm clusters all service sequences in the service sequence set into K groups, then finds a service sequence that is the most similar with the original service sequence among the medoids of K groups; finally the recommended service sequence is the one with the maximum product $SSim(S_0, S_i) \times T(S_i)$ in that group.

Only finding recommended service sequences in the group with the medoid that is the most similar with the original service sequence is according to the nonstrict transitivity of service sequence similarity; that is, if the original service sequence is similar with the medoid, then it is more likely to be similar with the service sequences that are in the same cluster with the medoid (the value of $SSim(S_0, S_i)$ is more likely to be high). Our target is to maximize $SSim(S_0, S_i) \times T(S_i)$; it will be more likely to be large when

$SSim(S_0, S_i)$ is large, although it may not be able to attain the maximum value in the BKSR algorithm.

Algorithm KSC Algorithm

Input: R: service sequence set; K: number of groups; LP_{max}: maximum loop count

Output: $G_1, G_2, ..., G_k$: K service sequence groups; $C_1, C_2, ..., C_k$: K medoids

1:   for j=1 to K do

2:        C_j=Random(R)

3:   end for

4:   LP=0

5:   While $LP < LP_{max}$ and $C_1, C_2, ..., C_k$ have changed do

6:       for j=1 to K do

7:          G_j={}

8:       end for

9:       for all S_i in R do

10:         $SSim_{max}$=0

11:         for j=1 to K do

12:            $SSim_j = SSim(S_i, C_j)$

13:            if $SSim_j > SSim_{max}$ then

14:               $SSim_{max}=SSim_j$, t=j

15:            end if

16:         end for

17:         $G_t = G_t \cup \{S_i\}$

18:       end for

19:       for j=1 to K do

20:         $SSim_{max}$=0

21:         for all S_i in G_j do

22:            $SSim_i = \Sigma_{S_p \in G_j} SSim(S_i, S_p)$

23:            if $SSim_i > SSim_{max}$ then

24:               $SSim_{max}=SSim_i$, $C_j = S_i$

25:            end if

26:         end for

27:       end for

28:       LP=LP+1

29:   end while

Before describing the BKSR algorithm, we have to introduce the K-medoids service clustering (KSC) algorithm. The KSC algorithm clusters service sequences according to the service sequence similarity $SSim(S_i, S_j)$ by using the K-medoids clustering algorithm. We also introduce the maximum loop count LP_{max} to restrict the loop count of the algorithm.

The KSC algorithm loops LP_{max} times at most, and every loop consists of two steps. In the first step, K medoids are randomly selected, and all sequences in the candidate set are clustered into K groups according to the similarity between service sequence and each medoid (lines 11−16). Assume that there are m service sequences in the service sequence set, and the average length of service sequences is n, then the time complexity of the first step is $O(m \times K \times \bar{n})$. The second step is to recalculate the medoids for each group. Specifically, we determine the new medoid of a cluster according to the sum of the similarity between the target sequence with other service sequences in this cluster (lines 21−26). Assume that there are $\bar{g}$ service sequences in one group on average, and the time complexity of the second step is $O(K \times \bar{g}^2 \times \bar{n})$. Therefore, the time complexity of each loop is $O(K \times \bar{n} \times (m + \bar{g}^2))$, and the total time complexity is $O(LP_{max} \times K \times \bar{n} \times (m + \bar{g}^2))$. Although the time complexity of the KSC algorithm is not low, the algorithm can be run offline. Therefore, it will not affect the efficiency of the BKSR algorithm.

Algorithm BKSR Algorithm

Input: S_0: original service sequence; K: number of groups; $G_1, G_2, ..., G_k$: K service sequence groups; $C_1, C_2, ..., C_k$: K medoids

Output: S: recommended service sequence

1:   $SSim_{max} = 0$
2:   for j=1 to K do
3:       $SSim_j = SSim(S_0, C_j)$
4:       if $SSim_j > SSim_{max}$ then
5:          $SSim_{max} = SSim_j$, G=G_j
6:       end if
7:   end for
8:   Return S=$SSR(S_0, G)$

Service sequences are clustered into K groups by using a KSC algorithm, which provides the foundation for the BKSR algorithm. Similar to the KSC algorithm, the BKSR algorithm consists of two steps. In the first step, it finds the medoid C_j that is the most similar to the original service sequence S_0 among K medoids and takes the service sequences in group G_j as candidates (lines 1−7). The second step is to find the recommended service sequence with the maximum product $SSim(S_0, S_i) \times T(S_i)$ among candidates (line 8).

The time complexity of the first step of BKR algorithm is $O(K \times n)$ for an n-length original service sequence, while the time complexity of the second step is $O(\bar{g} \times n)$ by calling the SSR algorithm to find the recommended service sequence. Therefore, the total time complexity is $O(n \times (\bar{g} + K))$. Because $\bar{g}$ is the average number of service sequence in a group, $\bar{g}$ can be expressed as $\frac{m}{K}$. In this way, the total time complexity is transformed into $O\left(n \times \left(\frac{m}{K} + K\right)\right)$. Apparently, the time complexity of BKSR reaches its minimum value $O(n \times \sqrt{m})$ when the number of clusters is $K = \bar{g} = \sqrt{m}$. Compared with the time complexity of the SSR algorithm ($O(n \times m)$) and the BSR algorithm ($O(n^{D+1} \times \bar{L}^D)$), the BKSR algorithm outperforms the SSR algorithm and is better than the BSR algorithm when $\sqrt{m} < n^D \times \overline{L}^D$. As discussed above, the value of $n^D \times \overline{L}^D$ is smaller than m most of the time. And we also find the value of $n^D \times \overline{L}^D$ is larger than $\sqrt{m}$ empirically. Therefore, most of time, the efficiency order of these three algorithms is $BKSR > BSR > SSR$.

6.2.5 Experiments

6.2.5.1 Experiment setup

To evaluate the performance of these three algorithms, we prepared a service repository containing 10,000 services for the experiment. We artificially created all services. Among these services, besides the reflexive ones, there are 99,990,000 service pairs. We counted the symmetrical pairs repeatedly; that is, we regarded (A, B) and (B, A) as two different pairs, because it can simplify the calculation of the average number of services that similar with one service. Specifically, the similarities of the symmetrical pairs are the same.

From the left part of Figure 6.4, it can be observed that almost all similarities concentrate between 0 and 0.1, while only a small percent of similarities are larger than 0.5. Specifically, we counted the average number of services that have a similarity with one service that is greater than 0.5. Among the 9999 services, there are an average 3.199 services with a similarity larger than 0.9 to the target service, and an average 14.216 is larger than 0.8, an average 35.943 is larger than 0.7, an average 72.741 is larger than 0.6, and an average 132.054 is larger than 0.5.

The right part of Figure 6.4 shows the distribution of services' QoS. Similar to previous studies [13,14], we normalize the QoS of the composite service to one value that is in the range of [0,1]; the higher the value is, the higher the QoS is. It can be seen that for most services, QoS is on the high side. About 90% of the services' QoS are greater than 0.6, and the percentage of services which have a QoS between 0.7 and 0.9 exceeds 50%.

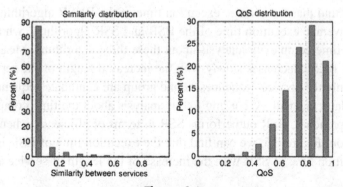

Figure 6.4
Similarity and QoS distribution in dataset.

Furthermore, we prepared a service execution log that records 73,242,650 executions of 100,000 different service sequences, which are generated based on the 10,000 atomic services. In particular, the length of these service sequences varies from 5 to 20, and there are $\frac{100,000}{16} = 6250$ service sequences for each length. As for the input of the recommendation system (original service sequences), we generate 1600 service sequences that have lengths varying from 5 to 20, and there are 100 service sequences for each length.

Our experiments ran on a desktop PC with Intel Core 2 Duo CPU E7200 2.53 GHz, 4GB-memory, and Ubuntu Server 10.10 OS. The experiment program is written in Java and runs on OpenJDK 1.6.0 update 20. To minimize the experimental error, all evaluations were executed in a robust benchmark framework[1] for the Java program.

6.2.5.2 Efficiency evaluation

In this group of experiments, we compared the efficiency of the SSR algorithm, BSR algorithm, and BKSR algorithm. Except for the SSR algorithm, some parameters are introduced in the execution of the other two algorithms. Therefore, we also evaluated the impact of these parameters, (1) maximum edit distance, (2) minimum similarity, and (3) cluster number, and analyzed the evaluation results.

First, we compared the efficiencies by varying the length of the service sequence, because the time complexities of these three algorithms are all affected by the length of the service sequence. In particular, the setup of other parameters is $Ed(edit\ distance) = 2$, $Sim_{min}(similarity\ threshold) = 0.8$, and $K(number\ of\ groups) = 318$. It should be noted that 318 is the square root of the number of different service sequences (100,000), which means 318 is the optimal value of the number of groups for the BKSR algorithm according to our analysis. Without a loss of generality, the execution time in all experiments means the time used to complete the recommendation based on all original service sequences.

In Figure 6.5, we find that the average execution time of the BKSR algorithm is obviously smaller than the average execution time of the BSR and SSR algorithms, which demonstrates our time complexity analysis about these three algorithms. Meanwhile, the execution time of BKSR increases slowly with the increased length of the service sequence. This is because only the service sequences in one group are candidate sequences and the number of candidates is small. According to our analysis about the time complexity of the SSR and BSR approaches, BSR outperforms SSR in terms of efficiency when $n^D \times \overline{L}^D < m$. From Figure 6.5, we can find that the execution time of BSR is progressively close to the execution time of SSR with the increase of the length of service sequence and

---

[1] http://www.ibm.com/developerworks/java/library/j-benchmark2/.

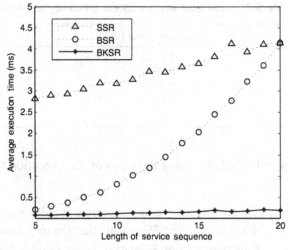

Figure 6.5
Efficiency comparison.

Table 6.1: Parameter impact to the efficiency of BSR

	Execution Time of BSR (s)		
$Sim_{min}\backslash Ed$	1	2	3
0.9	0.01337	0.14934	2.291
0.8	0.03506	2.59695	187.391
0.7	0.07916	14.0971	2501.287

even exceeds the execution time of SSR when the length of service sequence exceeds 20. The trend of these two curves also demonstrates our analysis in the previous section.

The parameters Ed and Sim_{min} affect the efficiency of the BSR algorithm according to the time complexity of BSR $O(n^{D+1} \times \overline{L}^D)$. In this experiment, we also evaluated the detailed impact of these two parameters. In particular, the execution time in Table 6.1 is the sum of the execution time over all types of service sequence lengths (from 5 to 20). Obviously, the execution time of BSR in Table 6.1 increases with the increase of the maximum edit distance (Ed). It is easy to explain, because the value of Ed stands for the value of D in the time complexity equation of $O(n^{D+1} \times \overline{L}^D)$. Meanwhile, the execution time of the BSR algorithm increases with the decrease of the service similarity threshold Sim_{min}, which is used to control the value of $\overline{L}$. Because the decrease of Sim_{min} increases the value of L, the execution time of the BSR algorithm increases respectively.

The idea of BKSR is using a K-medoid clustering approach to improve the efficiency of the BSR algorithm. Therefore, the parameter K is important to the performance of the

Table 6.2: Parameter impact to the efficiency of BKSR

K	Execution Time (s)	Volatility
32	1.0212	—
100	0.4741	−53.57%
318	0.2149	−54.67%
1000	0.1221	−43.18%
3162	0.1511	+23.75%

BKSR algorithm. In the Table 6.2, we show the trend of the execution time of BKSR with the variance of K.

In Table 6.2, the volatility reflects the change of the current issue compared with the former one. For instance, the value of -53.57% means that the execution time decreases 53.57% when the value of K increases from 32 to 100. From Table 6.2, we can find that the curve of K's impact to BKSR's efficiency fits our analysis; that is, the execution time first decreases and then increases with the increase of K. However, this curve reaches its wave trough when K has a value between 1000 and 3162, but not 318 ($\sqrt{m}$, $m = 100,000$). This is caused by the impact of a constant that is ignored in the analysis of time complexity.

6.2.5.3 Effect evaluation

In this group of experiments, we evaluated the practical effectiveness of these three algorithms. The robustness of the recommended service sequences has no occasion to be evaluated because the Bayes approach guarantees the plentiful execution times of the recommended service sequence. Although QoS itself has incommensurability and contradictoriness and stands for explicit quality only, we still chose QoS as the metric to measure the effect of the recommendation algorithms because it is objective and is measurable, while the implicit quality is subjective and immeasurable. In this experiment, we measured the effectiveness of the recommendation algorithm by comparing the incremental QoS of the recommended service sequence against the original service sequence. The QoS of the service sequence here is the sum of QoS of all services in the service sequence. The following experiments are all implemented based on 1600 original service sequences with lengths from 5 to 20, and the average increments of QoS are average increment QoS values of 1600 recommended service sequences compared with 1600 original service sequences.

Figure 6.6 shows the QoS of service sequences recommended by using the SSR algorithm, compared with the QoS of original service sequences. In Figure 6.6, the length of the brown bar means the percentage of recommended service sequences with incremental QoS is in a certain range. For instance, the first brown bar means that about 42% recommended

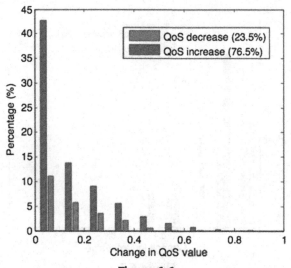

Figure 6.6
QoS increment of SSR algorithm.

service sequences have a higher QoS than the original service sequence, and the incremental QoS is in the range of [0,0.1]. From Figure 6.6, we can find that a large percentage of recommended service sequences obtain a higher QoS (brown, 76.5%) and a small percentage obtain a lower QoS (dark, 23.5%). The reason why some service sequences' QoS decreases is that there are some implicit qualities besides QoS. Nevertheless, we can see that the QoS of service sequences increases after recommendation in general, by an 0.06212 average, and more than 65% of QoS increments are concentrated between 0 and 0.3. The reason why the QoS increments are small is that the QoS of services are generally high. In particular, besides the increment of QoS, a larger improvement of our recommendation algorithm compared with existing service recommendation algorithms is that the robustness of the recommended service can be guaranteed.

Similarly, we also evaluated the effect of the BSR algorithm, as shown in Figure 6.7. In particular, the parameter setting of Figure 6.7 is $Sim_{min} = 0.8$, $Ed = 2$. Compared with the effect of the SSR algorithm, the performance of BSR is apparently worse than the SSR algorithm, because the percentage of QoS increase of BSR is smaller than the one of SSR. Meanwhile, the average QoS increment of BSR is 0.018, which is also smaller than the average QoS increment of the SSR algorithm. It should be noted that the SSR algorithm is based on an exhaustion approach. Despite the execution time of the SSR algorithm being longer than the BSR algorithm, the effect of SSR is better.

In this subsection, we also evaluate the impact of two parameters (Sim_{min} and Ed) to the effect of the BSR algorithm. Table 6.3 shows the trend of the average QoS increment of

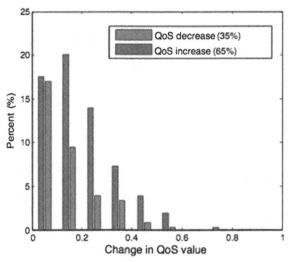

Figure 6.7
QoS increment of BSR algorithm.

Table 6.3: Parameter impact to the effect of BSR

	Average QoS Increment of BSR		
$Sim_{min} \backslash Ed$	1	2	3
0.9	0.00253	0.00307	0.00346
0.8	0.01343	0.01815	0.01977
0.7	0.02438	0.03802	0.04178
0.6	0.03261	0.05515	0.05897
0.5	0.03399	0.05832	0.06212

BSR algorithm with the variance of Sim_{min} and Ed. From Table 6.3, we can find that the average QoS increment increases with the increase of Ed because the increase of Ed stands for the increase of the number of candidate service sequences. Meanwhile, the average QoS increment increases with the decreases of Sim_{min} for a similar reason. The decrease of the service similar threshold increases the number of candidate service sequences. It can be found that the performance of BSR is progressively close to SSR with the increase of Ed and Sim_{min} and even equal to SSR when $Ed = 3$, $Sim_{min} = 0.5$.

Figure 6.8 shows the distribution of the service sequences on the increment of QoS with the BKSR algorithm. Similar to the SSR and BSR algorithms, some recommended service sequences' QoS increase, while the rest decrease. In particular, the parameter setting of Figure 6.8 is $K = 318$. The QoS of service sequences increases by 0.061567 on average,

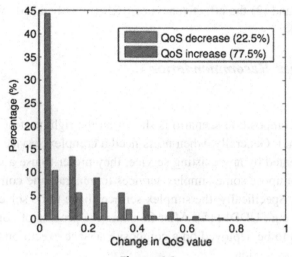

Figure 6.8
QoS increment of BKSR algorithm.

Table 6.4: Parameter impact to the effect of BKSR

K	Average QoS Increment	Volatility
1	**0.062127**	—
32	0.061881	−0.395%
100	0.061407	−0.766%
318	0.061567	+0.26%
1000	0.060726	−1.36%
3162	0.061452	+1.19%

and more than 58% of QoS increments concentrate between 0 and 0.4. As discussed above, the BKSR algorithm calculates the approximate maximum $SSim(S_0, S) \times T(S)$ by using less time. Therefore the effectiveness of BKSR should be a little worse than the SSR algorithm. To demonstrate this analysis, we do more experiments by varying the number of K to get a detailed performance for BKSR.

As for the parameter impact to the effect of the BKSR algorithm, we implement a series of experiments by varying the value of K. Table 6.4 shows the trend of the average QoS increment with the change of K. With the increase of the value of K, the average QoS increment of the BKSR algorithm decreases. In particular, the BKSR algorithm is just the SSR algorithm when $K = 1$. As discussed previously, the effect of the SSR algorithm is the best for the reason of the exhaustion approach. Meanwhile, the incremental QoS of BKSR with $K = 32, 100, 318, 1000, 3162$ are all smaller than 0.06217.

Compared with the SSR and BSR algorithm, BKSR should be the preferred recommendation algorithms for two reasons: (1) efficiency of BKSR is far better than the other two algorithms and (2) the effectiveness of BKSR is only a little worse than SSR and is better than BSR.

6.3 Instant Service Recommendation

6.3.1 Overview

A traditional service composition scenario is shown on the right part of Figure 6.9 (to the right of the dashed line). Generally, when users need a complex service and the function has not been implemented by any existing service, they prefer to use a service composition tool to compose some simplex services to generate the composite service that fulfills their demands. Specifically, the simplex services have to be selected from a service repository or registry, e.g., UDDI [15]. After finishing the process of composition, the composite service has to be deployed on a composite service execution engine (e.g., Apache ODE [7]) for execution.

As described above, traditional service composition schema have three main drawbacks: (1) some professional domain knowledge is essential to select simplex services for composition; (2) knowledge about service description language is needed for composing services to satisfy users' demands; and (3) manually selecting simplex services is a time-consuming job. Although the appearance of some service

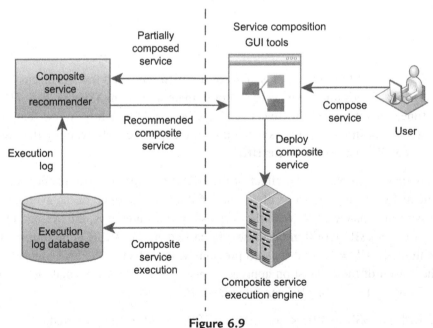

Figure 6.9

Overview of instant recommendation for web service composition.

composition tools such as Eclipse BPEL Designer [16] overcome the second drawback, professional domain knowledge is still a roadblock for nonprofessional users to do web service composition. Furthermore, the reliability of composite service generated by traditional service composition schema cannot be guaranteed. This is because traditional service composition approaches are mainly concerned with the matchmaking of interfaces and functionalities, which cannot guarantee the reliability of the composite service.

Inspired by Instant Search, Spelling Suggestion, and Autocomplete by Google [17], we propose a novel web service composition schema, WSCRec, that is faster and smarter than traditional solutions. Similar to Google Instant Search, a bunch of appropriate services will be instantly recommended to users, along with the incrementally implemented composition processes. According to these services recommended by WSCRec, users refine their partially composed services as well as complete the composition task.

The newly introduced components of the proposed WSCRec approach are shown in the left part of Figure 6.9. There are mainly two new components: (1) composite service recommender, which recommends a list of candidate composite services to the user according to the partially composed service and execution logs; specifically, it can be implemented as a local component of the service composition GUI tools (e.g., an Eclipse plugin) or a remote service for it and (2) execution log database, which records the execution information of each composite service running on the Composite Service Execution Engine. When a user attaches a new service to the partially composed service, the information of the partially composed service will be promptly sent to the composite service recommender. Then the composite service recommender tries to obtain a list of proper composite services according to the execution log of the composite services from the execution log database, and send it back to the service composition GUI tools for users to choose. If a user does not choose the recommended composite service, while a new service is attached, the above process will be repeated.

Compared with the traditional service composition schema, the benefit of our approach is threefold:

1. Instant recommendation—Dynamically present recommendations relevant to the partially composed service. Helps users formulate a better service composition by providing instant feedback.
2. Smart prediction—Professional domain knowledge is not essential. Even when users do not know exactly which web service they are looking for, predictions help guide their discovery. The top prediction will present beside the user's partially composed service, thus they can stop discovering as soon as they see what they need.

3. Guaranteed reliability—A bunch of frequently used web services have been proved to be more reliable and robust and have higher probability to fulfill the user's demand.

In the following section, we first provide the essential definitions and form the problem, and then propose four different recommendation algorithms. Finally, experimental results with different algorithms are presented.

6.3.2 Definition and Problem Description

In this section, we introduce some definitions that are related to the Composite Service Recommendation concept.

Definition 9: Web service (ws). A web service *ws* can be defined by a tuple as $ws = (N, F, I, O, CI, CO, QoS)$, in which N is the name of the service, F is the function, I is the input list, O is the output list, CI is the precondition list, CO is the post-condition list, and QoS is the quality of the service.

QoS consists of nonfunctional attributes of the service that describe the features of the service, such as availability, reliability, response time, and so on [8]. QoS can be presented as a vector consisting of the values of the QoS attributes.

Definition 10: Composite service. A composite service is defined by a directed acyclic graph of services as $G = (V, E)$, in which V and E are the sets of vertices and edges in the graph, respectively.

Each vertex in the graph represents a service involved in the composition. This condition should be held on all vertices of the graph: For each $WS_i \in V$, in which WS_i is a service that has at least one incoming edge, let $WS_{i1}, WS_{i2}, \ldots, WS_{in}$ be the vertices from which there is a directed edge pointing to WS_i. Then $I_i \subseteq (O_{i1} \cup O_{i2} \cup \ldots \cup O_{im})$ and $CI_i \leftarrow (CO_{i1} \cap CO_{i2} \cap \ldots \cap CO_{im})$, in which $\subseteq$ is the subsumption relation and is the implication relation. In other words, a service at any stage of the composition has its inputs from the outputs of its predecessors, and its preconditions should be implied by the post-conditions of its predecessors.

Definition 11: Service sequence (S). Service sequence S is a special kind of composite service. A composite service is a service sequence if there is only an order relation between any adjacent services and no self-circular services in the composition.

A service sequence can be defined by a tuple as $S = (WS_1, WS_2, \ldots, WS_n)$, in which for each $i \in [1, \ldots, n]$, WS_i is one of the services composing the service sequence, and WS_i is executed before WS_{i+1}. Service sequence is a simple and commonly used type of composite service in the real world. In this chapter, we focus only on the instant recommendation of service sequence and leave the other variants (e.g., parallel, conditional, and loops) for our future work.

For an instant composite service recommendation, we want to find the composite service that the user wants most, based on the service composed by the user. Formally speaking, given the fully composed service q from the user, we want to find the composite service s' with the highest probability $p(s|q)$ among all composite services s. By applying the Bayes theorem, we can express the problem as the following equation:

$$s' = \text{argmax}_s p(s|q) = \text{argmax}_s p(q|s)p(s) \tag{6.9}$$

Here, $p(q|s)$ is the probability that the composite service the user wants most is s, but he prefers to compose q. We assume that the more similar s and q are, the higher probability the user will prefer to compose q. So the probability $p(q|s)$ can be measured by the similarity between s and q that is represented as $Sim(s, q)$. Assume s and q are service sequences with the same length n, and they can be represented as $s = (s_1, s_2, \ldots, s_n)$ and $q = (q_1, q_2, \ldots, q_n)$, in which s_k and q_k are the k-th services of s and q, respectively. Then $Sim(s, q)$ can be calculated as:

$$Sim(s, q) = \prod_{k=1}^{n} Sim(s_k, q_k), \tag{6.10}$$

in which $Sim(s_k, q_k)$ is the similarity between the services s_k and q_k. Currently, there are some methods for service similarity computation [18–20]. In this chapter, we use a modified version of the method introduced by Khalid Elgazzar et al. [20] to calculate the similarity between services. We will give more details on this modified method in the following section.

In Eqn (6.9), $p(s)$ is the prior probability of s. $p(s)$ is usually measured by the frequency of occurrence of s, that is, the frequency of execution of s. In this chapter, we measure $p(s)$ with the linear combination of the relative execution frequency and QoS of s as:

$$p(s) = \alpha \cdot Q(s) + \beta \cdot f(s) \tag{6.11}$$

in which $Q(s)$ is the QoS utility [21] of the composite service s, $f(s)$ is the frequency of execution of s, which can be easily obtained from the composite service execution log, α and β are parameters, and $\alpha + \beta = 1$, $\alpha \geq 0$, $\beta \geq 0$. As for the computation of QoS utility, it involves scaling the QoS attribute values to allow a uniform measurement of the multidimensional service qualities independent of their units and ranges. And the approach for the QoS utility computation [21] is widely accepted.

The reason we use the linear combination of $Q(s)$ and $f(s)$ to calculate $p(s)$ instead of just using $f(s)$ is that, $p(s)$ represents how much users may want the service sequence s, and we assume that it does not only depend on how often s is executed, but also how high the QoS of s is (for convenience, we will not distinguish between QoS and QoS utility in the rest of this chapter).

We use the utility function from [21] to calculate $Q(s)$, which normalizes the QoS attributes of s into one single value, allowing a uniform measurement of the multidimensional QoS. The QoS vector of s with r attributes is defined as $qos(s) = (qos_1(s), \ldots, qos_r(s))$, in which $qos_i(s)$ is the value of the i-th attribute QoS attribute of s and can be calculated as:

$$qos_i(s) = F^n_{j=1} qos_i(s_j) \tag{6.12}$$

in which s_j is the j-th service of s, and F is an aggregation function depending on the QoS attribute as shown in [21]. For instance, the availability of s can be calculated as:

$$qos_i(s) = \prod_{j=1}^{n} qos_i(s_j) \tag{6.13}$$

Then the overall QoS utility of s is computed as:

$$Q(s) = \sum_{i=1}^{r} \frac{qos_i(s) - \min_{s \in R} qos_i(s)}{\max_{s \in R} qos_i(s) - \min_{s \in R} qos_i(s)} \cdot w_i, \tag{6.14}$$

in which R is the set of all composite services that have been ever executed, and $\sum_{i=1}^{r} w_i = 1, w_i \geq 0$ is the weight of $qos_i(s)$ to represent the user's priority. It can be observed that $Q(s) \in [0,1]$.

We use the following equation to calculate the relative execution frequency $f(s)$:

$$f(s) = \frac{t(s) - \min_{s \in R} t(s)}{\max_{s \in R} t(s) - \min_{s \in R} t(s)}, \tag{6.15}$$

in which $t(s)$ is the execution times of s. Obviously $f(s) \in [0,1]$, therefore $p(s) \in [0,1]$. Therefore, Eqn (6.9) can be rewritten as:

$$s' = \text{argmax}_s \left(\prod_{k=1}^{n} Sim(s_k, q_k) \times (\alpha \cdot Q(s) + \beta \cdot f(s)) \right) \tag{6.16}$$

Now for the instant composite service recommendation, we are given only the partially composed service $\bar{q}$, which is the prefix of the potential fully composed service q. The objective is to find the composite service s' with the highest probability $p(s|q)$ among all composite services s and q that extend $\bar{q}$. Similar to Eqn (6.9), we want to find:

$$s' = \text{argmax}_{s,q|q=\bar{q}\ldots} p(s|q) = \text{argmax}_{s,q|q=\bar{q}\ldots} p(q|s)p(s) \tag{6.17}$$

in which $q = \bar{q} \ldots$ denotes that $\bar{q}$ is a prefix of q. We can see that the only difference between Eqns (6.17) and (6.9) is that it is given only the prefix $\bar{q}$ instead of the entire q.

So we can view the offline composite service recommendation as a special case of the more general instant composite service recommendation.

Note that the analysis on offline composite service recommendation is also applicable to instant composite service recommendation. Thus, Eqn (6.17) can be transformed to:

$$s' = \operatorname{argmax}_{s,q|q=\overline{q}...} \left(\prod_{k=1}^{n} Sim(s_k, q_k) \times (\alpha \cdot Q(s) + \beta \cdot f(s)) \right) \tag{6.18}$$

Among all composite service q that extend $\overline{q}$, when $s_{|\overline{q}|+1} = q_{|\overline{q}|+1}, s_{|\overline{q}|+2} = q_{|\overline{q}|+2}, ..., s_n = q_n$, that is, $Sim(s_{|\overline{q}|+1}, q_{|\overline{q}|+1}) = 1, ..., Sim(s_n, q_n) = 1$, in which $|\overline{q}|$ is the length of $\overline{q}$, $Sim(s, q)$ will be the maximum for any s. Then the task of the instant composite service recommendation is transformed to the following:

$$s' = \operatorname{argmax}_s \left(\prod_{k=1}^{|\overline{q}|} Sim(s_k, \overline{q}_k) \times (\alpha \cdot Q(s) + \beta \cdot f(s)) \right) \tag{6.19}$$

6.3.3 Recommendation Algorithms

6.3.3.1 Exhaustion search-based algorithm

To solve Eqn (6.19), the easier way is to going through every service sequence s in R, calculating the value of $Sim(s_k, \overline{q}_k) \times (\alpha \cdot Q(s) + \beta \cdot f(s))$, and obtaining the top-$k$ results with maximum value as return. We call this algorithm an exhaustion-based algorithm, or *E-WSCRec* algorithm. The pseudo-code of *E-WSCRec* is shown in the following algorithm.

First, the algorithm creates a class called TopKList to maintain top-k service compositions with maximum probability (line 1). There is a method *add(s, p)* in class TopKList to add service composition into result, in which s represents the service composition to add and p is the probability of s. Class TopKList implements a heap structure to maintain the result. When the add method is called, if the number of the service composition in the heap is smaller than k, add s directly to the heap; if the number of the service composition is equal to k, then compare p to the item in the heap with minimum probability. Delete the item if its probability is smaller than p, and add the new item to the heap, or do nothing. The time complexity of the add method is $O(logk)$. Notice that the number of the items in the heap should not be larger than k. And then, the algorithm goes through every service composition s in set R (line 2). As long as the length of s is larger than or equal to the length of prefix $\overline{q}$ (line 3), calculate the probability of s (line 4) and add s to result. Notice that in Eqn (6.19) implicit is the condition $|s| \geq \overline{q}$, which should be prejudged before calculation. Eventually the algorithm would return the result set (line 8).

Algorithm E-WSCRec Algorithm

Input: service sequence prefix $\bar{q}$, service composition set R, integer k
Output: top k recommended service sequences for $\bar{q}$
$Result$ = new TopKList(k)
for each s in R **do**
  if $|s| \geq |\bar{q}|$ **then**
    $p = Sim(s_k, \bar{q}_k) \times (\alpha \cdot Q(s) + \beta \cdot f(s))$
    $Result.add(s, p)$
  end if
end for
return $Result$

6.3.3.2 Replacement-based algorithm

Replacement-based algorithm, or algorithm called *R-WSCRec*, tries to maximize the posterior probability by maximizing the similarity and uses similar services to replace the ones in $\bar{q}$ to speed up the maximization of similarity.

Since the similarity of $\bar{q}$ and itself is one, if we replace a few of the services as similar (similarity close to one) of the service in $\bar{q}$, the similarity of service we got and q will be close to one. Then we check whether the service we got is known already; if it is, then we get a service highly similar to $\bar{q}$, and its posterior probability is likely to be great. *R-WSCRec* tries to find similar solutions among known service composition by exhaustive possible replacement. The pseudo-code of the *R-WSCRec* algorithm is shown in the following algorithm.

Algorithm R-WSCRec Algorithm

1: Input:service sequence prefix $\bar{q}$, the minimum similarity M_{min}, the maximum
   replacement number M_{rep}, integer k
2: Output: top k recommended service sequences for $\bar{q}$
3: $Result$ = new TopKList(k)
4: R-WSCRec_Recursive($\bar{q}$, M_{min}, M_{rep},0,1,$Result$)
5: **return** $Result$

The algorithm creates a TopKList class (see Section 3.1.2) instance to maintain the result set (line 1), then calls the *R-WSCRec* recursive, a recursive function to solve the problem (line 2). Finally, the program returns the result set (line 3). The pseudo-code of the *R-WSCRec* recursive is shown in the following algorithm.

At first, the program determines whether the number of services that have been replaced exceed the maximum number of replacements (line 1). If it is not exceeded, then it searches S to find the service with prefix $\bar{q}$ by function *findWithPrefix*. We can create a hash table with different prefixes of services in advance, so that *findWithPrefix* could find the result in $O(1)$ time. Notice that the set S is empty if there is no result. And then the program traverses every service composition s in set S (line 3), calculates the posterior probability of s (line 4), and adds s to the result set (line 5). Then the function checks whether the number of services that has been replaced is less than the maximum number of replacements (line 8), to determine if it is allowed to continually replace the services. If so, it starts from the index and goes through every item in q (line 9). And then it traverses each service ws with a similarity with $\overline{q_i}$ that is greater than or equal to M_{min} (line 10). For each ws, it copies q to q' (line 11) to prevent the modification of q; then it replaces the i'-th item of $q_{i'}$ by ws (line 12). Finally, call function recursively (line 13), which replaces the prefix of services by q', increases the replaced number, and starts the index by 1. Notice that because M_{min} is a constant in practice, the set $\{ws|Sim(ws,\overline{q_i}) \geq M_{min}, ws \neq \overline{q_i}\}$ in line 10 can be calculated in advance, so that the function can be run in $O(1)$'s time to get this collection.

Algorithm R-WSCRec_Recursive algorithm

1: Input:service sequence prefix $\bar{q}$, the minimum similarity M_{min}, the maximum replacement number M_{rep}, integer r for replaced service number, start index $from$, result list $Result$
2: **if** $r \leq M_{rep}$ **then**
3:    $S = findWithPrefix(\bar{q})$
4:    **for each** s in S **do**
5:       $p = Sim(s_k, \bar{q}_k) \times (\alpha \cdot Q(s) + \beta \cdot f(s))$
6:       $Result.add(s, p)$
7:    **end for**
8: **end if**
9: **if** $r < M_{rep}$ **then**
10:    **for** $i = from$ to $|\bar{q}|$ do **do**
11:       **for each** ws in $\{ws - Sim(ws, \bar{q}_i) \geq M_{min}, ws \neq \bar{q}_i\}$ **do**
12:          $\bar{q}' = clone(\bar{q})$
13:          $\bar{q}_i' = ws$
14:          R-WSCRec_Recursive($\bar{q}'$, M_{sim}, M_{rep}, $r+1$, $i+1$, $Result$)
15:       **end for**
16:    **end for**
17: **end if**

6.3.3.3 Improved replacement-based algorithm

The problem of the *R-WSCRec* algorithm is that the result of replacing several items of $\bar{q}$ is highly possible to be an unknown service composition, so the program may deal with many irrelevant service compositions. The improved online service composition recommend algorithm based on replacement (or algorithm called *IR-WSCRec*) uses a so-called search trie data structure to ensure that the result of replacement is always a known services in the collection, to avoid that unnecessary calculations of unrelated service compositions.

Let's take a look at the search trie structure. Figure 6.10 shows the construction of a search trie of service compositions listed in Table 6.5 (each letter represents a service).

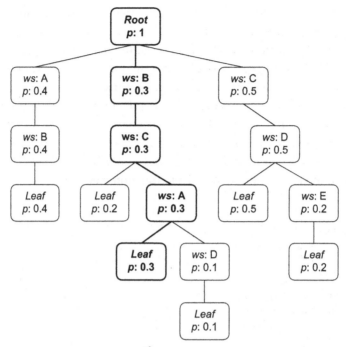

Figure 6.10
An example of service trie.

Table 6.5: Service sequence execution log

Service Sequence s	$p(s)$
AB	0.4
BC	0.2
BCA	0.3
BCAD	0.1
CD	0.5
CDE	0.2

Search trie is a multibranch data structure. Each internal (nonroot, nonleaf) node represents a service in some service compositions, while root and leaf nodes are placeholders. Any path from the root to leaf represents a combination of known services, and the entity of services is stored in the leaf node. For example, Figure 6.10 highlights a path that represents a composition of service "BCA" (ignore the probability p). Clearly, the search trie can be constructed with $O(|R| \cdot n_{max})$ offline.

The *IR-WSCRec* algorithm traverses the search trie by depth first search. In the meantime, it calculates the similarity of service $\bar{q}$ and notes in the search trie and limits the range of similarity (must be greater than or equal to M_{min}) and the number of different services (i.e., up to M_{rep}) to achieve the effect of pruning. So we get a more effective *R-WSCRec* algorithm. The pseudo-code of the *IR-WSCRec* function is shown in the following algorithm.

Algorithm IR-WSCRec algorithm

1: Input:service sequence prefix $\bar{q}$, the minimum similarity M_{min}, the maximum replacement number M_{rep}, search trie T, integer k
2: Output:top k recommended service sequences for $\bar{q}$
3: $Result$ = new TopKList(k)
4: IR-WSCRec_Recursive($\bar{q}$, M_{min}, M_{rep}, 0, 1,$T.root$, $Result$)
5: **return** $Result$

At first, we create a TopKList class instance to maintain the result set (line 1). Then we call the *IR-WSCRec* recursive, a recursive function to solve the problem (line 2). Finally, we return the result set (line 3). The pseudo-code of the *IR-WSCRec* recursive is shown in the following algorithm.

Algorithm IR-WSCRec_Recursive algorithm

1: Input:service sequence prefix $\bar{q}$, the minimum similarity M_{min}, the maximum replacement number M_{rep}, integer r for replaced service number, current index i, result list $Result$
2: **if** $r \leq M_{rep}$ **then**
3:   **if** node is a leaf and $i > |\bar{q}|$ **then**
4:     $s = node.s$
5:     $p = Sim(s_k, \bar{q}_k) \times (\alpha \cdot Q(s) + \beta \cdot f(s))$
6:     $Result.add(s, p)$
7:   **end if**
8: **else if** *node* is not a leaf **then**
9:   **for** each child of node **do**
10:     **if** $i \leq |\bar{q}|$ and child is not a leaf and $Sim(child.ws, \bar{q}_i) \geq M_{sim}$ **then**
11:       **if** $child.ws = \bar{q}_i$ **then**
12:         $r' = r$
13:       **else**
14:         $r' = r + 1$
15:       **end if**
16:       IR-WSCRec_Recursive($\bar{q}$, M_{sim}, M_{rep}, r', $i+1$, $child$, $result$)
17:     **else**
18:       IR-WSCRec_Recursive($\bar{q}$, M_{sim}, M_{rep}, r, $i+1$, $child$, $result$)
19:     **end if**
20:   **end for**
21: **end if**

First, the program determines whether the number of services that have been replaced is less than or equal to the maximum number of the replacement (line 1). If it is, then you can continue the search, or otherwise return. Then, if the current node is a leaf node and the current index exceeds the length of q (line 2), get the combination of services that corresponds to the leaf node (line 3), calculate the posterior probability (line 4), and add to the result set (line 5). If the current node is not a leaf node (line 6), then traversal each child node of the current node (line 7). For each child, if the current subscript does not exceed $|q|$ (i.e., q_i is effective), and the child is not a leaf node (i.e., the node that services *child.ws* is effective), and the similarity of *child.ws* and q_i is greater than or equal to M_{min} (line 8), then recursively call this function (line 9), which increases the current index by one. And when *child.ws* and q_i are the same, keep replacements unchanged, otherwise, the replace number increases by one (line 9). If the current index is more than $|q|$ (line 10), then directly call this recursive function (line 11), which increases the current index by one.

6.3.3.4 Heuristic search-based algorithm

To solve Eqn (6.19), we apply the A* search algorithm on a trie of service. In the following subsections, we introduce the search trie again with service probabilities. Then we present the A* search algorithm to find the service sequence maximizing Eqn (6.19) on the service trie. Last we discuss the pruning technique to speed up the A* search. This algorithm is mainly inspired by the work of Huizhong et al. on instant spelling correction for query completion [22].

The A* search algorithm traverses the input service sequence one service by one service from the beginning and tries to match it with the ones in the execution log. To make the searching efficient, we hold all service sequences in the execution log with their probabilities in the service trie. Note that the service trie can be built offline, and the update is easy and efficient. The service trie can be updated periodically instead of each time a service sequence is executed. The heuristic function used in the A* search algorithm is:

$$h(\bar{s}, i) = p_{max}(\bar{s}) \times \begin{cases} \prod_{k=1}^{i} Sim\left(\overline{s_k}, \overline{q_k}\right) & \text{if } i \leq |\bar{q}| \\ \prod_{k=1}^{|\bar{q}|} Sim\left(\overline{s_k}, \overline{q_k}\right) & \text{otherwise} \end{cases} \tag{6.20}$$

in which $\bar{s}$ is a prefix with length i of some service sequences in the execution log, and $p_{max}(\bar{s})$ is the maximum value of $p(s)$ among all service sequences extending $\bar{s}$. $p_{max}(\bar{s})$ can make sure that the search will tend to find the path with larger probability $p(s)$. When $\bar{s}$ is an entire service sequence, i.e., $\bar{s} = s$, Eqn (6.20) is equal to Eqn (6.19). Therefore the heuristic can lead to the objective function.

Equation (6.20) can be rewritten in a recursive form:

$$h(\overline{s'}, i+1) = h(\bar{s}, i) \times \left(p_{max}\left(\overline{s'}\right)/p_{max}(\bar{s})\right) \times \begin{cases} Sim\left(\overline{s'_{i+1}}, \overline{q_{i+1}}\right) & \text{if } i+1 \leq |\bar{q}| \\ 1 & \text{otherwise} \end{cases} \tag{6.21}$$

in which $\overline{s'}$ is a prefix with length $i+1$ that extends $\bar{s}$ by one service.

Given the service sequence prefix $\bar{q}$, the service trie t, and an integer k, the A* search algorithm is applied to find the top-k service sequences with the largest probabilities. We use a triple (p, i, n) to represent each intermediate search state, in which p is the probability of the current path, which is actually the value of the heuristic function, i is the index of the current service in the service sequence, and n is the current node in the service trie. The pseudo-code of the algorithm is shown in the following algorithm.

Algorithm H-WSCRec algorithm

1: Input:service sequence prefix $\bar{q}$, service trie t, integer k
2: Output:top k recommended service sequences for $\bar{q}$
3: $result$ = an empty list
4: $queue$ = an empty priority queue
5: add state $(p = 1, i = 0, n = t.root)$ to $queue$
6: **while** $queue$ is not empty and $|result| < k$ **do**
7:     $current$ = get and remove the top entry from $queue$
8:     **if** $current.i \geq |\bar{q}|$ and $current.n$ is leaf **then**
9:         add $current.n.s$ to $result$
10:    **else**
11:        **for** each $child$ of $current.n$ **do**
12:            $index = current.i + 1$
13:            **if** $index \leq |\bar{q}|$ **then**
14:                $prob = current.p \times Sim(\bar{q}_{index}, child.ws) \times child.p/current.n.p$
15:            **else**
16:                $prob = current.p \times child.p/current.n.p$
17:            **end if**
18:            add state $(p = prob, i = index, n = child)$ to $queue$
19:        **end for**
20:    **end if**
21: **end while**
22: **return** $result$

The algorithm mainly relies on a priority queue (line 4) of the intermediate search states, sorted by decreasing p, the value of the heuristic function. So in each step of the search, the state with the current largest p is always processed. The search starts from the root of the service trie, so the state with $p = 1$ (the probability of the *root* is always one), $i = 0$, $n = root$ is first added to the *queue* (line 5). The search repeats until there are no states left in the queue or the top-k service sequences are found (line 6). In each step of the search, the state with the largest probability is retrieved from the *queue* first (line 7). If the leaf node is reached, which means we have already found a path, the corresponding service sequence is added to the *result* list (lines 8 and 9). Otherwise we iterate over all child nodes of the current node to expand states (line 11). For each child node, the *index* is moved forward by one service (line 12). Then we calculate the probability of the child node according to the heuristic function (this is explained later; lines 13−17). And the new state with the child node is added to the *queue* (line 18). Finally, the top-k service sequences with the largest probabilities are returned (line 22).

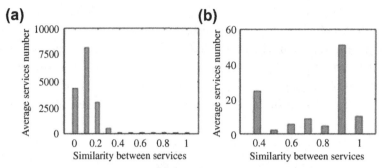

Figure 6.11
Service similarity distribution in dataset.

6.3.4 Experiments

6.3.4.1 Experiment setup

To evaluate the performance of the instant composite service recommendation algorithm, we took 15,959 web services from seekda.[2] In this dataset, we have the name, provider, country, WSDL file, and availability for each web service. The service name and WSDL file is used to calculate similarities between services. Because only the availability of service is available in the dataset, it is used as a representative for QoS, and the QoS utility of service sequence can be calculated as Eqns (6.13) and (6.14) with $r = 1$ and $w_1 = 1$.

Figure 6.11 shows the service similarity distribution in the dataset. It shows how many services on average yield similarities in each range with one service. In Figure 6.11, 0 on the x-axis indicates similarity in the range of [0,0.1], 0.1 indicates the range of [0.1,0.2], and so on; 1 indicates that the similarity equals to 1. From Figure 6.11(a), it can be observed that almost all similarities concentrate between 0 and 0.3, while only a small number of similarities are larger than 0.3; that is, most pairs of services are not similar. Figure 6.11(b) is a zoom-in of Figure 6.11(a), with similarities between 0.3 and 1. Specifically, there are an average 60.367 services with similarity larger than 0.9, i.e., counterintuitive. We examined the dataset and found that a number of the services are generated by Microsoft Office, and their names and the WSDL files are almost the same. This explains the counterintuitive situation.

Furthermore, we prepared an execution log that records 75,228,237 executions of 100,000 different service sequences, which are generated based on the 15,959 web services. The lengths of these 100,000 service sequences are uniformly distributed from 5 to 20. As for

---

[2] http://webservices.seekda.com/.

the input service sequences of the recommendation algorithm, we generate 1000 service sequences, the lengths of which vary from 5 to 20.

As for the *IR-WSCRec* algorithm and *H-WSCRec* algorithm needs, we constructed a service trie based on 100,000 service compositions. The number of son nodes of service trie rapidly decrease with height; the number of son nodes of the first layer is 10,141, and the average number of branches of the second layer is 9,841 and 1,002 for the third layer. Our experiments run on a desktop PC with Intel Core 2 Duo E7400 2.80 GHz CPU and 3 G memory, and Windows 7 OS. The program is written in Java and runs on Sun JDK 6 Update 27. To minimize the experimental error, all evaluations are executed in a robust benchmark framework[3] for Java program.

6.3.4.2 Efficiency evaluation

In this group of experiments, we evaluated the efficiency of the three algorithms, *E-WSCRec*, *IR-WSCRec*, and *H-WSCRec* (not *R-WSCRec*, because we have an improved algorithm) and analyzed the evaluation results. We adjusted the parameters of each algorithm and tested the algorithm's execution time and the relationship between these parameters. Finally, we have the execution time of three algorithms for the horizontal comparison. The average execution time of the experiments is the average execution time of 1000 inputs.

The execution time of the *E-WSCRec* algorithm and the relationship between the parameter α is shown in Figure 6.12. Note that because $\beta = 1 - \alpha$, we only need to adjust the parameter α. As can be seen from Figure 6.12, the largest difference of algorithm's execution time is not more than 0.06 ms. Thus, ignoring measurement error, we can conclude that the parameter α of *E-WSCRec* has no effect on the algorithm execution time.

Figure 6.13(a) shows the impact of parameters M_{rep} (maximum number of replacements) on the *IR-WSCRec* algorithm, in which M_{rep} ranges from 0 to 10, M_{min} is 0.1, and α is 0.5. From the figure we can see, the execution time rapidly increases with the M_{rep} and then gently increases when M_{rep} is larger than 4. The increase of execution time is due to the increase of M_{rep}; the algorithm would be able to search the higher of the service trie with more and more paths. And then the execution time goes flat, because the branches of the trie have only 0 or 1 nodes when the search reaches a certain level. Then the algorithm will not search more branch paths, but only goes down to reach the leaf node. So when $M_{rep} = 4$, the parameter M_{rep} has less impact on the execution time.

Figure 6.13(b) shows the relationship of parameters M_{min} (minimum similarity) and *IR-WSCRec* algorithm execution time, in which M_{rep} is fixed to 10, and α is fixed to 0.5. We can see that the algorithm execution time decreases rapidly with the increase of M_{min},

---

[3] http://www.ibm.com/developerworks/java/library/jbenchmark2/.

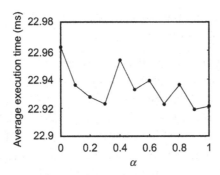

Figure 6.12
Efficiency of *E-WSCRec.*

then gently increases after $M_{min} = 0.5$. With the increase of M_{min}, the services with a similarity greater than or equal to M_{min} rapidly decline, so the number of paths the algorithm would search also decreases rapidly, and the corresponding algorithm execution time is reduced. There are a few services that have the similarity greater than or equal to 0.5, so when $M_{min} \geq 0.5$, the parameter has little impact on the execution time.

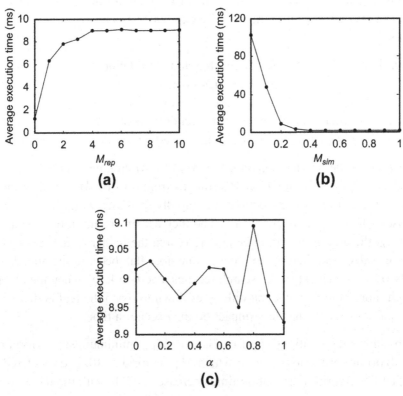

Figure 6.13
Efficiency of *IR-WSCRec.*

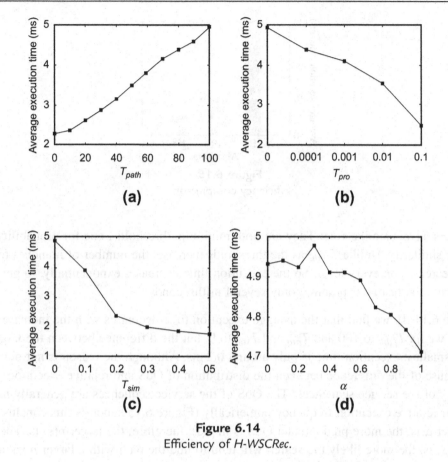

Figure 6.14
Efficiency of *H-WSCRec.*

The relationship of the parameter α and *IR-WSCRec* algorithm execution time is shown in Figure 6.13(c), in which M_{rep} and M_{min} are fixed to 10 and 0.1, respectively. It is obvious that the parameter α has little impact on the *IR-WSCRec* algorithm execution time.

Figure 6.14(a) shows that the average execution time increases linearly with the increase of $T_{path}(\alpha = 0.5, T_{pro} = 0, T_{sim} = 0)$, while theoretically it should increase exponentially. This is because the branch number (number of children for a node) in the service trie decreases rapidly along with the increase of depth. The branch number of the first level (direct children number of the root node) is 10141, the second level is 9.841 on average, the third level is average 1.002, etc. Therefore, when $T_{path} \geq 10$, the pruning impacts little on/after the second level, and the execution time mainly depends on the number of branches to search on the first level, which is equal to T_{path}.

As shown in Figure 6.14(b) ($\alpha = 0.5$, $T_{path} = 100$, $T_{sim} = 0$) and Figure 6.14(c) ($\alpha = 0.5$, $T_{path} = 100$, $T_{pro} = 0$), both of the average execution times decrease exponentially with the increase of T_{pro} (note that the x-axis is logarithmic) and T_{sim}, because these two

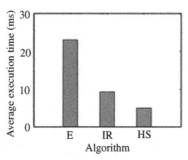

Figure 6.15
Efficiency comparison.

parameters have a similar role: They are both minimum thresholds, one for probability, the other for similarity. Unlike T_{path}, as the thresholds increase, the number of branches to search decreases on every level. So the execution time decreases exponentially. In general, the algorithm is fast after pruning, only several milliseconds.

In Figure 6.14(d), we find that the average execution time decreases with the increase of α, while we fix T_{path} to 100 and T_{pro} and T_{sim} to 0, but the difference between the largest and the smallest execution time is only around 0.2 ms. Although the reason is not obvious, it is because of the difference between the distribution of QoS and relative execution frequency of the service sequences. The QoS of the service sequences are generally higher than their relative execution frequency numerically (Figure 6.13 supports this conclusion). The larger α is, the more predominant QoS is in $p(s)$; therefore, the larger $p(s)$ is. The larger $p(s)$ is, the more likely the search will tend to find the path with a larger p value, which yields less attempts to other paths, and then the search is faster. Nevertheless, the impact α on execution time is small.

Figure 6.15 shows the three algorithms' execution time comparison (E for $E\text{-}WSCRec$ algorithm, IR for $IR\text{-}WSCRec$ algorithm, HS for $H\text{-}WSCRec$ algorithm), in which $\alpha = 0.5$, $K = 316$, $M_{rep} = 10$, $M_{min} = 0.1$, $T_{path} = 100$, $T_{pro} = T_{sim} = 0$.

It can be seen from the figure, the $E\text{-}WSCRec$ algorithm execution time is significantly higher than that of the other two algorithms. The $H\text{-}WSCRec$ algorithm and $IR\text{-}WSCRec$ algorithm require a few milliseconds, while the $E\text{-}WSCRec$ algorithm requires 20 ms. In general, the execution time of the $IR\text{-}WSCRec$ algorithm and $H\text{-}WSCRec$ algorithm is less than 10 ms, and meets the requirements of an online recommendation.

6.3.4.3 Effect evaluation

$E\text{-}WSCRec$ selects the services with highest probability from all service compositions, therefore the $E\text{-}WSCRec$ algorithm is the best standard algorithm. It represents the best results the algorithm can achieve.

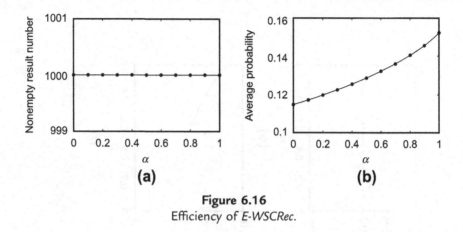

Figure 6.16
Efficiency of *E-WSCRec*.

Figure 6.16(a) shows the relationship of parameter α and the nonempty results of the *E-WSCRec* algorithm. Obviously, the *E-WSCRec* algorithm can always return a nonempty result and therefore is not related to the parameters α.

The relationship of the parameter α and the average probability of the *E-WSCRec* algorithm is shown in Figure 6.16(b). We can see that the average probability increases with the increasing of α. The value of QoS of the service compositions is generally larger than the frequency. So when α increases, the prior probability will increase accordingly, so that the posterior probability increases.

Figure 6.17(a) shows the impact of parameter M_{rep} on the nonempty result of the *IR-WSCRec* algorithm, and Figure 6.17(b) shows the impact of parameter M_{rep} on the average probability of the algorithm, in which $M_{min} = 0.1$, $\alpha = 0.5$. The number of nonempty results of the *IR-WSCRec* algorithm increased with the increase of M_{rep}, because the more services that need to be replaced, the more paths to search, so there will be more nonempty results. Note that even when $M_{rep} = 10$, not all inputs return nonempty results. The average probability of the algorithm rapidly increases with the increase of M_{rep} at the beginning and then gently increases after the $M_{rep} \geq 3$. Rapid increases are the result of the newfound results having higher probability, and then the leveling off is the result of the newfound result with a probability that has a distribution similar to the average.

Figure 6.17(c) and 6.17(d) shows the relationship of the parameter M_{min} and the number of nonempty results and average probability of the algorithm, in which $M_{rep} = 10$ and $\alpha = 0.5$. The number of nonempty results rapidly declines with the increase of M_{min}, then gently increases after the $M_{min} \geq 0.4$, and reaches the minimum when $M_{min} = 1$. The average probability has a similar situation, and it has much lower values than the other

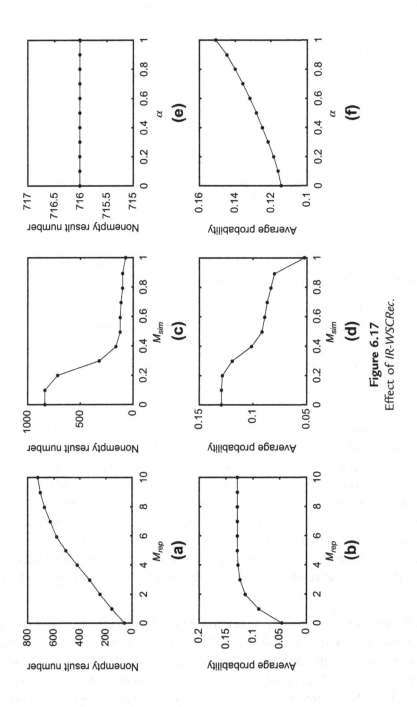

Figure 6.17
Effect of *IR-WSCRec.*

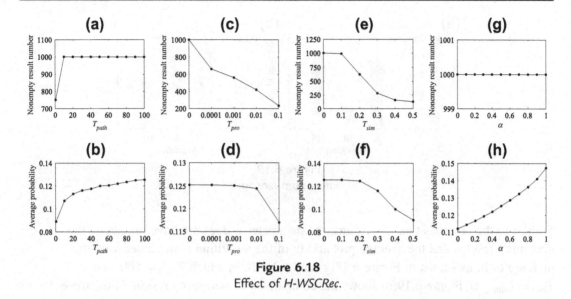

Figure 6.18
Effect of *H-WSCRec*.

when $M_{min} = 1$, because the increase of minimum similarity leads to the reduction of the number of paths.

Parameter α of the *IR-WSCRec* algorithm does not have an affect on the number of nonempty results, and the average probability of the algorithm increases with increasing α, as shown in Figure 6.17(e) and 6.17(f), in which $M_{rep} = 10$ and $M_{min} = 0.1$. However, the *IR-WSCRec* algorithm does not always return nonempty results.

Figure 6.18(a) and 6.18(b) show the relationship between parameter T_{path} and the number of nonempty results and average probability of the algorithm, in which $T_{pro} = T_{sim} = 0$ and $\alpha = 0.5$. It can be seen that when $T_{path} = 1$, the number of nonempty results and the value of probability are quite low; the reason is that the algorithm only searches the path with the highest probability of the first layer of branches. When $T_{path} \geq 10$, the algorithm almost always returns nonempty results, while the average probability increases slowly along with the T_{path}. While $T_{path} \geq 10$, it has less impact on the algorithm.

As Figure 6.18(c) (in which $T_{path} = 100$, $T_{sim} = 0$, $\alpha = 0.5$) and Figure 6.18(e) (in which $T_{path} = 100$, $T_{pro} = 0$, $\alpha = 0.5$) show, the number of nonempty results of the *H-WSCRec* algorithm decreases with the increase of parameter T_{pro} and parameters T_{sim}. Similarly, Figure 6.18(d) (in which $T_{path} = 100$, $T_{sim} = 0$, $\alpha = 0.5$) and Figure 6.18(f) (in which $T_{path} = 100$, $T_{pro} = 0$, $\alpha = 0.5$) show that the number of nonempty results of the *H-WSCRec* algorithm decreases with the increase of parameter T_{pro} and parameters T_{sim}. This is due to increased restrictions, so that the path to the search reduces. So the return result has less nonempty results and lower average probability.

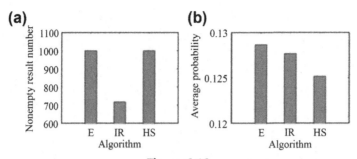

Figure 6.19
Effect comparison.

Similar to the previous two algorithms, the parameter α does not have impact on the nonempty results, and the average probability of the algorithm is increased with the increase of α, as shown in Figure 6.18(g) and 6.18(h), in which $T_{path} = 100$, and $T_{pro} = T_{sim} = 0$. Figure 6.19(a) shows the comparison of nonempty results of the three algorithms, and Figure 6.19(b) shows the comparison of average probability of the three algorithms, in which $\alpha = 0.5$, $K = 316$, $M_{rep} = 10$, $M_{min} = 0.1$, $T_{path} = 100$, and $T_{pro} = T_{sim} = 0$. Notice that except for the *IR-WSCRec* algorithm, the other two algorithms always return nonempty results. And there is no doubt that the average probability of the *E-WSCRec* algorithm is the highest. The average probability of the IR-WSCRec algorithm is very close to the maximum result; however, the number of its nonempty results is much lower than that of the other two algorithms.

6.4 Summary

Traditional solutions to the service recommendation problem propose to recommend optimized services based on accurate service (functionality) matchmaking. Similar to the expert system, these solutions will meet bottlenecks as long as they develop to a certain extent. To handle this problem, we propose a Bayes-based approach, by recommending composite services based on the service execution logs that contain diverse information such as service functionality, QoS record, execution order, etc. Based on this collective knowledge, the recommended service is more optimized, and the robustness can be guaranteed as well.

Further, inspired by Google Instant Search, we propose an instant service recommendation approach, *WSCRec*, in which a list of candidate composite web services are instantly recommended to the user according to the partially composed service. Specifically, service execution logs and the Bayes theorem are adopted for calculating the probabilities of candidate composite services, while an A*-based algorithm is proposed for generating top-k composite services.

References

[1] Z. Zheng, H. Ma, M.R. Lyu, I. King, QoS-aware web service recommendation by collaborative filtering, IEEE Trans. Serv. Comput., to be published.

[2] X. Chen, X. Liu, Z. Huang, H. Sun, Regionknn: a scalable hybrid collaborative filtering algorithm for personalized web service recommendation, in: International Conference on Web Services, 2010, pp. 9–16.

[3] D. Liu, X.W. Meng, J.L. Chen, A framework for context-aware service recommendation, in: International Conference on Advanced Communication Technology, 2008, pp. 2131–2134.

[4] L. Liu, L. Lecue, N. Mehandjiev, L. Xu, Using context similarity for service recommendation, in: International Conference on Semantic Computing, 2010, pp. 277–284.

[5] R. Wang, G. Zeng, An efficient service recommendation using differential evolutionary contract net for migrating workflows, Expert Syst. Appl. 37 (2) (2009) 1152–1157.

[6] J.M. Bernardo, A.F.M. Smith, Bayesian theory, Meas. Sci. Technol. 12 (2) (2001).

[7] Apache ODE, http://ode.apache.org/.

[8] G.E. Mathew, J. Shields, V. Verma, QoS based pricing for web services, in: 5th International Conference on Web Information Systems Engineering (WISE), 2004, pp. 264–275.

[9] Y. Wang, E. Stroulia, Semantic structure matching for assessing web service similarity, in: 1st International Conference on Service-oriented Computing (ICSOC), 2003, pp. 194–207.

[10] X. Dong, A. Halevy, J. Madhavan, E. Nemes, J. Zhang, Similarity search for web services, in: Proc. 30th International Conference on Very Large Data Bases (VLDB), 2004, pp. 372–383.

[11] S. Dasgupta, S. Bhat, Y. Lee, SGPS: a semantic scheme for web service similarity, in: 18th International World Wide Web Conference (WWW), 2009, pp. 1125–1126.

[12] J. Wu, Z. Wu, Similarity-based web service matchmaking, in: IEEE International Conference on Services Computing (SCC), 2005, pp. 287–294.

[13] L.-H. Vu, M. Hauswirth, K. Aberer, QoS-based service selection and ranking with trust and reputation management, in: OTM Confederated International Conferences CoopIS, DOA, and ODBASE, 2005, pp. 466–483.

[14] Y. Liu, A.H. Ngu, L. Zeng, QoS computation and policing in dynamic web service selection, in: Proc. 13th International World Wide Web Conference (WWW), 2004, pp. 66–73.

[15] UDDI, http://www.uddi.org/pubs/uddi v3.htm.

[16] Web services business process execution language, http://docs.oasis-open.org/wsbpel/2.0/wsbpel-v2.0.html.

[17] Google Instant, http://www.google.com/instant/.

[18] Y. Wang, E. Stroulia, Semantic structure matching for assessing web-service similarity, in: International Conference on Service-oriented Computing, 2003, pp. 194–207.

[19] J. Wu, Z. Wu, Similarity-based web service matchmaking, in: International Conference on Service Computing, 2005, pp. 287–294.

[20] K. Elgazzar, A.E. Hassan, P. Martin, Clustering WSDL documents to bootstrap the discovery of web services, in: Proc. of the 2010 IEEE International Conference on Web Services (ICWS), 2010, pp. 147–154.

[21] M. Alrifai, D. Skoutas, T. Risse, Selecting skyline services for QoS-based web service composition, in: Proc. of the 19th International Conference on World Wide Web (WWW), 2010, pp. 11–20.

[22] H. Duan, B.-J.P. Hsu, Online spelling correction for query completion, in: Proc. of the 20th International Conference on World Wide Web (WWW), 2011, pp. 117–126.

[23] D. Wu, B. Parsia, E. Sirin, J. Hendler, D. Nau, Automating DAML-S web services composition using SHOP2, in: International Semantic Web Conference, 2003, pp. 195–210.

[24] L. Chen, Y. Feng, J. Wu, Z. Zheng, An enhanced qos prediction approach for service selection, in: Proceedings of the Eighth International Conference on Service Computing (SCC), 2011, pp. 727–728.

[25] J. Wu, L. Chen, Y. Feng, Z. Zheng, M. Zhou, Z. Wu, Predicting quality of service for selection by neighborhood-based collaborative filtering, IEEE Trans. Syst. Man Cybernet. Part A 43 (2) (March 2013) 428–439.

[26] A. Paliwal, B. Shafiq, J. Vaidya, H. Xiong, N. Adam, Semantics based automated service discovery, IEEE Trans. Serv. Comput. 5 (2) (2012) 260–275.

[27] L. Zeng, B. Benatallah, M. Dumas, J. Kalagnanam, Q.Z. Sheng, Quality driven web services composition, in: Proc. of the 12th International Conference on World Wide Web (WWW), 2003, pp. 411–421.

[28] L. Zeng, B. Benatallah, A.H.H. Ngu, M. Dumas, J. Kalagnanam, H. Chang, QoS-aware middleware for web services composition, IEEE Trans. Softw. Eng. (2004) 311–327.

[29] M. Klusch, A. Gerber, M. Schmidt, Semantic web service composition planning with OWLS-XPlan, in: Proc. of the First International AAAI Fall Symposium on Agents and the Semantic Web, 2005.

[30] S. Sohrabi, N. Prokoshyna, S.A. Mcilraith, Web service composition via generic procedures and customizing user preferences, in: International Semantic Web Conference, 2006, pp. 597–611.

[31] S. Sohrabi, N. Prokoshyna, S.A. Mcilraith, Web service composition via the customization of Golog programs with user preferences, Conceptual Model. Found. Appl. (2009) 319–334.

[32] A.B. Hassine, S. Matsubara, T. Ishida, A constraint-based approach to horizontal web service composition, in: International Semantic Web Conference, 2006, pp. 130–143.

[33] Z. Zheng, H. Ma, M.R. Lyu, I. King, QoS-aware web service recommendation by collaborative filtering, IEEE Trans. Serv. Comput. (2011) 140–152.

[34] Y. Jiang, J. Liu, M. Tang, X. Liu, An effective web service recommendation method based on personalized collaborative filtering, in: International Conference on Web Services, 2011, pp. 211–218.

[35] P.C. Xiong, Y.S. Fan, M. Zhou, QoS-aware web service configuration, IEEE Trans. Syst. Man Cybernet. Part A 38 (4) (July 2008) 888–895.

[36] P.C. Xiong, Y. Fan, M. Zhou, Web service configuration under multiple quality-of-service attributes, IEEE Trans. Autom. Sci. Eng. 6 (2) (April 2009) 311–321.

[37] W. Tan, Y. Fan, M. Zhou, A petri net-based method for compatibility analysis and composition of web services in business process execution language, IEEE Trans. Autom. Sci. Eng. 6 (1) (January 2009) 94–106.

[38] W. Tan, Y. Fan, M.C. Zhou, Z. Tian, Data-driven service composition in building SOA solutions: a petri net approach, IEEE Trans. Autom. Sci. Eng. 7 (3) (July 2010) 686–694.

[39] P. Wang, Z. Ding, C. Jiang, M. Zhou, Automated web service composition supporting conditional branch structures, Enterp. Inform. Syst. (June 2011) 121–146. Available online.

[40] J. Wu, L. Chen, Y. Xie, Z. Zheng, Titan: a system for effective web service discovery, in: International World Wide Web Conference, Demo Track, 2012, pp. 441–444.

[41] L. Chen, L. Hu, Z. Zheng, J. Wu, J. Yin, Y. Li, S. Deng, WTCluster: utilizing tags for web services clustering, in: International Conference on Service-oriented Computing, 2011, pp. 204–218.

[42] N. Thio, S. Karunasekera, Automatic measurement of a QoS metric for web service recommendation, in: Australian Software Engineering Conference, 2005, pp. 202–211.

[43] A. Moraru, C. Fortuna, B. Fortuna, R. Slavescu, A hybrid approach to QoS-aware web service classification and recommendation, in: Intelligent Computer Communication and Processing, 2009, pp. 343–346.

Service Composition

Chapter Outline

Service Computing: Concepts, Methods and Technology. http://dx.doi.org/10.1016/B978-0-12-802330-3.00007-2

7.1 Introduction

A web service is a software application that is network distributed and identified by a uniform resource identifier (URI) and can be programmatically accessed through the web [1]. As the Internet progresses toward cloud computing, the evolution of web services presents new trends. First, more and more enterprises provide services on the Internet, and thus the number of web services increases rapidly. Second, semantic information is introduced into web services to describe their functionalities in a computer readable way. Finally, besides the functionalities, quality of services (QoS) draws more and more attention when web services are chosen to build applications. As a result, it becomes a challenge for users to locate and find a proper service quickly from so many candidate services on the Internet. So, a good service discovery method is needed, and semantic and QoS information of services must be considered during the discovery process [2,3]. Moreover, it should support composing services with different functions into a large service to meet user requests when no single service can fulfill those requests. For example, if the output parameters of one service can be used as the input parameters of another service, these two services can be connected as a new service with input parameters that are the same as the input parameters of the first single service and output parameters that are the same as the output parameters of the second single one. This new service is called a composed service or composite service, and the elemental services are referred to as the member services or component services. This triggers another important issue, i.e., service composition, in the research area of service computing [4].

Generally speaking, web service composition problems can be divided into two categories: manual composition and automatic composition. Manual web service composition needs to select component services and build the workflow logic by hand. Therefore, it could not handle a situation in which thousands of web services are available for composition. On the contrary, automatic web service composition generates the composite service intelligently by artificial intelligence (AI) planning methods or search methods without human intervention. However, it is more difficult than manual web service composition and requires much more research effort. As the number of web services increase dramatically, it is already beyond human ability to manually generate the composed service. Thus, the automatic web service composition aiming at finding a composed service to satisfy the user request becomes an important technique to reuse existing resources and accelerate the development of web applications. The automatic service composition problem can be perfectly mapped into the AI planning problem, in which services correspond to operators in the planning domain, the user request includes the planning goal, and the composition corresponds to the plan [5]. So, many approaches based on different kinds of AI planning techniques were used to solve the composition problem. These included situation calculus [6,7], state space search [8−11], problem deduction [12−14], automatic theorem proving [15−17], and the planning-graph [18−23]. These techniques have different features and can be applied in different situations. Most planning techniques can model all kinds of web services, including information-providing services and world-altering services. However, even if heuristic functions are used to guide the planning process, the running time still increases exponentially in the optimal searching problem when the search space increases rapidly. Therefore, efficiency improvement is the key issue for these approaches with classical planning techniques.

Approaches based on the planning-graph technique filtered active services into layers (the planning-graph) to prune the search space. A planning graph is a very useful and powerful search space in which layers with proposition are connected with directed arcs. Propositions are symbols presenting the state of real-world targets. Thus, they have a much higher performance than approaches with the classical planning techniques. Although planning-graph-based approaches mainly model the information-providing services (mutual exclusion is not considered), they still have a good application prospect because information-providing services are the major category of web services on the Internet. Consequently, approaches based on the planning-graph are the most efficient approaches to solve the large-scale (tens of thousands of services) automatic composition of information-providing services.

Up till now, there has been a great deal of successful research performed on service composition; we review representative approaches with different planning techniques. McIlraith and Son [6] extended the Golog language for automatic composition. Golog is a logic programming language built on top of the situation calculus. This approach addresses the web service composition problem through the provision of high-level generic procedures and customizing constraints. Some researchers used a state space search technique to solve the composition problem [8−11]. For these approaches, the design of a heuristic function is very important. Oh et al. [8] used QoS as a factor for the heuristic function, but the value of the estimation function is always less than 1, thus it has little effect in guiding the search process. Wu et al. [10] used the distance between parameters to design the heuristic function, and it is applicable when the service repository is not very large. Sirina et al. [12] proposed an approach by using SHOP2 that was a successful hierarchical task network (HTN) planning system for problem deduction. This approach is applicable because the concept of task decomposition in HTN planning is very similar to the concept of composite process decomposition in OWL-S process ontology. In other words, if we cannot provide decomposition information (e.g., we only describe web services by WSDL), then this approach is not available any more. Based on the HTN approach, many variants emerged. Paik and Maruyama [13] proposed a framework combining logical composition and physical composition for automatic service composition. Chen et al. [14] proposed a model of combining a Markov decision process model and HTN planning to address web services composition. Some authors modeled the automatic composition problem as a theorem-proving vproblem [15−17]. Li and Chen [15] used a theorem prover named Otter to solve the planning problem. Like other approaches, using the existing AI planner directly makes the performance uncontrollable.

As mentioned before, efficiency improvement is the key issue of all approaches with classical planning techniques. However, a planning-graph can solve an AI planning problem effectively and efficiently. It iteratively expands itself one level at a time until either it reaches a level where the proposition set contains all goal propositions or a fixed-point level. The goal cannot be attained if the latter happens first. Otherwise, the planning-graph searches backward from the last level of the graph for a solution. Instead of pruning the planning-graph by a backward search, Zheng and Yan [18] provided four strategies to remove the redundant web services during a forward planning-graph generating process. They attempted to find a solution in the shortest time. However, without the backward pruning, the solutions may contain some redundant web services. Moreover, they did not consider QoS and semantics. WSPR is another planning-graph-based algorithm [19], which adopted a backward search with a heuristic-based greedy algorithm to minimize the number of web services in a solution and to remove all the redundant services. Li et al. [20] focused on the semantic matching problem in the planning-graph-based composition algorithms. In the forward search, it used the concept similarity and some predefined threshold to calculate the service matching degrees, which were added into the planning-graph as the weights of services. In addition, it removed services producing the same parameter, but with lower weights to keep the planning-graph as simple as possible. Just like other methods, it adopted a backward search to prune the redundant services. Unfortunately, the threshold is not so easy to define, and this limits the application of this method. Li et al. [21] defined the semantic matching between concepts by two simple but effective relationships: the "sameAs" relationship and the "subClassOf" relationship. In addition, they took the overall QoS of the composed service into account. In the forward search, they enhanced the traditional planning-graph to store the source service of every parameter in the state layer, the cost of the source service, and the semantic candidates of every parameter. After that, a backward indexing algorithm was used to find the web service composition chain according to the overall QoS of services. This approach can find a solution with better overall QoS. However, the solution cannot be guaranteed to be optimal. Furthermore, the way of calculating the overall QoS of the composed service is too simple. The approach proposed in [22,23] aimed at finding the solution with the best overall QoS. Compared with the study in [21], it computed the overall QoS with different types of QoS measures and different composition patterns. In the forward search, this approach used a hash table to store the best QoS computed for a particular parameter and its corresponding provider. In the backward search, it found the optimal composition result from the end node to the start node by the hash table constructed in the forward search.

As service composition techniques are being more widely used, more and more problems arise. These problems present new challenges to traditional service computing technologies:

1. Most of the existing approaches are designed to return only one optimal composition with the best QoS. This has several limitations and may cause users some inconvenience. For example, when some service in the optimal composition becomes unavailable, the whole composition is void and a re-composition is needed. Besides, returning only one optimal result cannot satisfy users' preferences for more alternatives. Hence, providing top-k service composition solutions that enjoy top-k QoS values, among all feasible solutions, can avoid these limitations.

2. Traditional service composition approaches are almost always based on a central mechanism. With the number of web services growing so much, it may lead to a performance bottleneck due to the explosion of the planning and searching space. To improve the efficiency of the automatic web service composition with large-scale data-intensive web services, it should be optimized in a decentralized way to ensure that the composition process is executed in parallel.

3. Traditional service composition schemata require professional domain knowledge. Some professional domain knowledge is essential to select simplex services for composition; knowledge about service description languages are needed for composing services to satisfy users' demands. However, professional domain knowledge is a roadblock for nonprofessional users to do web service composition. Furthermore, the reliability of composite services generated by traditional service composition schemata cannot be guaranteed.

To address the above challenges, this chapter introduces three composition methods: an efficient method for top-k service composition [24], a parallel optimization for service composition [25], and a service composition based on historical records [26].

7.2 Top-k QoS Composition

This section introduces a novel approach based on the planning-graph to solve the top-k QoS-aware automatic composition problem of semantic web services. The approach includes three sequential stages: a forward search stage to generate a planning-graph to greatly reduce the search space of the following two stages; an optimal local QoS calculating stage to compute all the optimal local QoS values of services required in the planning; and a backward search stage to find the top-k composed services with optimal QoS values according to the planning-graph and the optimal QoS value. To validate this approach, experiments are carried out based on the test sets offered by the WS-Challenge competition 2009. The results show that this approach cannot only find the same optimal solutions as the champion system from the competition, but also can provide more alternative solutions with the optimal QoS for users.

7.2.1 Problem Formalization

In this section, we give clear definitions to the key concepts in QoS-aware automatic web service composition problems.

In semantic web services, every parameter of services corresponds to a concept in the ontology that formally represents knowledge as a set of concepts within a domain and the relationships between those concepts.

Definition 1: Ontology tree. An ontology tree, OT, is a pair, $OT = (C, R)$, in which C is a set of concepts represented by nodes in the tree, and R is a set of direct inheritance relationships represented by edges in the tree. If a concept c_1 inherits from another concept c_2 directly or indirectly, it can be denoted as $c_1 \rightarrow c_2$.

Definition 2: Semantic match. Given two sets of concepts, S and T, if $\forall s \in S \cdot (\exists t \in T \cdot (t \rightarrow s \lor t = s))$, then we say S semantically matches T, denoted as $S \sqsubseteq T$.

Definition 3: Web service. A web service, w, is a triple, $w = (I, O, Q)$, in which I is a set of input parameters, each of which corresponds to a concept in the ontology tree; O is a set of output parameters, each of which also corresponds to a concept; and Q is the QoS value of w. For every parameter p, the corresponding concept is denoted as $CON(p)$.

Definition 4: Composed web service. A composed web service, cw, is a sequence of sets of web services, $cw = <W_1, W_2, ..., W_N>$, satisfying the following conditions:

1. W_1 contains only one service *start*, such that $start.I = \emptyset$ and $start.Q = 0$;
2. W_N also contains one service *end*, such that $end.O = \emptyset$ and $end.Q = 0$;
3. let

$$Out_i = \bigcup_{1 \le j \le |W_i|} w_i^j.O$$

- $1 < i < N$, $|W_i|$ represents the number of elements of W_i, w_i^j is an element of W_i, such that

$$w_i^j.I \sqsubseteq \bigcup_{1 \le k \le i-1} Out_k$$

$1 < i < N+1$, $1 \le j \le |W_i|$, w_i^j is an element of W_i.

From an abstract perspective, a composed web service is still a web service. Its input parameters are the output parameters of the *start* service, its output parameters are the input parameters of the *end* service, and its QoS can be calculated according to the QoS of its member services (see in the next subsection).

Definition 5: QoS of web service. The QoS of a web service is a value representing the nonfunctional property of the web service, such as response time, throughput, price cost, reputation, etc. The QoS properties can be categorized into two classes. One is negative—the higher the value, the lower the quality—such as response time and price cost. The other is positive—the higher the value, the higher the quality—such as throughput and reputation.

In this section, we focus on the single QoS dimension. For multiple QoS dimensions, one possible but not perfect approach is using the weighted sum of all dimensions to transform all the QoS values into a single aggregate value.

Definition 6: Global QoS computing rules. Given a composed web service, *cw*, the global QoS of *cw* is computed as follows: $GQ(cw) = LQ(cw.end)$, in which *cw.end* represents the *end* service in *cw*, and the function *LQ* calculates the local QoS of every service in *cw*. *LQ* is defined as follows:

$$LQ\left(w_i^j\right) = F_2\left(F_1\left(LQ\left(pre\left(w_i^j\right)\right)\right), w_i^j.Q\right)$$

in which:

1. *pre* is a set of services producing parameters that can be consumed by w_i^j in the composed service *cw*, $pre(w_i^j) = \{w_x^y | \forall p \in w_i^j.I \cdot \exists q \in w_x^y.O \cdot (CON(q) \rightarrow CON(p)),$ $x < i, 1 \le y \le |W_i|\}$;

2. F_1 and F_2 are functions in the set of $\{\sum, \prod, MAX, MIN\}$. They depend on the QoS type taken into account, as shown in Table 7.1. For example, if the QoS type is response time, then $F_1 = MAX$, $F_2 = \sum$.

According to the definition of the composed web service, we can calculate the local QoS of services in their sequence order. First, calculate the local QoS of the *start* service in W_1; then calculate the local QoS of services in W_2; and finally, we get the local QoS of the *end* service, which is exactly the global QoS of the composed service.

Definition 7: Top-k QoS-aware automatic composition. Given an ontology tree *OT*, a set of web service *W*, and a user request $req = (I, O)$ find the top-k-composed services according to the global QoS, each of which (denoted as *cw*) satisfies the following conditions:

1. $\forall w_i^j \in cw.W_i \cdot (w_i^j \in W)$;
2. $req.I = cw.start.O, req.O = cw.end.I$.

Table 7.1: F_1, F_2, and QoS type

F_1	F_2	QoS Type
MAX	$\sum$	Response time
MIN	$\sum$	Throughput
$\sum$	$\sum$	Cost
$\prod$	$\prod$	Reputation

QoS, quality of services.

7.2.2 Composition Algorithm

7.2.2.1 Framework overview

In this subsection, we describe the framework of our automatic composition algorithm. The automatic composition algorithm (algorithm 1) takes OT (an ontology tree), W (a set of web services), req (a user request), and K (a number) as inputs and returns the top-k solutions in terms of their global QoS values. In most cases, it includes three stages: a *ForwardSearch* stage, a *CalculateOptimalLocalQoS* stage, and a *BackwardSearch* stage. In the *ForwardSearch* stage, the algorithm generates a planning-graph. If the planning-graph does not contain the *end* service, it will return an empty set (no more stages are needed); otherwise it will calculate the optimal local QoS for every service in the planning-graph and use this to find the solutions in the *BackwardSearch* stage. Details about algorithms in these stages are given in the following subsections.

Algorithm 1 *TopK_AutomaticComposition*

Input:	OT, W, req, K
Output:	*solutions*

Comments: *start* and *end* are two virtual services contained in the composed services.

1. $start.I=\emptyset$; $start.O=req.I$; $start.Q=0$;
2. $end.I=req.O$; $end.O=\emptyset$; $end.Q=0$;
3. $W=W\cup\{start,end\}$;

4. $[AS, PS\_Map]=ForwardSearch(OT, W)$;
5. **if** $(end\notin AS)$ **then**
6.   **return** $\emptyset$;
7. **else**
8. $OptLQ\_Map =CalculateOptimalLocalQoS(AS, PS\_Map)$;
9. $solutions=BackwardSearch(OptLQ\_Map, PS\_Map, K)$;
10.   **return** *solutions*;

7.2.2.2 Forward search

Before we describe the detail of the *ForwardSearch* algorithm (algorithm 2), we need to introduce a key data structure (map) that is the basis for many other data structures (ending with the suffix_*Map*).

Definition 7−8: Map. A map is a triplet, $m = (Keys, Values, f)$, in which *Keys* and *Values* are sets of objects and f is a function $f:Keys \mapsto Values$. In other words, a map is a set of key−value pairs.

Three operations can be defined on a map: *Put(m, k, v)*, *Get(m, k)*, and *PutS(m, k, o)*. The *Put(m, k, v)* operation adds a new pair (k, v) into m if k does not appear in the *Keys* set of *m*; otherwise, it updates the corresponding object in the *Values* set with *v*. The *Get*(*m, k*) operation returns the object corresponding to *k* in *m*. When objects in the *Values* set are also sets, the *PutS*(*m, k, o*) adds a new object, *o*, into the set corresponding to *k*.

The *ForwardSearch* algorithm is a filtering algorithm based on the planning-graph. It takes *OT* and *W* corresponding to actions in the planning-graph as its inputs and gives *AS* and *PS_Map* as outputs, in which *AS* is an ordered set of services corresponding to actions in the action levels of the planning-graph, and *PS_Map* is a map that maps a service parameter into a set of source services that produce that same parameter. Initially, *W* is assigned to *valid*, which records the services that can be examined during the expansion of the planning-graph, and *P* is set to be empty, which is a set of parameters corresponding to propositions of the planning-graph (lines 1 and 2). Then, the algorithm expands the planning-graph iteratively while some services are still valid for expansion (lines 3−14). During each iteration, every valid service, *w*, is examined (line 5), if its input parameters semantically match *P* (line 6), it will be added into the *AS* and *PS_Map* (service *w* will not be examined any more; lines 7−9), otherwise it will be added into *stillValid*, which stores all valid services for the next iteration (line 11). At the end of each iteration, the algorithm checks whether the planning-graph reaches its fixed point (i.e., it cannot be expanded any more). If this does happen, the algorithm will break the expansion (line 12), otherwise it will prepare for the next iteration (line 14). Finally, *AS* (services not in *AS* are filtered out) and *PS_Map* are returned for further processing.

Algorithm 2 *ForwardSearch*

Input:	*OT, W*
Output:	*AS, PS_Map*

Comments: *W* contains two virtual services (*start* and *end*). *OT* can be used in the semantic matching.

1. $AS=\emptyset$; $PS\_Map=\emptyset$;
2. $valid=W$; $P=\emptyset$;

3. **while** $(valid\neq\emptyset)$ **do**
4. $newP=\emptyset$; $stillValid=\emptyset$;
5.   **for** $w\in valid$ **do**
6.   **if** $(w.I\subseteq P)$ **then**
7. $AS=AS\cup\{w\}$; $newP=newP\cup w.O$;
8.   **for** $o\in w.O$ **do**
9. $PS\_Map=PutS(PS\_Map, o, w)$;
10.   **else**
11. $stillValid=stillValid\cup\{w\}$;
12.   **if** $(valid==stillValid)$ **then break;**
13.   **else**
14. $P=P\cup newP$; $valid=stillValid$;

15. **return** *AS, PS_Map*;

7.2.2.3 QoS calculation

The ordered set *AS* (a sequence of services) returned by the *ForwardSearch* algorithm is a trivial solution to the automatic composition problem. However, it may contain some redundant services that have no contribution to the user-requested output parameters or if its global QoS is not optimal. Therefore, it is not exactly what we want. To solve these two problems, we use the *CalculateOptimalLocalQoS* algorithm (algorithm 3) to calculate the optimal global QoS value of all solutions, even without enumerating all of them, and use the *BackwardSearch* algorithm (algorithm 4) to find the real top-k solutions without redundant services.

According to the computing rules (definition 6), a local QoS value of a service is relative to a composed service. In other words, the same service in different composed services related to the same composition problem may have different local QoS values. Thus, an optimal local QoS value of a service w (denoted as $B(w)$) must exist. Additionally, if the QoS property is positive, the optimal value is the maximum of all possible local QoS values; otherwise it is the minimum.

Theorem 1. Given a service w, the optimal local QoS of w satisfies:

$$B(w) = F_2(F_1(\{G(\{B(sv)|sv \in Src(i)\})|i \in w.I\}), w.Q)$$

in which F_1 and F_2 are functions in the set of $\{\sum, \prod, MAX, MIN\}$, G is a function in $\{MAX, MIN\}$, which depends on the QoS property (*MAX* for positive property and *MIN* for negative property), and $Src(i)$ is a set of services producing i.

This theorem indicates that if we know the optimal local QoS of the source services for every input parameter of a service w, we can easily calculate the optimal local QoS of w. For example, assume a service w_1 has two input parameters, i_1 and i_2, i_1 has two source services, w_2 and w_3, and i_2 also has two sources services, w_4 and w_5, as shown in Figure 7.1. If the QoS property is response time, then $F_1 = MAX$, $F_2 = \sum$, and $G = MIN$, thus we can calculate $B(w_1)$ as follows:

$$B(w_1) = \sum(MAX(MIN(B(w_2), B(w_3)), MIN(B(w_4), B(w_5))), w_1.Q)$$

$$= MAX(MIN(B(w_2), B(w_3)), MIN(B(w_4), B(w_5))) + w_1.Q.$$

Proof: We take response time as an example to prove this theorem, and when other QoS properties are considered, it can be proven in a similar way.

When the response time property is taken into account, $F_1 = MAX$, $F_2 = \sum$, and $G = MIN$. For every i in $w.I$, let $q(i)$ be the number of its source services. Let $w_{i,j}$

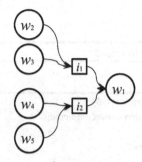

Figure 7.1
An example.

$(1 \leq j \leq q(i))$ be a source service of i and $w_{i,m(i)}$ be the source service with the minimum local QoS value. Assume theorem 1 does not hold; this means:$(\exists i \cdot a(i) \neq m(i)) \wedge (MAX(w_{i,a(i)}) < MAX(w_{i,m(i)}))$

However, if $MAX(w_{i,m(i)}) \leq MAX(w_{i,a(i)})$, it is contradictory to the former one; thus theorem 1 must hold.

AS is an invocation sequence of services, thus we can calculate the optimal local QoS of services by their invocation order in the sequence. However, when we apply theorem 1 to compute the optimal local QoS of some service *w*, the optimal local QoS of its source services may be unknown. If this does happen, we just ignore the unknown values and compute a temporary value for *w*, which will then be put back into the *unCompleted* queue for recalculation. Algorithm 3 uses *AS* and *PS_Map* as its inputs and returns a map, *OptLQ_Map*, which records the optimal local QoS values for every service in *AS*. Initially, the optimal local QoS of the *start* service is set to be 0, and other services in *AS* are put into the *unCompleted* queue for calculation (lines 1 and 2). Then, the algorithm calculates the optimal local QoS of services in *unCompleted* iteratively (lines 3−12). During each iteration, *current* holds all services needed to be calculated, and every service of *current* is processed by the algorithm *Calculate*, which is an application of theorem 1 (line 6). If the calculating result is a temporary value, the service will be put it into the *next* queue for calculation in the next iteration (lines 7 and 8). After calculating all services in the *current* queue, if the current queue reaches its fixed point (no services are removed from *current* and no calculating values of services in *current* are updated), the algorithm will break out; otherwise it begins the next iteration (lines 9–12). Finally, the algorithm stops and returns the *OptLQ_Map*.

Algorithm 3 *CalculateOptimalLocalQoS*

Input: *AS, PS_Map*
Output: *OptLQ_Map*

1. *OptLQ_Map=Put(OptLQ_Map, start, 0);*
2. *unCompleted=AS-{start}; current=unCompleted;*
3. **while** *(current≠∅)* **do**
4.   *updateFlag=**false**; next=∅;*
5.   **for** *w∈current* **do**
6.   *[unCompleted, updateFlag, OptLQ_Map]=*
            Calculate(w, unCompleted, updateFlag, OptLQ_Map, PS_Map);
7.   **if** *(w∈unCompleted)* **then**
8.   *next=next∪{w};*
9.   **if** *(current==next ∧ updateFlag==**false**)* **then**
10.   **break;**
11.   **else**
12.   *current=next;*
13. **return** *OptLQ_Map;*

The implementation of *Calculate* (algorithm 4) depends on the QoS property considered by us. We will use the response time property as an example to elaborate this algorithm and prove the correctness of *CalculateOptimalLocalQoS* (algorithm 3).

As we mentioned above, if the QoS property is response time, then $F_1 = MAX$, $F_2 = \sum$, and $G = MIN$; therefore algorithm 3 first calculates the minimum value of the source services for every input parameter of service w (lines 3–13) and then calculates the maximum value of all these minimum ones (lines 14 and 15). In addition, if any optimal local QoS value of the source services is unknown (line 7) or just a temporary value (line 12), the *minFlag* of the corresponding parameter will be set to be true. The *maxFlag* records the *minFlag* of the parameter, the *min* value of which is the maximum one among all *min* values (line 15). The *maxFlag* determines whether the value should be recalculated (lines 20 and 21). After all calculations, if the calculated value is better than the existing one, it will be updated in the *OptLQ_Map* (lines 17–19).

Algorithm 4 *Calculate*

Input: *w, unCompleted, updateFlag, OptLQ_Map, PS_Map*

Output: *unCompleted, updateFlag, OptLQ_*Map

---

1. *max*=0; *maxFlag*=**false**;
2. **for** *i*∈*w.I* **do**
3.   *min*=∞; *minFlag*=**false**;
4.   *srcSvs*=*getAllSemanticCompitableSvs*(*i, PS_Map*);
5.   **for** *sv*∈*srcSvs* **do**
6.   *svMin*=*Get*(*OptLQ_Map, sv*);
7.   **if** (*svMin*==**null**) **then**
8.   *minFlag*=**true**;
9.   **else**
10.   **if** (*svMin*<*min*) **then**
11.   *min*=*svMin*;
12.   **if** (*sv*∈*unCompleted*) **then**
13.   *minFlag*=**true**;
14.   **if** (*min*>*max*) **then**
15.   *max*=*min*; *maxFlag*=*minFlag*;
16.   *newQ*=*max*+*w.Q*; *oldQ*=*Get*(*OptLQ_Map, w*);
17.   **if** (*newQ*<*oldQ*) **then**
18.   *updateFlag*=**true**;
19.   *OptLQ_Map*=*Update*(*OptLQ_Map, w, newQ*);
20. **if** (*maxFlag*==**false**) **then**
21.   *unCompleted*=*unCompleted* - {*w*};
22. **return** *unCompleted, updateFlag, OptLQ_*Map;

7.2.2.3.1 Correctness proof

Algorithm 3 must terminate in some limited time. Because the local QoS value of every service is bounded and discrete and only better values are updated (algorithm 4), the *OptLQ_Map* must enter its fixed point after some finite calculating iterations.

When the algorithm stops, the result values in *OptLQ_Map* must conform to theorem 1. If any of the result values is not the optimal one, there must be some source service with a value that is not optimal either. The number of services is limited; thus a cycle must appear among all these services in the same composed service. According to definition 4, no cycles can appear in a composed web service; therefore all result values must be the optimal local QoS values.

7.2.2.4 Backward search

After we get all the optimal local QoS values of every services in *AS*, we use the *BackwardSearch* algorithm to find the top-k solutions. Before we introduce the algorithm, we need to introduce a key concept.

Definition 9: Source combination. Given a service w, a source combination SC of w is a set of services, which satisfies the following conditions:

1. $\forall wsc \in SC \cdot (wsc.O \cap w.I \neq \emptyset)$;
2. $\forall i \in w.I \cdot (\exists w_i \in SC \cdot (w_i.O \sqsupseteq \{i\}))$, and w_i is the only one.

A source combination produces all input parameters of a service semantically and every service in the source combination has its contribution to the producing process. Take Figure 7.1 as an example, w_1 has four different source combinations: $\{w_2, w_4\}$, $\{w_2, w_5\}$, $\{w_3, w_4\}$, and $\{w_3, w_5\}$.

The basic idea of the *BackwardSearch* algorithm is using a threshold to reduce the search space to improve the efficiency. In other words, the *BackwardSearch* algorithm prunes all search branches with global QoS values (calculated on the composition result in the leaf of the search branch) that are larger than the threshold. This strategy can find all solutions that have global QoS values that are not larger than the threshold, but how can we determine the value of the threshold to make sure the number of solutions is not less than K if there does exist more than K solutions? We use a list of thresholds in ascending order (the *delts* list) to solve this problem. First, we use the optimal global QoS value (i.e., the optimal local QoS value of the *end* service) as a threshold to find some optimal solutions (but not all) quickly (line 1). Fortunately, if the number of the solutions is larger than K, we will return the solutions (lines 2 and 3). Otherwise, we will change the source combination of every service in the composed services to generate some new solutions with slight changes, and insert the global QoS values of these new solutions into the *delts* list in ascending order (line 5). After this, we use *delts*, one by one, as thresholds to search solutions until the number of solutions is not less than K (line 6). More details of algorithms used in algorithm 5 can be found in later paragraphs.

Algorithm 5 *BackwardSearch*

Input: *OptLQ_Map, PS_Map, K*
Output: *solutions*

---

1. [*strictSols, strictPreSvs_Map*]=*SearchBeforehand(OptLQ_Map, PS_Map, K)*;
2. **if** (|*strictSols*| ≥ *K*) **then**
3.   *solutions=strictSols*; **return** *solutions*;
4. **else**
5.   *delts=CalculateDelts(OptLQ_Map, PS_Map, strictSols, strictPreSvs_Map)*;
6.   *solutions=SearchTopK(OptLQ_Map, PS_Map, delts, K)*;
7.   **return** *solutions*;

The *SearchBeforehand* algorithm is used for finding the optimal solutions as quickly as possible. It uses *strictPreSvs_Map* to keep the sets of source combinations for every service. The number of source combinations for every service is limited up to *width*, which is initially set to be 3 (lines 1 and 2). Then, it enters a loop (line 3) and uses the *findStrictPreSvs* algorithm to find the strict source combinations for every service. A strict source combination for a service w must satisfy the following condition: the sum of the optimal local QoS value of each service in the strict source combination and the QoS value of the service w are not larger than the optimal local QoS value of the service w (line 4). After storing the strict source combinations in *strictPreSvs_Map*, it estimates the number of solutions by multiplication of numbers of source combinations for every service (line 5). If the estimated number is larger than K or no more source combination can be added into *strictPreSvs_Map*, it will break out of the loop; otherwise it will increase *width* by one and go back to add more source combinations into *strictPreSvs_Map* (lines 6–9). The purpose of the loop (line 3) is to keep the number of strict solutions close to K. After the loop, the *SearchBeforehand* algorithm uses *findStrictSolutions* to construct all possible solutions according to *strictPreSvs_Map* (line 10). The *findStrictSolutions* algorithm at first puts the *end* service into the solution structure, then tries each source combination of the *end* service and adds it into the solution structure. This process continues until all services in the solution can be generated from the *start* service directly or indirectly. The *findStrictSolutions* algorithm is a recursive algorithm.

Algorithm 6 *SearchBeforehand*

Input: *OptLQ_Map, PS_Map, K*
Output: *strictSols, strictPreSvs_Map*

---

1. *width=3; oldCount=0;*
2. *strictPreSvs_Map=Put(strictPreSvs_Map, start, ∅);*
3. **while (true) do**
4.   *strictPreSvs_Map=findStrictPreSvs(OptLQ_Map, PS_Map, width);*
5.   *newCount=estimateSolNum(strictPreSvs_Map);*
6.   **if** (*newCount>K* ∨ *newCount==oldCount*) **then**
7.   **break;**
8.   **else**
9.   *oldCount=newCount; width=width+1;*
10. *strictSols=findStrictSolutions(strictPreSvs_Map, K);*
11. **return** *strictSols, strictPreSvs_Map;*

The *CalculateDelts* algorithm calculates thresholds in an ascending order by relaxing the constraints in finding the source combinations of every service. First, it adds every service in the *strictSols* found by algorithm 6 into *svInStrictSols* (lines 1–3). Then, for every service *sv* in *svInStrictSols*, the algorithm just finds all the source combinations of *sv* (lines 5–9) and removes the strict source combinations that have been considered in *strictSols* (lines 10 and 11). It calculates new values according to the rules defined in definition 6 and inserts all these values into *delts* in an ascending order (lines 12 and 13).

Algorithm 7 CalculateDelts

Input: *OptLQ_Map, PS_Map, strictSols, strictPreSvs_Map*
Output: *delts*

---

1. *svInStrictiSols=∅; delts=∅;*
2. **for** (*cw ∈strictSols*) **do**
3.   *svInStrictSols=svInStrictSols∪DAG_GetAllNodes(cw);*
4. **for** (*sv ∈svInStrictSols*) **do**
5.   *paraSrcSvs_Map=∅;*
6.   **for** *i ∈sv.I* **do**
7.   *srcSvs=getAllSemanticCompitableSvs(i, PS_Map);*
8.   *paraSrcSvs_Map=PutS(paraSrcSvs_Map, i, srcSvs);*
9.   *allPreSvs=CombineParaSrcSvs(paraSrcSvs_Map, -1);*
10.   *strictPreSvs =Get(strictPreSvs_Map, sv);*
11.   *allPreSvs =allPreSvs -strictPreSvs;*
12.   *LQs=CalculateLQ(sv, allPreSvs, OptLQ_Map);*
13.   *delts=delts∪LQs;*
14. **return** *delts;*

The *SearchTopK* algorithm uses *delts* as the thresholds to find all solutions with a global QoS value that is not larger than the threshold. It searches for the top-k solutions iteratively until all values in *delts* have been considered (line 2) or the top-k solutions have been found (line 8). During each of these iterations, it gets the head of *delts* (the smallest value) as the current threshold and constructs all solutions in this way in algorithm 8 (lines 4–6). The only difference is that here we use *thresholds_Map* to keep the upper bound of the local QoS value for every service. When we find the source combinations of a service, we should make sure that the local QoS value of this service is not larger than the upper bound recorded in *threshold_Map*. After finding all solutions under the current threshold, if the number of solutions is larger than *K*, the algorithm will return the top-k solutions ordered by their global QoS values; otherwise, the next iteration will begin (lines 7–10).

Algorithm 8 *SearchTopK*

Input: *OptLQ_Map, PS_Map, delts, K*
Output: *solutions*

---

1. *delt=RemoveHead(delts);*
2. **while** (*delt≠***null**) **do**
3.   *solutions=∅;*
4.   *open={end}; closed=∅; DAG_AddNode(cw, end);*
5.   *thresholds_Map=Put(thresholds_Map, end, delt);*
6.   *solutions=OneByOne(solutions, OptLQ_Map, PS_Map, open, closed, cw,*
      thresholds_Map);
7.   **if** (|*solutions*|≥*K*) **then**
8.   **return** *TopK(solutions, K);*
9.   **else**
10.   *delt=RemoveHead(delts);*
11. **return** *solutions;*

7.2.3 Experimental Evaluation

7.2.3.1 Preparation

We use the competition test sets provided by WS-Challenge 2009 to validate our algorithm. Each test set contains four different files: an OWL file that gives the ontology tree used in the whole test set; a WSDL file that lists all invocation interfaces of web services; a WSLA file that describes the QoS value of every service; and a CHALLENGE file that includes a user request. Although the competition only provides five different test sets, these sets have some important features. First, semantics is taken into account, and every parameter in the service interfaces references to a concept in the ontology tree. Second, the numbers of services in these test sets vary from 500 to 15,000, thus considering all large-scale services. At last, two major QoS properties are given: the response time and the throughput.

After choosing the test sets, we implement our automatic composition algorithm with Java, which is a famous independent platform programming language. Except for the classes used for reading the XML files in the test sets, we do not use any other third-party packages; therefore, it is really easy for other researchers to rebuild our experimental environment to validate our result data or do some further experiments. The hardware used for our experiments is the Lenovo ThinkPad X200 (2.26 GHz*2, 3GB RAM).

7.2.3.2 Results and analysis

Since our automatic composition algorithm has three stages, we use different metrics for each stage. Although two QoS properties are given in the test sets, we just record experimental results with the response time property, because the throughput property has similar results. Additionally, we run our algorithm five times for each test set, and the average value is given in the result.

7.2.3.2.1 Stage 1

This stage filters active services that participate in the planning-graph and make contributions to generate the goal stated for all the services, thus we take the number of active services and the number of all the services as metrics to prove its effectiveness. Moreover, the running time for this stage is used to analyze its performance. The results are shown in Figure 7.2.

From these results, we see that our filtering algorithm can prune a lot of redundant services (98.44% at most). Therefore, it greatly improves the total performance. In addition, the function between the number of all services and the running time is almost linear, and this proves that the time complexity of this stage is polynomial.

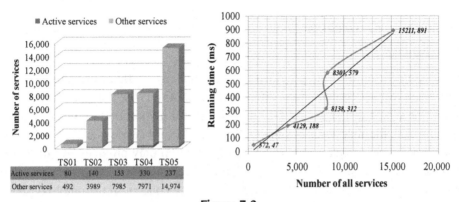

Figure 7.2
Results of stage 1.

7.2.3.2.2 Stage 2

This stage calculates the optimal local QoS value of every active service iteratively, thus we use the optimal local QoS value of the *end* service (i.e., the optimal global QoS value), the number of iterations, and the running time as metrics. The optimal global QoS value can be used to compare with the result given by the champion system in the WS-Challenge competition. The number of iterations and the running time can be used for performance analysis. The results are shown in Table 7.2 and Figure 7.3−7.8.

According to these results, we find that the calculating stage for the test sets can finish in a short time, because the number of active services returned by the first stage is small. In addition, the optimal values are exactly the same as the ones found by the champion system of the WS-Challenge 2009. The function between $M*N*N$ (M is the number of iterations, and N is the number of active services) and the running time is almost linear; this proves the time complexity is $O(M*N*N)$, just as we analyzed.

Table 7.2: Results of stage 2

Test Set	Optimal Global QoS	Number of Iterations	Running Time (ms)
01	500	2	0
02	1690	3	17
03	760	2	5
04	1470	2	47
05	4070	1	13

QoS, quality of services.

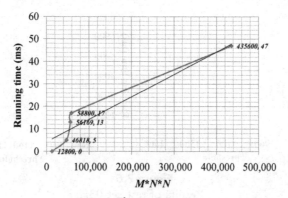

Figure 7.3
The running time in stage 2.

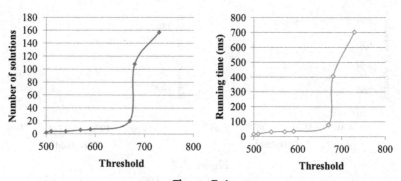

Figure 7.4
Results of test set 01.

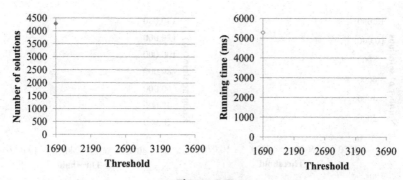

Figure 7.5
Results of test set 02.

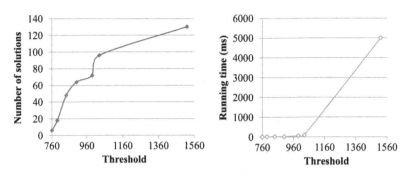

Figure 7.6
Results of test set 03.

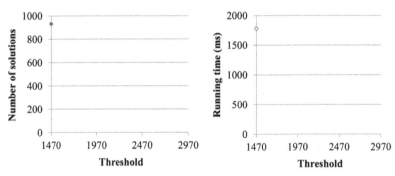

Figure 7.7
Results of test set 04.

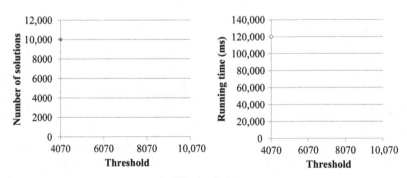

Figure 7.8
Results of test set 05.

7.2.3.2.3 Stage 3

This stage uses some QoS thresholds to find the top-k solutions. Unlike the previous stages, the search space of this stage depends on the value of K. Therefore, we set K to be 50, 100, and 150 to record as many iterations as possible. Moreover, the threshold and the number of solutions for every iteration are used as metrics.

From these results, we find that the number of solutions increases with an increase in the threshold, because a larger threshold causes a larger search space. This stage searches all the solutions under the threshold; thus, if the number of solutions under some threshold is larger than K, we can grant the top-k solutions (not just approximate). Moreover, the running time for each iteration is almost linear with the threshold, and this proves that the threshold significantly improves the performance.

However, we still find that in some test sets (02, 04, 05) there are too many solutions with the same optimal global QoS value. This causes our algorithm not to be able to stop in an acceptable time (2 min). If K is less than the number of optimal compositions, then the top-k problem will be meaningless. The best test set for the top-k problem is the one having a large number of compositions, but the global QoS of these compositions are quite different. Therefore, we conclude that some large test sets of the WS-Challenge competitions are not suitable for the top-k composition problem.

7.3 Parallel Optimization for Service Composition

With the number of services growing very quickly, it may lead them to a performance bottleneck due to the explosion within the planning and searching space. To improve the efficiency of the automatic web service composition with large-scale services, this section introduces an extension of Automatic Web Service Planner (AWSP). AWSP is extended by combining the state space and the planning-graph and optimized with a decentralized method that causes the composition process to execute in parallel. This approach takes the advantages of the state space approach and the planning-graph approach to form a parallel composition framework based on multi-agents. The parallel composition framework consists of a central agent and several planning agents. The central agent is the interface between the whole composition system and the outside application system. It distributes the planning task to all the planning agents and keeps the workload of all the planning agents stable. The planning agent is responsible for searching the results in their local state space. Experiments show that the decentralized system can work stably and improve the composition efficiency.

7.3.1 Problem Formalizing

In this section, we extend the formal definitions for solving the automatic web service composition problem.

Definition 10: State. A state s is a two-tuple (O, P), in which O is the set of objectives represented as "*name:type*," and P is the set of first-order predicates represented as "*predicate object*."

Definition 11: Operator. For any service, it can be represented as an operator in the state space. An operator p is a four-tuple (*In, Out, Pre, Effect*), in which:

- *In* is the set of input objectives;
- *Out* is the set of output objectives;
- *Pre* represents the precondition of the operator and consists of the predicates of the input objectives;
- *Effect* represents the change in the global state after the operator's execution, which consists of two categories: positive effect, *Effect*$^+$, and negative effect, *Effect*$^-$. The positive effect consists of the predicates of the output objectives, and the negative effect consists of the predicates of the input objectives.

Definition 12: Coordination operators. Given a state s, suppose that the operators p_1 and p_2 can be executed with s, and the execution instances are p_1' and p_2'. We say that p_1 and p_2 are coordination operators in the state s if and only if the following conditions are met:

- Set $o = p_1'.In \cap p_2'.In$,
  then $p_1'.Effect^+(o) = \varnothing$
  or $p_2'.Effect^+(o) = \varnothing$
  or $p_1'.Effect^+(o) = p_2'.Effect^+(o)$;
- $p_1'.Effect^- \cap (p_2'.Pre \cup p_2'.Effect^+) = \varnothing$;
- $p_2'.Effect^- \cap (p_1'.Pre \cup p_1'.Effect^+) = \varnothing$

Definition 13: Expansion function. Given a state s and a set of operators $P = \{p_1, p_2, ...p_n\}$, suppose that all the operators of P can be executed with s, and the execution instances are $P' = \{p_1', p_2', ...p_n'\}$. If any two operators in P are coordination operators, then the following state can be achieved through the expansion function $f_{expansion}(s, P')$:

$$s - \bigcup_{1 \le i \le n} p_i'.In - \bigcup_{1 \le i \le n} p_i'.Effect^- + \bigcup_{1 \le i \le n} p_i'.Out + \bigcup_{1 \le i \le n} p_i'.Effect^+$$

The expansion function here can cause a series of coordinated services to be executed in a certain state. Thus you can increase the number of operators for each expansion and reduce the searching width, which may improve the searching efficiency.

Definition 14: Planning subgraph. Begin with a start state s_0, let a sequence of operator sets $\prod = <P_1, P_2, ..., P_n>$ function on s_0 by the expansion function in order, and then reach a final state s_N. Then $s_i = f_{expansion}(s_{i-1}, P_i')$ is called a planning subgraph of the sequence of operator sets from s_0 to s_N.

Definition 15: Automatic web service composition problem. An automatic web service composition problem ψ is a six-tuple (S, s_0, S_G, P, T, Π) in which:

- S is the set of all states.
- $s_0 \in S$, s_0 is the initial state that corresponds to the input objectives and predicates of user requests.
- $S_G \subseteq S$, S_G contains all possible goal states. Each state in S_G contains output objectives and predicates.
- P is a set of operators.
- T represents the set of reasoning relationships among the predicates.
- Π represents a planning subgraph from the initial state to the goal state. It is actually a solution for the planning problem.

7.3.2 Composition Algorithm

The extended algorithm AWSP-E is illustrated as follows. It takes four inputs: user-requested input s_0, user-requested output s_G, a set of services P, and a set of predicate reasoning T; and it generates a planning subgraph Π as the output. The main process, the heuristic function, and the primary data structures in AWSP-E are the same as AWSP. We mainly make two extensions:

1. The searching states are extended. In AWSP-E, the searching states contain not only the type of the objective, but also the name and attributes of the objective. Thus you can make the searching result more accurate, and more possible solutions can be achieved.
2. The operators are extended. In AWSP-E, coordination operators are applied in a certain state. Compared to AWSP, the searching width is reduced. Then the searching space is reduced, and the searching efficiency is improved.

Algorithm 9 *AWSP-E (Automatic Web Service Planner - Extension)*

Input:	s_0, s_G, P, T
Output:	Π

1. *Open=$\emptyset$; Closed=$\emptyset$; Graph=$\emptyset$; Tree=$\emptyset$;*
2. *Graph.addV(s_0); Tree.addNode(s_0);*
3. calculate $f_{heuristic}(s_0)$; *Open.insert(s_0);*
4. **while** (*Open != $\emptyset$*) **do**
5. *c=Open.getHead();*
6. *Closed.insert(c);*
7. **if** (*c$\supseteq s_G$*) **then**
8.   *Π=path from s_0 to c in Tree;*
9.   **return** *Π;*
10. **else**
11.   *pIns*=all operator instance which can be applied on current state *c*;
12.   *ES=findAllExpansionSets(pIns);*
13.   **for every** *P'* in *ES* **do**
14.   *t=$f_{expansion}(c, P')$;*
15.   **if** (*Open$\supseteq t$*) **then**
16.   *Graph.addE(c, t);*
17. $f^{new}=g_{heurstic}(c) + 1 + 10 * h_{heuristic}(t)$;
18.   **if** ($f^{new} < f_{heuristc}(t)$) **then**
19.   change the parent node of *t* to be *c*;
20.   label the path between *c* and *t* to be *P'*;
21.   recalculate $f_{heuristc}(t)$;
22.   replace *t* in *Open*;
23.   **else if** (*Closed$\supseteq t$*) **then**
24.   *Graph.addE(c, t);*
25. $f^{new}=g_{heurstic}(c) + 1 + 10 * h_{heuristic}(t)$;
26.   **if** ($f^{new} < f_{heuristc}(t)$) **then**
27.   change the parent node of *t* to be *c*;
28.   label the path between *c* and *t* to be *P'*;
29.   recalculate $f_{heuristc}(t)$;
30.   *adjust(t);*
31.   **else**
32.   *Graph.addV(t); Graph.addE(c, t);*
33.   *Tree.addNode(t); Tree.addParent(c, t);*
34.   label the path between *c* and *t* to be *P'*;
35.   calculate $f_{heuristic}(t)$;
36.   *Open.inert(t);*

7.3.3 Parallel Optimization

In this section, we introduce the parallel optimization approach for automatic web service composition based on the AWSP-E.

7.3.3.1 Parallel composition framework

The architecture of the parallel composition framework is outlined in Figure 7.9. This parallel composition system consists of a central agent and several planning agents. The central agent is the interface between the whole composition system and the outside application system. It distributes the planning tasks to all the planning agents and keeps the workload of all the planning agents stable. The planning agent is responsible for searching results in their local state space. The number of planning agents can be dynamically adjusted according to the workload of the tasks.

The main process flow of the parallel composition framework is as follows. First, the central agent will distribute the composition task to free planning agents when the user request arrives. Then the planning agents start to search for solutions with AWSP-E. Once a solution is found, the result is returned to the central agent, and the central agent notifies the other planning agents to terminate their tasks. Finally, the central agent returns the result to the user.

7.3.3.2 Central agent

The central agent, as the interface between the parallel composition system and the user request, needs to implement the following functions:

- Service registry and management—Before the execution of the composing process, web services from external applications should register in the parallel composition system.

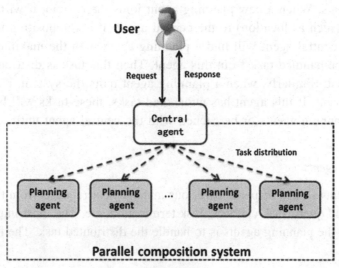

Figure 7.9
The parallel composition framework.

The central agent is responsible for the registry of web services, and then a catalog of services is maintained. So when a planning agent wants to query an available service, it only needs to send the query request to the central agent, which can save a great deal of storage space for the planning agents. In general, the central agent should maintain and manage the description documents of the registered services and provide access interfaces for the planning agents.

- Handling a composition request—When the user request arrives, the central agent constructs an initial task and distributes it to a free planning agent. Then the planning agent starts to plan the task. When other free planning agents are available, the central agent will extract some tasks and distribute them to these planning agents. The formal definition of a task is as follows.

Definition 16: Task. A task for a planning agent distributed by the central agent is represented as a five-tuple $t = (Graph, Tree, Open, Closed, curState)$, in which $Graph$ is the state space graph, $Tree$ is the generated tree of the state space, $Open$ is the set of unvisited vertexes, $Closed$ is the set of visited vertexes, and $curState$ is the start state of the task.

- Handling a composition result—The central agent is also responsible for receiving a planning result from a planning agent and sending it to the user. If a planning agent acquires a planning result, it will send the result to the central agent. As soon as the central agent receives a planning result, it will first notify the other planning agents to terminate their tasks and reclaim the computation resources. Then, the central agent will feedback the planning result to the user.
- Management of planning agents—To fulfill the scalability of the distributed computing, agents in the parallel composition system can dynamically join or quit the system. So the central agent should be in charge of the dynamic change of the planning agents. When a new planning agent joins the system, it will provide its information (such as location) to the central agent. If a composition task is being handled, the central agent will find a planning agent with the maximum load and extract a to-be-handled task from this agent. Then this task is distributed to the new planning agent. Similarly, when a planning agent quits the system, it should notify the central agent. If this agent has unhandled tasks, these tasks will be distributed to other free planning agents or be cached with the central agent until a planning agent is free.

7.3.3.3 Planning agents

The planning agents should respond to various management requests from the central agent, such as load query, task callback, task termination, etc. The most important responsibility for the planning agents is to handle the distributed task. The task handling is based on the AWSP-E, and several tasks for multiple planning agents can be executed in parallel. The parallel algorithm for AWSP-E is as follows:

Algorithm 10 *ParaAWSP-E (Parallel Automatic Web Service Planner-Extension)*

Input:	*Graph, Tree, Open, Closed, curState*
Output:	Π

1.   *localOpen={curState}*;
2.   **while** *(localOpen != $\emptyset$)* **do**
3.   *c=localOpen.getHead()*;
4.   *Closed.insert(c)*;
5.   **if** *($c \supseteq s_G$)* **then**
6. Π=path from s_0 to c in *Tree*;
7.   invoke the service of the central agent to get Π;
8.   **return** Π;
9.   **else**
10.   *pIns*=all operator instance which can be applied on current state c;
11.   *ES=findAllExpansionSets(pIns)*;
12.   **for every** *P'* in *ES* **do**
13. $t=f_{expansion}(c, P')$;
14.   **if** *(Open$\supseteq$t)* **then**
15.   *Graph.addE(c, t)*;
16. $f^{new}=g_{heurstic}(c) + 1 + 10 * h_{heuristic}(t)$;
17.   **if** *($f^{new}<f_{heuristc}(t)$)* **then**
18.   change the parent node of t to be c;
19.   label the path between c and t to be P';
20.   recalculate $f_{heuristc}(t)$;
21.   **if** *(localOpen$\supseteq$t)* **then**
22.   replace t in *localOpen*;
23.   **else**
24.   *localOpen.insert(t)*;
25.   **else if** *(Closed$\supseteq$t)* **then**
26.   *Graph.addE(c, t)*;
27. $f^{new}=g_{heurstic}(c) + 1 + 10 * h_{heuristic}(t)$;
28.   **if** *($f^{new}<f_{heuristc}(t)$)* **then**
29.   change the parent node of t to be c;
30.   label the path between c and t to be P';
31.   recalculate $f_{heuristc}(t)$;
32.   *adjust(t)*;
33.   **else**
34.   *Graph.addV(t); Graph.addE(c, t)*;
35.   *Tree.addNode(t); Tree.addParent(c, t)*;
36.   label the path between c and t to be P';
37.   calculate $f_{heuristic}(t)$;
38.   *Open.inert(t)*;
39.   *localOpen.insert(t)*;
40.   inform the central agent that the current planning agent is free;

Table 7.3: Datasets of WS-challenge 2009

Dataset	Number of Services
Test01	572
Test02	4,129
Test03	8,138
Test04	8,301
Test05	15,211

The algorithm takes the distributed task as the input and tries to get a planning result. If a result is achieved, the planning will invoke the result receiving function of the central agent (line 7). In contrast, the planning agent will inform the central agent that it is free if no result is found so that another task can be distributed to it.

7.3.4 Experiments

To validate the feasibility of the proposed approach in this section, we implemented it in JAVA and conducted a series of experiments using the datasets of WS-Challenge 2009 and large-scale test sets generated by WSBen [27]. The parallel composition system we built for the experiments consists of a central agent and four planning agents. The execution environment is Intel Core2 P7370 2.0 GHZ with 4GB RAM, Windows 7, jdk1.6.0.

We first use the datasets of WS-Challenge 2009 to compare the performance of AWSP and ParaAWSP-E. The details of the five datasets of WS-Challenge 2009 are shown in Table 7.3, and the comparison results are shown in Table 7.4 and Figure 7.10.

From the comparison results, we can conclude that: (1) when the scale of the test set is larger, the parallel composition system can improve the composition efficiency. However, when the scale of the test set is small as Test01, the parallel composition system will take more time to get a result. The reason is that the communication between the central agent and planning agents would cost the parallel composition system some time. Therefore, for a small-scale test set, the time cost of the communication is more than that for planning. So the efficiency of the parallel composition system is reduced and (2) although the scale of

Table 7.4: Execution time of AWSP and ParaAWSP-E

Dataset	AWSP (ms)	ParaAWSP-E (ms)
Test01	47	102
Test02	188	197
Test03	312	243
Test04	579	398
Test05	891	689

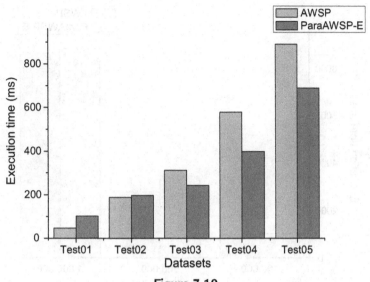

Figure 7.10

Performance comparison.

the test set is large enough, as shown in Test05, the performance improvement of the parallel composition system could not reach $1/N$ as expected. That's because the internal management and communication in the parallel composition system will cost some time, which can impact the execution performance of the whole system.

Besides the datasets of WS-Challenge 2009, we also used WSBen to generate three groups of large-scale test sets. Each group has five test sets, and the service number of each group is set as 100,000, 500,000, and 1,000,000. The average execution time for these test sets is shown in Table 7.5 and Figure 7.11.

From the above results, we can conclude that: (1) for the super-large-scale test sets, the parallel composition system can also improve its efficiency and (2) during the execution for these test sets, all four planning agents are almost fully loaded all the time. Besides, with the increase of the service number, the performance improvement of the parallel composition system becomes less and less. The reason is that the number of planning agents is small for the super-large-scale test sets. However, for the limitation of the

Table 7.5: Execution time with super-large-scale test sets

Dataset Scalibity	AWSP (ms)	ParaAWSP-E (ms)
100,000	1021	978
500,000	3458	2786
1,000,000	8834	8654

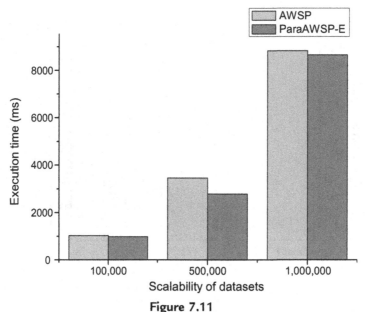

Figure 7.11
Performance comparison with super-large-scale test sets.

experiment's environment, we can hardly get more planning agents. We may consider extending the scalability of the parallel composition system in any future work.

7.4 Service Composition Based on Historical Records

Previous studies are less aware of the potential value and the hidden knowledge of the service usage data for assisting users with their service composition tasks. Frequently used web services (FUWS) have the following advantages. They carry users' previous experiences, have higher probability to fulfill users' requirements, and have been proved to be more reliable and robust. Furthermore, composite services that share the same FUWS may have similar composition process or functionality. By reusing such types of verified knowledge, it will dramatically increase the correctness and rationality of composed services and accelerate their rapid application development. By analyzing the historical composition records in a historical service-composition dataset (HSD), some similar FUWSs could be recommended to the user as candidates for selection according to the user's partially composed service. Further, if the user's partially composed service share the same FUWS with composite services in HSD, they may have a similar composition process in the forwarding step, which could also be recommended to the user to facilitate the composition task. To handle the above scenario, this section proposes a graph mining based approach to model and explore the hidden knowledge from a HSD. More specifically, the approach includes the following: We modeled an executed service transaction or a bunch of web services that compose together and register in a service repository by using a directed labeled graph. We adopted and extended the graph mining approach gSpan to identify FUWSs among those directed labeled graphs. Then, we explored and located those web services that share the same FUWSs with the user's partially composed services. After that, we proposed a model to estimate how likely it will be for a service that shares the same FUWSs to be able to meet the user's needs. Based on the likelihood, we recommended some web services as candidates for a user's composition task, and then selected the optimal ones with consideration of the overall QoS by using a skyline approach. Technically, to address the issue of frequent subgraph mining (e.g., FUWS identification), we adopted and extended gSpan to discover frequent substructures efficiently without costly subgraph isomorphism tests and a costly candidate generation. To the best of our knowledge, this work is the first attempt to exploit such efficient frequent structured pattern mining techniques to identify FUWSs with their connecting structure, which could provide instant and smart suggestions to facilitate the composition of Web services.

7.4.1 Framework Based on Graph Mining

Web service recommendations can accelerate and facilitate the process of service composition. Suppose a user is composing some web services, our objective is to understand the intent of the user based on the semifinished (i.e., partially composed) composite web service, so as to recommend appropriate web services to the user to help them finish the composition. Moreover, to ensure the effectiveness of the recommendations, we try to enlarge the probability that users select the recommended extensions.

In this section, we propose a novel graph mining-based service recommendation framework to help facilitate service composition. Generally, there are three main stages in the proposed framework: data preparation stage, data processing stage, and service recommendation stage, as illustrated in Figure 7.12.

1. Data preparation stage: In this stage, web services with the same or similar function-ality are clustered and marked with the same class label. Then the executed composite web services (i.e., historical composition records) are modeled into directed labeled graphs.
2. Data processing stage: In this stage, we use a graph mining algorithm to identify frequent subgraphs (i.e., FUWS), representing the key components of web services that are often executed together.
3. Service recommendation stage: We propose a model to estimate the probability that a directed labeled graph (e.g., a composition of web services) will meet the user's needs, and then select the optimal composite service.

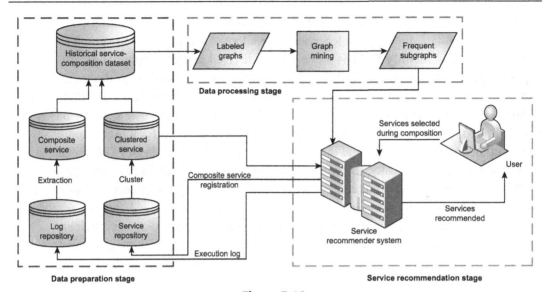

Figure 7.12
The process for service recommendation based on graph mining.

7.4.2 Processing Stages

The data preparation stage and data processing stage are the bases for the service recommendation stage. In this section, we will give a detailed description of data preparation stage and data processing stage.

7.4.2.1 Data preparation stage

The data preparation stage can be divided into two steps: (1) clustering web services and (2) modeling historical composition records with directed labeled graphs.

Before identifying FUWSs, we need to cluster similar web services, because the usage data are very sparse, and the clustering results can help to provide diverse candidates to users. There are many approaches for web service clustering. In this section, we use the K-medoids clustering algorithm to group together web services with the same function.

Definition 17: Clustered web service. After service clustering, a web service can be formally defined by a five-tuple, *WS = (WS-ID, In, Out, QoS, Cluster-ID)*, in which:

- *WS-ID* is the unique identifier of the web service;
- *In/Out* is the input/output interface;
- QoS is the quality of service;
- *Cluster-ID* is the unique identifier of the cluster that the web service belongs to, and all the web services belonging to the same cluster have the same *Cluster-ID*.

In most situations, a single web service cannot meet users' needs, and service composition is inevitable. Once a composite web service is invoked by a user, we can construct a corresponding graph for this composite web service, in which the links are built according to the execution order between the component web services. For the sake of simplicity, in this approach, we focus on directed acyclic graphs. The formal definitions of a composite web service and composite service graph are given as follows.

Definition 18: Composite web service. A composite web service can be represented by a two-tuple, $CS = (WSS, WSR)$, in which:

- WSS is the set of component web services included in this composite web service;
- $WSR \subseteq WSS \times WSS$ represents the relation between two web services, i.e., $(WS_i, WS_j) \in WSR$ when WS_j is executed on the neck of WS_i.

Definition 19: Directed labeled graph for composite service. A directed labeled graph for composite service can be represented by a four-tuple, $G = (V, E, LV, lV)$, in which:

- V is the vertex set of the graph, in which each vertex refers to a component web service;
- $E \subseteq V \times V$ is the edge set of the graph, in which each edge represents the execution order between two web services;
- LV is the label set for the vertex set, which is comprised by *Cluster-IDs*;
- lV is a function mapping from a vertex to a label. Because each vertex represents a web service and each web service has a *Cluster-ID*, each vertex's label is just the corresponding *Cluster-ID*.

For example, Figure 7.13(a) gives a sample of a composite web service invoked by the user, and Figure 7.13(b) shows *Cluster-ID for* each web service in Figure 7.13(a), then we can construct the corresponding composite service graph as Figure 7.13(c) shows. In particular, $WS2$ and $WS3$ are in the same cluster $C2$.

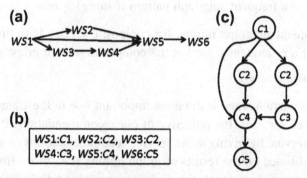

Figure 7.13
Construction of composite service graph.

7.4.2.2 Data processing stage

The data processing stage is responsible for the acquisition of the web service clusters that are often executed together. To achieve this goal, we use graph mining algorithms to mine frequent subgraphs from the composite service graphs.

Before introducing the proposed method, we first define the subgraph isomorphism for composite service graphs.

Definition 20: Subgraph isomorphism for composite service. Given two composite service graphs $G = (V, E, L_V, l_V)$ and $G' = (V', E', L_V, l_V)$, a subgraph isomorphism from G to G' is an injective function $f:V \rightarrow V'$, such that:

1. for any vertex $u \in V$, $l_V(u) = l_V(f(u))$, i.e., the two corresponding web services represented by u and $f(u)$ belong to the same cluster;
2. for any edge $(u,v) \in E$, $(f(u), f(v)) \in E'$.

If there exists a subgraph isomorphism from G to G', then G is a subgraph of G' and G' is a supergraph of G, denoted as $G \sqsubseteq G'$.

Based on the definition of subgraph isomorphism, we can give the definition of a frequent subgraph mining as follows.

Definition 21: Frequent subgraph mining for composite service. Given a composite service graph dataset $D = \{G_1, G_2, ..., G_n\}$, and a minimum support min_sup, assume $sup(g)$ denotes the support of g in D, then:

$$sup(g) = \sum_{G_i \in D} I(g, G_i), 1 \le i \le n, \quad \text{where}$$

$$I(g, G) = \begin{cases} 1, & \text{if } g \text{ is a subgraph of } G; \\ 0, & \text{if } g \text{ is not a subgraph of } G. \end{cases}$$

A subgraph g is called a frequent subgraph pattern if $sup(g) \ge min\_sup$.

The objective of frequent subgraph mining for composite service is to find the complete set of subgraphs that are frequently used in the composite service graph dataset D.

7.4.2.3 Service composition stage

The service recommendation stage is the most important one in the framework. When a user is composing web services, the objective of our recommendations is to extend the partially composed service by giving some service recommendations or suggestions. Our approach is proposed based on the results of graph mining (i.e., those frequent subgraphs obtained in the data processing stage). For each frequent subgraph g, find the frequent subgraph g' that is the supergraph of g, such that the probability for g' appearing together with g is larger. That is to say, when the frequent subgraph g appears in the user's partially composed service, we extend it to g', because the probability that the user will need g' is high. Thus, for the user's partially composed service, we find the frequent subgraphs it contains and extend these frequent subgraphs to those corresponding supergraphs, such that the extensions of the partially composed service are realized. For each extension, we need to replace it with concrete web services. Because there will be many corresponding concrete web services for each extension, we have to select and compose the optimal composite web service according to both the satisfaction probability and QoS. Thus, this stage can be divided into two steps: (1) determine frequent subgraphs for the recommendations and (2) select the optimal composite web service. These two steps are described in the following subsections.

According to the user's partially composed service, we can construct the corresponding directed labeled graph as described in Section 7.4.2.1. This directed labeled graph is used as an original graph G_o. We enumerate all subgraphs of G_o to find subgraphs that are in the result set of graph mining. To make it clear, the set comprising these subgraphs is denoted as S_o, and the result set of graph mining is denoted as FS. Formally, $S_o = \{g | g \sqsubseteq G_o \text{ and } g \in FS\}$.

For one graph g, if another graph g' can be obtained by adding one edge to g, then g' is the child of g. And the child of g' is the descendant of g. For each graph g in S_o, we enumerate all descendants of g to find those descendants that are also in FS. The set of those descendants with respect to g is denoted as $Des(g)$. Formally, $Des(g) = \{g' | g' \text{ is the descendant of } g \text{ and } g' \in FS\}$.

Then, we need to find the graph in $Des(g)$ with the highest probability that is extended from g. For each graph g' in $Des(g)$, the probability that g' appears when g appears can be denoted as $P(g'|g)$. According to the Bayesian formula, probability $P(g'|g)$ can be transformed as follows:

$$P(g'|g) = \frac{P(g|g') \times P(g')}{P(g)}, \tag{7.1}$$

in which $P(g|g')$ represents the probability that g appears when g' appears. Because g' is the descendant of g, g must appear when g' appears. Namely, the value of $P(g|g')$ is one. Then, Eqn (7.1) can be transformed as follows:

$$P(g'|g) = \frac{P(g')}{P(g)} = \frac{sup(g')}{sup(g)} \tag{7.2}$$

According to Eqn (7.2), the probability $P(g|g')$ is larger when g' has fewer edges, and we cannot get those extensions with more edges. Thus, by introducing the edge count, Eqn (7.2) is transformed into Eqn (7.3), the value of which is denoted $Score(g',g)$.

$$Score(g', g) = \frac{(|E(g')| + 1)^\alpha \times sup(g')}{(|E(g)| + 1)^\alpha \times sup(g)} \qquad (7.3)$$

Next, we need to find the graph in $Des(g)$ with the highest score and denote it as g_b, which is a candidate for our recommendation. The list of candidates for recommendations is denoted as CFS, in which each graph g_{ib} is the graph in $Des(g_i)$ that has the highest score. All graphs in CFS will be ranked according to $Score(g_{ib}, g_i)$. The higher the score, the higher the ranking. If scores are equal, we will consider the extended edge count. The extended edge count for g_{ib} is calculated by Eqn (7.4).

$$N_e\big(g_{ib}, g_i\big) = \big|E\big(g_{ib}\big)\big| - \big|E\big(g_i\big)\big| \qquad (7.4)$$

The larger the extended edge count, the higher the ranking. If the extended edge counts are equal, a minimum DFS code is considered. The smaller the minimum DFS code, the higher the ranking. The number of candidates for recommendations may be large. We set a parameter k to limit the number of frequent subgraphs recommended for users. If the number of candidates is larger than k, we just return top k in CFS, otherwise, we return all the candidates. The list of recommended frequent subgraphs is denoted as RFS_k. For each graph in FS, its descendant with the highest score can be calculated offline, so that we can speed up the online service recommendation stage.

To make it more convenient for the user, the final recommendation is based on the graphs that are acquired by joining each graph in RFS_k with G_o, and the list of these graphs is denoted as RG_k.

For example, Figure 7.14(a) shows the user's partially composed service, and Figure 7.14(b) shows the *Cluster-ID* of each web service in Figure 7.14(a). After that, we can construct the corresponding original graph G_o, which is given in Figure 7.14(c). Figure 7.14(d) shows the graphs in S_o. For each graph in Figure 7.14(d), its descendant with the highest score are given in Figure 7.14(e), and the corresponding scores and extended edge counts are given in Figure 7.14(f) and 7.14(g), respectively. Then the list of recommended frequent subgraphs is given in Figure 7.14(h), in which each graph has already been ranked. Please note that the value of α and k in this example are two and five, respectively. Figure 7.15 shows the graphs in RG_5, in which the solid lines represent the edges in Figure 7.14(c), and the dotted lines represent the edges in corresponding graph in Figure 7.14(h).

For a graph g in RG_k, the label of each vertex in g is *Cluster-ID*. For the vertices of g that are also in G_o, they are replaced by the corresponding web services already selected by the user. For other vertices of g, they can be replaced by any web service in the corresponding cluster. Thus, we can get many composite web services for g with different replacements.

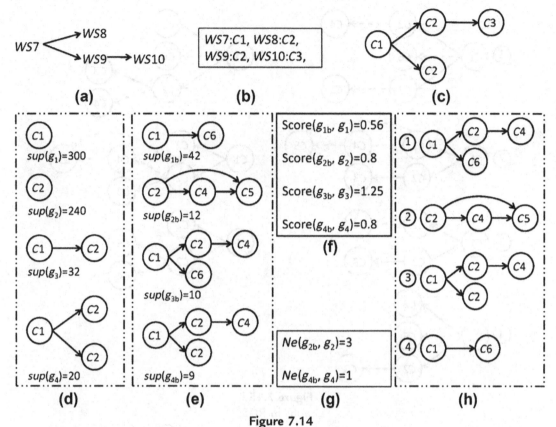

Figure 7.14
Determination of recommended frequent subgraphs.

A criterion is needed to measure the quality of composite web services, so that we can select the optimal composite web service.

In this approach, we consider six dimensions of QoS, which are shown in Table 7.6. For all the web services in the service repository, we use the function: $y = (x - min(x))/(max(x) - min(x))$ to normalize each dimension of QoS into the range [0,1]. Without explicit mentioning, QoS discussed below is normalized as QoS.

For each composite web service, we can calculate its QoS in six dimensions according to its structure and the QoS of the component web services. According to definition 18, we can use $CS = (WSS, WSR)$ to denote one composite web service. The formulas to calculate the QoS of CS in six dimensions will be presented next. Because the branch relationship in composite web services is a common relationship and its calculation is more complicated, we focus on branch relationships in this approach. However, it is not hard to cover other relationships in composite web services.

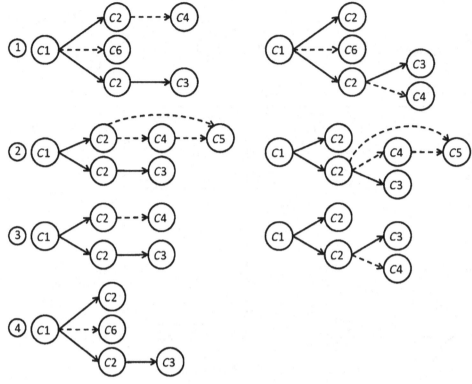

Figure 7.15
Graphs in RG5.

Table 7.6: QoS parameters

Parameter Name	Description	Units
Response time (RT)	Time taken to send a request and receive a response	ms
Availability (AV)	Number of successful invocations/total invocations	%
Throughput (TP)	Total number of invocations for a given period of time	#/s
Successaibility (SU)	Number of response/number of request messages	%
Reliability (RE)	Ratio of the number of error messages to total messages	%
Latency (LA)	Time taken for the server to process a given request	ms

QoS, quality of services.

To compute the QoS of *CS* in six dimensions for each component web service *WS* in *CS*, the number of its direct predecessors is called its *indegree*, denoted as $deg^-(WS)$, and the number of its direct successors is called its *outdegree*, denoted as $deg^+(WS)$. In additon, we add two more web services, WS_s and WS_f, which represent the initial service and final service, respectively. In addition to the relationships in *WSR*, each web service with an *indegree* of 0 has a relationship from WS_s, and each web service with an *outdegree* of 0 has a relationship to WS_f. Thus in *CS*, WS_s is the only web service with an *indegree* of 0, and WS_f is the only web service with an *outdegree* of 0. It should be noted that response time and latency of WS_s and WS_f are 0, and the availability, throughput, successability, and reliability of WS_s and WS_f are 1.

1. Response time for composite web service: For each component web service *WS* in the composite web service *CS*, its response time can be denoted as $RT(WS)$. The aggregated response time of *WS*, denoted as $Agg\_RT(WS)$, is the response time that an execution starting from WS_f will terminate at *WS*. For a web service WS_i, $Agg\_RT(WS_i)$ can be defined recursively as follows:

   If $deg^+(WS_i) \neq 0$, then $Agg\_RT(WS_i) =$

   $$RT(WS_i) + \frac{1}{deg^+(WS_i)} \sum_{j,(WS_i, WS_j) \in WSR} Agg\_RT(WS_j).$$

   Otherwise, $Agg\_RT(WS_i) = RT(WS_i)$. Namely, $Agg\_RT(WS_f) = RT(WS_f) = 0$.

   Thus, the response time of the composite web service *CS* is the aggregated response times of the component web services with an *indegree* of 0. Formally, we use $RT(CS)$ to represent the response time of *CS*, and it can be calculated as follows:

   $$RT(CS) = Agg\_RT(WS_s).$$

2. Availability for composite web service: For each component web service *WS* in the composite web service *CS*, its availability can be denoted as $AV(WS)$. The aggregated availability of *WS*, denoted as $Agg\_AV(WS)$, is the availability that an execution starting from WS_s will terminate at *WS*. For a web service WS_j, $Agg\_AV(WS_j)$ can be defined recursively as follows:

   If $deg^-(WS_j) \neq 0$, then $Agg\_AV(WS_j) =$

   $$AV(WS_j) \times \sum_{i,(WS_i, WS_j) \in WSR} \frac{1}{deg^+(WS_i)} Agg\_AV(WS_i).$$

   Otherwise, $Agg\_AV(WS_j) = AV(WS_j)$. Namely, $Agg\_AV(WS_s) = AV(WS_s) = 1$.

Thus, the availability of the composite web service *CS* is the aggregated availability of component web services with an *outdegree* of 0. Formally, we use *AV(CS)* to represent the availability of *CS*, and it can be calculated as follows:

$$AV(CS) = Agg\_AV(WS_f).$$

3. Throughput for composite web service: For each component web service *WS* in the composite web service *CS*, its throughput can be denoted as *TP(WS)*. The aggregated throughput of *WS*, denoted as *Agg_TP(WS)*, is the throughput that an execution starting from WS_s will terminate at *WS*. For a web service WS_j, $Agg\_TP(WS_j)$ can be defined recursively as follows:
    If $deg^-(WS_j) \neq 0$, then

$$Agg\_TP\left(WS_j\right) = min\left(TP\left(WS_j\right), \sum_{i,\left(WS_i,WS_j\right) \in WSR} \frac{1}{deg^+\left(WS_i\right)} Agg\_TP\left(WS_i\right)\right).$$

Otherwise, $Agg\_TP(WS_j) = TP(WS_j)$. Namely, $Agg\_TP(WS_s) = TP(WS_s) = 1$.

Thus, the throughput of the composite web service *CS* is the aggregated throughput of component web services with an *outdegree* of 0. Formally, we use *TP(CS)* to represent the throughput of *CS*, and it can be calculated as follows:

$$TP(CS) = Agg\_TP(WS_f).$$

4. Successability for composite web service: For each component web service *WS* in the composite web service *CS*, its successability can be denoted as *SU(WS)*. The aggregated successability of *WS*, denoted as *Agg_SU(WS)*, is the successability that an execution starting from WS_s will terminate at *WS*. For a web service WS_j, the method for calculating $Agg\_SU(WS_j)$ is similar to $Agg\_AV(WS_j)$. It can be defined recursively as follows:

If $deg^-(WS_j) \neq 0$, then $Agg\_SU(WS_j) =$

$$SU\left(WS_j\right) \times \sum_{i,\left(WS_i,WS_j\right) \in WSR} \frac{1}{deg^+\left(WS_i\right)} Agg\_SU\left(WS_i\right).$$

Otherwise, $Agg\_SU(WS_j) = SU(WS_j)$. Namely, $Agg\_SU(WS_j) = SU(WS_s) = 1$. Thus, the successability of the composite web service *CS* is the aggregated successability of component web services with an *outdegree* of 0. Formally, we use *SU(CS)* to represent the successability of *CS*, and it can be calculated as follows:

$$SU(CS) = Agg\_SU(WS_f).$$

5. Reliability for composite web service: For each component web service *WS* in the composite web service *CS*, its reliability can be denoted as *RE(WS)*. The aggregated reliability of *WS* denoted as *Agg_RE(WS)* is the reliability that an execution starting from WS_s will terminate at *WS*. For a web service WS_j, the method for calculating $Agg\_RE(WS_j)$ is similar to $Agg\_AV(WS_j)$. It can be defined recursively as follows:

If $deg^-(WS_j) \neq 0$, then $Agg\_RE(WS_j) =$

$$RE(WS_j) \times \sum_{i,(WS_i,WS_j) \in WSR} \frac{1}{deg^+(WS_i)} Agg\_RE(WS_i).$$

Otherwise, $Agg\_RE(WS_j) = RE(WS_j)$. Namely, $Agg\_RE(WS_s) = RE(WS_s) = 1$.

Thus, the reliability of the composite web service *CS* is the aggregated reliability of component web services with an *outdegree* of 0. Formally, we use *RE(CS)* to represent the reliability of [EQUATION], and it can be calculated as follows:

$$RE(CS) = Agg\_RE(WS_f).$$

6. Latency for composite web service: For each component web service *WS* in the composite web service *CS*, its latency can be denoted as *LA(WS)*. The aggregated latency of *WS*, denoted as *Agg_LA(WS)*, is the latency that an execution starting from WS_f will terminate at *WS*. For a web service WS_i, the method for calculating $Agg\_LA(WS_i)$, is similar to $Agg\_RT(WS_i)$. It can be defined recursively as follows:

If $deg^+(WS_i) \neq 0$, then $Agg\_LA(WS_i) =$

$$LA(WS_i) + \frac{1}{deg^+(WS_i)} \sum_{j,(WS_i,WS_j) \in WSR} Agg\_LA(WS_j).$$

Otherwise, $Agg\_LA(WS_i) = LA(WS_i)$. Namely, $Agg\_LA(WS_f) = LA(WS_f) = 0$.

Thus, the latency of the composite web service *CS* is the aggregated latency of the component web services with an *indegree* of 0. Formally, we use *LA(CS)* to represent the latency of *CS*, and it can be calculated as follows:

$$LA(CS) = Agg\_LA(WS_s).$$

For example, Figure 7.16(a) gives a sample composite web service *CS*. According to the formulas we defined above, we can calculate its QoS in six dimensions, as illustrated in Figure 7.16(b).

After calculating the QoS of the composite web services, we select the composite web service that has a QoS that is optimal for the recommendation. To select an optimal composite web service, we unite the six dimensions of QoS into one value ranging

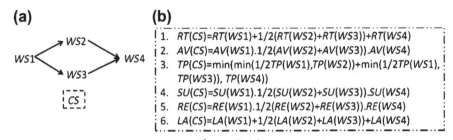

Figure 7.16
Calculation of QoS of a composite web service. Qos, quality of services.

between [0,1], and the greater the value, the higher the quality of the composite web service. A weight vector $W = (w_1, w_2, w_3, w_4, w_5, w_6)$ is introduced to represent the importance of the QoS in each dimension. For response time and latency, the higher the value is, the lower is the quality of the composite web service. For other dimensions of QoS, the higher the value is, the higher is the quality of the composite web service. Thus, for a composite web service CS, its QoS can be calculated as follows:

$$QoS(CS) = w_1 \cdot \frac{1}{RT(CS)+1} + w_2 \cdot AV(CS) + w_3 \cdot TP(CS) + w_4 \cdot SU(CS) + w_5 \cdot RE(CS)$$
$$+ w_6 \cdot \frac{1}{LA(CS)+1},$$

where $\sum_{i=1}^{6} w_i = 1$ and $w_i \geq$ for $1 \leq i \leq 6$.

For a graph g in RG_k, we assume that it has N vertices that are not in G_0 (i.e., N clusters), and there are M web services in each cluster. The total number of corresponding composite web services is M^N. The computation cost of selecting an optimal composite web service is $O(M^N)$. Such an approach is impractical for large N and M.

However, from those formulas in Section 7.4.2.3, we can find that the QoS of the composite web service is only better when the component web services' QoS is better. Thus, we can use *skyline* to boost the selection of optimal composite web services. First, we use *skyline* to select web services with a higher QoS in each cluster. And these web services are the skyline services of each cluster. Then, each vertex is just replaced with the skyline services instead of any service in the corresponding cluster, so that we can reduce the computation cost. For example, for each graph in Figure 7.15, we replace each vertex with corresponding web services to get those composite web services, which are shown in Figure 7.17. Then we can calculate QoS of each composite web service in Figure 7.17 and get optimal composite web services. Please note that the process for computing skyline services in each cluster can be finished offline.

7.4.3 Experimental Evaluation

7.4.3.1 Experiment setting

We prepare a service repository containing 1530 services for the experiments. All services are selected from the QWS dataset. As mentioned in Section 7.4.2.1, we adopt the K-medoids clustering algorithm and get 100 clusters at last. While clustering, we use the modified version of the method in [28] to calculate service similarity. The main modifications are those features considered and the method for calculating the web service name similarity. Particularly, we consider these features including *WSDL types*, *WSDL messages*, *WSDL ports*, and *web service name*, while the feature *WSDL contents* is not considered. This is because the implementation for the feature *WSDL contents* is very complex, and this feature is less important. While calculating *web service name* similarity, we do not use Normalized Google Distance (NGD) [29], but use the Lin measure of WordNet similarity [30]. However, the effectiveness of the Lin measure of WordNet similarity is not better than NGD, because for those words not in WordNet, there will be no similarity. The main reason we do not use NGD is that we have 1530 services, and the emphWeb service name of these services has more than 1000 words. NGD needs a search engine to search the number of any two words to both appear, and there will be more than 1000^2 searches. Current search engines do not allow that

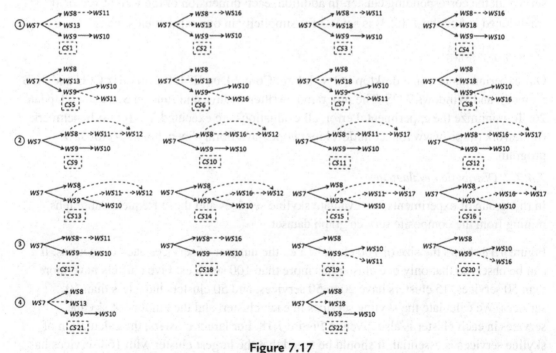

Figure 7.17

Candidates of composite web service for recommendation.

many uses of auto-search (i.e., machine search, not manual search), so we use the Lin measure of WordNet similarity to calculate *Web service name* similarity. For each word not in WordNet, its similarities with other words are all set to 0.

Furthermore, we prepare a log repository containing 10,000 executed composite services, which are generated based on the service repository. So the size of the composite service graph dataset is 10,000. The edge count of each graph in the composite service graph dataset is uniformly distributed in the range [5,30].

In addition, we generate 1000 composite services, and those corresponding 1000 composite service graphs are used as a test set, in which the edge count of each graph is uniformly distributed in the range [10,60]. Then we select half of each graph in the test set as an input set for recommendation, i.e., each graph in the input set like G_o mentioned in Section 7.4.2.3. Thus, the edge count of each graph in the input set is uniformly distributed in the range [5,30].

While evaluating the efficiency and effectiveness of our approach, random recommendation is used as a baseline. Random recommendation with skyline means that each vertex is replaced with a randomly selected skyline service in the corresponding cluster. And random recommendation without a skyline means each vertex is replaced with a randomly selected service in the corresponding cluster. In addition, each dimension of the weight vector W (mentioned in Section 7.4.2.3) is set to $\frac{1}{6}$ for simplicity in our experiments, i.e.,

$$W = \left(\tfrac{1}{6}, \tfrac{1}{6}, \tfrac{1}{6}, \tfrac{1}{6}, \tfrac{1}{6}, \tfrac{1}{6}\right).$$

Our experiments run on a desktop PC with Intel Core 2 Duo E7400 2.80 GHz CPU and 3GB memory, and Windows 7 OS. The program is written in Java and runs on Sun JDK 6 Update 26. To minimize the experimental error, all evaluations are executed in a robust benchmark framework (http://www.ibm.com/developerworks/java/library/jbenchmark2/) for Java program.

7.4.3.2 Distribution evaluation

In this group of experiments, we evaluate skyline services and those frequent subgraphs mining from the composite service graph dataset.

Figure 7.18 shows the size of 100 clusters, i.e., the number of services each cluster has. It can be observed that only one cluster has more than 100 services. Five clusters have more than 50 services, 15 clusters have 20 to 50 services, and 50 clusters have less than 10 services. We calculate the skyline services in each cluster, and the number of skyline services in each cluster is also given in Figure 7.18. For larger clusters, the calculation of skyline services is essential. It should be noted that the largest cluster with 168 services has 28 skyline services.

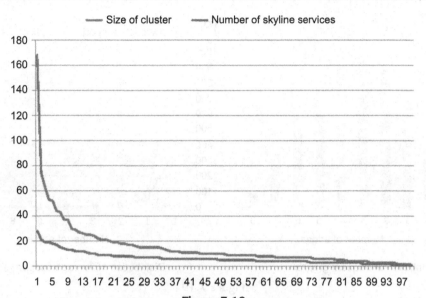

Figure 7.18
The distribution of clusters and skyline services.

Then, we evaluate the frequent subgraphs, mining from the composite service graph dataset. The minimum support is set to 3.

Figure 7.19(a) shows the distribution of frequent subgraphs on the number of edges. Please note that the y-axis is in logarithmic scale. As the number of edges increases, the number of corresponding frequent subgraphs first increases exponentially. When the number of edges reaches three, the number of corresponding frequent subgraphs reaches a peak. Then, as the number of edges increases, the number of corresponding frequent subgraphs decreases exponentially. The result is consistent with our understanding.

We calculate the average support of frequent subgraphs with respect to the number of edges. To get the suitable value of α in Eqn (7.3), we use function $y = c \cdot (x + 1)^{-\beta}$ to fit the data. The reason we use this function is that we hope the result of Eqn (7.3) is around one and the impact of the edge count for support can be eliminated. Figure 7.19(b) shows the results. We can observe that the average support of the frequent subgraphs decreases exponentially as the number of edges increases. And we determine that the value of c is 336.853, and the value of β is 2.516. So when the minimum support is 3, the suitable value of α is 2.516.

7.4.3.3 Efficiency evaluation

In this group of experiments, we evaluated the efficiency of our approach. Because the data preparation stage and data processing stage can be completed offline, we just study the time of service recommendation stage.

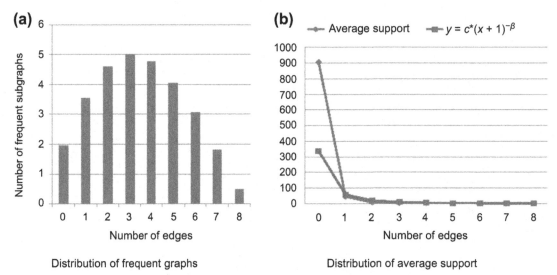

Figure 7.19
The distribution of frequent subgraphs.

As mentioned in Section 7.4.2.3, we first determined the frequent subgraphs for the recommendation. Then, we replaced each vertex with the corresponding cluster's skyline services to find the optimal composite web service for each frequent subgraph. We test the average time when we use or do not use skyline services to obtain the optimal recommendation. Meanwhile, we also test the average time of the random recommendation with or without skyline. The results are shown in Table 7.2. For the optimal recommendation, the average time without skyline is eight times more than the average time with skyline. Thus, using skyline services is efficient for an optimal recommendation. Further, it can be observed that skyline does not affect the average time of the random recommendation. The average time of the random recommendation is much less than that of the optimal recommendation, which is consistent with our understanding. Assume that there are N vertices and each vertex can be replaced with M web services; the time complexity of the random recommendation is $O(N)$, while the optimal recommendation is $O(M^N)$.

7.4.3.4 Effect evaluation

In this group of experiments, we evaluate the practical effectiveness of the proposed approach. First, we evaluate the extended edge count of the recommendation, as illustrated in Figure 7.20. In Figure 7.20(a), the extended edge count decreases when the minimum support increases. This is because the edge count of frequent subgraphs decreases with the increase of the minimum support. It should be noted that for different minimum support, the suitable value of α is set according to the method mentioned in Section 7.4.3.2. When

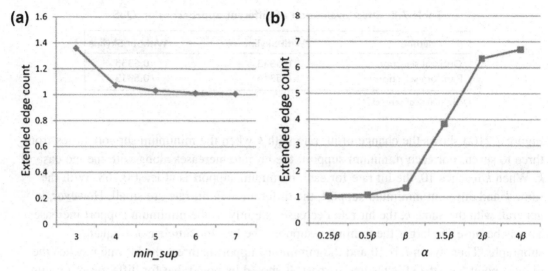

Figure 7.20
Effect evaluation on extended edge count.

the minimum support varies from three to seven, the suitable value of α is 2.516, 2.572, 2.676, 2.804, and 2.72. In Figure 7.20(b), the extended edge count increases along with the increase of α. This is because when α is small, the result of Eqn (7.3) is mainly affected by the support. The graphs with larger support often have fewer edges. It should be noted that the minimum support is set to 3 in Figure 7.20(b) (Table 7.7).

Then, we evaluate the hit rate of the recommendation that mainly considers functionality. That is to say, we concern the structure of the recommended composite web services (i.e., these corresponding composite service graphs). For one graph G_l in the test set, we denote its corresponding graph in the input set as G_s. Thus, $E(G_s) = \frac{1}{2}E(G_l)$. For G_s, we denote its list of recommended graphs as $RG_{G_{s,k}}$, in which k is the parameter limiting the number of frequent subgraphs recommended for users (mentioned in Section 7.4.2.3). If one graph in $RG_{G_{s,k}}$ is isomorphic to the corresponding subgraph in G_l, this recommendation is hit. For the entire test set and input set, there will be 1000 recommendations. We can get the number of hit recommendations, and the hit rate is the corresponding percentage.

Table 7.7: Average time of different approaches (ms)

Method	With Skyline	Without Skyline
Optimal selection	36.379	308.291
Random selection	0.661	0.661

Table 7.8: Effect evaluation of different approaches on QoS

Method	With Skyline	Without Skyline
Optimal selection	0.5333	0.5333
Random selection	0.5316	0.5313

QoS, quality of services.

Figure 7.21(a) shows the change of hit rate with k when the minimum support varies from three to seven. For each minimum support, the hit rate increases along with the increase of k. When k reaches 10, the hit rate for each minimum support is at least 0.768. With the same k and different minimum support, the differences in hit rate are small. However, in general, with the same k, the hit rate decreases slightly as the minimum support increases. This is because the larger the minimum support, the less the number of frequent subgraphs. Thus, when k is 10 and the minimum support is three, the hit rate reaches the highest point, i.e., the effectiveness is best. It should be noted that for different minimum support, the suitable value of α is set according to the method mentioned in Section 7.4.3.2.

We evaluate the impact of α on the hit rate, by setting the minimum support to three. The results are shown in Figure 7.21(b). For each value of α, the hit rate increases with the increase of k. With the same k, when $\alpha \geq \beta$ the hit rate decreases rapidly along with the increase of α. Because the result of Eqn (7.3) is mainly affected by the edge count, graphs for the recommendation should have more edges. However, the larger the number of edges, the smaller the support. Thus, the hit rate is low. With the same k, when $\alpha \geq \beta$, the difference in hit rate is small for a different α.

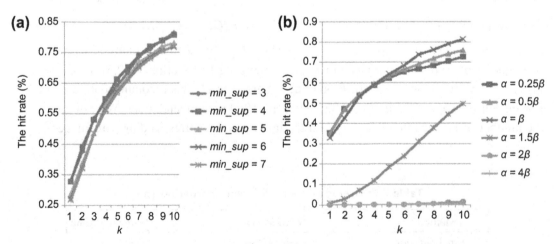

Figure 7.21
Effect evaluation on hit rate.

This is because the result of Eqn (7.3) is mainly affected by the support. However, when $k \geq 5$ and $\alpha \leq \beta$, with the same k, the hit rate increases as α increases. Thus, when $k > 5$, the suitable value of α, is β.

Furthermore, we evaluate the recommended composite web services' average QoS. The results are given in Table 7.8. For the optimal recommendation, these recommended composite web services' average QoS of the approach with skyline is the same with the one without skyline. That is to say, the optimal composite web service is in the candidates of the composite web services replaced with skyline services, which means our approach is feasible and correct. For the random recommendation, these recommended composite web services' average QoS is better with skyline, because skyline services' QoS is not worse than any service in the same cluster. These recommended composite web services' average QoS of the optimal recommendation is better than that of the random recommendation, which is consistent with our understanding.

7.5 Summary

The issue of web service composition has grown to be a hot topic and has attracted many researchers to work on it. This chapter first introduces a novel planning-graph-based algorithm to address the top-k QoS-aware automatic composition problem of semantic web services. This method cannot only return required solutions for users, but also gets top-k QoS solutions for users. Thus we can bring more convenience for users' selection and improve the availability of the composition solutions. Then a parallel composition method is introduced, which can avoid a performance bottleneck due to the explosion of the planning and searching space and improve the efficiency of automatic web service compositions with large-scale services. Finally, this chapter introduces a graph mining-based recommendation approach to model and explore the hidden knowledge to facilitate the users' service composition task.

In the future, with advancement of technologies and newly emerging concepts, we predict that service composition will be quite different. Traditionally, services are mostly running on enterprise servers. But along with the progress in modern smart devices, they can now become service providers as well. They can provide certain services that cannot be supplied by traditional providers. Services provided by mobile providers will be quite different from conventional computation-intensive services. They could be moving location-based or context-aware services' sensing and providing, through their sensors, immediate real world information. Furthermore, they can also act as intermediaries for people to enable them to become movable "human-provided services." Forced by these new trends, defining a new service model to substitute an obsolete triangle service-oriented architecture model is now required. Next, to composition, nonfunctional aspects uniquely belonging to mobile devices or applications, such as mobility prediction, may become a real concern for future mobile service composition, instead of the QoS or transaction property that are of interest in traditional composition works. Identifying and analyzing unknown mobile nonfunctional aspects is significant because, to modern software users, nonfunctional requirements are usually more important than prior functional requirements. In the future, a composite service probably may blend traditional as well as mobile services, and the architecture of the composite services may not always be a typical "pipe and filter." We imagine that how to define process and aggregate nonfunctional features will be a baffling problem.

References

[1] Z.H. Wu, S.G. Deng, Y. Li, J. Wu, Computing compatibility in dynamic service composition, Knowl. Inf. Syst. 19 (1) (2009) 107–129.

[2] J. Wu, L. Chen, Z.B. Zenf, M.R. Lyu, Z. Wu, Clustering web services to facilitate service discovery, Knowl. Inf. Syst. (2012) to appear.

[3] P.C. María, B. Rafael, S. Ismael, M.J. Aramburu, A semantic approach for the requirement-driven discovery of web resources in the life sciences, Knowl. Inf. Syst. (2012).

[4] M. Papazoglou, P. Traverso, S. Dustdar, F. Leymann, Service-oriented computing: state of the art and research challenges, IEEE Comput. 40 (11) (2007) 38–45.

[5] J. Peer, Web Service Composition as AI Planning—a Survey, 2005. http://logicstanford.edu/serviceplanning/readinglist/pfwsc.pdf.

[6] S. McIlraith, T.C. Son, Adapting Golog for composition of semantic web services, in: International Conference on Knowledge Representation and Reasoning, 2002, pp. 482–493.

[7] M. Phan, F. Hattori, Automatic web service composition using ConGolog, in: IEEE International Conference on Distributed Computing Systems Workshops, 2006, pp. 17–22.

[8] S.C. Oh, J.Y. Lee, S.H. Cheong, S.M. Lim, M.W. Kim, S.S. Lee, WSPR*: web-service planner augmented with A* algorithm, in: International Conference on Commerce and Enterprise Computing, 2009, pp. 515–518.

[9] S.C. Oh, B.W. On, E.J. Larson, D. Lee, BF*: web services discovery and composition as graph search problem, in: IEEE International Conference on e-Technology, e-Commerce and e-Service, 2005, pp. 784–786.

[10] B. Wu, S.G. Deng, Y. Li, J. Wu, J. Yin, AWSP: an automatic web service planner based on heuristic state space search, in: International Conference on Web Services, 2011, pp. 403–410.

[11] M. Naseri, A. Tomhidi, QoS-aware automatic composition of web services using AI planners, in: International Conference on Internet and Web Applications and Service, 2007, pp. 29–35.

[12] E. Sirina, B. Parsiab, D. Wu, J. Hendler, D. Nau, HTN planning for web service composition using SHOP2, Web Semant. Sci. Serv. Agents World Wide Web 1 (4) (2004) 377–396.

[13] I. Paik, D. Maruyama, Automatic web services composition using combining HTN and CSP, in: International Conference on Computer and Information Technology, 2007, pp. 206–211.

[14] K. Chen, J.Y. Xu, S. Reiff-Marganiec, Markov-HTN planning approach to enhance flexibility of automatic web services composition, in: International Conference on Web Services, 2009, pp. 9–16.

[15] Y. Li, J.L. Chen, Automatic composition of semantic web services—a theorem proof approach, in: Asian Conference on the Semantic Web, 2006, pp. 481–487.

[16] J.H. Rao, P. Kungas, M. Matskin, Application of linear logic to web service compo-sition, in: International Conference on Web Services, 2003, pp. 3–9.

[17] J.H. Rao, P. Kungas, M. Matskin, Logic-based web services composition: from service description to process model, in: International Conference on Web Services, 2004, pp. 446–453.

[18] X.R. Zheng, Y.H. Yan, An efficient syntactic web service composition algorithm based on the planning-graph model, in: International Conference on Web Services, 2008, pp. 691–699.

[19] S.C. Oh, D. Lee, S.R.T. Kumara, Web service planner (WSPR): an effective and scalable web service composition algorithm, Int. J. Web Serv. Res. 4 (1) (2007) 1–23.

[20] W.Q. Li, X.M. Dai, H. Jiang, Web services composition based on weighted planning-graph, in: International Conference on Networking and Distributed Computing, 2010, pp. 89–93.

[21] X.G. Li, Q.F. Zhao, Y. Dai, A semantic web service composition method based on an enhanced planning-graph, in: International Conference on e-Business and e-Government, 2010, pp. 2288–2291.

[22] Z.Q. Huang, W. Jiang, S.L. Hu, Z. Liu, Effective pruning algorithm for QoS-aware service composition, in: IEEE Conference on Commerce and Enterprise Computing, 2009, pp. 519–522.

[23] W. Jiang, C. Zhang, Z.Q. Huang, M. Chen, S. Hu, Z. Liu, QSynth: a tool for QoS-aware automatic service composition, in: International Conference of Web Services, 2010, pp. 42–49.

[24] S. Deng, B. Wu, J. Yin, Z. Wu, Efficient planning for top-K web service composition, Knowl. Inf. Syst. 36 (3) (2013) 579–605.

[25] S. Deng, L. Huang, B. Wu, L.R. Xiong, Parallel optimization for data-intensive service composition, J. Internet Technol. (2013).

[26] J. Wu, L. Chen, Y. Xie, L. Ji, Z. Wu, Modelling and exploring historical records to facilitate service composition, Int. J. Web Grid Serv. 10 (1) (2014) 54–79.

[27] S.-C. Oh, H. Kil, D. Lee, S.R. Kumara, WSBen: a web services discovery and composition benchmark, in: Proc. IEEE International Conference on Web Services, Salt Lake City, USA, July, 2006, pp. 239–248.

[28] K. Elgazzar, A.E. Hassan, P. Martin, Clustering WSDL documents to bootstrap the discovery of web services, in: 2010 IEEE International Conference on Web Services (ICWS 2010), 2010, pp. 147–154.

[29] R.L. Cilibrasi, P.M. Vitanyi, The Google similarity distance, IEEE Trans. Knowl. Data Eng. 19 (3) (2007) 370–383.

[30] D. Lin, An information-theoretic definition of similarity, in: Proc. of the 15th International Conference on Machine Learning (ICML 1998), 1998, pp. 296–304.

CHAPTER 8

Service Verification and Dynamic Reconfiguration

Chapter Outline

Service Computing: Concepts, Methods and Technology. http://dx.doi.org/10.1016/B978-0-12-802330-3.00008-4

8.1 Introduction

Presently, service composition has become an increasingly important way for IT enterprises to rapidly develop their applications that not only satisfy customer business requirements but also deliver an expected quality of service (QoS) [1,2]. However, developing various composite services is not the only critical step in service composition. To the best of our knowledge, two additionally urgent challenges have been addressed. One is how to verify whether the composed services can run correctly and achieve their predefined business goals [3,4]. The other is how to adjust service-based applications to meet highly dynamic environments (e.g., in a cloud environment) and fast-changing business requirements [5,6]. This chapter first gives an overview of service verification and dynamic reconfiguration. Then it introduces an approach to verify the substitutability between different granularity services. At last, it presents a quality of service (QoS)-driven dynamic reconfiguration method.

8.1.1 Overview of Service Verification

During the past years, service verification has become a significant research issue in service-oriented computing. Analyzing compatibility [3,4] and substitutability/ replaceability/equivalence [3,7−14] are of great importance to web services verification technology. Service compatibility allows for exploiting the correctness of the interactive relationship between two services. It is the key to ensure that web services, especially large granularity services, are run correctly and achieve their predefined business goals. Additionally, because composite services are by nature heterogeneous, dynamic, and collaborative, they can be recovered by service substitution when one or several of their component services fail. As a result, service substitutability/replaceability/ equivalence is a key for ensuring that a composite service, once assembled, can reliably run.

Since 2000 years, a large number of approaches for service verification exist [3,8−14]. Most of them are based on formal methods, such as Petri Net, automata, or process algebra, etc. Taher et al. [8] determined the similarity in two services based on their interface descriptions (specified in WSDL). This work assumed the formation of communities of services that provide similar functionality, and hence can be substituted by only analyzing syntactical and semantic similarity between services.

Furthermore, various efforts have been devoted to exploring the equivalence between web services at the behavioral level. Vallecillo and Vasconcelos et al. [9] showed how session types not only allow high-level specifications of complex object interactions, but also allow the definition of powerful interoperability tests at the protocol level, namely compatibility and substitutability of objects. The idea of simulation equivalence is applied by Benatallah et al. [10] for determining compatibility and substitutability of web services. Mario Bravetti and Gianluigi Zavattaro [11] related the theory of contracts with the notion of choreography conformance, used to check whether an aggregation of services correctly behaves according to a high level specification of their possible conversations. Filippo Bonchi and Antonio Brogi et al. [12] defined a new behavioral equivalence for web services, based on bisimilarity and inspired by recent advances in the theory of reactive systems, in which the proposed equivalence is compositional and decidable. Martens [3] defined the notion of equivalence based on that of usability of a module: a module N' simulates a module N if for each M that the composition of N and M is a weak sound, then the composition of N' and M is also a weak sound; N' and N are equivalent if N' and N simulate each other. Based on the behavioral analysis, Lucas Bordeaux et al. [13] proposed two types of substitutability: context-dependent and context-independent substitutability, in which the former requires that service N' is compatible with a particular M that is compatible with N; and the latter requires that N' is compatible with any M that is compatible with N. However, neither the formal condition of substitutability (i.e., replaceability) nor an algorithm for verifying substitutability is presented in most of the above-mentioned studies. It turns out to be quite hard to automatically analyze substitutability between web services according to these notions.

Researchers continued in-depth discussion on a clear and decidable notion of substitutability for web services. Based on the Petri-net theory, Xitong Li et al. [14] introduced a formal definition of context-independent similarity and showed that a web service can be substituted by an alternative peer of similar behavior without intervening other web services in the composition. Therefore, the cost of verifying service substitutability is largely reduced. Jyotishman Pathak et al. [7] determined substitutability of a service by reducing it to the satisfaction of the quotient mu-calculus formulas. Amit K. Chopra et al. [15] outlined an approach for verifying the correctness of commitment protocols and their compositions that exploits the well-known software engineering technique of model checking. Christian Stahl et al. [16] proposed three notions of substitutability for services and further presented a decision algorithm for substitutability based on the concept of an operating guideline, which is an abstract representation of all environments that a given service can cooperate with. Wombacher et al. [17] proposed to formalize a service with automata extended by logical expressions associated with states and the formalization that explicates message sequence and allows for more precise matchmaking than current approaches that are limited to matching only individual messages. However, it turns out to be a trace-based equivalence, which is too weak. Foster and Uchitel [18] discussed a model-based approach to verifying process interactions for coordinated web service compositions. The approach used finite state machine representations of web service orchestrations and assigns semantics to the distributed process interactions.

However, these approaches suffer from some limitations. First, most of them are limited to atomic or simple services, which can be called small granularity services. However, due to the significant progress of service composition technology, more and more composed services, which are called large granularity services, are being built at different platforms, published by different people, and possibly with different uses in mind. In contrast to the former, the latter have more complex business logic and provide more functions. Thus, it becomes a new challenge to judge the compatibility and substitutability between large granularity services or different granularity services. Second, most of the verification approaches can only better describe the behavior of services and exactly judge behavior substitutability. However, due to the lack of syntax and semantics, the existing approaches only capture the ordering of message exchanges in a service or multiple interactions between services. If two services with different functions have similar behavior, this may lead to an overestimate of their substitutability. Therefore, there is still a dearth of overall analysis and verification of web services from syntax, semantics, and behavior.

8.1.2 Overview of Dynamic Reconfiguration of Service-Based Application

In dynamic environments, service composition needs to support the recovery service-based applications from unexpected violations of not only function but also QoS. Therefore, holding the original overall QoS constraints of service-based applications has caused a big challenge that needs to be addressed. Up to now, although there existed many valuable works, most of these focused on providing essential services and functions in the presence of runtime environment changes [19−22]. With the ever increasing amount of service-based applications that are now adopted in a wide range of critical domains (such as, real-time system, navigation system, and online payment system), it has become increasingly important for enterprises to make service-based applications deliver a desirable QoS. Due to many inevitable factors, such as network fault, host exception, and replacement of failed component services, delivered QoS from service-based applications may not comply with their original claims at runtime. Once this happens, service-based applications should be recovered immediately to continue holding the original QoS. Moreover, most enterprises would like to recover their applications with lower cost and better efficiency, so that their customers undergo as few unexpected business shutdowns as possible. Thus, providing QoS consistent service-based applications has become a huge challenge.

Although service-based applications can be recovered by recomposition, service recomposition is extremely time-consuming and may lead to system shutdown, since the optimal service selection is an non-deterministic polynomial hard (NP-hard) problem [23]. Recently, researchers have introduced and extended the traditional dynamic reconfiguration technology [21] to service-based applications [19−21,24−26]. Some studies have looked at dynamic reconfiguration of service-based applications, but without considering QoS [19−21,26]. For example, Tsai et al. [19] presents an innovative dynamic reconfiguration technology that can be embedded into a service-oriented application to make the application reconfigurable. Onyeka Ezen-woye et al. [21] presented a hybrid model of service composition which supports the dynamic reconfiguration for data-intensive applications.

Recent works on dynamic reconfiguration for service composition have begun studies to hold the original overall QoS constraints. Yu et al. [25] presented an approach to conduct dynamic process reconfiguration under end-to-end QoS constraints. They use the replacement path idea to reconfigure a business process to avoid only one faulty service. Yanlong Zhai et al. [24] presented an approach for repairing multiple failed services by replacing them with new services and ensuring the new system satisfies the end-to-end QoS constraints. However, they only limit dealing with the case of violation of some of the component services. Due to some inevitable factors (such as, network fault, host exception), the delivered QoS from individual services may not always meet their predefined QoS at runtime. As a result, the delivered QoS from service-based applications may deviate from their initial QoS constraints. Once that happens, the methods in [24,25] will be invalid. This is due to the fact that with no service violations, reconfiguration regions cannot be found. Their idea is to construct a reconfiguration region based on only failure services and replace the services to meet the original QoS constraints in the region.

8.2 Service Verification

Considering service substitutability has become a significant research issue in service verification. In this section, we focus on the substitutability between different granularity services [27]. By analyzing the large granularity services, we found that not all inputs are imperative for clients to get some output. However, for an existing service model, each output is defaulted to be fully dependent on all the inputs. Thus, we propose the notion of interface inverted dependence to capture data dependencies from an output to inputs within a web service. Next, a formal model is built by Martin_Löf's type theory (MLTT) [28] to describe different granularity services from two aspects: input, output, precondition, and effect (IOPEs) and behavior. Due to the correspondence between types and logics, IOPEs are clearly described using existing types in MLTT, for example, dependent record type (DRT), product type, function type, etc. The formalism of DRT is applied to semantics of the services (ontological knowledge) to get a better expressivity. In addition, the service behavior type, proposed in our previous work [29], is improved to formalize the behavior of services. Besides our model, few existing models can describe not only the behavior of services, but also the syntax and semantics. And then the subtyping rules of the improved service behavior type are given. Based on these rules, we propose the notion of substitutability between different granularity services with different stringency through considering the context of services. Furthermore, because subtyping can be checked by a type checking mechanism, the substitutability can be determined automatically.

8.2.1 Basic Theory

8.2.1.1 Martin_Löf's type theory

MLTT [28] was originally developed with the aim of being a clarification of constructive mathematics, but unlike most other formalizations of mathematical type theory, it is not based on first-order predicate logic. Instead, predicate logic is interpreted within the type theory through the correspondence between propositions and sets. The idea behind propositions as sets is to identify a proposition with the set of its proofs. MLTT has a basic type and two type formers. The basic type is the type of sets. For each set S, the elements of S form a type.

Predicates and relationships are seen in type theory as functions yielding propositions as output. In addition to sets, propositions are inductively defined. So, a proposition is determined by the rules that construct its proofs. To prove a proposition P, we have to construct an object of type P. In other words, a proposition is true if we can build an object of type P, and it is false if the type P is not inhabited. We write "Prop" to refer to the type of propositions. Furthermore, the way propositions are introduced allows us to identify propositions and sets, and then we usually write "Set" instead of Prop.

In MLTT, there is a correspondence between types and logics. This is summarized in Table 8.1:

Table 8.1: The correspondence between types and logics

Logics	Types
$A\&B$	Product type ($\times$)
$A \vee B$	Sum type ($+$)
$A \rightarrow B$	Function type ($\prod(A,(x)B)$)
$\forall\, (x : A)B(x)$	Dependent product type ($\prod(x : A)B(x)$)
$\exists\, (x : A)B(x)$	Dependent sum type ($\sum(x : A)B(x)$)
False	Bottom type
True	Unit type

8.2.1.2 Dependent record types

DRT [30] is an extension of dependent product types ($\prod$-type) and dependent sum types ($\sum$-type), in which types are expressed in terms of data. DRT is much more flexible than simple dependent types such as $\prod$-types and $\sum$-types.

The syntax of DRT is extended with record types $\langle\rangle$ and $\langle R;\ l:A\rangle$ and records $\langle\rangle$ and $\langle r;\ l=a:A\rangle$, in which we overload $\langle\rangle$ to stand for both the empty record type and the empty record. Records are associated with two operations: *field selection r.l* that selects the field labeled by l and *first projection* (or *restriction*) $[r]$ that removes the last component of record r.

Figure 8.1 provides the rules for DRT. L is a finite set of labels. *RType* denotes all DRTs.

Formation Rules	Introduction Rules	Elimination Rules	Equality Rules
$\dfrac{\Gamma valid}{\Gamma\mid-\langle\ \rangle:RType[\phi]}$	$\dfrac{\Gamma valid}{\Gamma>\langle\ \rangle:\langle\ \rangle}$	$\dfrac{\Gamma>r:\langle R,l:A\rangle}{\Gamma>[r]:R}$	$\dfrac{\Gamma>\langle r,l=a:A\rangle:\langle R,l:A\rangle}{\Gamma>[\langle r,l=a:A\rangle]=r:R}$
$\dfrac{\Gamma>R:RType[L]\quad \Gamma>A:(R)Type\ l\notin L}{\Gamma>\langle R,l:A\rangle:RType[L\cup\{l\}]}$	$\dfrac{\Gamma>\langle R,l:A\rangle:RType\quad \Gamma>r:R\ \Gamma\quad a:A(r)}{\Gamma>\langle r,l=a:A\rangle:\langle R,l:A\rangle}$	$\dfrac{\Gamma>r:\langle R,l:A\rangle}{\Gamma>r.l:A([r])}$	$\dfrac{\Gamma>\langle r,l=a:A\rangle:\langle R,l:A\rangle}{\Gamma>\langle r,l=a:A\rangle.l=a:A(r)}$

Figure 8.1
Rules for DRT.

8.2.2 Modeling for Different Granularity Services

Currently, the models of web services have evolved from traditional black-box models, such as WSDL, into multiviews models, such as OWL-S (http://www.w3.org/Submission/OWL-S/) and WSMO (http://www.w3.org/Submission/WSMO/). The latter describes every aspect of web services by defining the different profiles. However, they still regard a service as a whole. As a result, to use a service, you need to provide all the inputs of the service to get some output of the service. Although they cater for the specification of the small granularity services, the large-granularity services are not clearly described. Because not all inputs are compulsory for each output for large-granularity services, too strict criteria for service substitutability may be introduced.

To avoid the limitation of existing service models, we propose a new model of services using the notion of interface inverted dependence (proposed in Section 3.2). The model can clearly describe not only the small granularity services but also the large granularity services. Some basic definition should be given first before the model is introduced.

8.2.2.1 Basic definition

8.2.2.1.1 IOPEs of web services

The functions of services are often described by IOPEs. IOPEs involve not only syntactic information of services interfaces, but also their semantic information. To describe syntactic and semantic information, we give some necessary definitions as follows.

Definition 1: Domain-specific term. Given a set of labels, $L \equiv \{l_1, ..., l_n\}$, and all terms $\{c_1, ..., c_n\}$ in the ontology U, for $\forall ci \in U$, and the DRT $C := \langle R, l: L \rangle$, c_i is an object of C.

Inspired by the work [29], definition 1 applies the formalism of DRT to ontological knowledge (domain-specific term) to get a better expressivity. DRT realizes a continuum of precision from the basic assertions we are used to expect from types, up to a complete specification of a representation (e.g., a context). Also, DRT can gather all the knowledge related to a semantic concept within a single structure.

The following example is given to show how to formalize ontological knowledge. Figure 8.2 provides a part of ontology for a travel domain.

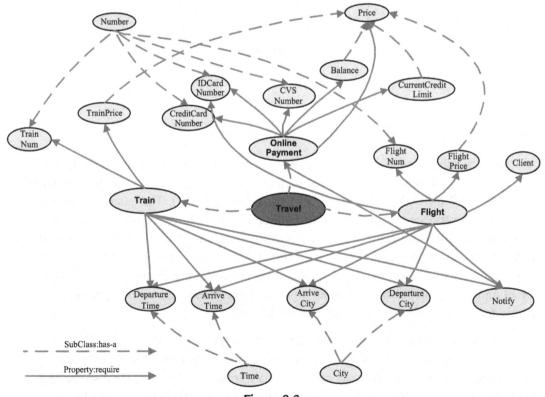

Figure 8.2
The partial ontology for a travel domain.

The domain-specific term in Figure 8.2 is formalized as:

1. DepartureCity = $\langle$l$_1$: City, l$_2$: $\sum$(Train, Require), l$_3$: $\sum$(Flight, Require)$\rangle$
2. ArriveCity = $\langle$l$_1$: City, l$_2$: $\sum$(Train, Require), l$_3$: $\sum$(Flight, Require)$\rangle$
3. CreditCardNumber = $\langle$l$_1$: Number, l$_2$: $\sum$(OnlinePayment, Require)$\rangle$
4. CVSNumber = $\langle$l$_1$:Number, l$_2$: $\sum$(OnlinePayment, Require)$\rangle$
5. Client = $\langle$l$_1$: $\sum$(Flight, Require)$\rangle$
6. ArriveTime = $\langle$l$_1$: Time, l$_2$: $\sum$(Train, Require), l$_3$: $\sum$(Flight, Require)$\rangle$
7. DepartureTime = $\langle$l$_1$: Time, l$_2$: $\sum$(Train, Require), l$_3$: $\sum$(Flight, Require)$\rangle$
8. TrainNumber = $\langle$l$_1$: Number, l$_2$: $\sum$(Train, Require)$\rangle$
9. TrainPrice = $\langle$l$_1$: Price, l$_2$: $\sum$(Train, Require)$\rangle$
10. FlightNumber = $\langle$l$_1$: Number, l$_2$: $\sum$(Flight, Require)$\rangle$
11. FlightPrice = $\langle$l$_1$: Price, l$_2$: $\sum$(Flight, Require)$\rangle$
12. CurrentCreditlimit = $\langle$l$_1$: Price, l$_2$: $\sum$(OnlinePayment, Require)$\rangle$
13. Balance = $\langle$l$_1$: Price, l$_2$: $\sum$(OnlinePayment, Require)$\rangle$
14. IDCardNumber = $\langle$l$_1$: Number, l$_2$: $\sum$(OnlinePayment, Require), l$_3$: $\sum$(Flight, Require)$\rangle$
15. Notify = $\langle$l$_1$: $\sum$(Train, Require), l$_2$: $\sum$(OnlinePayment, Require), l$_3$: $\sum$(Flight, Require)$\rangle$

Inputs and outputs specify the data transformation produced by one service.

Definition 2: Input of service. Given a service S and the set $I \equiv \{i_1, ..., i_n\}$ of all its inputs, for $\forall i_i \in I$, i_i is an object of the product type $ION \times c_i$, denoted as $i_i \equiv \langle n_i, r_i \rangle$: $ION \times c_i$, in which ION is name type, $ION := Name:Type$.

Definition 3: Output of service. Given a service S and the set $O \equiv \{o_1, ..., o_n\}$ of all its outputs, for any o_i in O, o_i is an object of the product type $ION \times c_i$, denoted as $o_i \equiv \langle n_i, r_i \rangle :ION \times c_i$, in which ION is name type, $ION := Name:Type$.

Using a product type, one input or output is defined as a pair which contains two elements, the name and the corresponding semantics. The ordinary projection operators are defined by: $fst\langle x,y \rangle = x$, $snd\langle x,y \rangle = y$.

Based on the relevance of elements in pairs, such pairs can represent that the semantics is annotated to each input or output of a service in definitions 2 and 3.

By definitions 2 and 3, the inputs and outputs of service FT in Figure 8.3 can be formalized as:

I$_{FT}$ = {$\langle$Date,Time$\rangle$, $\langle$DCity,DepartureCity$\rangle$, $\langle$ACity,ArriveCity$\rangle$, $\langle$CCnum, CreditCardNumber$\rangle$, $\langle$CVSnum,CVSNumbe$\rangle$, $\langle$Fnum,Number$\rangle$, $\langle$Fprice,Price$\rangle$, $\langle$CName,Client$\rangle$, $\langle$CID,IDCardNumber$\rangle$}

O$_{FT}$··$\langle$FATime, ArriveTime$\rangle$··$\langle$FDTime, DepartureTime$\rangle$ · $\langle$Fnum, Number$\rangle$ · $\langle$FPrice, Price$\rangle$,$\langle$··x,CurrentCreditlimit$\rangle$,$\langle$Available, balance$\rangle$,$\langle$FInfo, Notify$\rangle$·

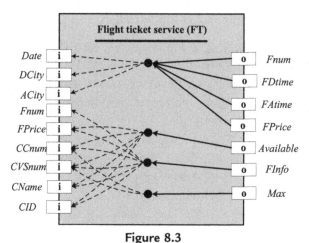

Figure 8.3
Inverted interface dependence of service *FT*.

A service can be performed correctly unless the precondition is true. Thus, the precondition should be a boolean expression.

Definition 4: Precondition. Precondition is defined as *P:=bexp:Type*, in which *bexp* is a boolean expression.

Effect of service shows what result will be produced for some given condition. Thus, we can use function type to formalize it.

Definition 5: Effect. Effect of service is denoted as $E \equiv \prod(A,(x)O_r)$, in which A:Type, $x \in O_r$, and $O_r \equiv \{o_1, ..., o_n\}$.

Effect is defined as a function type that returns the elements in O_r (some output of one service). For example, the function $(\lambda(s: Int).\text{if } s > 0 \text{ then } O.l_i = s - 1 \text{ else } O.l_i = s + 1)$ is the object of E.

8.2.2.1.2 Behavior of web services

The behavior of a service can clearly show how a service interacts with other services. This has been an important aspect related to specification of services. Currently, many existing formal approaches have focused on behavioral analysis. However, those approaches only regard the behavior of service as the sequences of abstract message passing. Due to a lack of semantics, they may overestimate the substitutability between services.

To solve the problem, we improve the service of the behavior type, which is proposed in our previous study [31], by: (1) introducing a domain-specific term *C*; (2) adding an assignment type and redefining the loop type; (3) reviewing the operational semantics; and (4) redefining the subtyping rules of the service behavior type. The two latter improvements will be introduced in Section 8.4. The syntax of the improved service behavior type is as follows:

T: Service Behavior Type:=

```
|BSkip: T |BAss: ION → ION → T | BAss: ION → T | BSeq:Seq T
|BRev: ⟨l₁: ION,.......,lₓ: ION ⟩→T
| BSed: ⟨l₁: ION,...,lₓ: ION ⟩→T
|BAny: T → T → T |BIf: bexp → T→ T → T
|BWhile: bexp → T→ T
```

where ION: = Name: Type

BSkip is the Skip Type and represents inaction. For our convenience, it is denoted as τ.

BAss is the Assignment Type. It represents the fact that some output of a service is assigned to some input of another service and is denoted as $n_i = n_j$.

BSeq is the Sequence Type. It represents the sequence pattern in a composition or the behavior of a service and is denoted as $\{c_1;c_2\}$.

BRev is the Input Type. It represents a message sequence that is received and is denoted as $\downarrow \langle l_1:fst(m_1), ..., l_n:fst(m_n)\rangle$, where $m_1, ..., m_n$: M, M:=ION × C, The definition of C refers to Section 8.2.1.1.

BSed is the Output Type. It represents the fact that a message sequence is sent. It can be denoted as $\uparrow \langle l_1:fst(m_1), ..., l_n:fst(m_n)\rangle$.

BAny is the Parallel Type. It represents a parallel pattern in a composition or the behavior of a service and is denoted as $(b,h_1||h_2||...)$, in which $b:Int$, $h_1,h_2:T$.

BIf is the Selection Type. It represents a select pattern in a composition or the behavior of a service and is denoted as $\{If\ b\ then\ c\ else\ d\}$, in which $b:bexp$, $c:T,d:T$.

BWhile is the Loop Type. It represents a loop pattern in a composition or the behavior of a service and is denoted as $\{While\ b\ do\ c\}$, in which $b:bexp$, $c:T$.

Definition 6: Service behavior. Given a service S, the behavior $\mathbb{B}_s$ of S is an object of T, denoted as $\mathbb{B}_s:T$.

8.2.2.2 Interface inverted dependence

The notion of interface inverted dependence shows which inputs of a service have to be provided to produce one output of that service. It captures data dependencies from an output to inputs within a service, especially, a large granularity service.

Figure 8.3 provides the interface inverted dependencies of the service *FT* that provides the flight querying and the flight ticket booking. The users can pay for their tickets by credit cards. Given a departure date (*Date*), a departure city (*DCity*), and an arrival city (*ACity*), providing the flight number (*Fnum*), the departure time (*FDtime*), the arrival time, and (*FAtime*) provides the ticket price (*FPrice*) of all available flights. Given the flight number (*Fnum*), the ticket price (*FPrice*), a credit card number (*CCnum*), the CVS number of the credit card (*CVSnum*), the name of the owner holding the credit card (*CName*), and his ID card number (*CID*), providing the credit limit (*max*), the balance (*Avaiable*), and a flight ticket reservation notice (*FInfo*). The effect shows that the balance (*available*) is equal to the credit limit (*max*) minus the flight ticket (*FPrice*) when credit limit (*Max*) is greater than the flight ticket (*FPrice*). In the right area of Figure 8.3, all outputs of the service *FT* are shown. In its left area, all inputs of the service are shown. The arrows show these inputs are indispensable to some output.

Service *FT* can be viewed as a large-granularity service due to the various functions that are involved. Through the inverted interface dependences of service *FT*, clients can use some or all of the functions, for example, querying a flight or booking flight tickets or both querying a flight and booking a flight ticket. Thus, inverted interface dependence can give more clear descriptions of their functions for both small and large granularity services.

Definition 7: Interface inverted dependence. Given a service *S*, the set *I* of inputs of *S*, the set *O* of outputs of *S*, an interface inverted dependence d_i of *S* is an object of *D*, denoted as $d_i{:}D$, in which:

> *D* is the record type, $D := \langle I: \langle l_1 : I_r, l_2 = p : P \rangle, \; O: \langle l_1 : n'_i, l_2 = e: E \rangle \rangle$;
> n'_i is the name of some output o_i of *S*, and $n'_i = fst\,(o_i)$;
> I_r is the set of the indispensable inputs, in order to get o_i, and $I_r = \{\, fst(i_1),\ \ldots,\ fst(i_m)\,\}$;
> *e* is the effect of o_i;
> *p* is the precondition.

Then, the set DI_s of all interface inverted dependences of *S* can be obtained and denoted as $\mathbb{R}_s \equiv \{d_j | 1 \le j \le n\}$.

The interface inverted dependence of Service *FT* can be formalized as:

```
d₁≡ ⟨I= ⟨l₁={DCity,ACity,Date}),O= ⟨l₁=FATime⟩⟩
d₂≡ ⟨I= ⟨l₁=⟨DCity,ACity,Date}),O= ⟨l₁=FDTime⟩⟩
d₃≡ ⟨I= ⟨l₁=⟨DCity,ACity,Date}),O= ⟨l₁=FPrice⟩⟩
d₄≡ ⟨I= ⟨l₁={DCity,ACity,Date})i0= ⟨l₁=FNum⟩⟩
d₅≡ ⟨I= ⟨l₁={CCnum,CVSnum}),O=⟨l₁= Max⟩⟩
d₆≡ ⟨I=⟨l₁={CCnum,CVSnum,CName,CID,Fnum,FPrice}), O= ⟨l₁=Available,l₂=· x: balance,
      y: flightprice, z: currentcreditlimit. If z.l₄≥y.l₂ then x.l₄=z.l4 −y.l₂)⟩
d₇≡ ⟨I= ⟨l₁={CCnum,CVSnum,CName,CID,Fnum, FPrice}), O=⟨l₁=FInfo⟩⟩
```

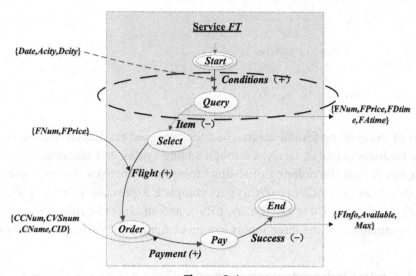

Figure 8.4
The business logic of service *FT*.

Thus, the set of interface inverted dependence of service *FT* can be obtained and denoted as $\mathbb{R}_{FT} \equiv \{d_j | 1 \leq j \leq 7\}$.

8.2.2.3 Modelling for different granularity services

Based on the above-mentioned definitions, the model is proposed for specification of different granularity services in this section.

Definition 8: Complete service behavior. Given a service *S*, if the behavior covers all business logics of *S*, it is defined as the complete behavior of *S* and denoted as $\mathbb{B}_s^c$, in which $\mathbb{B}_s^c : T$.

Figure 8.4 provides the complete business logic of service *FT*. It first receives the querying requests from clients. If the satisfied results are queried, the flight information is returned to the clients. Then, the clients select the satisfied flight and input their bank account information to pay for the ticket. If the payment is completed, the ticket information is sent to the clients. In Figure 8.4, "+" denotes message receiving and "−" denotes message sending. By definition 8, the complete behavior of service *FT* can be formalized using the improved service behavior type as follows:

$\mathbb{B}_{FT} ::= \{\alpha; \beta\}$:BSeq
$\alpha :: = \downarrow \langle l_1 = \text{Date}, l_2 = \text{ACity}, l_3 = \text{DCity} \rangle$:BRev
$\beta :: = \{\varphi; \varepsilon\}$:BSeq
$\varphi :: = \uparrow \langle l_1 = \text{FNum}, l_2 = \text{FPrice}, l_3 = \text{FDtime}, l_4 = \text{FAtime} \rangle$:BSed
$\varepsilon :: = \{\pi; \kappa\}$:BSeq

$\Pi::=\downarrow\langle l_1 = \text{FNum}, l_2 = \text{FPrice}\rangle$:BRev
$\kappa::=\{\lambda;\psi\}$:BSeq
$\lambda::=\downarrow\langle l_1 = \text{CCNum}, l_2 = \text{CVSNum}, l_3 = \text{CName}, l_4 = \text{CID}\rangle$:BRev
$\psi::=\text{if currentcreditlimit}.l_4 \geq \text{FlightPrice}.l_2 \text{ then } \gamma$:BIf
$\gamma::=\{\nu;\rho\}$:BSeq
$\nu::=\uparrow\langle l_1 = \text{FInfo}, l_2 = \text{Available}, l_3 = \text{Max}\rangle$:BSed
$\rho::=\tau$:BSkip

Unlike most of the existing formal approaches, the proposed service behavior type can describe the business logics of services through adding syntax and semantics information, rather than the ordering of abstract message exchanges. For example, for $\alpha: = \downarrow\langle l_1 = Date, l_2 = ACity, l_3 = DCity\rangle$, its complete expression is $\alpha::=\downarrow\langle l_1 = \langle Date, \text{Time}\rangle, l_2 = \langle ACity, City\rangle, l_3 = \langle DCity, City\rangle\rangle$, and an object of *BRev* type. And then, the semantics of the three inputs can be computed by the *snd* operation of the pairs.

Definition 9: Context-independent service model. Given a service S, the set $\mathbb{R}_s$ of all its interface inverted dependences, and its complete behavior $\mathbb{B}_s^c$, the context-independent model of S is denoted as $S \equiv \langle \mathbb{R}_s, \mathbb{B}_s^c \rangle$.

Definition 10: Partial service behavior. Given a service S, all its interface inverted dependences $\mathbb{R}_s \equiv \{d_j | 1 \leq j \leq n\}$, and $\mathbb{R}_s$ is the subset of $\mathbb{R}'_s$, if the behavior covers the business logics of S, which are triggered by the inputs involved in DI'_s and all the product outputs involved in $\mathbb{R}'_s$, it is defined as a partial behavior of S corresponding to $\mathbb{R}'_s$ and is denoted as $\mathbb{B}_s^{\mathbb{R}'_s}$, in which $\mathbb{B}_s^{\mathbb{R}'_s}: T$.

For example, in the dashed ellipse in Figure 8.3, the partial behavior of *FT* can be described as:

$\mathbb{B}_{FT}^{\mathbb{R}'_s} ::= \{\alpha;\beta\}$:BSeq
$\alpha::=\downarrow\langle l_1 = Date, l_2 = ACity, l_3 = DCity\rangle$:BRev
$\beta::=\uparrow\langle l_1 = \text{FNum}, l_2 = \text{FPrice}, l_3 = \text{FDtime}, l_4 = \text{FAtime}\rangle$:BSed

in which $\mathbb{R}'_s = \{d_j | 1 \leq j \leq 4\}$.

Definition 11: Context-dependent service model. Given a composition M, its component service S, the set $\mathbb{R}'_s$ of the interface inverted dependences of S in M, and the partial behavior $\mathbb{B}_s^{\mathbb{R}'_s}$ of S in M, then the context-dependent model of S in M is denoted as $S^M \equiv \langle \mathbb{R}'_s, \mathbb{B}_s^{\mathbb{R}'_s} \rangle$.

8.2.3 Determining Substitutability between Different Granularity Services

In this section, we propose the notions of substitutability between different granularity services with different stringencies through considering the context of services based on subtyping theory.

8.2.3.1 *Subtyping rules for semantics of services*

Definition 12: Semantics subtyping. Given $c_i, c_j : C$, there can only exist the coercion $\Phi: \langle R, l:A \rangle \rightarrow R$, so that c_i is a subtype of c_j, denoted as $c_i <:_c c_j$.

In definition 12, coercive subtyping for dependent-type theories is introduced. In coercive subtyping, A is a subtype of B if there is a coercion $c: (A)B$, expressed by $A <:_c B$. In other words, if A is a subtype of B via coercion c, then any object of type A can be regarded as (an abbreviation of) the object $c(a)$ of type B [30].

Theorem 1: Transitivity of semantics subtyping. Let $c_1, c_2, c_3 : C$, if $c_1 <:_c c_2$ and $c_2 <:_c c_3$, $c_1 <:_c c_3$.

Proof: Using proof by contradiction, the theorem obviously holds.

Definition 13: Semantics similarity. Given the set $U \equiv \{c_1, ..., c_n\}$ of all terms in an ontology G, and $c_i, c_j, c_k : C$, if they satisfy the conditions as follows:

1. $c_i <:_c c_j$;
2. $c_i <:_c ... <:_c c_k$ and $c_j <:_c ... <:_c c_k$,

then the terms c_i is similar with c_j.

8.2.3.2 *Subtyping rules of the improved service behavior type*

8.2.3.2.1 Operation semantics of the improved service behavior type

The section introduces the operation semantics of the improved service behavior type.

$seval$:Type: $=$

```
BESkip|BEAss|BESeq|BESed|BERev|BEAny|BEIfTrue|BEIfFalse|BEWhileEnd|BEWhileLoop
BESkip:BESkip →T:=···
···ss:BAss →T:= forall n₁ n₂ l, BEAss l n₁ → BEAss n₂ l, where n₁ n₂:ION, l:DataType
BESeq:BSeq →T:= forall t₁ t₂...tₙ,vseqrec({t₁ t₂...tₙ},a,e)→seval a, where t₁,
                t₂,...,tₙ:T
BESed:BSed →M:=forall m₁ m₂...mₙ t, ⟨l₁:fst(m₁),...,lₙ:fst(mₙ)⟩.l→t, where m₁ m₂,...,mₙ:M,
                M:ION × C, t:T, the definition of C seen in Section 2.1
BERev:BRev →M:=forall n₁ n₂ ... nₙ t,⟨l₁:fst(n₁),...,lₙ:fst(nₙ)⟩.l→t, where n₁,
                n₂,...,nₙ:M, M:ION × C, t: T
BEAny:BAny→T:= forall t₁ t₂...tₙ, aeval b=i→seval t₁, where t₁ t₂,...,tₙ:T, b, i:Int
BEIfTrue:BIf→T:=forall b₁ t₁ t₂,beval b₁ = true → seval t₁, where b₁:bexp,t₁,t₂:T
BEIfFalse:BIf→T:=forall b₁ t₁ t₂,beval b₁ = false → seval t₂, where b₁:bexp, t₁, t₂:T
BEWhileEnd:BWhile→T:=forall b₁ t₁,beval b₁ = false → seval t₁, where b₁:bexp, t₁,
                t₂:T
BEWhileLoop:BWhile→id→T:=forall b₁ t₁,beval b₁ = true → seval t₁ →seval, while b₁ do
                t₁, where b₁:bexp, t₁ : T
```

S-Seq:

$$\frac{t,s : BSeq \quad BESeq\ t <: BESeq\ s}{t <: s}$$

S-Any:

$$\frac{\begin{array}{l} t,s : BAny \\ t = (a, t_1 \| ... \| t_n) \\ s = (b, s_1 \| ... \| s_{m+n}) \\ \forall a.BEAny\ t <: \exists b.BEAny\ s \end{array}}{t <: s}$$

S-Sed:

$$\frac{t,s : BSed \quad snd(BESed\ t) <:_c snd(BESed\ s)}{t <: s}$$

S-Sel1:

$$\frac{\begin{array}{l} t,s : BIf \\ t = \text{If } b_1 \text{ then } c_1 \text{ esle } c_2 \\ s = \text{If } b'_1 \text{ then } c'_1 \text{ esle } c'_2 \\ b_1 \to b'_1 \\ BEIfTrue\ t <: BEIfTrue\ s \\ BEIfFalse\ t <: BEIfFalse\ s \end{array}}{t <: s}$$

S-Sel2:

$$\frac{\begin{array}{l} t,s : BIf \\ t = \text{If } b_1 \text{ then } c_1 \text{ esle } c_2 \\ s = \text{If } b'_1 \text{ then } c'_1 \text{ esle } c'_2 \\ b_1 \to \neg b'_1 \\ BEIfTrue\ t <: BEIfFalse\ s \\ BEIfFalse\ t <: BEIfTrue\ s \end{array}}{t <: s}$$

S-Rev:

$$\frac{t,s : BRev \quad snd(BESed\ t) <:_c snd(BESed\ s)}{t <: s}$$

S-Sel3:

$$\frac{t : BIf \quad s : T \quad BEIfFalse\ t <:\ s}{t <: s}$$

S-Sel4:

$$\frac{t : BIf \quad s : T \quad BEIfTure\ t <:\ s}{t <: s}$$

S-Sel5:

$$\frac{t : BIf \quad s : T \quad s <:\ BEIfFalse\ t}{s <: t}$$

S-Sel6:

$$\frac{t : BIf \quad s : T \quad s <:\ BEIfTure\ t}{s <: t}$$

S-WhileR:

$$\frac{s : T \quad t : BWhile \quad s <: BEWhileLoop\ t}{s <: t}$$

S-WhileL:

$$\frac{s : T \quad t : BWhile \quad BEWhileLoop\ t <: s}{t <: s}$$

S-While:

$$\frac{\begin{array}{l} s,t : BWhile \\ s = \text{While } a \text{ do } b \\ t = \text{While } a' \text{ do } b' \\ a \to a' \\ BEWhileLoop\ s <: BEWhileLoop\ t \end{array}}{s <: t}$$

S-Idle:

$$\frac{}{T <: \tau}$$

Figure 8.5

The subtyping rules of services behavior types.

In *BEAny*, the parameter b is used to decide which parallel branch is run. b is the index of a branch in a parallel pattern. In *BEWhileLoop*, the parameter i is used to assign the times of a loop.

8.2.3.2.2 Subtyping rules of the improved service behavior type

Based on these operation semantics, the subtyping rules of the improved service behavior type are given in Figure 8.5. The meaning of these rules is also easy to understand, we also do not cover them in detail here due to limited space.

Theorem 2: Transitivity of service behavior type. Let $t_1, t_2, t_3 : T$; if $t_1 <: t_2$ and $t_2 <: t_3$, $t_1 <: t_3$.

Proof: Using proof by contradiction, the theorem obviously holds.

8.2.3.3 Defining substitutability between different granularity services

This section provides the notions of the substitutability that have different stringencies, considering the context of a composition and catering for different granularity services.

Definition 14: Context-independent substitutability of complete IOPEs. Given service $s_1 \equiv \langle R_{s_1}, \mathbb{B}^c_{s_1} \rangle$ and $s_2 \equiv \langle R_{s_2}, \mathbb{B}^c_{s_1} \rangle$, the sets of all inputs of s_1 and s_2 are $I_1 = \{i_1, ..., i_n\}$ and $I_2 = \{i'_1, ..., i'_m\}$, respectively, and the sets of all outputs of s_1 and s_2 are $O_1 = \{o_1, ..., o_p\}$ and $O_2 = \{o'_1, ..., o'_q\}$, respectively, if $\exists O'_1 \subset O_1, O'_2 \subset O_2$, and satisfy:

1. for $\forall oi \in O'_1, \exists o'_i \in O'_2, snd(o_i) <<: snd(o'_i)$ holds;
2. for $\forall i'_i \in I'_2, \exists i_i \in I'_1, snd(i_i) <<: snd(i'_i)$ holds;

Then s_2 can substitute for s_1 on the complete IOPEs of s_1, denoted as $s_2 \sim {}_w s_1$.

Definition 15: Context-independent substitutability of complete behavior. Given service $s_1 \equiv \langle R_{s_1}, \mathbb{B}^c_{s_1} \rangle$ and $s_2 \equiv \langle R_{s_2}, \mathbb{B}^c_{s_1} \rangle$, for some behavior $\mathbb{B}_{s_2}$ of s_2, if $\mathbb{B}^c_{s_1} <: \mathbb{B}_{s_2}$, s_2 can substitute s_1 on the complete behavior of s_1, denoted as $s_2 \sim {}_n s_1$.

Definition 16: Context-independent substitutability of partial IOPEs. Given service $s_1 \equiv \langle R_{s_1}, \mathbb{B}^c_{s_1} \rangle$ and $s_2 \equiv \langle R_{s_2}, \mathbb{B}^c_{s_1} \rangle$, the sets of all inputs of s_1 and s_2 are $I_1 = \{i_1, ..., i_n\}$ and $I_2 = \{i'_1, ..., i'_m\}$, respectively, and the sets of all outputs of s_1 and s_2 are $O_1 = \{o_1, ..., o_p\}$ and $O_2 = \{o'_1, ..., o'_q\}$, respectively, if $\exists O'_1 \subset O_1, O'_2 \subset O_2$ and satisfy:

1. for $\forall oi \in O'_1, \exists o'_i \in O'_2, snd(o_i) <<: snd(o'_i)$ holds;
2. for $\forall o'_i \in O'_2, \exists o_i \in O'_1, snd(o_i) <<: snd(o'_i)$ holds;
3. Let $\mathfrak{R}'_{s1}$ and $\mathfrak{R}'_{s2}$ be respectively the sets of interface inverted dependences of s_1 and s_2 corresponding to O'_1 *and* O'_2, the compulsive inputs of s_1 and s_2 are $I'_1 \subset I_1$ and $I'_2 \subset I_2$, respectively, for $\forall i'_i \in I'_2, \exists i_i \in I'_1, snd(i_i) <<: snd(i'_i)$ holds, then s_2 can substitute s_1 on $\mathbb{R}'_{s_1}$ and $\mathbb{R}'_{s_2}$, denoted as $s_2 \approx {}_w s_1$.

Definition 17: Context-independent substitutability of partial behavior. Given service $s_1 \equiv \langle R_{s_1}, \mathbb{B}^c_{s_1} \rangle$ and $s_2 \equiv \langle R_{s_2}, \mathbb{B}^c_{s_1} \rangle$, for the partial behavior $\mathbb{B}_{s_1}^{R'_{s_1}}$ of s_1 and $\mathbb{B}_{s_2}^{R'_{s_2}}$ of s_2, if $\mathbb{B}_{s_1}^{R'_{s_1}} <: \mathbb{B}_{s_2}^{R'_{s_2}}$, s_2 can substitute s_1 on the partial behavior $\mathbb{B}_{s_1}^{R'_{s_1}}$ of s_1 and $\mathbb{B}_{s_2}^{R'_{s_2}}$ of s_2, denoted as $s_2 \approx {}_n s_1$.

Definition 18: Context-dependent substitutability of IOPEs. Given a composition M, its component service $s_1 \equiv \langle R_{s_1}, \mathbb{B}^c_{s_1} \rangle$ and $s_2 \equiv \langle R_{s_2}, \mathbb{B}^c_{s_1} \rangle$, the set of all inputs of s_2 is $I_2 = \{i'_1, ..., i'_m\}$, and the set of all outputs of s_2 is $O_2 = \{o'_1, ..., o'_q\}$. Let the part of s_1 in

M be $s_1^M \equiv \langle \mathbb{R}'_{s_1}, \mathbb{B}_{s_1}^{\mathbb{R}'_{s_1}} \rangle$, the sets of the inputs and outputs s_1 in M are $I_M = \{i_1, ..., i_n\}$ and $O_M = \{o_1, ..., o_p\}$ respectively. If:

1. for $\forall o_i \in O'_M$, $\exists o'_i \in O'_2$, $snd(o_i) <<: snd(o'_i)$ holds;
2. for $\forall i'_i \in IM$, $\exists i_i \in I'_i$, $snd(i_i) <<: snd(i'_i)$ holds,

then under the context of M, s_2 can substitute s_1 on IOPEs, denoted as $s_2 \infty_w^M s_1$.

Definition 19: Context-dependent substitutability of behavior. Given a composition M, its component service $s_1 \equiv \langle \mathbb{R}_{s_1}, \mathbb{B}_{s_1}^c \rangle$ and $s_2 \equiv \langle \mathbb{R}_{s_2}, \mathbb{B}_{s_2}^c \rangle$, Let part of s_1 in M be $s_1^M \equiv \langle \mathbb{R}'_{s_1}, \mathbb{B}_{s_1}^{\mathbb{R}'_{s_1}} \rangle$, if there exits $\mathbb{B}_{s_2}$, and $\mathbb{B}_{s_1}^{\mathbb{R}'_s} <: \mathbb{B}_{s_2}$, then under the context of M, s_2 can substitute s_1 on the behavior, denoted as $s_2 \infty_n^M s_1$.

From definitions 14−19, we can find some important relationships between different notions of substitutability as follows: (1) substitutability on behavior is stricter and implies substitutability of IOPEs; (2) substitutability on the complete IOPEs or behavior is stricter than substitutability of the partial IOPEs or behavior; (3) context-independent substitutability is stricter than context-dependent substitutability; and (4) context-dependent substitutability on IOPEs or behavior is one case of substitutability of the partial IOPEs or behavior. Therefore, some theorems can be proposed.

Theorem 3: If $s_2 \sim_w s_1$, then $s_2 \approx_w s_1$.

Proof: Let $s_1 \equiv \langle \mathbb{R}_{s_1}, \mathbb{B}_{s_1}^c \rangle$ and $s_2 \equiv \langle \mathbb{R}_{s_2}, \mathbb{B}_{s_2}^c \rangle$, there must exist subsets $\mathbb{R}'_{s_1}$ and $\mathbb{R}'_{s_2}$ of $\mathbb{R}_{s_1}$ and $\mathbb{R}_{s_2}$, respectively, so that s_2 can substitute s_1 on $\mathbb{R}'_{s_1}$ and $\mathbb{R}'_{s_2}$ by definitions 14 and 16. Thus $s_2 \approx_w s_1$ holds.

Similarly, theorem 4 can be obtained.

Theorem 4: If $s_2 \sim_w s_1$, then $s_2 \infty_w^M s_1$.

Proof: Ignored.

Theorem 5: If $s_2 \sim_n s_1$, then $s_2 \approx_n s_1$.

Proof: Let $s_1 \equiv \langle \mathbb{R}_{s_1}, \mathbb{B}_{s_1}^c \rangle$ and $s_2 \equiv \langle \mathbb{R}_{s_2}, \mathbb{B}_{s_2}^c \rangle$, in which $\mathbb{B}_{s_1}^c = \{t'_{11}, t'_{12}, ..., t'_{1n}\}$ and $\mathbb{B}_{s_2}^c = \{t'_{21}, t'_{22}, ..., t'_{2m}\}$, we can obtain $\mathbb{B}_{s_1}^c <: \mathbb{B}_{s_2}^c$ by $s_2 \sim_n s_1$, thus $t_{11} <: t_{21}, ..., t_{1n} <: t_{2n}$, so that $s_2 \approx_n s_1$ holds by definition 17.

Similarly, theorem 6 can be obtained.

Theorem 6: If $s_2 \sim_n s_1$, then $s_2 \infty_n^M s_1$.

Proof. Ignored.

Theorem 7: If $s_2 \infty_w^M s_1$, then $s_2 \approx_w s_1$.

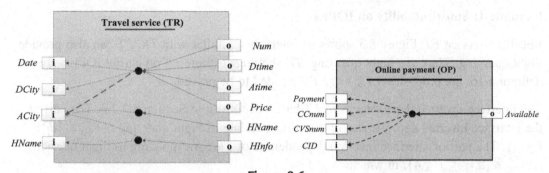

Figure 8.6

Service travel service (TR) and online payment (OP).

Proof: Let the part of s_1 in M be $s_1^M \equiv \langle \mathbb{R}'_{s_1}, \mathbb{B}_{s_1}^{\mathbb{R}'_{s_1}} \rangle$ and $s_2 \equiv \langle \mathbb{R}_{s_2}, \mathbb{B}_{s_2}^c \rangle$, we can obtain that there exists the subset $\mathbb{R}'_{s_1}$ of $\mathbb{R}_{s_2}$ by $s_2 \infty_w^M s_1$, so that $s_2 \approx_w s_1$ holds by definition 16.

Theorem 8: If $s_2 \infty_w^M s_1$, then $s_2 \approx_n s_1$.

Proof: Let the part of s_1 in M be $s_1^M \equiv \langle \mathbb{R}'_{s_1}, \mathbb{B}_{s_1}^{\mathbb{R}'_{s_1}} \rangle$ and $s_2 \equiv \langle \mathbb{R}_{s_2}, \mathbb{B}_{s_2}^c \rangle$, in which $\mathbb{B}_{s_1}^{\mathbb{R}'_{s_1}} = \{t'_{11}, t'_{12}, ..., t'_{1n}\}$ and $\mathbb{B}_{s_2}^c = \{t'_{21}, t'_{22}, ..., t'_{2m}\}$, we can obtain that there exists the behavior $\mathbb{B}_{s_2}$ of s_2 and $\mathbb{B}_{s_2} = \{t'_{21}, t'_{22}, ..., t'_{2j}\}, j \leq m$, so that $\mathbb{B}_{s_1}^{\mathbb{R}'_{s_1}} <: \mathbb{B}_{s_2}$ by $s_2 \infty_w^M s_1$, thus $s_2 \approx_n s_1$ holds by definition 17.

8.2.4 Case Study

The section gives some examples to show the effectiveness of the proposed notions of the substitutability for different granularity services.

8.2.4.1 Judging the substitutability between large-granularity services

Figure 8.6 provides the travel service *TR* and the online payment service *OP*. *TR* is a large granularity service. Given the date (*Date*), the departure city (*DCity*), and the arrival city (*ACity*), it provides the train or flight number (*Num*), the departure time (*Dtime*), the arrival time (*Atime*), and the ticket price (*Price*) of all available trains or flights. Given the arrival city (*ACity*), it provides the names (*HName*) of all hotels in the city. Given the arrival city (*ACity*) and the name of a hotel, it provides the information on the hotel. *OP* is a small granularity service. Given the price (*Payment*), the credit card number (*CCnum*), the CVS number of the credit card (*CVSnum*), and the ID number of the owner holding the credit card (*CID*), it provides a balance (*avaiable*).

Example 1: Substitutability on IOPEs

Recalling service *FT*, Figure 8.3 shows its interfaces. Similar with *TR*, *FT* can also provide flight querying. Thus, for flight querying, *TR* should substitute *FT* on partial IOPEs. By definition 16, the proposition $TR \approx_w FT$ is needed to be proved.

The interface inverted dependences of *FT* have been given in Section 8.2.2.3. The part of the interface inverted dependences of *FT* corresponding to flight querying is $\mathbb{R}'_{FT} \equiv \{d_j | 1 \leq j \leq 4\}$. The part of interface inverted dependences of *TR* corresponding to flight querying is $\mathbb{R}'_{TR} \equiv \{d'_j | 1 \leq j \leq 4\}$, in which:

```
d'₁≡ ⟨I=⟨l₁={DCity,ACity,Date}⟩,O=⟨l₁=ATime⟩⟩
d'₂≡ ⟨I=⟨l₁={DCity,ACity,Date}⟩,O=⟨l₁=DTime⟩⟩
d'₃≡ ⟨I=⟨l₁={DCity,ACity,Date}⟩,O=⟨l₁=Price⟩⟩
d'₄≡ ⟨I=⟨l₁={DCity,ACity,Date}⟩,O=⟨l₁=Num⟩⟩
```

The inputs and outputs of *FT* and *TR* in $\mathbb{R}'_{FT}$ and $\mathbb{R}'_{TR}$ are respectively:

```
I'FT={ ⟨Date,Time⟩,⟨DCity,DepartureCity⟩,⟨ACity,ArriveCity⟩ }
O'FT={ ⟨FATime,ArriveTime⟩,⟨FDTime,DepartureTime⟩,⟨Fnum,Number⟩,⟨FPrice,
       FlightPrice⟩ }
I'TR={ ⟨Date,Time⟩,⟨DCity,DepartureCity⟩,⟨ACity,ArriveCity⟩ }
O'TR={ ⟨ATime,ArriveTime⟩,⟨DTime,DepartureTime⟩,⟨num,Number⟩,⟨Price,Price⟩ }
```

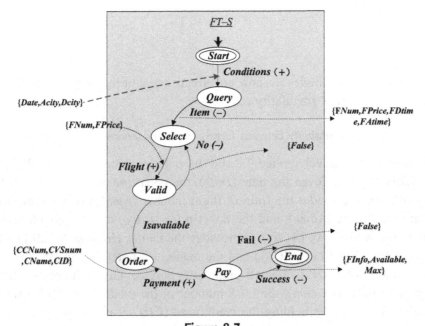

Figure 8.7
The behavior of service *FT-S*.

To judge $TR \approx wFT$, two subgoals need to be obtained:

1. for $\forall i_i \in I'_{FT}$, only one $i'_j \in I'_{TR}$, $snd(i_i) <<: snd(i'_j)$ holds.
2. for $\forall o_i \in O'_{FT}$, only one $o'_j \in O'_{TR}$, $snd(o_i) <<: snd(o'_j)$ holds.

Due to the same semantics of all inputs of FT and TR in $\mathbb{R}'_{FT}$ and $\mathbb{R}'_{TR}$, the first subgoal obviously can be obtained. Similarly, there are the same semantics of some outputs of FT and TR in $\mathbb{R}'_{FT}$ and $\mathbb{R}'_{TR}$. Thus, $FlightPrice <<: Price$ can be obtained by definition 13.

By $FlightPrice = \langle l_1: Price, l_2: \sum(Flight, Require) \rangle$ (referred to Section 8.2.1.1) and definition 12, we can obtain $FlightPrice <:_c Price$, in which the coercion $c:\langle l_1:Price, l_2: \sum(Flight, Require) \rangle \rightarrow Price$. Thus, the second subgoal is proved. By the two subgoals, we can obtain $TR \approx wFT$.

Example 2: Substitutability on behavior

Figure 8.7 provides the behavior of service *FT-S*. *FT-S* has similar behavior with service *FT*. However, unlike service *FT*, *FT-S* can check if there are any tickets left. Thus, *FT-S* should substitute *FT* on the complete behavior of *FT*, that is $FT \sim {}_n FT\text{-}S$.

The complete behavior of *FT-S* can be formalized as:

```
𝔹ᶜ_FT-S ::= {α';β'}                                                    :BSeq
α'::=↓⟨l₁=Date, l₂=ACity, l₃:DCity⟩                                     :BRev
β'::={ φ';ε'}                                                           :BSeq
φ'::=↑⟨l₁=FNum, l₂=FPrice, l₃=FDtime, l₄=FAtime⟩                        :BSed
ε'::={γ'; ρ'}                                                           :BSeq
γ'::=↓⟨l₁=FNum,l₂=FPrice⟩                                               :BRev
ρ'::=if seat⟩0 then μ' else κ'                                          :BIf
μ'::={π';θ'}                                                            :BSeq
π'::=↓⟨l₁=CCNum, l₂=CVSNum, l₃=CName, l₄=CID⟩                           :BRev
θ'::=if currentcreditlimit.l₄≥FlightPrice.l₂ then γ'elseκ'              :BIf
γ'::={υ';σ'}                                                            :BSeq
υ'::=↑⟨l₁=FInfo, l₂=Available, l₃=Max                                   :BSed
σ'::=τ                                                                  :BSkip
κ'::=↑⟨l₁=False⟩                                                        :BSed
```

To get $FT \sim {}_n FT\text{-}S$, $\mathfrak{I}^c_{FT} <: \mathfrak{I}^c_{FT-s}$ should be proved by definition 15. The proving process is as follows:

$$\cfrac{\{\alpha; \beta\} <: \{\alpha'; \beta'\} \quad by \ S-Seq}{\cfrac{\left(\begin{array}{c} \downarrow\langle l_1 = Date, l_2 = ACity, l_3 : DCity \rangle <: \\ \downarrow\langle l_1 = Date, l_2 = ACity, l_3 : DCity \rangle \end{array} \right) {}_{by \ S-Rev}}{\substack{Time<<:Time \quad ArriveCity<<:ArriveCity \quad DepartureCity<<:DepartureCity}} \qquad \substack{\beta<:\beta' \\ \cdots}}$$

$$\alpha<:\alpha'$$

Obviously, we can obtain $\alpha <: \alpha'$. For $\beta <: \beta'$, the proving process is as follows:

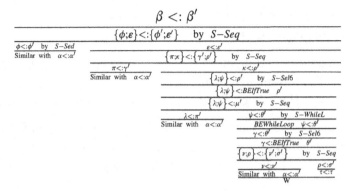

$$\beta <: \beta'$$

8.2.4.2 Judging the substitutability between small and large-granularity services

Example 3: Substitutability of IOPEs

In recalling the small granularity service OP in Figure 8.6 and the large granularity service FT in Figure 8.3 from Figures 8.3 and 8.6, we find that both OP and FT can provide online payment. However, unlike OP, FT can also query the balance of the credit card. Thus, FT can substitute OP in the complete IOPEs of OP; that is, $TR \prec wOP$. Obviously, we can obtain it by definition 12. The proving process is similar with example 1.

Example 4: Substitutability of behavior

Figure 8.8 provides a composition M composed by two services FT and OP. FT can provide flight querying in M, while OP provides online payment.

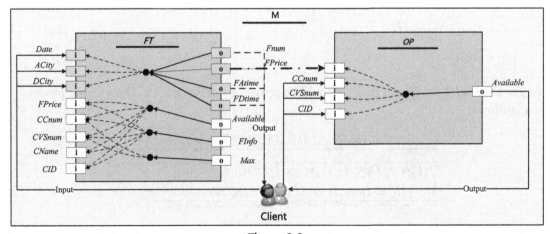

Figure 8.8
The composition M.

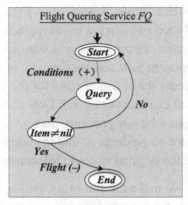

Figure 8.9
The behavior of service flight quering (*FQ*).

Suppose *FT* fails in runtime. To recover *M*, a substitution service is expected to replace *FT*. The behavior $\mathfrak{J}_{FT}^{\mathcal{R}_s'}$ of *FT* in *M* is shown in the dashed ellipse of Figure 8.4 and has been formalized in Section 8.2.2.3. Service *FQ* is a small granularity service and only provides flight querying. However, the behavior of *FQ* is more complex than the partial behavior of *FT* in *M*, because *FQ* can allow clients to perform another request when the querying result is null. The complete behavior of *FQ* is shown in Figure 8.9 and is formalized as:

$$
\begin{aligned}
\mathfrak{J}_{FQ}^c &::= \{\alpha; \beta\} & &: \text{BSeq} \\
\alpha &::= \downarrow \langle l_1 = \text{Date}, l_2 = \text{ACity}, l_3 : \text{DCity} \rangle & &: \text{BRev} \\
\beta &::= \text{If item} \neq \text{nil then } \phi \text{ else } \alpha & &: \text{BIf} \\
\phi &::= \uparrow \langle l_1 = \text{FNum}, l_2 = \text{FPrice}, l_3 = \text{FDtime}, l_4 = \text{FAtime} \rangle & &: \text{BSed}
\end{aligned}
$$

To judge the substitutability between *FQ* and *FT* in *M*, that is $FT \propto_n^M FQ$, the subgoal $\mathfrak{J}_{FT}^{\mathcal{R}_s'} <: \mathfrak{J}_{FQ}^c$ needs to be proved by definition 19. We can apply *S-Seq*, *S-Rev*, *S-Sel6*, and *S-Sed* to obtain the subgoal. Thus, $FT \propto_n^M FQ$ holds. The complete proving process is not given due to limited space.

8.3 The Dynamic Reconfiguration of a Service-Based Application

We now present a QoS-driven dynamic reconfiguration method [32]. In the rest of this section, the term component QoS and overall QoS are used to refer to QoS of a component service and QoS of an application, respectively. The method involves two subprocesses as follows: one is to deal with the original overall QoS violation that is caused by degradation of the component QoS, and the other is to deal with the original overall QoS violation caused by the violation of one or multiple component services in a service-based application at runtime. When degradation of the component QoS leads to a violation of the original overall QoS, we always try to replace the d component services that have the biggest reconfiguration factor, as long as they are reconfigured to deliver the original QoS. When some component services are violated, our method first replaces them with new services, and then repeats the above process for the rest of the component services. In this way, our method can recover overall QoS with less attempts and shorter response time. Meanwhile, inspired by our previous work [33], the notion of the reconfiguration factor is presented to guide us to find the component services that are replaced to most likely achieve the original overall QoS constraints.

For the clarity of this research, we make the following assumptions: all candidate services of each component services have been given for services based applications; they can provide functions similar with its corresponding component service; this can be checked based on substitutability of services that were studied in the above section.

8.3.1 QoS Metrics

In this chapter, we use the existing QoS model that is presented in [34]. Moreover, four QoS attributes of web services are considered as follows: *Response Time (T_s), Cost (C_s), Reliability (R_s), Availability (A_s).*

Given a service-based application S, its QoS model is denoted $Q_s = (T_s, C_s, R_s, A_s)$, and $S_1, \ldots, S_n$ are its component services. For some component service S_i, its QoS model is denoted $Q_{si} = (T_{si}, C_{si}, R_{si}, A_{si})$. To calculate QoS of S, four types of structure patterns are considered in our study: sequence, parallel, condition, and loop.

1. Sequence (Figure 8.10(a))

$$T_s = \sum_{i=1}^{n} T_{si}, \quad C_s = \sum_{i=1}^{n} C_{si}, \quad R_s = \prod_{i=1}^{n} R_{si}, \quad A_s = \prod_{i=1}^{n} A_{si}; \tag{8.1}$$

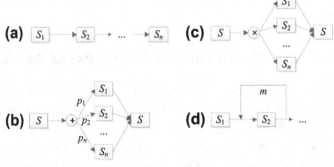

Figure 8.10
Structure pattern.

2. Condition (Figure 8.10(b))

Suppose the execution probability for the *i-th* branch is p_i, and $\sum_{i=1}^{n} p_i = 1$.

$$T_s = \sum_{i=1}^{n} T_{si} p_i, \quad C_s = \sum_{i=1}^{n} C_{si} p_i, \quad R_s = \sum_{i=1}^{n} R_{si} p_i, \quad A_s = \sum_{i=1}^{n} A_{si} P_i; \tag{8.2}$$

3. Parallel (Figure 8.10(c))

Two following types of parallel structures are discussed in this chapter: and parallel and or parallel.

In and parallel, *Response time* equals the maximal response time of all components, while other QoS attributes can be calculated by Eqn (8.1). Equation (8.3) shows the calculation of *Response Time*.

$$T_s = Max\ (T_{s1}, ..., T_{sn}) \tag{8.3}$$

In or parallel, the QoS attributes of *Response Time*, *Cost*, and *Availability* can be computed using Eqn (8.2). Equation (8.4) shows the calculation of *Reliability*.

$$R_s = 1 - \prod_{i=1}^{n} [1 - R_{si}]. \tag{8.4}$$

4. Loop (Figure 8.10(d))

Suppose the loop body T_{si} executed m times for some time.

$$T_s = m * T_{si}, \quad C_s = m * C_{si}, \quad R_s = (R_{si})^m, \quad A_s = (A_{si})^m. \tag{8.5}$$

8.3.2 Quality of Service-Driven Dynamic Reconfiguration Method

8.3.2.1 Subprocess for degradation of component QoS

In this section, algorithm RecDeg is presented to maintain the original QoS constraints when component QoS degrades at runtime. Once the original overall QoS constraints are broken, the algorithm first computes reconfiguration factors for all component services in a service-based application, and sorts all component services according to their reconfiguration factor (steps 3 and 4). The reconfiguration factor is introduced in Section 8.3. Next, the reconfiguration process is divided into two phases as follows:

(1) Individual service replacement: We try to replace individual component services one by one in the descending order of the reconfiguration factor only if there exists some candidate service for which the QoS is not worse than the predefined QoS of the replaced service (steps 6–13). Obviously, the original overall QoS constraints can also be satisfied by such replacement.

If such a replacement cannot be found in this phase, then move to the second phase. (2) Multiple services replacement: We begin to try to replace the d component services with a reconfiguration factor that is the highest among all component services. QoS of the substitutions of the d component services is the best among all their respective candidate services. The range bound of d starts from two and increases gradually until a replacement is found to deliver the original overall QoS (steps 14−24).

Algorithm: **RecDeg**

Input: all replaceable component services $\{S_1,...,S_n\}$ in a services based application S.

Output: the replaced services $R_S \subseteq \{S_1,...,S_n\}$ and their substitutions $R_D \subseteq \{CS_i\}$.

Require: candidate services $CS_i=\{CS_{i1},...,CS_{im}\}$ of service S_i.

1: **SET** $R_S=\varphi$, $R_D=\varphi$, $S_r=\varphi$, $D_g[i]$=null;
2: **FOR** (INT $i = 0$; $i < n$; $i++$){
3:      $D_g[i]$=CalDg(S_i); }/*CalDg(S_i) is to calculate reconfiguration factor of S_i */ (See Section 3.3)
4: $S' =$ Sort(S); /*Sort(S) sorts $S_1,...$, S_n in ascending order according to $D_g[]$*/
5: **SET** $j = n$;
6: While($j > 0$) {
7:      $S_k =$ Get($S'.j$); /* GetS$_r$(j) is to get the j-th element in S'*/
8:      **IF** ($\exists CS_{kp} \in CS_k$ && QoS of CS_{kp} is not worse than the pre-defined QoS of S_k){
9:          **SET** $j = 0$;
10:         $R_S = R_S \cup \{S_k\}$; $R_d = R_d \cup \{CS_{kp}\}$; **Goto 27**;
11:         }**Else**{ $j = j - 1$;
12:     }
13: }
14: **SET** d=2;
15: **Do**{
16:     **FOR**(INT $l = 0$; $l < d$; $l++$){
17:         $R_s[l] = R_s[l] \cup \{$Get($S'.j-l$) $\}$;
18:         $R_D[l] = R_D[l] \cup \{$Select($S'.j-l$) $\}$; /*Select a service CS_{kp} for $M[l]$ whose QoS is the best among all its candidates*/
19:         Replace $M[l]$ with CS_{kp}
20:     }
21:     **IF** (the current QoS of S comply with the original overall QoS of S){ **Goto 27**;
22:         }**Else**{ $d = d+1$;
23:     }
24: }**While** ($d < n + 1$);
25: **RETURN** $RS[]$,$RD[]$;

Once it happens, no such reconfigurations can deliver the original overall QoS in the current given candidate services repository. A recomposition should be needed to achieve original overall QoS for service-based applications. But this goes beyond our current study.

8.3.2.2 Subprocess for violation of component services

Component services may fail at runtime. This may lead to a violation of the original overall QoS constraints. In this section, algorithm RecViol is presented to repair failed component services by replacing them with new services and ensuring that the new service-based applications still meet the original overall QoS constraints. In the algorithm, we first replace each failed service with the substitution with a QoS that is the best among all candidate services of the failed services (steps 2−7). Next, if the delivered overall QoS by the new service-based application still does not satisfy the original overall QoS, the algorithm RecDeg will be called to reconfigure the rest of the component services (steps 8−11).

Algorithm: RecViol

Input: normal component services $Sn = \{Sn_n,...,Sn_{n-p}\}$ and fault component services $Sf = \{Sf_1,...,Sf_p\} \subseteq \{S_1,...,S_n\}$ in a services based application S at runtime.

Output: the replaced services $R_S \subseteq \{S_1,...,S_n\}$ and their substitutions $R_D \subseteq \{CS_i\}$.

Require: candidate services $CS_i = \{CS_{i1},...,CS_{im}\}$ of service Sf_i.

1: **SET** $R_S = \varphi$, $R_D = \varphi$, $S_r = \varphi$;
2: **FOR** ($\forall Sf_i \in Sf$){
3:      $R_D[l] = Select(Sf_i)$;/*Select a service CS_{kp} for Sf_i whose QoS is the best among all its candidates*/
4:      Replace Sf_i with CS_{kp};
5:      $R_D[l] = R_D[l] \cup \{CS_{kp}\}$;
6:      $R_s = Sf$;
7: }
8: **IF** (the current QoS of S comply with original QoS ´ of S){ **Goto 12;**
9:      }Else{
10:         Call **RecDeg**(Sn);(Algorithm **RecDeg**)
11: }
12: **RETURN** $RS[]$,$RD[]$;

8.3.3 Reconfiguration Factor

For our method, we would like to find and replace the most promising component services so that the original overall QoS can be delivered with as few attempts and as soon as possible. Thus, all component services in a service-based application need to be evaluated from the two following aspects: QoS degradation level and QoS global significance.

8.3.3.1 Relative QoS degradation value of component services

The relative QoS degradation value of a component service shows the degree of its QoS actual degradation relative to other component service. When the original overall QoS constraints are violated, the bigger the relative degradation value of a component service is, the bigger its contributions to the violation are.

In this section, we calculate relative QoS degradation value of a component service by the following steps:

1. To compute the actual QoS degradation rate of a component service by Eqn (8.6):
   Given a service-based application Ω and all its component services $S_1, \ldots, S_n$,

$$\overline{\Delta_K^{S_i}} = \frac{\sum\limits_{j \leq m} \Delta_{Kj}^{S_i}}{m} \times \frac{m}{n},$$ (8.6)

in which $\overline{\Delta_K^{S_i}}$ is the actual degradation rate of the QoS property $K \in \{T_{S_i}, C_{S_i}, R_{S_i}, A_{S_i}\}$ from S_i; n is the monitored time in a period (user defined) before violation of the original overall QoS constraints; $m(m \leq n)$ is the degradation time; and $\Delta_{Kj}^{S_i}$ is the actual degradation value of QoS property $K \in \{T_{S_i}, C_{S_i}, R_{S_i}, A_{S_i}\}$ from S_i.

2. To sort $S_1, \ldots, S_n$ according to the QoS actual degradation rate: Four sorts are obtained as follows: $\Delta_T[], \Delta_C[], \Delta_R[],$ and $\Delta_A[]$. They are the descending sorts of the actual degradation value of *Response time, Cost, Reliability,* and *Availability.* And then a 4*n matrix G is built by the four sorts and is denoted as $[\Delta_T[], \Delta_C[], \Delta_R[], \Delta_A[]]^T$. Every column in the matrix is assigned to a weight. The weight of the *j*-th column is set to $(n - j + 1)/n$.

3. To set the effective weight of $S_1, \ldots,$ and S_n: Effective weight of S_i is a vector $WE_i = (WE_{Ti}, WE_{Ci}, WE_{Ri}, WE_{Ai})$. WE_i components are the column weights of S_i in G.

Thus, the relative QoS degradation value DV_i of S_i equals the sum of all components of its effective weights. The equation is as follows:

$$DV_i = \frac{WE_{Ti} + WE_{Ci} + WE_{Ri} + WE_{Ai}}{4}$$ (8.7)

For example, Figure 8.10 gives an online store system that is built by JTangComponent in [33]. The system is composed of eight services as follows: *Login(S_1), CheckforRecieve(S_2), PaytoSeller(S_3), CheckforSatifaction(S_4), Search(S_5), AddtoCart(S_6), PaytoThirdParty(S_7),* and *Logout(S_8).* Suppose QoS actual degradation Δ_4 of S_4 is $(a, 0, b, c)$, and Martix G is as follows:

$$
\begin{array}{cccccccc}
Weight & 1 & \frac{7}{8} & \frac{6}{8} & \frac{5}{8} & \frac{4}{8} & \frac{3}{8} & \frac{2}{8} & \frac{1}{8}
\end{array}
$$

$$
G = \begin{bmatrix}
S_8 & S_7 & S_4 & S_1 & S_6 & S_3 & S_5 & S_2 \\
S_7 & S_8 & S_6 & S_1 & S_2 & S_4 & S_3 & S_5 \\
S_4 & S_5 & S_6 & S_3 & S_8 & S_1 & S_2 & S_7 \\
S_4 & S_5 & S_6 & S_3 & S_8 & S_2 & S_1 & S_7
\end{bmatrix}
\begin{matrix}
\Delta T[\ ] \\
\Delta C[\ ] \\
\Delta R[\ ] \\
\Delta A[\ ]
\end{matrix}
$$

The column weights of S_4 in G are $(\frac{6}{8}, \frac{3}{8}, 1, 1)$. Due to $\Delta_{T4} = 0$, the effective weight WE_4 of S_4 is $(\frac{6}{8}, 0, 1, 1)$. Thus, the relative QoS degradation value DV_4 of S_4 is 2.75.

8.3.3.2 QoS global significance of component services

The QoS global significance shows how the changes of the component QoS influence the changes of the overall QoS. This has been reported in our previous work [33]. A partial derivative is used to calculate the QoS global significance. For a component service, the greater QoS global significance means that the component QoS has a greater influence on the overall QoS. Here, it is used to compute the reconfiguration factor for component services as another indispensable element.

Computing the global significance of a component service depends on the following four types of attribute significances: *Response Time* significance D_t, *Cost* significance D_c, *Reliability* significance D_r, and *Availability* significance D_a. Given a service-based application Ω, attribute significances of its component service A can be derived from the following equations:

$$D_t(\Omega, A) = \frac{\partial T(\Omega)}{\partial T(A)} = \frac{\partial T(\Omega)}{\partial T(S)} * \frac{\partial T(S)}{\partial T(A)}, \quad D_c(\Omega, A) = \frac{\partial C(\Omega)}{\partial C(A)} = \frac{\partial C(\Omega)}{\partial C(S)} * \frac{\partial C(S)}{\partial C(A)},$$

$$D_r(\Omega, A) = \frac{\partial R(\Omega)}{\partial R(A)} = \frac{\partial R(\Omega)}{\partial R(S)} * \frac{\partial R(S)}{\partial R(A)}, \quad D_a(\Omega, A) = \frac{\partial A(\Omega)}{\partial A(A)} = \frac{\partial R(\Omega)}{\partial R(S)} * \frac{\partial R(S)}{\partial R(A)} \qquad (8.8)$$

Now we will discuss how to compute attribute significance values in different structures in detail.

8.3.3.2.1 Sequence

Suppose that a sequence S consists of the component C_1, C_2, ..., C_n. By Eqn (8.1) and Eqn (8.7), we can derive:

$$D_t(S, C_i) = \sum_{j=1}^{n} \left[D_t(C_j, C_i) \right], \quad D_c(S, C_i) = \sum_{j=1}^{n} \left[D_c(C_j, C_i) \right],$$

$$D_r(S, C_i) = \sum_{j=1}^{n} \left[D_r(C_j, C_i) * \prod_{k=1, k\neq j}^{n} R(C_k) \right],$$

$$D_a(S, C_i) = \sum_{j=1}^{n} \left[D_a(C_j, C_i) * \prod_{k=1, k\neq j}^{n} A(C_k) \right] \qquad (8.9)$$

8.3.3.2.2 Condition

Suppose a condition S is composed of component C_1, C_2, ..., C_n, and the probability of each branch is $P(C_1)$, $P(C_2)$, ..., $P(C_n)$, respectively. By Eqn (8.2) and Eqn (8.7), the following equations are obtained:

$$D_t(S, C_i) = \sum_{j=1}^{n} \left[D_t(C_j, C_i) * P(C_j) \right],$$

$$D_c(S, C_i) = \sum_{j=1}^{n} \left[D_c(C_j, C_i) * P(C_j) \right],$$

$$D_r(S, C_i) = \sum_{j=1}^{n} [D_r(C_j, C_i) * P(C_j)],$$

$$D_a(S, C_i) = \sum_{j=1}^{n} [D_a(C_j, C_i) * P(C_j)], \quad \text{where} \quad \sum_{j=1}^{n} P(C_j) = 1 \qquad (8.10)$$

8.3.3.2.3 Parallel

For And Parallel, we use Eqn (8.8) to calculate the significance values of *Cost*, *Reliability*, and *Availability*. If *Response time* of a service is the maximum among all individuals, its significance value of *Response Time* is set to one; otherwise the value is zero.

For Or Parallel, the significance value of *Response Time*, *Cost*, and *Availability* are obtained by Eqn (8.10). And Eqn (8.11) is adopted to compute the attribute significance value of *Reliability*.

$$D_r(S, C_i) = \sum_{j=1}^{n} D_r(C_j, C_i) * \prod_{k=1, k \neq j}^{n} [1 - R(C_k)] \qquad (8.11)$$

8.3.3.2.4 Loop

Suppose the loop structure L from a service-based application S, and m is the execution times of L. Then Eqn (8.12) is given to compute the attribute significances:

$$D_t(S, L) = m, D_c(S, L) = m, \; D_r(S, L) = m * R^{m-1}(L), \; D_a(S, L) = m * A^{m-1}(L), \qquad (8.12)$$

To calculate the global significance of each component service, all component services need to be sorted in descending order according to each of the types of attribute significances. This chapter uses Γ_t, Γ_c, Γ_r, and Γ_a to represent the sorts of *Response Time*, *Cost*, *Reliability*, and *Availability*, respectively. Then a 4*n matrix can be built and be denoted as $[\Gamma_t, \Gamma_c, \Gamma_r, \Gamma_a]^T$. The weight of the j-th column is set to $(n - j + 1)/n$. Suppose there are n existing component services in Ω, and w_1, w_2, w_3, and w_4 are the column weights of its component service A in G. The global significance of A can be calculated by Eqn (8.13):

$$D_g(A) = w_1 * D_t(\Omega, A) + w_2 * D_c(\Omega, A) + w_3 * D_r(\Omega, A) + w_4 * D_a(\Omega, A) \qquad (8.13)$$

Finally, reconfiguration factor λ_i of S_i can be computed as follows:

$$\lambda_i = DV_i \times D_g(S_i) \qquad (8.14)$$

8.3.4 Evaluation

To evaluate the efficiency and effectiveness of our proposed method, three groups of tests are conducted.

Test case generation: We use a service test collection from JTangComponent previously built in [26], in which 1056 services have been included to generate the needed application in the test. In addition, to support the test, QoS of candidate services is simulated and produced in the following way: *Cost* and *Response Time* are randomly generated with a uniform distribution from one to 100; *Availability* and *Reliability* are randomly generated with a uniform distribution from zero to one and are assigned to each candidate service.

Test A: With the increasing number of candidate services from 20 to 1000, the run time of algorithm RecDeg is given in Figure 8.11. Furthermore, to illustrate the effects of different QoS constraints on the runtime, a QoS constraint number from one to four is applied to algorithm RecDeg to test the runtime. In the test, the application is the online store system that has been built by the JTangComponent in [33] (see Figure 8.12).

The test results are shown in Figure 8.11. The following conclusions can be drawn: (1) Although the runtime of algorithm RecDeg is near when the QoS constraints number is one and two, the runtime of algorithm RecDeg is proportionate to the QoS constraints number on the whole. (2) With the gradual increase in the number of candidate services, the run time of the algorithm fluctuates. Furthermore, the trends of fluctuation are different for the different QoS constraints numbers. The reason for the fluctuations lies in the different number of candidate services. The more candidate services there are, the more are the times for traversing all candidate services. For example, when the QoS constraints number is four, the run time declines sharply, with the number of candidate services

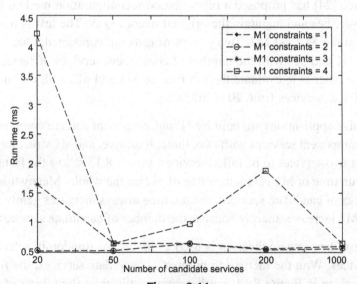

Figure 8.11

Run time of algorithm RecDeg with different QoS constraints.

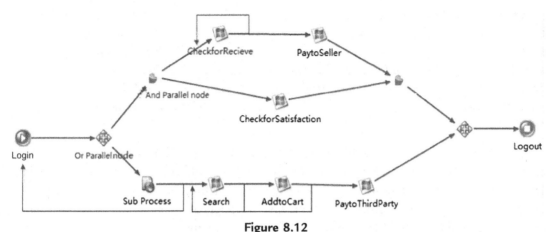

Figure 8.12
The structure of online store system.

increased from 20 to 50. The reason is that the original overall QoS is satisfied only through replacing an individual component service when the number of candidate services is 50, while multiple component services need to be replaced when the number of candidate services is 20. The run time slowly increases again when the number of candidate services increases from 50 to 100. This is because more time needs to be spent on selecting a suitable one from all the candidate services when the number of candidate services is 100. Although, the test is done based on a given composite service, we can still conclude that the number of candidate services has a greater influence on the run time.

Test B: Reference [24] has proposed a region-based reconfiguration method to repair multiple failed services and maintain the original overall QoS. The test is to compare the performance between M1 and M2. Two groups of tests are conducted. One is to evaluate the run time of M1 and M2 with the number of component services of service-based applications. The other is to evaluate the run time of M1 and M2 with the increasing number of candidate services from 20 to 1000.

In the first test, five applications are built by JTangComponent and are composed of 5, 10, 15, 20, and 25 component services with two, three, four, five, and six structure patterns. Randomly select two services to be failed services. Figure 8.13 shows the test results. Obviously, the run time of M1 is less than that of M2 on the whole. Meanwhile, with the increasing number of candidate services, the run time always increases gently for M1; while the run time of M2 increases sharply because the number of candidate services is 10.

In the second test, the same application is used as in Test A. Randomly select two services to be failed services. With the increasing number of candidate services, the run time of M1 and M2 are given in Figure 8.14. Furthermore, to illustrate the effects of different QoS constraints on the runtime, two and four QoS constraints are applied to test the run time.

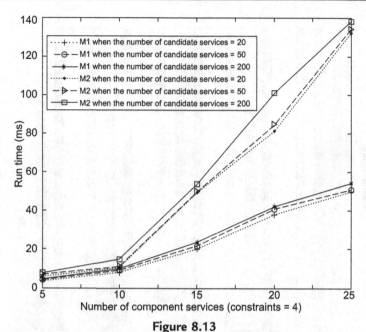

Figure 8.13
Performance comparison between M1 and M2 with different component services (M1 and M2 refer to algorithm RecViol and the method in [12]).

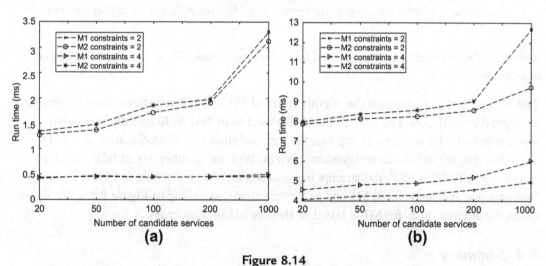

Figure 8.14
Performance comparison between M1 and M2 with different candidate services.

Figure 8.14(a) shows that the run time of M1 and M2 satisfy the predefined overall QoS. Otherwise Figure 8.14(b) shows that for the run time of M1 and M2, the predefined overall QoS is not satisfied. The former can show which method is faster to maintain the original overall QoS, while the latter can show their single complete execution time. Thus,

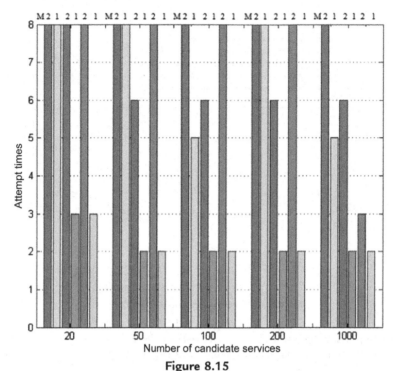

Figure 8.15

Comparison of attempt times between M1 and M2 with different candidate services.

under the above conditions, our method takes less time than [24] to maintain the original overall QoS.

Test C: This test is to compare the attempt times of M1 and M2 with three different groups of original overall QoS. The application is still used as in Test A. Randomly select two services to be faulty services. Using M1, the three original overall QoS can be satisfied by only replacing the individual component services. With the number of candidate services increasing from 20 to 1000, the attempt times of M1 and M2 are shown in Figure 8.15. Numbers one and two refer to M1 and M2, respectively, at the top of Figure 8.15. The figure shows the attempt times for M1 is less than that for M2 in most cases.

8.4 Summary

In this chapter, we proposed an approach to verify the substitutability between different granularity services. We proposed the notion of interface inverted dependence to make up for the specification of large granularity services by the existing service description languages. Interface inverted dependence captures data dependencies from output to inputs within a large-granularity web service. Also, we built a model to formally describe different granularity services by applying and extending MLTT. Unlike other existing formal models that are built by Pi-calculus, Petri-net, automata, etc., this model can also describe syntax and semantics information of services except for behavioral information of services. Based on subtyping theory, we proposed the notions of substitutability between different granularity services with different stringencies through considering the context of services. Furthermore, because subtyping can be judged by a type-checking mechanism, the substitutability can be determined automatically. Compared to other studies, we take advantage of the formalization, type theory and the substitutability between formalized services that can be analyzed from not only behavior, but also from syntax and semantics. Furthermore, considering large-granularity services and the context of services, we defined the substitutability between different granularity services with their different stringencies.

Additionally, we discussed how to ensure that the composite services can run reliably in dynamic environments. Due to failed services or degradation of component QoS, the original QoS of service-based applications may be broken. Once that happens, it is undesirable to halt and recompose service-based applications. Service-based applications should be recovered as soon and as efficiently as possible. The chapter proposes a QoS-driven dynamic reconfiguration method to maintain the original QoS of service-based applications. The key to our method is the reconfiguration factor of component services that can guide us to find the component services which provide the most contributions to the violations of the overall QoS. The results of our evaluation show that our method can recover the original overall QoS by reconfiguring only a small number of services with fewer attempts in an acceptable time frame. We believe this is a feasible and effective way to make service-based applications adaptive to QoS violations. Compared to our study, other studies are limited to recovery when component services become faulty; while they become invalid when the delivered QoS of component services degrades. Furthermore, our test has shown the performance of our method is better than the other proposed studies.

References

[1] L.J. Zhang, J. Zhang, H. Cai, Services Computing, Springer & Tsinghua University Press, 2007.
[2] M. Brian Blake, W. Tan, Florian Rosenberg, composition as a service, IEEE Internet Comput. 14 (1) (2010) 78–82.
[3] A. Martens, On compatibility of web services, Petri Net Newsl. 65 (2003) 12–20.
[4] H. Foster, S. Uchitel, J. Magee, J. Kramer, Compatibility verification for web service choreography, in: Proc. of International Conference on Web Service (ICWS), 2004, pp. 738–741.
[5] M. Aoyama, S. Weerawarana, H. Maruyama, C. Szyperski, K. Sullivan, D. Lea, Web services engineering: promises and challenges, in: Proc. ICSE 2002, Orlando, 2002, pp. 647–648.
[6] W. Vambenepe, C. Thompson, V. Talwar, et al., Dealing with scale and adaptation of global web services management, Int. J. Web Serv. Res. 3 (2007) 65–84.
[7] J. Pathak, S. Basu, V. Honavar, On context-specific substitutability of web services, in: 5th IEEE International Conference on Web Services (ICWS), Beijing, China, 2007.

[8] Y. Taher, D. Benslimane, M.-C. Fauvet, Z. Maamar, Towards an approach for web services substitution, in: 10th Intl. Database Engineering and Applications Symposium, Delhi, India, 2006.

[9] A. Vallecillo, V.T. Vasconcelos, A. Ravara, Typing the behavior of software components using session types, Fund. Inform. 4 (2006) 583–598.

[10] B. Benatallah, F. Casati, F. Toumani, Representing, analysing and managing web service protocols, Data Knowl. Eng. 58 (3) (2006) 327–357.

[11] M. Bravetti, G. Zavattaro, Towards a unifying theory for choreography conformance and contract compliance, in: Proc. of 6th Symposium on Software Composition, Braga, Portugal, 2007.

[12] F. Bonchi, A. Brogi, S. Corfini, F. Gadducci, A behavioural congruence for web services, in: International Symposium on Fundamentals of Software Engineering, Tehran, Iran, 2007.

[13] L. Bordeaux, G. Salaun, D. Berardi, M. Mecella, When are two web services compatible? in: VLDB-TES, Toronto, Canada, 2004.

[14] X. Li, Y. Fan, Q.Z. Sheng, Z. Maamar, H. Zhu, A petri net approach to analyzing behavioral compatibility and similarity of web services, IEEE Trans. Syst. Man Cybernet. Part A Syst. Hum. 41 (3) (2011) 510–521.

[15] N. Desai, Z. Cheng, A.K. Chopra, M.P. Singh, Toward verification of commitment protocols and their compositions, in: The 6th International Joint Conference on Autonomous Agents and Multiagent Systems, Honolulu, Hawaii, USA, 2007.

[16] C. Stahl, P. Massuthe, J. Bretschneider, Deciding substitutability of services with operating guidelines, Trans. Petri Nets Other Models Concurrency II Spec. Issue Concurrency Process Aware Inf. Syst. 2 (5460) (2009) 172–191.

[17] A. Wombacher, P. Fankhauser, B. Mahleko, E. Neuhold, Matchmaking for business processes based on choreographies, Int. J. Web Serv. Res. 1 (4) (2004) 14–32.

[18] H. Foster, S. Uchitel, J. Magee, J. Kramer, Compatibility verification for web service choreography, in: The Intl. Conf. on Web Service, San Diego, California, USA, 2004.

[19] W. Tsai, W. Song, Y. Chen, R. Paul, Dynamic system reconfiguration via service composition for dependable computing, in: Reliable Systems on Unreliable Networked Platforms, 2007, pp. 203–224.

[20] P. Avgeriou, Run-time reconfiguration of service-centric systems, in: Proc. of the European Pattern Languages of Programming (EuroPLOP), 2006.

[21] O. Ezenwoye, S. Busi, S.M. Sadjadi, Dynamically reconfigurable data-intensive service composition, WEBIST (2010) 125–130.

[22] Y. Yan, P. Poizat, L. Zhao, Repair versus recomposition for broken service compositions, ICSOC (2010) 152–166.

[23] L. Zeng, B. Benatallah, A.H.H. Ngu, M. Dumas, J. Kalagnanam, H. Chang, QoS-aware middleware for web services composition, IEEE Trans. Softw. Eng. 30 (5) (2004) 311–327.

[24] Y.L. Zhai, J. Zhang, K.-J. Lin, SOA middleware support for service process reconfiguration with end-to-end QoS constraints, in: The IEEE International Conference on Web Services (ICWS), 2009, pp. 815–822.

[25] T. Yu, K.J. Lin, Adaptive algorithms for finding replacement services in autonomic distributed business processes, in: Proc. of the 7th International Symposium on Autonomous Decentralized Systems, 2005.

[26] Y.Y. Yin, Y. Li, J.W. Yin, et al., Ensuring correctness of dynamic reconfiguration in SOA based software, in: 2009 Congress on SERVICES-I, 2009, pp. 599–606.

[27] Y. Yin, S. Deng, Analysing and determining substitutability of different granularity web services, Int. J. Comput. Math. 90 (11) (2012) 2201–2220.

[28] B. Nordstrom, K. Petersson, J.M. Smith, Programming in Martin-Löf Type Theory: An Introduction, Oxford University Press, 1999.

[29] Y.I.N. Yu-yu, L.I. Ying, D.E.N.G. Shui-guang, Y.I.N. Jian-wei, Determining on consistency and compatibility of web services behavior, Acta Electron. Sin. 37 (3) (2009) 433–438 (in Chinese).

[30] Z. Luo, Manifest fields and module mechanisms in intensional type theory, in: Types for Proofs and Programs, Proc. of Inter. Conf. of TYPES '08, Torino, Italy, 2008.

[31] R. Dapoigny, P. Barlatier, Towards a conceptual structure based on type theory, in: The International Conference on Computational Science (ICCS) 2008, Krakow, Poland, 2008.

[32] Y. Yin, Y. Li, Towards dynamic reconfiguration for QoS consistent services based applications, ICSOC (2012) 771–778.

[33] Y. Li, Y.L. Lu, Y.Y. Yin, et al., Towards QoS-based dynamic reconfiguration of SOA-based applications, APSCC (2010) 107–114.

[34] Y.T. Liu, A.H.H. Ngu, L.Z. Zeng, QoS computation and policing in dynamic web service selection, in: Proc. of the 13th International World Wide Web Conference, 2004, pp. 66–73.

Complex Service Computing

Chapter Outline

Service Computing: Concepts, Methods and Technology. http://dx.doi.org/10.1016/B978-0-12-802330-3.00009-6

9.1 Introduction

The development of the human economy, after the agricultural economy and industrial economy, ushered in the era of the service economy in 1950s. In recent years, with the popularization of the computer, Internet, mobile communications, and especially the development and application of new information technology such as cloud computing and the Internet of Things, the service economy has shown a new trend of crossover development.

9.1.1 Crossover Service

"Crossover" means breaking the existing boundaries and realizing collaborations that take place in and out of bounds. Crossover marketing, crossover consumption, crossover design, crossover music, crossover cars, etc., have arisen. All the above proves that crossover has become a new trend and fashion. With the support of the new revolution of information technology, the modern service industry not only promotes the crossover industry integration development of the first, the second, and the third industry, but also promotes the mutual penetration and fusion of different enterprises.

Crossover service is a concept of multiple subjects, which can be understood as a new economic phenomena and economic activity in the modern service industry. It also can be regarded as the new content and new form of modern enterprise management. Furthermore, it is also the new application scenario of the information technology age for the modern service industry. Crossover services have three "C" characteristics: Crossover, Convergence, and Complex.

9.1.1.1 Crossover

Crossover is the basic characteristic of crossover services. Crossover services are services provided across different business areas, different industries, and different industrial domains. Intangible products formed or derived from crossover services are always cross-domain. For example, banks begin to cross the traditional banking business to provide ticket selling services; traditional network carriers start to provide broadcasting services; Internet enterprises begin to set foot in the field of mobile communication; etc. All the above reflects the natural attribute of crossover services.

9.1.1.2 Convergence

Modern enterprises provide crossover services on the premise of realizing convergence. Convergence occurs among different industries and gradually forms a new crossover industry through interaction and mutual infiltration. Convergence is a dynamic development process, in which there will be technology convergence, product convergence, service convergence, enterprise convergence, and market convergence. Intangible products formed or derived from crossover services are the result of convergence. For example, Apple Corp, the IT industry upstart, has made great achievements in business thanks to its culture and creativity being converted into products. The convergence innovation of technology and culture makes Apple stand out among the crowd.

9.1.1.3 Complex

Compared with traditional services, crossover services are more complicated in the innovation process, development process, and operation process. It is difficult for the providers of crossover services not only to cross the boundaries of different industries and integrate all kinds of resources into industries or areas in which they are not familiar, but also to conduct a series of innovative activities such as service innovation and business pattern design by combining their advantages of resources, market, and technology. Furthermore, these enterprises already existing in the market have advantages in marketing, technology, and services, which brings more risks and challenges to the crossover service providers.

9.1.2 Complex Service Computing

Service computing is an emerging discipline that is moving toward a dynamic, changeable, and complex Internet environment, which takes web services and service-oriented architecture as the supporting technology, takes service composition as the main methods for developing software, and takes the service-oriented software analysis and design principles as the basic concepts for innovative development. It is a basic subject across the computer and information technology, business management, and consulting services. Service computing, the goal of which is to use science and technology to eliminate the gap between business services and information technology services, can provide technical support for crossover service innovation patterns. The 3 "C" characteristics of crossover services lead the traditional service computing to the complex service computing with the characteristics of large-scale, high dynamic, crossover, and integration.

To explore the three major characteristics of crossover services, we propose a technical framework of complex service computing by combining the basic theories and methods of economics, management, and information science. The technical framework includes three phases of crossover services design, implementation, and operation, which contains relevant theoretical models, techniques, methods, and a tools platform.

1. In the design phase, the support technology enables the capability assessment of enterprise crossover services, crossover services pattern design, business pattern value analysis, and risk prediction and assessment.
2. In the implementation phase, the support technology provides information technical support for the construction and implementation of specific crossover services. Specifically, the main realization is for the management and application of the huge amounts of enterprise data, processes, and services.
3. In the operation phase, the support technology is responsible for the daily operation and optimizing the crossover services for enterprises and provides a series of related technology for enterprises to carry out crossover services value analysis, business model bottlenecks mining, a new round of service innovation, and business pattern design.

From the prospect of information technology, we think that the study of complex service computing has three important technical challenges: big data management for crossover services, complex environment of crossover services, and service pattern models for crossover services.

9.1.2.1 Big data management

Big data management refers to the data processing in a scale of PB (10^{15}), EB (10^{18}), or ZB (10^{21}) and/or greater size. Traditional file systems, relational databases, and parallel processing techniques can hardly deal effectively with big data calculations. Big data management is also known as big enough computing or extreme-scale computing. Recently, a large number of big data platforms have emerged, including Oracle's Big Data Appliance, EMC Greenplum, Hadoop, etc. At the same time, there are more and more applications in three-dimensional data, medical imaging, network video service, remote sensing information processing, intelligent transportation, and other fields. The emergence of crossover services increases the requirements and demands for large data processing. On one hand, big data computing provides new technical means for crossover services. On the other hand, crossover services also bring new technical challenges to big data computing.

9.1.2.2 Complex computing environment

As crossover services enable collaborations across multiple domains, future service computing will no longer be limited under traditional context and environments; it should be more flexible and complex. For example, service computing techniques will be extended to cloud environments, mobile environments, Internet of Things, etc. New problems will arise when using traditional service-computing techniques in these complex computing environments. For example, services provided by mobile providers will be different from conventional computation-intensive services. They could be moving location-based or context-aware services for sensing and providing, through their sensors, immediate real-world information. Therefore, it is essential to study new service-computing techniques for complex computing environments.

9.1.2.3 Service management

Cloud computing has been increasingly applied and deployed in the industrial environment. This new paradigm and service model has had great influence on modern enterprise information. In the process of enterprise information based on cloud computing, service management will become the support technology for a modern enterprise to build and operate crossover business applications. However, crossover services create new requirements for this technology. Compared to traditional business, an enterprises' crossover business is more complex, and the service involved is large-scale, various, and multi-granularity. This brings new challenges to the enterprise service resources management, such as how to realize service sharing, invocation, composition, and collaboration. To support the efficient collaboration of crossover business process flow, data flow, logistics, transaction flow, and workflow, is the key issue of complex service computing to support crossover services.

To address the above challenges, this chapter introduces three exploring methods: a service discovery method by using the big data of services, a service composition method in mobile environments, and a service pattern model analysis method.

9.2 Service Computing with Big Data

With the prevalence of service computing and cloud computing, more and more services are emerging on the Internet, generating huge volumes of data, such as trace logs, quality of service (QoS) information, service relationship, etc. The overwhelming service-generated data become too large and complex to be effectively processed by traditional approaches. How to use, manage, and create values from the service-oriented big data becomes an important research problem. Web service tags, i.e., terms annotated by users to describe the functionality or other aspects of web services, are being treated as collective user knowledge for web service mining. Since user tagging is inherently uncontrolled, ambiguous, and overly personalized, a critical and fundamental problem is how to measure the relevance of a user-contributed tag with respect to the functionality of the annotated web service. In this section, we propose a hybrid mechanism by using Web Services Description Language (WSDL) documents and service-tag network information to compute the relevance scores of tags by using a semantic computation and hyperlink-induced topic search (HITS) model, respectively. Further, we introduce tag relevance measurement mechanisms into three applications of web service mining: (1) web service clustering; (2) web service tag recommendation; and (3) tag-based web service retrieval. To evaluate the accuracy of tag relevance measurement and its impact on web service mining, experiments are implemented based on Titan, which is a web service search engine constructed and based on 15,968 real web services. Comprehensive experiments demonstrate the effectiveness of the proposed tag relevance measurement mechanism and its active promotion to the usage of tagging data in web service mining.

9.2.1 Tagging Data Relevance Measurement

In this section, we first give an overview of the proposed web service tag relevance measurement (WS-TRM) approach and then introduce the computation of semantic tag relevance and HITS-based tag authority. Finally, we introduce the computation of final tag relevance by integrating semantic tag relevance and tag authority.

9.2.1.1 Overview of web service tag relevance measurement

Figure 9.1 presents an overview of our proposed WS-TRM mechanism, which mainly consists of two parts: (1) semantic relevance computation and (2) tag authority computation by using the HITS model. Given a tag list associated with one web service, we first compute the relevance score of each tag by evaluating the sematic relevance between each tag and the WSDL document of the corresponding service. In particular, we extract a content vector (i.e., a set of keywords) from the WSDL document for semantic

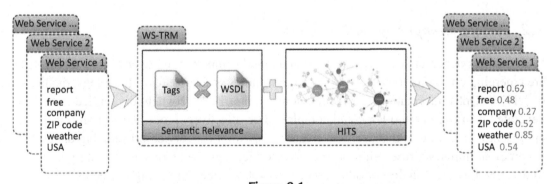

Figure 9.1
An overview of web service tag relevance measurement (WS-TRM) mechanism.

relevance computation between a tag and service. Although the relevance scores obtained in this way reflect the semantic relevance between tags and services, the relationships in STNet have not been considered. In the second part, the HITS model is used to explore the relationships in STNet to compute the authorities of tags, which reflect the meaningfulness of tags. In particular, phSTNet is constructed by using the association relationship between tags and web services. Finally, the relevance score of a tag is generated by integrating semantic relevance and tag authority.

9.2.1.2 *Semantic relevance computation*

A WSDL document, which describes the functionality of a web service, is actually an XML-style document. Therefore, we can use some information retrieval (IR) approaches to extract a vector of meaningful content words that can be used as a feature for semantic relevance computation. This concept has been demonstrated to be effective in some previous works [1−3]. In this section, we build the content vector in four steps:

1. **Building original vector**. In this step, we split the WSDL content according to the white space to produce the original content vector. For a term such as "WeatherReport," we split it into two single words "Weather" and "Report."
2. **Suffix stripping**. Words with a common stem will usually have the same meaning; for example, connect, connected, connecting, connection, and connections all have the same stem, "connect" [4]. For the purpose of convenient statistics, we strip the suffix of all the words that have the same stem by using a Porter stemmer [5].
3. **Pruning**. In this step, we propose removing two types of words from the content vector. The first type of words to be removed are XML tags, e.g., s:element and s:complex-Type, which are not meaningful for the semantic relevance computation. The second type of words to be removed is function words that have little or no contribution to the meaning of texts. Poisson distribution is used to model word occurrence in documents for the purpose of distinguishing function words [6]. Typically, a way to decide whether a word w in the content vector is a function word is computing the degree of over-estimation of the observed document frequency of the word w, denoted by n_w, using Poisson distribution. The overestimation factor can be calculated as follows:

$$\Lambda_w = \frac{n_w}{\overline{n_w}}, \tag{9.1}$$

in which $\overline{n_w}$ is the estimated document frequency of the word w. Specifically, the word with a higher value of Λ_w has a higher possibility to be a content word. In this section, we set a threshold Λ_T for Λ_w, and take the words that have Λ_w higher than the threshold as content words. The value of threshold Λ_T is as follows:

$$\Lambda_T = \begin{cases} \text{avg}[\Lambda] & \text{if}(\text{avg}[\Lambda] > 1) \\ 1 & \text{otherwise} \end{cases} \tag{9.2}$$

in which avg[Λ] is the average value of the observed document frequency of all words being considered. After the process of pruning, we can obtain a new content vector, in which both XML tags and function words are removed.

4. **Refining**. Words with a very high frequency occurrence are likely to be too general to discriminate between web services. After the step of pruning, we implement a step of refining, in which words with too general meanings are removed. Clustering-based approaches were adopted to handle this problem in some related work [2,4]. In this section, we choose a simple approach by computing the frequencies of words in all WSDL documents and setting a threshold to decide whether a word has to be removed.

After the above four steps, we can obtain the final content vector. Through our observation, the dimension of the content vector of most web services for experiments (i.e., 15,968 real web service) is in the range of 10−30.

As mentioned above, WSDL is an XML structure document. Thus the position of a content word taken in the XML structure should be considered in the process of semantic relevance computation. That is, the importance of content words in different positions of the structure should be discriminated. In this section, we classify the positions of content words in an XML structure into four categories:

1. **Name property**. In the definition of elements or other objects (e.g., message, type, operation) in a WSDL document, there is always a name property. Take this record <s:element name = "GetWeatherResponse"> as an example; the positions of "Get," "Weather," and "Response" are all name properties.
2. **Value property**. Similar to name property, value property is another kind of property for an element or other objects in a WSDL document.
3. **Text**. There is always some text description for the operation in WSDL. We call this kind of position text.
4. **Annotation**. At the beginning of a WSDL document, there may be some annotation given by a service provider. In annotation, some information about the service provider or the functionality of service is presented.

In this section, we use c_1, c_2, c_3, and c_4 to represent name property, value property, text, and annotation, respectively. And f_1, f_2, f_3, and f_4 are their corresponding weights for different position categories, $f_1 + f_2 + f_3 + f_4 = 1$. Given a content vector *content* (consists of a set of words, $w_1,...,w_n$) and a tag t, the semantic relevance between t and *content* is computed as follows:

$$SR(t,content) = \frac{\sum_{i=1}^{n} Sim(t,w_i)\sum_{j=1}^{4} f_j \times Occur_{ij}}{\sum_{i=1}^{n}\sum_{j=1}^{4} f_j \times Occur_{ij}}, \qquad (9.3)$$

in which $Occur_{ij}$ means the occurrence number of word w_i in position c_j, and $Sim(t,w_i)$ means the semantic similarity between t and w_i. In this section, normalized Google distance (NGD) [7] is used to compute the semantic similarity between two words:

$$Sim(t,w_i) = 1 - \text{NGD}(t,w_i)$$

$$\text{NGD}(t,w_i) = \frac{\max\{\log f(t), \log f(w_i)\} - \log f(t,w_i)}{\log N - \min\{\log f(t), \log f(w_i)\}}, \tag{9.4}$$

in which $f(w_i)$ denotes the number of pages containing w_i, and $f(t,w_i)$ denotes the number of pages containing both t and w_i, as reported by Google. N is the total number of web pages searched by Google.

By using Eqns (9.3) and (9.4), we can obtain the semantic relevance between tag t and the content vector extracted from the WSDL document of service s, and we set $SR(t,s) = SR(t,content)$ as the semantic relevance of t to s. Because the number of words left in the content vector is limited after the above four steps, the time cost for semantic relevance computation can be accepted.

9.2.1.3 STNet-adapted hyperlink-induced topic search

HITS (also known as hubs and authorities) is a link analysis algorithm that rates web pages and was developed by Kleinberg. It is a precursor to PageRank. The idea behind HITS stemmed from a particular insight into the creation of web pages when the Internet was originally forming. Compared with PageRank, the authority value computed by the HITS algorithm is more appropriate to reflect the importance of tag, while the meaning of the value computed by PageRank is more general. Thus, we propose to obtain the authority of a tag based on the STNet, which could reflect the importance of a tag. In the following, we first introduce how to build STNet, and then present a STNet-adapted HITS algorithm for tag authority computation.

9.2.1.3.1 STNet building

STNet can be modeled as a weighted directed graph G, in which node s_i means a service, and node t_i means a tag. For each node in G, it has two values, i.e., hub and authority. There are three kinds of directed edges in G:

Edge from a service node to tag node. Given a service s_1 annotated with three tags t_1, t_2, and t_3, then there is a directed edge from s_1 to t_1, t_2, and t_3, respectively. In particular, the weight of this kind of edge is one.

Edge from a service node to service node. Given two services s_1 and s_2, if there is one or more than one common tag annotated to these two services, we create one directed edge from s_1 to s_2 and one directed edge from s_2 to s_1. These two edges have the same weight, which depends on the common tags; i.e., $w(s_1,s_2) = w(s_2,s_1) = \frac{|t_{s_1} \cap t_{s_2}|}{|t_{s_1} \cup t_{s_2}|}$, in which t_{s_1} and t_{s_2} mean the set of tags annotated to s_1 and s_2, respectively.

Edge from a tag node to tag node. Given two tags t_1 and t_2, these two tags are annotated to one or more than one service. Similarly, we create one directed edge from t_1 to t_2 and one directed edge from t_2 to t_1. The weight of edge also depends on the common services; i.e., $w(t_1,t_2) = w(t_2,t_1) = \frac{|s_{t_1} \cap s_{t_2}|}{|s_{t_1} \cup s_{t_2}|}$, in which s_{t_1} and s_{t_2} mean the set of services containing t_1 and t_2, respectively.

In this way, we obtain STNet by building a weighted directed graph. It should be noted that the reputation of taggers and web services will be helpful to make the weights of edges more accurate. However, these types of data cannot be crawled as of yet.

9.2.1.3.2 Tag authority computation

HITS is a kind of iterative algorithm. We consider two types of updates as follows:

Authority update. For each node p (could be service node or tag node) in G, we update the authority of node p to be:

$$Auth(p) = \sum_{i=1}^{n} Hub(p_i) \times w(p_i,p), \tag{9.5}$$

in which $p_i(i = 1,...,n)$ means the node that points to p, and $w(p_i,p)$ is the weight of the edge from p_i to p; that is, the authority of node p that is the sum of all the weighted hub values of nodes that point to p.

Hub update. For each node p in G, we update the hub value of p to be:

$$Hub(p) = \sum_{i=1}^{n} Auth(p_i) \times w(p,p_i), \tag{9.6}$$

in which $p_i(i=1,...,n)$ means the node that p points to, and $w(p,p_i)$ means the weight of the edge from p to p_i.

9.2.1.4 Relevance integration

Semantic relevance score $SR(t,s)$ obtained in Section 9.2.1.2 reflects the semantic relevance between tag t and service s, while the authority of tag $Auth(t)$ obtained in Section 9.2.1.3 reflects the meaningfulness of tag t in the whole STNet. In this section, we integrate semantic relevance and tag authority to be the final relevance of the user-contributed tag t with respect to service s.

Given a service s with a set of tag T annotated to it, the relevance score of each tag $t \in T$ is computed as follows:

$$Score(t,s) = (1 - \lambda)SR(t,s) + \lambda Auth(t), \qquad (9.7)$$

in which λ is the weight of the tag authority. The range of λ is [0,1]. Specifically, WS-TRM only considers the semantic relevance of t to s when $\lambda = 0$, while WS-TRM ranks tags only according to the tag authority in STNet when $\lambda = 1$.

9.2.2 Tagging Data Recommendation

Similar to the multimedia tagging and document tagging, some inherent properties in web service tagging, e.g., uneven tag distribution, influence the effectiveness of tagging data in web service mining. This property is easily understood because tagging is a kind of user behavior. Hot web services are usually annotated with lots of tags, while less popular web services may be annotated with few or even no tags.

Tag recommendation technique is a widely accepted approach to handle this problem. Vote and sum are two classical tag recommendation approaches, in which tag co-occurrence is used to compute a score for each candidate tag and the top-K tags with the highest scores are selected as the recommended tags. Details about vote and sum can be found in [8]. In this section, we use the proposed WS-TRM to improve their performance by considering both tag relevance and co-occurrence in the process of web service tag recommendations. In particular, for a candidate tag t, the weighted average value of the normalized tag relevance $TR(t)$ and the normalized tag co-occurrence score $TC(t)$ are utilized for tag recommendations. To evaluate the impact of tag relevance, the following approaches are implemented:

- **Sum**. In this approach, tag co-occurrence score $TC(t)$, which is computed by using the *Sum* strategy, is used as the metric for tag recommendations.
- **Vote**. In this approach, $TC(t)$ is also used as the metric for tag recommendations, while it is computed by using the *Vote* strategy.
- **Sum$^+$**. In this approach, the tag relevance value $TR(t)$ is introduced to improve the performance of sum.
- **Vote$^+$**. In this approach, the tag relevance value $TR(t)$ is used to improve the performance of vote.

Before evaluating the performance of tag recommendations, we select 1800 web services that contain 1254 unique tags as the dataset for evaluation. The ground truth is manually created through a blind review pooling method, in which for each of the 1800 web services, the top 10 recommendations from each of the two strategies are taken to construct the pool. The volunteers are then asked to evaluate the descriptiveness of each of the recommended tags in context of the web services. We provide the WSDL documents and web service descriptions to volunteers to help them. The volunteers are then asked to judge the descriptiveness on a three-point scale: very good, good, not good. The distinction between very good and good is defined to make the assessment task conceptually easier for the user. Finally, we received 212 very good judgments (16.9%), 298 good judgments (23.7%), and 744 not good judgments (59.4%).

To evaluate the performance of the web service tag recommendations, we adopt two metrics that capture the performance in different aspects:

- **Success at rank K (S@K).** The success of rank K is defined as the percentage of good or very good tags taken in the top-K recommended tags, averaged over all judged web services.
- **Precision at rank K (P@K).** Precision of rank K is defined as the proportion of retrieved tags that is relevant, averaged over all judged web services.

Table 9.1 shows the S@K comparison of the four tag recommendation strategies, in which the given tag means the number of tags that the target web service has. Take the sum strategy as an example. When the given tag varies from 1 to 2, the average value of S@K is more than 0.7, which means that more than 70% of the recommended tags have good or very good descriptiveness. From Table 9.1, it can be observed that the introduction of tag relevance largely improves the performance of traditional tag recommendation strategies, because the S@K values of both Sum^+ and $Vote^+$ are larger than the S@K values of the original strategies. A trend can be identified, which is that in most cases, the S@K values of all four strategies decrease with the increase of K. This is because the most relevant tags have a high probability to be included in the tag recommendation list when K is

Table 9.1: S@K comparison of four tag recommendation strategies

Given Tag	Method	$K = 1$	$K = 2$	$K = 3$	$K = 4$	$K = 5$
1−2	*Sum*	0.8132	0.7081	0.6738	0.7087	0.7181
	Sum^+	0.8331	0.7192	0.7033	0.7221	0.7318
	Vote	0.6329	0.5949	0.6737	0.7005	0.6972
	$Vote^+$	0.6875	0.6112	0.6745	0.7143	0.7348
3−5	*Sum*	0.7534	0.7143	0.7380	0.6852	0.6720
	Sum^+	0.7745	0.7322	0.7449	0.7208	0.6775
	Vote	0.7867	0.6646	0.7042	0.7022	0.7103
	$Vote^+$	0.7958	0.7436	0.7323	0.7128	0.7219
>5	*Sum*	0.7632	0.7211	0.6944	0.6975	0.6647
	Sum^+	0.7822	0.7318	0.7098	0.7145	0.6897
	Vote	0.8136	0.7769	0.7749	0.7262	0.6973
	$Vote^+$	0.8364	0.8012	0.7943	0.7438	0.7012

Table 9.2: P@K comparison of four tag recommendation strategies

Given Tag	Method	$K = 1$	$K = 2$	$K = 3$	$K = 4$	$K = 5$
1−2	*Sum*	0.6933	0.5083	0.4277	0.3788	0.3562
	Sum$^+$	0.7612	0.5329	0.4879	0.4374	0.4038
	Vote	0.7879	0.5409	0.4503	0.3947	0.3689
	Vote$^+$	0.7945	0.5983	0.4832	0.4329	0.3925
3−5	*Sum*	0.6512	0.4857	0.4171	0.3654	0.3345
	Sum$^+$	0.6856	0.5134	0.4658	0.3765	0.3564
	Vote	0.7415	0.5414	0.4496	0.3925	0.3494
	Vote$^+$	0.7667	0.5934	0.5092	0.4333	0.3764
>5	*Sum*	0.5894	0.4656	0.4365	0.3451	0.3508
	Sum$^+$	0.6219	0.5043	0.4754	0.3922	0.3657
	Vote	0.7148	0.5478	0.4105	0.4026	0.3658
	Vote$^+$	0.7443	0.5874	0.4459	0.4322	0.3745

small, and some irrelevant tags may also be included in the top-K recommendation list when K is large.

Table 9.2 shows the comparison of four tag recommendation strategies in terms of P@K. Similarly, it can be found that the introduction of WS-TRM improves the performance of tag recommendations in terms of P@K. From Table 9.2, one trend can be identified, which is that the P@K values of all four strategies decrease when the given tags increase. This is because the number of relevant tags to one certain web service is limited. When the given tags increase, the number of still relevant tags decreases, which leads to the decrease of P@K. In addition, P@K achieves its largest value when $K = 1$, and decreases when K increases.

9.2.3 Tagging Data-Based Service Mining

Recently, web service clustering was used to handle the low recall of web service search engines, which is caused by the keyword matching [2,4]. In their opinion, if web services with similar functionality are placed into the same cluster, more relevant web services could be retrieved in the search result. In our prior work [1], a hybrid approach of using both WSDL documents and tags to cluster web services was proposed, and this approach outperformed the previous clustering approaches, in which only WSDL documents were used. Specifically, given two web services s_1 and s_2, not only the similarity between the WSDL of s_1 and the one of s_2 (i.e., $Sim_{wsdl}(s_1,s_2)$) is considered, but also the similarity between the tags of s_1 and the ones of s_2 (i.e., $Sim_{tag}(s_1,s_2)$) is considered. The detailed process of web service clustering can be found in [1].

However, the relevance of user-contributed tags with respect to the web services has not been considered in [1]; that is, the tags associated with web services were all treated as totally relevant, which may limit or even bring negative effects on the performance of tagging data in web service clustering. In this section, we propose to use WS-TRM to obtain tag relevance scores, and weight $Sim_{tag}(s_1,s_2)$ by the relevance of the corresponding tags. That is, the similarity between s_1 and s_2 is generated by integrating $Sim_{wsdl}(s_1,s_2)$ and weighting $Sim_{tag}(s_1,s_2)$.

To evaluate the impact of WS-TRM on web service clustering, we implement two versions of clustering; one version uses WS-TRM, while the other one does not use WS-TRM. In this experiment, we use the six categories of web services (i.e., weather, e-mail, stock, tourism, finance, and communication) to do web service clustering. To evaluate the performance of web service clustering, we introduce two metrics (precision and recall), which are widely adopted in the IR domain:

$$Precision_{c_i} = \frac{succ(c_i)}{succ(c_i) + mispl(c_i)}, \tag{9.8}$$

$$Recall_{c_i} = \frac{succ(c_i)}{succ(c_i) + missed(c_i)} \tag{9.9}$$

in which $succ(c_i)$ is the number of services successfully placed into cluster c_i, $mispl(c_i)$ is the number of services that are incorrectly placed into cluster c_i, and $missed(c_i)$ is the number of services that should be placed into c_i, but are placed into another cluster.

Figure 9.2 shows the performance comparison of the above two versions of web service clustering. From Figure 9.2, we can observe that clustering with WS-TRM outperforms clustering without WS-TRM in both precision and recall. Specifically, the average improvement caused by the use of WS-TRM achieves 16% in terms of precision and 10% in terms of recall. As we discussed above, the neglect of tag relevance limits or even brings a negative effect on the performance of tagging data. The results in Figure 9.2 demonstrate that the use of tag relevance facilitates web service clustering.

Tagging data was recently used to improve the performance of web object retrieval due to the rich semantic information included in the user-contributed tags, especially in the domain of multimedia. The performance of web service retrieval is also unsatisfied because the simplicity of the information source can be used for service retrieval, i.e., WSDL. Intuitively, tagging data associated with web services could be used to improve the performance of web service retrieval. In our prior work [1], a brief introduction to tagging data in web service retrieval is proposed. Figure 9.3 shows the tag cloud of the Titan web service search engine, in which the most frequently annotated tags are listed and the tags with higher frequency have larger fonts.

However, if the web service tag relevance is ignored, the use of web service tags may provide limited contribution or even have a negative effect on the performance of web service retrieval. To evaluate the impact of tag relevance on the performance of web

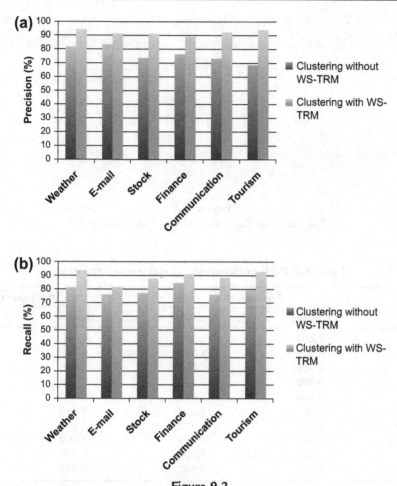

Figure 9.2

Impact of web service tag relevance measurement (WS-TRM) to the performance of web service clustering.

service retrieval, we implement two versions of service retrieval; one version does not use WS-TRM and treats the relevance of every tag as one (called baseline), while the other one uses WS-TRM and considers the relevance of tags in the process of service retrieval. Due to the limitation of space, we could not introduce the detailed process of service retrieval. As for the evaluation metric, we choose precision at K (P@K), which means the proportion of relevance instances in the top-K retrieved results.

Table 9.3 shows the results of the implemented evaluation based on the Titan web service search engine. In Table 9.4, for each query, we compare the performance of baseline and WS-TRM in terms of P@5 and P@20. From Table 9.3, it can be determined that WS-TRM largely outperforms baseline in most cases, in terms of P@5 and P@20. This is

Figure 9.3
Tag cloud of Titan web service search engine.

Table 9.3: P@K performance of web service retrieval

Query	Precision at 5		Precision at 20	
	Baseline	**WS-TRM**	**Baseline**	**WS-TRM**
Weather	0.800	1.000	0.650	0.900
sms	0.800	1.000	0.700	1.000
Tourism	0.400	0.800	0.500	0.650
Stock	0.800	0.800	0.750	0.900
ZIP	0.600	1.000	0.800	1.000
Location	0.400	0.800	0.550	0.750
Commercial	0.800	0.800	0.650	0.850
Bioinformatics	0.400	0.600	0.500	0.750
University	0.600	1.000	0.650	0.900
Average	0.640	0.840	0.645	0.845

Table 9.4: Integration rules for QoS of service composition

QoS Property	Ψ_1	Ψ_2
Cost	$\sum$	$\sum$
Response time	$\sum$	Max
Throughput	$\sum$	Min
Availably	$\prod$	$\prod$

because some user-contributed tags are imprecise, ambiguous, or even irrelevant. In baseline, all associated tags are treated as totally relevant, which limits the performance of tagging data in web service retrieval. On the other hand, by using WS-TRM, the effect of these imprecise, ambiguous, irrelevant tags are weakened in the process of tag-based web service retrieval.

9.3 Service Computing with a Complex Mobile Environment

As service-oriented applications have been increasingly developed and widely used, service-oriented architecture (SOA) becomes popular in more and more domains and the application environments become more complex. For example, SOA has stepped into mobile environments. Characteristics of the mobile environment, such as mobility, unpredictability, and variation of the mobile network's signal strength, present challenges in selecting optimal services for service composition. Traditional QoS-aware methods that select individual services with the best QoS may not always result in the best composite service, because constant mobility makes the performance of service invocation unpredictable and location-based. This section discusses the challenges of this problem and defines it in a formal way. To solve this new research problem, we propose a mobility model, a mobility-aware QoS computation rule, and a mobility-enabled selection algorithm with teaching-learning-based optimization (TLBO). The experimental simulation results demonstrate that our approach can obtain better solutions than current standard composition methods in mobile environments. The approach can obtain near-optimal solutions and has a nearly linear algorithmic complexity with respect to the problem size.

9.3.1 Motivating Scenarios

Because of the mobility of mobile users and the dynamics of mobile networks, service selection in a mobile environment is notably different from that in the traditional Internet environment. We will outline the differences using examples for single service selection and composite service selection.

9.3.1.1 Single service selection

Figure 9.4 illustrates an example of a single service selection in a mobile network.

Assume a mobile user, Tom, wants to invoke a hotel booking service when he is walking from base station A to base station B. Assume that the signal strength of B is stronger than A, the average data transmission rate between Tom's cellphone and A is 10 Kbps, and the data transmission rate between Tom's cellphone and B is 20 Kbps. A virtual service provider sp is responsible for selecting the service with the best response time for Tom. Suppose that sp finds two candidates that can provide hotel booking service, *Ctrip* and *Elong*, which are well-known hotel booking services in China. sp would make the selection decision for Tom depending on the QoS of each service. The booking confirmation wait time is 100 s for *Ctrip* and 120 s for *Elong*.

In the traditional Internet environment, it is intuitive that sp would select *Ctrip* for Tom because *Ctrip* performs faster than *Elong*. However, Tom is moving when he invokes the services. He sends the hotel booking request while at location A (we assume the time of

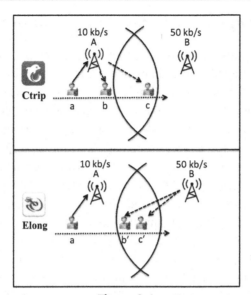

Figure 9.4
An example of single service selection in mobile networks.

sending a request is 1 s). If *sp* selects *Ctrip* for Tom, he would obtain the response when at location *B* and start receiving confirmation with 1000 KB of data. Because of the handover principles of cellular networks [9], Tom would not switch his connection to station *B* as soon as he gets into its coverage area. He would continue the connection with station *A* until its signal strength is lower than a threshold (we set it zero for simplification). Finally, Tom finishes receiving the confirmation at location *C*. Thus, the total service time of *Ctrip* is $1 \text{ s} + 100 \text{ s} + 1000/10 = 201$ s. If Tom selects the service *Elong*, he would have moved to location B' before he begins to receive the confirmation. Next, he would establish a connection with station *B* because of its stronger signal. Finally, Tom finishes receiving the confirmation at location C'; the total service time of *Elong* is $1 \text{ s} + 120 \text{ s} + 1000/20 = 171$ s. Thus, it is faster for Tom if *sp* selects *Elong*, although its execution time is longer.

Hence, we can see that service selection in a mobile environment is different from that in a traditional environment. It is essential to take a users' mobility into consideration when selecting services in mobile networks.

9.3.1.2 Composite service selection

Figure 9.5 illustrates a more complicated example of service selection for service composition.

This time Tom wants to arrange business travel to Beijing. He needs to know the weather conditions, book a flight, book a hotel, and pay. To this end, the virtual service provider *sp*

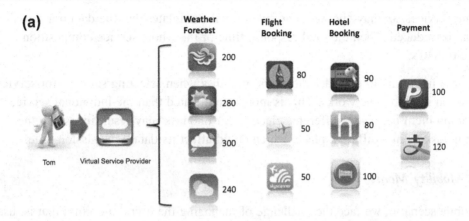

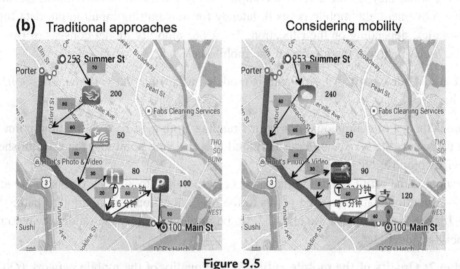

Figure 9.5

An example of service selection for service composition in mobile networks. (a) A services composition for arranging travel and (b) comparison of different solutions.

will compose multiple mobile services from different providers for Tom. Figure 9.5(a) shows the candidates for each task found by *sp*. Figure 9.5(b) shows that Tom will invoke the composed services when he goes to work by subway.

If *sp* used a traditional approach for service selection, the service composition would be composed of the fastest candidate for each task. However, data transmission time may vary as Tom travels to work. The data transmission time cannot be guaranteed by traditional methods. As Figure 9.5(b) shows, the total response time of the whole service composition is 850 s using traditional methods. If *sp* considers Tom's mobility when selecting services, *sp* may choose some suboptimal candidates, but the data transmission time can be reduced. Then the total response time of the whole service composition is now reduced to 830 s.

Hence, it is important to consider the users' mobility when selecting services for service composition in mobile networks. This is more complicated than the individual service selection problem because a different selection for one task may result in issuing the following task from a different place, which could affect its data transmission time.

9.3.2 Mobility Model

In a mobile scenario, we face the challenge of managing the users' mobility; that is, users are moving when they invoke a service composition in the mobile environment. During the users' movement, the mobile network latency for transmitting input/output data for services varies, depending on their location. Thus, our mobility model consists of two parts: the user's path and the quality of the mobile network.

Definition 1: User's path. A user's path is modeled as a triple $mp = (Time, Location, M)$, in which:

1. *Time* is the set of continuous time points ranging from t_0 to t_n, t_0 is the time point that the user starts the service composition, and t_n is the time point that the user finishes the service composition;
2. *Location* is the set of the user's locations corresponding to all time points in *Time*;
3. *M* is a function that maps time points to the user's locations on the motion path. *M: Time $\rightarrow$ Location*. The function *M* can be implemented by the random waypoint mobility model [10].

Definition 2: Quality of the mobile network. The quality of the mobile network (*QoMN*) usually describes the mobile signal strength at a specific location. In this section, we mainly consider the data transmission rate as the quality of the mobile network. The function *L* is used to map locations to *QoMN*, *L: Location $\rightarrow$ QoMN*.

Figure 9.6 shows an example that represents the mobility model in Figure 9.5(b). First, we can draw Tom's path in a two-dimensional space; we can obtain the location of Tom at any specific time point via function *M*. We can find the location where Tom starts to send or receive data for a service invocation by calculating the time points of the service invocations. For example, Tom starts invoking the weather forecast service at the time point t_0 and receives a response at time point t_1. Meanwhile, given a location, we can obtain the quality of the mobile network corresponding to this location. Thus, the mobile network latency for transmitting input/output data can be calculated. Lastly, the final response time of the whole service composition can be calculated.

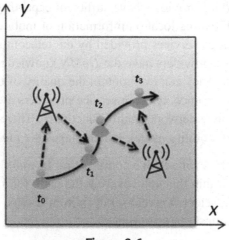

Figure 9.6
Mobility model.

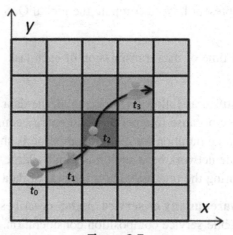

Figure 9.7
Mobility model grid.

To make the mobility model computable, we build an overlay grid on the two-dimensional space, as in Figure 9.7. Each cell of the grid corresponds to an area of constant *QoMN*. This is equivalent to the practical situation when the cells are infinitely small. We can approximately measure the *QoMN* of the area covering the user's path and build this grid by associating *QoMN* values with each cell. Based on the mobility model, we can define the problem that is the focus of this section.

Another challenge of adding a mobility model to service selection in composite services is the question of who is responsible for maintaining the model and generating service response time. Telecom service providers have sufficient capability to maintain the proposed mobility model. First, the location information of mobile users can be monitored by GPS or other location-based services provided by the telecom service providers. Additionally, telecom service providers have the *QoMN* knowledge through their monitoring of their network. They can even obtain the quality of the mobile network at a specific location in real time. Hence, telecom service providers are able to implement the path function *M* and the mobile network quality function *L*. Therefore, they are ideal maintainers of the proposed mobility model, which makes the model practical.

Definition 3: Service selection for service composition in mobile networks. Given a user's path and the *QoMN* within the area covering the path, for a service composition required by the mobile user, select concrete services from service candidates to obtain the optimal global QoS (the shortest response time).

9.3.3 Mobility-Aware Quality of Service Computation

In this section, we first introduce the concept of mobility-aware QoS (MQoS) based on the mobility model. Next, we present how to compute the global QoS of the mobile service composition.

Assumption 1. During the time of data transmission of each task, the *QoMN* remains constant.

The assumption can be justified as follows. On one hand, the data volume for a mobile service is normally not large because Internet fees and energy consumption must be controlled. Therefore, the time duration for data transmission is short. On the other hand, the covered area of a mobile network base station is usually large enough to ensure that the *QoMN* stays similar during the relatively short interval of data transmission.

Definition 4: Mobility-aware quality of service. *MQoS* describes the performance of a component service in a mobile service composition consideration. In this section, we consider only one property of QoS (response time). The *MQoS* of a component service *s* can be calculated as follows:

$$MQoS_s = t_{d_i} + Q_s + t_{d_o} \tag{9.10}$$

in which t_{d_i} is the mobile network latency of transmitting input data, Q_s is the execution time of *s*, and t_{d_o} is the mobile network latency of transmitting output data. t_{d_i} and t_{d_o} can be calculated as follows:

$$t_{d_i} = \frac{d_i}{QoMN_i}$$

$$t_{d_o} = \frac{d_o}{QoMN_o} \tag{9.11}$$

in which d_i is the volume of input data and $QoMN_i$ is the $QoMN$ at the location from which the user starts sending the input data. By assumption 1, $QoMN_i$ will not change during t_{d_i}. d_o and $QoMN_o$ are the corresponding variables for the output data.

Consider the example in Figure 9.5(b). To calculate the $MQoS$ of a weather forecast service s, we first need the time point tp when Tom starts to send the input data; Tom's location at the time point tp can be found through the function M: $location = M(tp)$. The quality of the mobile network at that location is derived through the function L: $QoMN = L(location)$. Next, t_{d_i} is calculated with Eqn (9.11). t_{d_0} is computed similarly. Finally, the $MQoS$ of s can be found with Eqn (9.10).

Definition 5: Global quality of service. Global QoS describes the performance of the entire service composition. The global response time of a service composition *so* can be calculated as follows:

$$GQoS = \underset{s \in so}{\psi} \; MQoS_s \tag{9.12}$$

in which ψ is an operator that integrates the values of local QoS. We adopt the QoS integration rules in [11] to implement ψ, as shown in Table 9.4, in which ψ_1 is the integration function for QoS of services in a sequential execution path. ψ_2 is the integration for QoS of multiple parallel paths. For the notations in the table, we only use their intuitive mathematic meanings. For example, "$\sum$" means summation, "$\prod$" means product, "max" means maximum, and "min" means minimum. The optimal QoS of a composition is the best value obtained from the integration rules. For simplicity, we consider only a one-dimensional QoS value (response time) in this section. It is not difficult to extend to other criteria by aggregating the overall QoS value of the service composition through the computation rules. If an efficient aggregating function of multiple QoS properties is provided, our proposal can also handle QoS values of multiple-dimensions.

9.3.4 Mobility-Enabled Selection Algorithm

Our selection algorithm is based on the TLBO, which belongs to the "swarm intelligence" optimization methods. First, we illustrate how our problem is transformed to an optimization problem. Then, we introduce our service selection algorithm based on TLBO.

9.3.4.1 Optimization problem

An optimization problem is to find the smallest $F(\Theta)$ with a feasible parameter vector Θ, which can be modeled as follows [12]:

$$\begin{aligned} \inf \quad & F(\Theta) \\ \text{subject to} \quad & \theta_i \in [1, N] \\ & \theta_i \in Z \end{aligned} \tag{9.13}$$

This means the feasible set of parameter vectors is constrained by $\theta_i \in [1, N]$ and is an integer. The optimal solution $\widehat{\Theta}$ satisfies the following conditions:

1. $\widehat{\Theta}$ belongs to the feasible set
2. $\forall \Theta, F(\widehat{\Theta}) \leq F(\Theta)$

The following theorem presents the relationship between this optimization problem and our mobility-aware service selection problem.

Theorem 1: Optimization problem. A mobility-aware service selection problem with a user's given path and a given quality of mobile network in this area is equivalent to the optimization problem described in Eqn (9.13).

Proof: For the problem of selecting optimal services with the shortest response time while considering mobility, the vector $\Theta = (\theta_1,...,\theta_m)$ can describe a possible solution as a service composition with m tasks. An element θ_i in Θ corresponds to a selected service from the candidates for the i-th task. The evaluation function for the parameter vector Θ can be implemented by Eqn (9.12):

$$F(\Theta) = \underset{\theta_i \in \Theta}{\psi} MQoS_{\theta_i} \tag{9.14}$$

The target of the mobility-aware service selection problem is to find a Θ to obtain the smallest $F(\Theta)$. Thus the problem is equivalent to the optimization problem described in Eqn (9.13).

The problem in Eqn (9.13) is an integer programming problem, which is a famous non-deterministic polynomial (NP) problem. Generally, there is no known algorithm with a non deterministic polynomial time complexity to solve such a problem. Thus, we propose a solution method based on the TLBO algorithm, which can achieve an approximately optimal solution in polynomial time.

9.3.4.2 Service selection algorithm

In this section, we give a basic overview of the TLBO algorithm. We then introduce our customizations of the algorithm for the problem of service selection for mobile service composition.

9.3.4.2.1 Overview of teaching-learning-based optimization algorithm

The TLBO was first proposed by Rao and Kalyankar [13]. Like other nature-inspired algorithms, TLBO is a population-based method that uses a population of solutions to proceed to the global solution. For TLBO, the population is considered to be a group or class of learners. For our mobile service composition problem, each learner in the

Table 9.5: Terms matching between teaching-learning-based optimization (TLBO) and service composition domain

Terms in TLBO	Terms in Service Composition Domain
Teacher	The optimal service composition
Learner	One feasible service composition
Class	The feasible set of service compositions
Subjects	Tasks in the service composition plan
Grade	Fitness (*GQoS*) of a service composition

population corresponds to a feasible service composition. Moreover, different tasks in the service composition plan are analogous to different subjects offered to learners; the learners' results are analogous to "fitness," as in other population-based optimization techniques. The teacher is considered to be the best solution obtained so far. Table 9.5 shows the analogous term matches between the TLBO and the service composition domains.

TLBO consists of two parts: "teacher phase" and "learner phase." The "teacher phase" means learning from the teacher, and the "learner phase" means learning through interactions between learners (Figure 9.8).

9.3.4.2.2 Initialization phase

One advantage of TLBO is that there are not as many parameters to be tuned, as in other population-based methods. Only two basic parameters need be decided in the initialization phase. One is the population size P, and the other is the maximum iteration number I. Next, the initial population is generated randomly.

For each learner in the class, $X^i = (x_1^i, x_2^i, ..., x_d^i)$ is generated randomly, in which

$i = (1, 2, 3,..., P)$, d is the number of tasks in the service composition plan, and x_j^i is the selected candidate for the j-th task in solution X^i, an integer that represents the selected candidate.

9.3.4.2.3 Teacher phase

In the teacher phase of TLBO, every learner X^i ($i = 1, 2, 3,..., P$) in the class learns from the teacher $X_{teacher}$ through the difference between the teacher $X_{teacher}$ and the mean value of the learners, *Mean*:

$$X_{new}^i = X_{old}^i + difference \qquad (9.15)$$

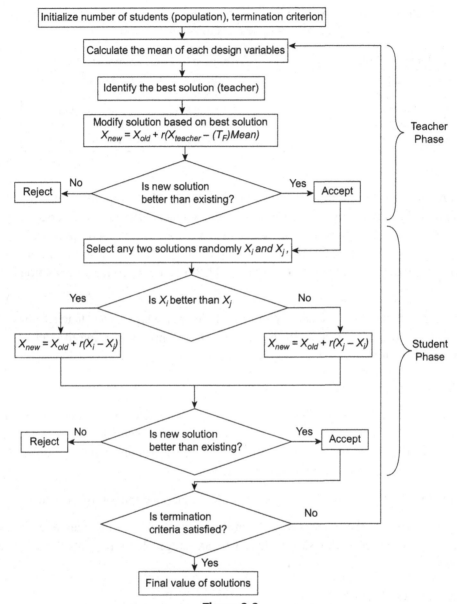

Figure 9.8

Teaching-learning-based optimization (TLBO) flow chart [13].

$$difference = r_i \times (X_{teacher} - TF_i \times Mean) \tag{9.16}$$

in which X_{old}^i and X_{new}^i is the i-th learner before and after learning from the teacher, $r_i = rand(0,1)$ is the learning step length, $TF_i = round[1 + rand(0,1)]$ is the teaching factor, and *Mean* is the average of all learners:

$$Mean = \frac{1}{P} \sum_{i=1}^{P} X^i \tag{9.17}$$

In our mobile service composition problem, each variable in a solution vector X must be an integer. We therefore add a *refine* operation for TLBO after each vector operation:

$$\begin{aligned}
&\text{def } refine\left(X^i\right): \\
&\quad \text{for } x_j \text{ in } X^i: \\
&\quad\quad x_j = round\left(x_j\right) \\
&\quad\quad \text{if } x_j > up: x_j = up \\
&\quad\quad \text{if } x_j < low: x_j = low
\end{aligned} \tag{9.18}$$

in which *up* and *low* are the upper and lower bounds of the candidates, respectively.

After learning from the teacher, all learners update themselves with the learned result:

$$\begin{aligned}
&\text{if } F\left(X^i_{new}\right) < F\left(X^i_{old}\right): \\
&\quad X^i_{old} = X^i_{new}
\end{aligned} \tag{9.19}$$

in which the function F is used to calculate the fitness of the learner according to Eqn (9.14).

9.3.4.2.4 Learner phase

Instead of learning from the teacher, learners increase their knowledge through interaction between themselves in the learner phase. A learner learns something new if another learner has more knowledge than he or she. This keeps the population diverse, which can avoid the algorithm converging too early to obtain a good result.

For each learner in the class, $X^i = (x^i_1, x^i_2, ..., x^i_d)$ will randomly choose a learning target $X^j = (x^j_1, x^j_2, ..., x^j_d) i \neq j$. X^i will analyze its difference between X^j, then make the learning decision:

$$X^i_{new} = \begin{cases} X^i_{old} + r_i \cdot \left(X^i - X^j\right) & F\left(X^j\right) > F\left(X^j\right) \\ X^i_{old} + r_i \cdot \left(X^j - X^i\right) & F\left(X^j\right) < F\left(X^j\right) \end{cases} \tag{9.20}$$

in which $r_i = \text{rand}(0,1)$ is the learning step length.

After learning between learners themselves, learners should also update as in Eqn (9.19).

9.3.4.3 Time complexity analysis

Suppose the number of learners in the population is P, the number of tasks in a service composition plan is d, and the maximum iteration number is I. The process of the proposed method can be summarized as follows:

1. Initialization: randomly generate P service compositions;
2. Calculate the fitness of every composition;

   for $i = 1:P$

3. Decide which is the teacher in the class;

for $j = 1{:}d$

4. Update the candidate for each task by learning from the teacher through Eqns (9.15) and (9.19);
5. Update the candidate for each task by teaching from other learners following Eqns (9.20) and (9.19);

EndFor

EndFor

6. If the iteration number reaches I, the algorithm terminates. Otherwise, return to step (2).

We can see that the main computation time is spent in steps (4) and (5): computing the difference between learners and the teacher/learners and then updating the candidates for each task. The time complexity of each of steps is $O(d)$. Thus, for each learner in the population, the time complexity of the teacher and learner phases is $O(d)$. Next, the time complexity for the whole population is $O(P*d)$. Finally, the overall time complexity with I iterations is $O(I*P*d)$.

9.3.5 Experimental Evaluation

In this section, we describe a series of simulations we conducted to evaluate and validate our proposed approach. The experiments were designed to answer the following questions:

1. Why is it necessary to consider user mobility when selecting services for service composition in a mobile environment? What is the impact of the mobility?
2. Compared with other metaheuristic algorithm-based methods, can our approach find more optimal results?
3. Compared with other metaheuristic algorithm-based methods, how does our approach perform as to scalability?

9.3.5.1 Setup

The evaluation was run on a machine with an Intel Core 2.3 GHz i7 CPU. All algorithms were implemented in Python 2.7 and evaluated sequentially; they were given up to a maximum of 8 GB of memory if needed. We generated our service compositions with randomly inserted tasks and control structures. For each task, we randomly created a number of candidate services, each with a different QoS. To avoid other factors affecting the evaluation results, we set it up so that the candidates for the same task required the same amount of input/output data. The execution time of each service was generated from a uniform distribution. Figure 9.9 depicts an example of a generated service composition with five tasks.

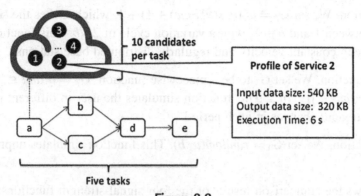

Figure 9.9
Example service composition with five tasks.

For all the implemented algorithms, the population size $P = 10$, and the maximum iteration number was 100; all the algorithms were run independently 50 times for unprejudiced statistical results.

9.3.5.2 Impact of mobility

To validate the necessity of considering mobility when making selections for mobile service composition, we compared our method with the standard composition method that considers only services' individual QoS. This method selects the candidate with the optimal execution time for each task without considering mobile network latency. For the experiments in this section, we generated service compositions with 50 tasks and 100 candidates available per task.

9.3.5.2.1 Impact of variation of signal strength

In the proposed mobility model, the two functions M and L determine the relationship between users' movements and the variation of signal strength. For our experiments, we combined the user movement function $location = M(time)$ and the mobile signal-strength function $QoMN = L(location)$ into one function of signal strength: $QoMN=G(time) = L(M(time))$, which gives the signal strength with increasing time. Because there are many factors affecting the variation of signal strength (such as a user's speed, distance from signal stations, properties of each signal station, etc.), the variation of signal strength in practice cannot be defined by any functions, and it is difficult to acquire the real data of signal strength. Therefore, we generated four different functions of signal strength to simulate the variation of signal strength during the users' movements:

G_1: constant function. We set $G_1 = a$. This function simulates a traditional environment and was used to evaluate how our method compares to the standard method for traditional service composition.

G_2: cosine function. We set $G_2 = a*(cos(b*time) + 1) + 1$, which makes the signal strength vary between 1 and $a + 1$, with a variation cycle of $2\pi/b$. This function simulates a user moving with constant velocity and regularly distributed base stations.

G_3: piecewise function. We set G_3 to be a piecewise function: $G_3 = a:time \in [0,t_1)|$ $b:time \in [t_1,t_2)|c:time \in [t_2,t_3)|$.... This function simulates the user in different periods and that the signal strength changes in each period.

G_4: random function. We set $G_4 = random(a, b)$. This function simulates unpredictable situations.

Figure 9.10 shows the comparison results of the four signal-strength functions; the x-axes are the iteration number and the y-axes are the response times of the service compositions found by the two methods. Figure 9.10(a) shows that the standard method can find better service compositions (with shorter response times) than our method. The standard method can guarantee to find the optimal solution with the shortest response time because the mobile network latency is always the same with function G_1. However, our method approaches the optimal result closely after a sufficient number of iterations, which validates that our method can find near-optimal solutions.

Figure 9.10(b)−(d) shows that our proposed method outperforms the standard method with the three variations of the signal strength function. This indicates that the standard method is not effective at finding compositions when signal strength varies in a mobile environment. We also find that our method performs better whether the signal strength varies regularly or randomly.

9.3.5.2.2 Impact of amplitude of variation of signal strength

In this experiment, we aim to evaluate the impact of the amplitude of the variation of signal strength (that is, how much the signal strength varied) on the improvement of our approach. To this end, we selected the cosine function G_2 as the variation function of signal strength because of the ease of adjusting the amplitude of variation through the tuning parameter a in G_2. We set the range of a from 60 to 120, and $b = 1$. We used the metric *improve_rate* to evaluate how much better our method is compared to the standard method.

$$improve\_rate = \frac{r_s - r_m}{r_s}$$

in which r_s is the optimal result achieved by the standard method, and r_m is the optimal result from our method.

Figure 9.11 shows the improvement of our method with different values of the amplitude of the variation of signal strength. The average improvement using our method is approximately 20% compared to the standard composition method. We observe that as the

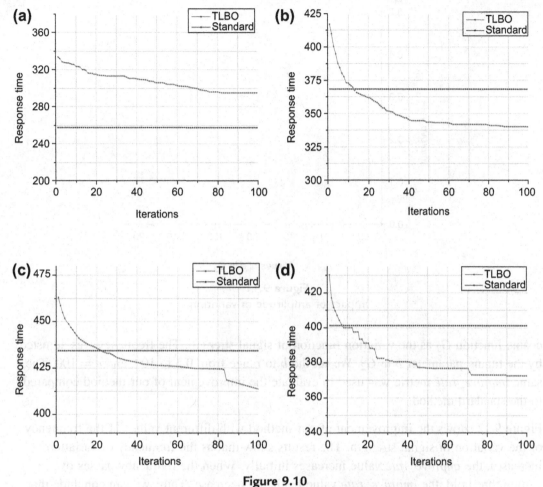

Figure 9.10

Comparison results with the standard method. (a) Under function G_1; (b) under function G_2; (c) under function G_3; and (d) under function G_4.

amplitude of variation increases, there is no obvious regularity in how *improve_rate* varies. This indicates that our method outperforms the standard method no matter how the amplitude of variation of signal strength varies, because the values of *improve_rate* are always positive. Furthermore, we note that the improvement fluctuates with different amplitude values; this is because the improvement of the mobile network latency cannot remain fixed under all conditions.

9.3.5.2.3 Impact of frequency of variation of signal strength

In addition to the amplitude, we also evaluated the impact of the frequency of the variation of signal strength on the improvement of our approach. Similarly, we also selected the

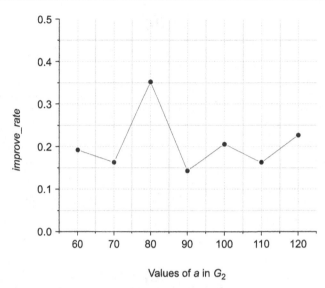

Figure 9.11
Impact of amplitude of variation.

cosine function G_2 as the variation function of signal strength. The frequency was adjusted by the tuning parameter b in G_2. We set the b to range from 0.5 to 100, and $a = 100$. The same *improve_rate* metric was used to evaluate the improvement of our method compared to the standard method.

Figure 9.12 shows the improvement of our method with different values of the frequency of the variation of signal strength. The results show that as the frequency of variation increases, the *improve_rate* value increases initially. When the frequency passes over a certain threshold, the *improve_rate* value begins to decrease. Thus, we can conclude that our method cannot continue to improve as signal strength changes more quickly. There are two reasons for this: (1) the initial increase of *improve_rate* confirms the intuitive notion that a relatively obvious variation of signal strength leads to better improvements and (2) when the variation frequency surpasses a certain threshold, it may cause the signal strength to vary so quickly that it returns to its previous value when the user re-issues a data request; thus there is less change in signal strength from the user's perspective.

9.3.5.3 Optimality evaluation

Because few studies have investigated the problem of service selection for mobile service composition, we have not found many existing methods for the problem to compare with ours. Because TLBO is a fundamental population-based algorithm, we chose several other population-based algorithms and compared their optimality with our method.

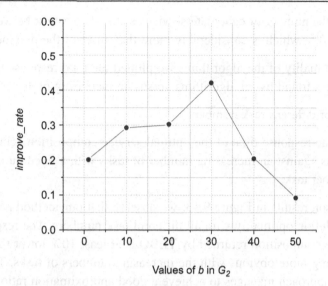

Figure 9.12
Impact of frequency of variation.

Genetic algorithm (GA): A search heuristic algorithm that mimics the process of natural selection [14]. This has been used by existing service composition approaches [15–17]. We extended it by adding mobility.

Particle swarm optimization (PSO): A computational method that optimizes a problem by iteratively trying to improve a candidate solution with regard to a given measure of quality [18]. PSO has also been widely used in service composition research [19–21].

Negative selection algorithm (NSA): NSA belongs to the field of artificial immune systems inspired by theoretical immunology and observed immune functions, principles, and models [22]. It has recently been used in solving service composition problems and proved to have high efficiency [23,24].

To compare the above algorithms with our approach, we tuned the parameters for each algorithm to achieve their best performance. The most suitable parameters are shown in Table 9.6. We generated service compositions with sizes between 10 and 100 (in steps

Table 9.6: Parameter setting of different algorithms

Algorithms	Parameter Setting
GA	Cross rate $= 0.7$; mutate rate $= 0.3$
PSO	$c_1 = c_2 = 2$; weight $= 0.8$
NSA	$\alpha = 0.1$; $\beta = 3$; $\rho = 1$

of 10). We varied the number of candidate services available per task between 100 and 1000 (in steps of 100), which is considerably more than most of the previous studies used.

To evaluate the optimality of the algorithms, we plotted the total response time of the service compositions found by all algorithms versus an increasing problem size.

9.3.5.3.1 Impact of different task number

Figure 9.13 plots the response time of the optimal service composition achieved by different algorithms against an increasing number of tasks with a fixed number (100) of services available per task.

From the comparison results in Figure 9.13, we observe that our method has outstanding performance of solution optimality with all different task numbers. The response time of the optimal service composition returned by TLBO is at least 10% lower than others, the advantages becoming more obvious with the increasing numbers of tasks. Thus, we can conclude that our approach manages to achieve a good approximation ratio of the optimal solution regardless of the composition size.

9.3.5.3.2 Impact of different numbers of candidates

Figure 9.14 shows that the optimal response time decreases slightly as the number of services per task increases. This is because there are more choices available as the number of services increases. We also observe that our method outperforms the others no matter what the number of candidate services are.

From the comparisons in this and the previous sections, we observe that our approach maintains good performance with large-scale datasets both for tasks and candidates. This

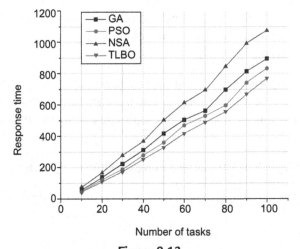

Figure 9.13

Response time of service composition with different numbers of tasks.

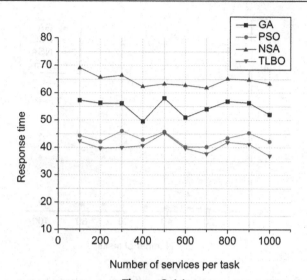

Figure 9.14

Response time of service composition with different numbers of services per task.

is because TLBO keeps the population diverse through the learning phase, which efficiently avoids converging to a suboptimal value too early. PSO performs better than GA because it has an evolution target in each generation, but this can also result in early convergence. For the problem we address, NSA performs worst, which is not consistent with previous research in [23]. This is because NSA-based methods focus more on local fitness, which is efficient in traditional service composition problems but not suitable in mobile environments. In summary, our proposed TLBO-based method has the best performance for optimality when compared to the other methods.

9.3.5.4 Scalability evaluation

In this section, we compared the scalability of our approach with the same other algorithms using the same settings as for optimality.

9.3.5.4.1 Impact of different numbers of tasks

Figure 9.15 shows that GA runs fastest compared to the other three algorithms. However, the qualities of its solutions are much worse than those of PSO and TLBO, although it takes much less than 100 ms to compute. It seems that GA is faster only because it fails to significantly improve the quality of its solutions, thus converging more quickly to a bad local optimum. Similarly, NSA also runs faster than PSO and TLBO, but the quality of NSA solutions are even worse than those of GA. PSO and TLBO obtain much better quality of solutions, but they sacrifice some runtime to improve their optimality.

Furthermore, TLBO takes longer than PSO. This is because TLBO adds a learning phase to avoid early convergence; this takes considerable runtime. Although TLBO uses a little

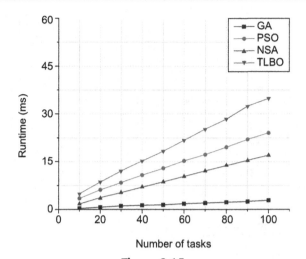

Figure 9.15
Runtime per iteration with different number of tasks.

more runtime than the other algorithms, it has a low algorithmic complexity, which is roughly linear with regard to the composition size. This observation validates the time complexity analysis in Section 9.3.4.3.

9.3.5.4.2 Impact of different numbers of candidates

In Figure 9.16 we note that the runtime of NSA increases significantly as the number of services per task increases. Thus, NSA quickly becomes unfeasible for practical purposes; it takes six times longer compared to the other algorithms for 1000 services per task. On

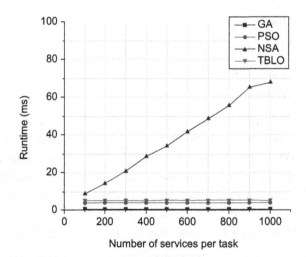

Figure 9.16
Runtime per iteration with different numbers of services per task.

the other hand, the runtimes of the other three algorithms do not change as much with an increasing number of services per task. Hence, all three algorithms scale well in this regard in our scenario.

9.4 Service Computing with Service Pattern Model

The research on how to model business patterns is a hot topic in recent years. It is an interesting problem to study the business model of service computing. There are three kinds of related models: classical service models, business process (BP) models, and the enterprise business (EB) models in management. However, none of them covers all the properties of the service business model. In this section, we define the business model of service as the combination of four kinds of strategies and name it the service pattern. We also propose a language named service pattern description language (SPDL) covering all the elements involved in these strategies. We formulate the language syntax and two basic extraction rules assisting economic analysis. Furthermore, we extend the business process model notation (BPMN) to support SPDL, which is named BPMN for service pattern (BPMN4SP). The example of a mobile application platform is studied in detail for a better understanding of SPDL.

9.4.1 Business Model and Service Computing

Nowadays the competition between businesses is not the competition of products but the competition of business models, just as Peter F. Drucker, the master in management, had said.

Taobao is a typical modern service company in China, which was established in 2003. The online mall (http://www.taobao.com) is the primary business of Taobao, which does not sell any goods, but it provides a platform service to sellers and attracts buyers. This business model is called customer to customer (C2C) in e-business. Taobao does not charge sellers for the basic platform service. The advertisement and the value-added services (e.g., website decorating service) are the major sources of income. Since the trading volume reaches 17.2 billion yuan (nearly 2.7 billion US dollars) in a single day, Taobao now is the largest online mall in China. The trading data (logs) are very valuable for helping to analyze customer behaviors. In recent years, the magic of this business model has attracted lots of researchers studying the business model. There are three basic questions on the business model:

- Q1: What is the business model of the service (e.g., Taobao)?
- Q2: How do you analyze the business model of a special service?
- Q3: How do you modify and redesign the business model of the service to provide a better benefit?

To address Q1, we define the business model of the service as the combination of four kinds of strategies: resources allocating (RA), activities organizing (AO), shareholders coordinating (SC), and productions designing (PD). We name the business model of this type of service the service pattern.

There are three types of models related to address Q2:

- Classical service model concentrates on the service function and quality, and it does not cover the business strategy and business process.
- Business process (BP) model defines the business process. Both Business Process Execution Language (BPEL) [25] and Business Process Model and Notation (BPMN) [26,27] solve the problem of business modeling and process optimization and have achieved great success in the last few years. However, the economic elements (e.g., resources) are not defined clearly in BP.
- Enterprise business (EB) model in management is a hot topic. EB does well in assisting to analyze the business strategy, while it is poor in process analysis. And EB cannot figure out the relationship between the business processes with the business strategy.

To address Q2, we extract four basic elements from these four strategies: resource from RA, activity from AO, role from SC, and entity from PD. In this section, we propose a language named SPDL covering these elements. Furthermore, we propose two basic analyzing tools based on SPDL. The SPDL is a high-level language that can bridge the gap between BP and EB. For better implementation, BPMN4SP is introduced, which extends the basic BPMN with the elements of SPDL. We replace the definition of resource and activity in BPMN. We have studied the basic idea of artifact-centric business process model (artifact BP) [28] and introduce the entity life cycle into our model.

To solve Q3, we need to first address Q1 and Q2. Both Q1 and Q2 are discussed in this section, while Q3 is left for a future study.

9.4.2 Service Pattern Description Language

This section formulates the key syntaxes and basic notions of SPDL. Figure 9.17 presents the relationship of basic notions through a Unified Modeling Language (UML) diagram. There are four basic elements (resource, activity, role, and entity) in service pattern strategies (RA, AO, SC, and PD). A role class owns many resources, and an entity class has many attributes and states. The concept of activity is redefined by adding roles and attributes. The step denotes the execution order, from one activity to another.

9.4.2.1 Basic set

We assume the existence of the following pair-wise disjoint countable infinite sets: T_P of primitive types, C_E of entity classes (names), AT of attributes (names), S of entity states,

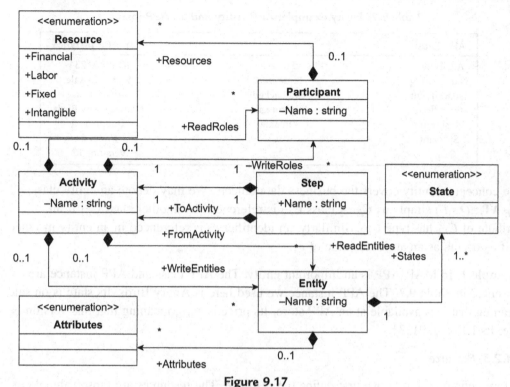

Figure 9.17
The UML diagram of basic notions.

$\mathbf{ID}_{C_E}$ of (entity) identifiers for each class $C_E \in C_E$, C_R of role classes (names), RE of resources (names), A of activities (names), and BR of business rules. A *type* is an element in the union $T = T_P \cup C_E$.

The domain of each type t in T, denoted as $\mathbf{DOM}(t)$, is defined as follows:

- if $t \in T_p$ is a primitive type, the domain $\mathbf{DOM}(t)$ is some known set of values (integers, strings, etc.);
- if $t \in C_E$ is an entity type, $\mathbf{DOM}(t) = \mathbf{ID}_t$.

9.4.2.2 Entity

Definition 6: Entity class. An entity class is a tuple $(C_E, \mathbf{AT}, \tau, Q, s, F)$ in which $C_E \in C_E$ is an entity class name, $\mathbf{AT} \subseteq AT$ is a finite set of attributes, $\tau : \mathbf{AT} \rightarrow T$ is a total mapping, $Q \subseteq S$ is a finite set of states, and $s \in Q$, $F \subseteq Q$ are initial *and* final states, respectively.

Definition 7: Entity instance. An entity instance of entity class $(C_E, \mathbf{AT}, \tau, Q, s, F)$ is a triple (e, μ, q) in which $e \in \mathbf{ID}_{C_E}$ is an identifier, μ is a partial mapping that assigns each attribute $AT \in \mathbf{AT}$ an element in its domain $\mathbf{DOM}(\tau(AT))$, and $q \in Q$ is the current state.

Table 9.7: Entity example: APP entity and an APP instance

APP Entity		An APP Instance
Attributes:	States:	ID:id391231
Name:string	Initialized	State: on sale
Quantity:int	Unchecked	Attributes:
Price:float	Not on sale	Name: Angry Birds
Version:int	On sale	Quantity: 5
Sales:int	...	Price: 0
...		Version: 12

The concept of entity covers the business data objects. We may denote an entity class $(C_E, \mathbf{AT}, \tau, Q, s, F)$ simply as C_E. A class C_{E2} is referenced by another class C_{E1} if an attribute of C_{E1} has type C_{E2}. Similarly, an identifier e_2 is referenced in an entity instance e_1 if e_2 occurs as an attribute value of e_1.

Example 1. In MAP, APP is an important entity. The APP class and APP instance are presented in Table 9.7. The APP instance we used here is Angry Birds. Its state is on sale, meaning that it is available at an APP store. Its price is zero, meaning that this version is free. Its ID is id391231.

9.4.2.3 Resource

Before defining the role, we first define the resource. The resources are those valuable in the process. There are four basic kinds of resources.

- The financial resource is the money in various forms.
- The fixed resource includes the houses, office equipment, etc.
- The labor resource is the resources of available manpower.
- The intangible resource includes the brand and information resources.

We define the type of each kind of resource as the basic float type for simplification.

9.4.2.4 Role

Definition 8: Role class. A role class is a triple $(C_R, \mathbf{RE}, \tau)$ in which $C_R \in C_R$ is the role class name, $RE \subseteq RE$ is a finite set of resources, and $\tau : RE \to T$ is a total mapping.

Definition 9: Role instance. The role instance of a role class $(C_R, \mathbf{RE}, \tau)$ is a two-tuple (r, μ) in which $r \in \mathbf{ID}_{C_R}$ is an identifier, and μ is partial mapping that assigns each resource $RE \in \mathbf{RE}$ an element in its domain $\mathbf{DOM}(\tau(RE))$.

In SPDL, the key characteristic of the role is owing resources (financial, fixed, labor, and intangible resources), and it is different from the concept of a participator in BP. An independent software company is a role, but a software engineer is only a participator.

Example 2. In MAP, there are four roles: customer, developer, platform and advertiser. Table 9.8 presents a develop role and an instance, which has an ID of id191231.

9.4.2.5 Schema

Definition 10: Entity schema. An entity schema is a finite set Γ_E of entity classes with distinct names such that every class referenced in Γ_E also occurs in Γ_E. The role schema followed Γ_E is a finite set Γ_R of role classes with distinct names such that every class is referenced in Γ_E. The schema is a finite set $\Gamma = \Gamma_E \cup \Gamma_R$.

9.4.2.6 Atom

Definition 11: Atom. An atom over a schema Γ is one of the following:

1. bolean expression,
2. $t_1 = t_2$, in which t_1, t_2 are instances of entity class (or role class) C in Γ,
3. **DEFINED**(t,D), in which t is an instance of the entity class C and D an attribute in C, or t is an instance of the role class C and D a resource in C,
4. **NEW**(t,D), in which t is an instance of the entity class C, and D is an entity typed attribute in C, or t is an instance of the role class C, and D is an entity typed resource in C or,
5. $s(t)$ (a (state) atom), in which t is an instance of the entity class C, and s is a state of C,
6. $\neg c$, in which c is an atom, and
7. $c_1 \wedge c_2$ and $c_1 \vee c_2$, in which $c1$ and $c2$ are atoms.

A condition is stateless if it contains no state atoms.

Example 3. An example of a condition is as follows:

DEFIND(id391231,APP.price) $\wedge$ on sale(id391231)

The condition is the combination of two atoms. The price of id391231 has been defined. id391231 is in the state of on sale.

Table 9.8: Role example: developer and developer instance

Developer	Developer Instance
Resources:	ID:id191231
Labor:float	Resource:
Financial:float	Labor: 20.3
Fixed:float	Financial: 32000
Invisible:float	Fixed: 1230000
	Invisible: 31233

9.4.2.7 Activity

Definition 12: Activity. An activity over schema Γ is a tuple $(n, V_{Er}, V_{Ew}, V_{Rr}, V_{Rw}, M, P, E)$, in which $n \in A$ is an activity name, V_{Er}, V_{Ew} are finite sets of variables of entity classes in Γ, V_{Rr}, V_{Rw} are finite sets of variables of role classes in Γ, P is a condition over V that does not contain **NEW**, M is a partial mapping from V_{Er} to V_{Ew}, and E is a conditional effect.

M describes the mapping as which input attributes influenced each output. Considering a sequence of input attributes $xe_1,...,xe_k$ and output attributes $ye_1,...,ye_l$ $(k,l \geq 1)$, $M \in R^{k \times l}$ is a matrix.

$$M_{i,j} = \begin{cases} 1 & \text{if } xe_i \text{ to } ye_j \text{ is a mapping in } M \\ 0 & \text{elsewise} \end{cases}$$

We denote $M(i,j) = M_{i,j}$.

Example 4. In MAP, an example of purchasing an APP is presented in Table 9.9. An entity instance (id391231) is used and two roles, namely id231441, id231357 have participated in this activity. This activity reads the price and sales of the APP as input attributes. It reads the financial resource of the customer and platform as input resources. The mapping relationship is that the sales of the APP influence itself. The precondition consists of three parts:

1. This APP has declared its price.
2. The price of the APP should be smaller than the amount of the customer's money.

Table 9.9: Activity example

Purchasing APP	
Entity:	id391231:APP
Role:	id231441:Customer, id231357:Platform
Read Attributes:	id391231.Price, id391231.sales
Write Attributes:	id391231.sales
Read Resource:	id231441.Financial, id231357.Financial
Write Resources:	id231441.Financial, id231357.Financial
Mapping Relation:	id391231.Sales → id391231.Sales
Precondition:	**DEFINED**($id391231,Price$)∧
	$id391231.Price \leq id231441.Financial$∧
	On sale($id391231$)
Effect:	$id391231.Sales = id391231.Sales+1$∧
	$id231357.Financial = id231357.Financial + id391231.Price$∧
	$id231441.Financial = id231441.Financial - id391231.Price$

3. The APP is in the state of on sale.

There are three effects of this activity:

1. The sales of the APP increases 1;
2. The money of the platform increases;
3. The money of the customer decreases.

9.4.2.8 Rule

Definition 13: Business rule. Given a schema Γ and a set of activities A, a business rule is an expression with one of the following two forms:

- "If ϕ invoke

$$\sigma(xe_1, \dots, xe_k; ye_1, \dots, ye_l; xr_1, \dots, xr_m; yr_1, \dots, yr_n)'', \text{ or}$$

- "If ϕ change state to φ,"

in which ϕ is a condition over variables $xe_1,\dots,xe_k;ye_1,\dots,ye_l;xr_1,\dots,xr_m;yr_1,\dots,yr_n(k,l,m,n \geq 1)$, σ is an activity in A such that $xe_1,\dots,xe_k$ are all entity variables to be read, $ye_1,\dots,ye_l$ are all entity variables to be written, $xr_1,\dots,xr_m$ are all role variables to be read, $yr_1,\dots,yr_n$ are all role variables to be written, and φ is a condition consisting of only positive state atoms over $ye_1,\dots,ye_l$.

9.4.3 Business Process Model Notation for Service Pattern

The BPMN4SP is the extension of BPMN 2.0 [26,27] for better support of SPDL. As mentioned in Table 9.2, there are three major extensions:

1. The entity extends the concept of data object with states. The entity can be created and modified from one state to another and archived at last. The process is the life cycle of the entity. In the model of artifact BP [29], the data with its life cycle is called artifact, and we use the entity instead. The entity class must be declared in the head of BPMN, and entity instances are defined in the process.
2. The participator is replaced by the role in our extension. The essential difference between participator and role is that the role owns resources and takes its resources into the service process to create (promote) values. Instead, the concept of participator cannot distinguish resources and normal attributes.
3. We extend the definition of activity with the reading and writing on the attributes of entities and the resources of roles, respectively.

Table 9.10 provides the detailed extension of BPMN4SP on BPMN.

Table 9.10: BPMN4SP extends BPMN

	BPMN2.0		BPMN4SP	
	Description	**Attributes**	**Description**	**Extended attributes**
Data object	Basic data object for processes		Replaced by entity	
Entity			Data attributes and states	Attributes, states
Participant	Partner entity or partner role	Name, processRef, partnerRoleRef, partnerEntityRef, interfaceRef, participantMultiplicity, endPointRefs	Replaced by role	
Role			Roles and its resources	Resources
Resource			Available source of wealth	
Task	Atomic activity	Name, isforcompensation	Replaced by activity	
Activity	Work performed within process	isForCompensation, loopCharacteristic, resources, default, ioSpecification, properties, boundaryEventRefs, dataInputAssociations, dataOutputAssociations, startQuantity, completeQuantity	Work performed within process	Name, readAttributes, writeAttributes, readResouces, writeResources, mapping, preCondition, conditionalEffect
Data object	Basic data object for processes		Replaced by entity	
Entity			Data attributes and states	Attributes, states
Participant	Partner entity or partner role	Name, processRef, partnerRoleRef, partnerEntityRef, interfaceRef, participantMultiplicity, endPointRefs	Replaced by role	
Role			Roles and its resources	Resources
Resource			Available source of wealth	

9.4.4 Case Study

This section discusses the example of MAP in detail. To analyze the value creation of each role in MAP, we format the process, which is presented in Figure 9.18.

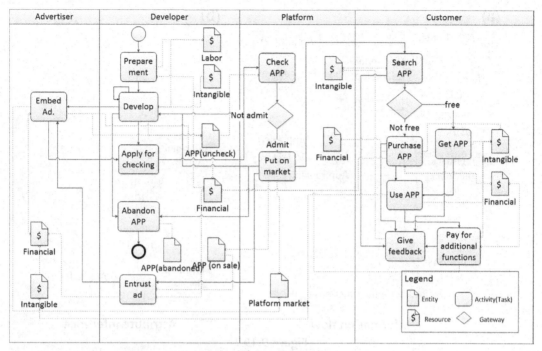

Figure 9.18
The swim lane diagrams of mobile application platform service example.

9.4.4.1 Information flow analysis

With the help of the extraction rule defined in Section 9.4.2, we can extract the *n*-th order attributes from the origin process in Figure 9.18. Figure 9.19 is the second-order attributes analysis result on feedback. Figure 9.19(a) is the information flow for the second-order attributes of feedback, and Figure 9.19(b) is the attributes influence diagram. We can see that feedback is directly influenced by the quality and price, and the feedback has an impact on the sales of APP by the influence of its ranking.

9.4.4.2 Value flow analysis

With the defined resources and roles, the value flow can be extracted from the origin diagram by the extraction rule defined in Section 9.4.2.8. Figure 9.20 presents the value flow of the MAP.

To quantitatively analyze the value flow of each role, we study the value flow of the advertiser. The value creation process can be divided into three parts.

- The investment phase is the first step. The advertiser uses 10 to buy fixed resources, 500 to employ programmers, and 30 to pay the advertising fee to the developer. The relative value of financial resource is $(-10) + (-500) + (-30) = -540$ now.

(a)   **(b)**

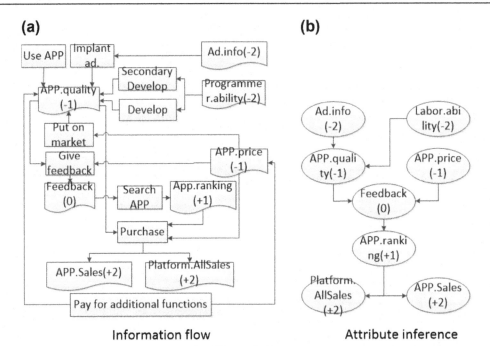

Information flow   Attribute inference

Figure 9.19
The second-order attributes information flow of feedback.

- The creation phase is the second step. The advertiser designs the advertisement and implants it into APP. In this step, 5 of 10 fixed resources and all 500 labor resources are used. The value promotion from the APP is 50. So the relative intangible resource is now $500 + 5 + 50 = 555$.

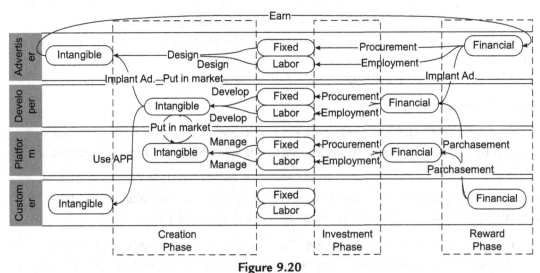

Figure 9.20
The value flow of four roles in mobile application platform.

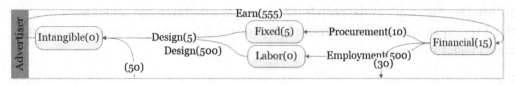

Figure 9.21
Advertiser value flow.

- The reward phase is the last step. The advertiser converts the value of the advertisement (555) to income. The financial resource is now $-540 + 555 = 15$.

After performing the three steps, we can see that the labor and intangible resources are not changed, but the financial and fixed resources increased. The last result is depicted in Figure 9.21. With the help of the value flow, we can now understand that the advertiser earns by such a process, and the return on investment is $(15 + 5)/(10 + 500 + 30) = 3.7\%$. The discussion on how to calculate each resource changing with the influence of activities and how to re-allocate the resources to get a higher return are beyond the scope of this section. It will be presented in a future study.

We have studied 62 enterprises from 355 public companies in the Growth Enterprise Market (GEM) in China and analyzed their service pattern [30]. The GEM is the second-board market, which is very similar to the NASDAQ Stock Market. We have extracted six types of service patterns: long tail service pattern, multiplatforms service pattern, free service pattern, secondary innovation service pattern, unbundling service pattern, and systematic service pattern.

9.5 Summary

The competition in the area of the modern service industry is becoming a focal point of the world's economic development. Service computing, which provides flexible computing architectures to support the modern service industry, has emerged as a promising research area. With the prevalence of cloud computing, more and more modern services are deployed in cloud infrastructures to provide rich functionalities. The number of services and service users are rapidly increasing. The issues in service computing become too large-scale and complex to be effectively processed by traditional approaches. This chapter first introduced the concept of crossover services and complex service computing. Then we analyzed three challenges of complex service computing. Then we introduced three of our studies on overcoming the above challenges. The study on tagging data service mining is a solution to use the big data generated in services. The study on service selection for mobile service composition is an example of service computing in complex environments. The study on a service pattern model is an innovation on service management. Above all, as the prevalence of service computing and information technology expand, the issues of service computing will become more complex and new research topics will emerge.

References

[1] L. Chen, L. Hu, Z. Zheng, J. Wu, Wtcluster: utilizing tags for web services clustering, in: Proc. of the Ninth International Conference on Service Oriented Computing (ICSOC), Springer, 2011, pp. 204–218.

[2] K. Elgazzar, A.E. Hassan, P. Martin, Clustering WSDL documents to bootstrap the discovery of web services, in: International Conference on Web Services, IEEE, 2009, pp. 147–154.

[3] R. Nayak, Data mining in web service discovery and monitoring, Int. J. Web. Serv. Res. 5 (1) (2008) 62–80.

[4] W. Liu, W. Wong, Web service clustering using text mining techniques, Int. J. Agent-Oriented Softw. Eng. 3 (1) (2009) 6–26.

[5] M.F. Porter, An algorithm for suffix stripping, Program 14 (3) (1980) 130–137.

[6] K. C, W. G, Inverse document frequency (IDF): a measure of deviations from Poisson, in: Proc. of the ACL Third Workshop on Very Large Corpora, Springer, 1995, pp. 121–130.

[7] R.L. Cilibrasi, P.M.B. Vitnyi, The Google similarity distance, IEEE Trans. Knowl. Data. Eng. 19 (3) (2007) 370–383.

[8] B. Sigurbjrnsson, R. van Zwol, Flickr tag recommendation based on collective knowledge, in: Proc. of the 17th International Conference on World Wide Web (WWW), ACM, 2008, pp. 327–336.

[9] S. Tekinay, B. Jabbari, Handover and channel assignment in mobile cellular networks, J. Commun. Mag. IEEE 29 (11) (1991) 42–46.

[10] D.B. Johnson, D.A. Maltz, Dynamic Source Routing in Ad hoc Wireless Networks[M]//Mobile Computing, Springer, 1996, 153–181.

[11] L. Zeng, B. Benatallah, A.H.H. Ngu, M. Dumas, J. Kalagnanam, H. Chang, QoS-aware middleware for web services composition, J. Softw. Eng. IEEE Trans. 30 (5) (2004) 311–327.

[12] F. Glover, Future paths for integer programming and links to artificial intelligence, J. Comput. Oper. Res. 13 (5) (1986) 533–549.

[13] R.V. Rao, V.J. Savsani, D.P. Vakharia, Teaching-learning-based optimization: a novel method for constrained mechanical design optimization problems, J. Computer-Aided Des. 43 (3) (2011) 303–315.

[14] Genetic algorithms and their applications, Proceedings of the Second International Conference on Genetic Algorithms[M], Psychology Press, 2013.

[15] M. Tang, L. Ai, A hybrid genetic algorithm for the optimal constrained web service selection problem in web service composition, in: [C]//Evolutionary Computation (CEC), 2010 IEEE Congress on, IEEE, 2010, pp. 1–8.

[16] Z. Ye, X. Zhou, A. Bouguettaya, Genetic Algorithm Based QoS-Aware Service Compositions in Cloud Computing[C]//Database Systems for Advanced Applications, Springer Berlin Heidelberg, 2011, 321–334.

[17] H. Jiang, X. Yang, K. Yin, S. Zhang, J.A. Cristoforo, Multi-path QoS-aware web service composition using variable length chromosome genetic algorithm, J. Inform. Technol. 10 (1) (2011) 113–119.

[18] M. Clerc, Particle Swarm Optimization[M], John Wiley & Sons, 2010.

[19] S. Wang, Q. Sun, H. Zou, F. Yang, Particle swarm optimization with skyline operator for fast cloud-based web service composition, J. Mob. Netw. Appl. 18 (1) (2013) 116–121.

[20] G. Kang, J. Liu, M. Tang, Y. Xu, An effective dynamic web service selection strategy with global optimal QoS based on particle swarm optimization algorithm, in: [C]//Parallel and Distributed Processing Symposium Workshops & PhD Forum (IPDPSW), 2012 IEEE 26th International, IEEE, 2012, pp. 2280–2285.

[21] H. Yin, C. Zhang, B. Zhang, Y. Guo, T. Liu, A hybrid multiobjective discrete particle swarm optimization algorithm for a SLA-aware service composition problem, J. Math Probl. Eng. 2014 (2014).

[22] D. Dasgupta, K. KrishnaKumar, D. Wong, M. Berry, Negative Selection Algorithm for Aircraft Fault Detection[M]//Artificial Immune Systems, Springer Berlin Heidelberg, 2004, 1−13.

[23] X. Zhao, Z. Wen, QoS-aware web service selection with negative selection algorithm, Knowl. Inf. Syst. 40 (2) (2013) 349−373.

[24] S. Deng, L. Huang, Y. Li, J. Yin, Deploying data-intensive service composition with a negative selection algorithm, Int. J. Web. Serv. Res. 11 (1) (2014) 76−93.

[25] C. Barreto, V. Bullard, T. Erl, J. Evdemon, D. Jordan, K. Kand, et al., Web Services Business Process Execution Language Version 2.0 Primer, OASIS Web Services Business Process Execution Language (WSBPEL) TC, OASIS Open, 2007.

[26] S.A. White, Business process modeling notation, Version 1.0, May 3, 2004. www.bpmn.org.

[27] S.A. White, Process modeling notations and workflow patterns, Work Handb. 2004 (2004) 265−294.

[28] K. Bhattacharya, C. Gerede, R. Hull, R. Liu, J. Su, Towards formal analysis of artifact-centric business process models, in: Business Process Management, Springer, 2007, pp. 288−304.

[29] D. Cohn, R. Hull, Business artifacts: a data-centric approach to modeling business operations and processes, Bull. IEEE Comput. Soc. Tech. Comm. Data Eng. 32 (3) (2009) 3−9.

[30] Z.H. Wu, X.B. Wu, M.M. Yao, Business Model Innovation of Modern Service Company a Value Network Perspective, 1st ed., Science Press, Beijing, 2013.

CHAPTER 10

JTang Middleware Platform

Chapter Outline

10.1 Overview of JTang

The software industry works as a country's basic strategic industry, which occupies an important position and role in the economic and social development of the country. Throughout the development of the global software industry, 2000s has seen a steady improvement in industrial sectors and also the trend of accelerated growth. One of the main reasons for the boosting in software industry is that middleware technology has been widely accepted and adopted.

Middleware has been regarded as one of the key components in fundamental software area, with operating systems and databases. It is located on the operating system, the network, and the database. It also works beneath the application tier, which hides the complexity of software structures and provides a unified development and runtime environment for the upper applications. Therefore, it can quickly help users build complex software applications with flexibility and efficiency. The last 10 years have seen a rapid development in middleware technology. It has transformed from early single type (messaging middleware, data access middleware, object middleware, etc.) to complex large-scale middleware. There are a variety of integrated middleware platforms, which are provided by many well-known middleware vendors, such as BEA, IBM, Oracle, and SAP.

The essential of a software platform is to partition complex systems into several tiers, which is to find the right midpoint between standardization and personalization. Currently, the middleware platform is the fundamental part of a national technology plan. In general, middleware platform software has two basic elements: one is to support the environment, and the other is to develop systems. The former part provides conditions for the development of application software and operating systems. The latter provides a range of basic tools for software management. Middleware software has been chosen as a fundamental supporting platform to accelerate the pace of software development and improve software reliability.

The JTang middleware software platform is developed in the background of the service-oriented research and development of the modern service industry. It was supported by China's "eleventh five-year" plan, a major project that was to support one of the topics in the "modern service support system and common technology demonstration project." The result is aimed at boosting modern service e-commerce, logistics, electronic finance, digital tourism, digital education, digital communities, and digital media sectors. During the eleventh five-year program, the JTang middleware platform was adopted in finance, securities, public services, e-government, e-commerce and industry, and other fields. In 2008, Zhejiang University worked with Hangzhou National Software Industry Base Co. and Alibaba Network Technology Co., Ltd, and 13 units to launch a JTang platform software industry alliance in Hangzhou, which aims to further expand the industrial impact of the JTang middleware platform.

10.2 Platform Architecture

The JTang modern services-oriented middleware platform is a large, integrated middleware platform software, including pond-based application servers, a service computing component library, and an integrated development environment with an integrated management console consisting of four parts. Its overall architecture structure is shown in Figure 10.1.

10.2.1 Basic Application Server

The JTang basic application server is a lightweight J2EE application server that provides object middleware, reliable messaging services, container security, object/relational

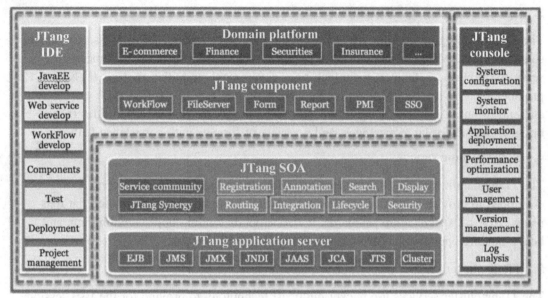

Figure 10.1
JTang middleware platform architecture.

mapping, and other basic services. It provides the basis for the calculation of the upper component library services and a variety of industry software components operating environments, following the introduction of the base application server, consisting of several core modules.

1. Micro-kernel services

The JTang micro-kernel is the core of the application server startup process, which is primarily responsible for the entire application server loading the system modules (registration, start, stop, cancel) and deploying the J2EE applications (EAR, EJB, WAR). The micro-kernel services uses inversion of control technology to achieve the dynamic loading of components among the application server modules.

2. JTang EJB container

The JTang EJB container is the basis for enterprise-class application server object middleware to provide transparency and security, transaction services, such as support for distributed enterprise-class Java object running calls. Compared with the widely used EJB application server, the JTang EJB container provides support for multiple network transport protocols (RMI, Socket, SSL, Http, IIOP, Https, etc.). Also it performs optimization and usability EntityBean, which integrates new object-relational mapping technology and other key features.

3. JTang messaging middleware

The JTang messaging middleware is consistent with Sun's JMS1.1 (Java Message Service) standardization. Messaging middleware provides reliable, high-performance messaging services for business, finance, manufacturing, government, and other sectors. It also provides security (user authentication authorization, message encryption and authentication) scalability (using interceptor technology), distributed capabilities (news bridge), support for large messages, and a variety of formats with persistence features.

4. JTang naming service

The JTang naming service is designed for a JTang-based application. Its server is developed to provide a lightweight naming service, through the use of a stored flat tree using JNDI 1.2 specification standards. It also supports binding objects, unbinding, and heavy-binding operation, and ensures stable and efficient features.

5. JTang cluster service

The JTang cluster services use packet multicast technology to provide for the EJB session bean. The session bean, load balancing, and other types of cluster services provide higher performance through a simple increase in the number of hardware servers.

6. Container security services

Based on the Java Authentication and Authorization Service authentication and access control system, this system provides secure authentication and authorization mechanisms. It achieves Java Authorization Contract for Containers declarative rights management, making the EJB module object access method the declared rights management, thereby providing fine-grained access control.

10.2.2 Service Computing Component Library

The JTang services computing library provides technical services for the calculation of basic components, tools, and methods, including visualization community service, enterprise service bus (ESB), messaging service component, file service components, portable management interface (PMI) security service component, process management services components, single sign-on service components, forms service components, and reporting services components.

1. Visualization services community

The JTang visualization community service provides an intuitive and convenient services organization and management component, improves service registration, offers classification services, and provides retrieval and efficiency operations. It provides a service management framework based on an Eclipse plug-in development technology, with full service registration, discovery, management and user management, category management, and other functions.

2. Message service component

The JTang message system works between service components using the service computing environment. The system provides news releases, news subscriptions, messaging, events, matching, event routing, and other functions, with loosely coupled and scalable features. It also supports efficient interaction with the news service system.

3. Distributed enterprise service bus

The JTang distributed ESB follows the Java Business Integration 1.0 specification, which is to provide business services to achieve integration of heterogeneous information systems based on the service-oriented architecture-based communications platform integration. The proposed container enterprise service bus (ESB container) operating in the platform concept designs and implements a fully distributed ESB engine, which provides integration reliability and throughput.

4. Distributed file storage service component

The JTang distributed file storage service component provides a distributed file storage service for the e-government and e-commerce requirements of massive document data. Based on a series of multisource downloading technology, virtual directory provides high-performance heterogeneous distributed file storage service, system backup and recovery, storage encryption, full-text search, and a series of back-office services.

5. PMI security service component

The JTang security services PMI is an enterprise-level rights management component that provides authentication and accesses control systems and other security-related applications. This component introduces grid technology, distributed architecture to improve the efficiency of system access privileges constrained by simplifying the mechanism, the use of Lightweight Directory Access Protocol (LDAP) data storage, and enterprise-class authority on request.

6. Process management service components

The JTang process management services is a generic process management system that provides Eclipse platform-based process design, process execution and process monitoring, and other functions, which can speed up the processing of business processes, increase productivity, and improve efficiency levels of the organization. The system proposes a service flow concept, the definition of support services, references, bindings, and combinations of a variety of ways to support third-party application integration and staff organization integration.

7. Single sign-on services component

The JTang single sign-on service is a single sign-in service component that can simplify access to different computing environment services and systems designs. This component provides a single point of landing multimode support for desktop applications, providing automated, unified, and secure login web services and also applications to improve the efficiency of development and access to complex distributed service systems.

8. Forms services components

The JTang forms services component provides automatic generation and deployment of electronic forms, information collection, and processing functions. The component supports Dreamweaver plug-in development and Eclipse plug-in development in two ways through the WYSIWYG visual customization form to simplify and speed up the modern service industry software required for data collection with the user interface design process.

9. Reporting services components

Reporting services is a set of network protocols. The JTang service components provide report design and deployment. They print through network report design components, providing convenient services for all types of industry report output software. This component uses B/S architecture. It supports dynamic selection of a variety of statistical chart types and a variety of report output formats, such as images, PDF files, and other Flash files.

10.2.3 Integrated Development Environment

The JTang integrated development environment works on the application server. JTang service computing components include JBuilder and the Eclipse integrated development environment, providing service components, and application software from modeling, designing, and development. It supports running and managing the necessary technical methods, in addition to tool support. Through this development environment, application software development and application integration using Unified Modeling Language (UML) modeling tools can provide the required environment, and model-driven (MDA) tools can be used to achieve application requirement descriptions, along with an automatic and semiautomatic code generation software system. It takes advantage of the service component development tools to allow someone to develop his own service components and do any necessary debugging and deployment. It takes advantage of the service package tools, services component assembly tools gray box, black box assembly tools for on-demand application assembly, deployment, and operation and dynamic tracing and debugging, thus speeding up the modern service industrial application software development.

10.2.4 Integrated Management Console

The JTang integrated management console is a web browser-based middleware platform. It supports configuration, monitoring, maintenance, and other functions in an integrated set of management tools that provide a platform for configuration, application deployment, performance monitoring, performance optimization, log management, security management, version management, and other management functions. The web application can help users to quickly and easily manage the JTang middleware platform, monitoring the operation of the platform and deploying a variety of external applications.

10.3 JTang Development Environment for Service Components

Compared with traditional binary components such as EJB and CORBA, service components provide functionalities with greater granularity, more independence, and a higher level of abstraction. How to design, develop, assemble, and manage service components in an agile way has become an important issue for a distributed computing software system structure. The JTang service component development environment provides UML service component modeling, code conversion, source-level Java component visual assembler, and service component lifecycle management. It includes MDA service component development tools, assembly tools, and services component library services.

Based on the concept of model driven, the JTang service component development environment provides user demand modeling and code conversion functionality. As a result, users do not need to be concerned with the code itself, but rather can focus on the requirement modeling. The service component assemble toolkit manages tools into the gray box and black box. The former box focuses on invasive methods, which provides a graphic way to achieve fine-grained service components assembler. The latter tool supports an encapsulation mechanism identifying the differences between the heterogeneous components, and also it provides graphic assembly methods, along with authentication and assembly models. Service component library management tools support semantic technology to provide registration services for different types of components, deployment, and other routine maintenance functions.

10.3.1 Model-Driven Development of Service Components

Based on MDA technology, the service component development method can, to some extent, simplify the work for developers. It only creates a platform-independent model, and then automatically converts to code through the model, thus completing the development work.

In the JTang service component development environment, the service component development toolkit uses a MDA service to provide a complete set of service components for functional transition from model to code through Eclipse plug-ins. It composes using UML tools, resources, tools, and MDA libraries form the core of the engine. First, the UML design tool supports UML2.0 standards to the MDA standard UML modeling process design models and adds a reference to the archives of MDA. MDA-related information is transferred to the design process. Second, the main components of the repository are responsible for storing PIM tools to provide a variety of functional MDA engineering project management. Finally, the MDA core engine consists of three parts: including the translation library, metafacade library, and template engines. The translation library, primarily Object Constraints Language, queries into various forms of language under this component and is mainly responsible for the conversion of the PIM model constraints content. The metafacade library contains metadata for each platform to achieve, a template engine configuration, and implementation cartridge script, a template based on the template's engine encapsulation technology, combined with model transformation rules metafacade objects, and ultimately generates a technology platform-specific model of products.

10.3.2 Assembling Service Component

Based on the fine-grain development method, the service component assembly method is a direct way by which service members have used r for the rapid development of large-grained granularity of service members. The JTang service component development environment offers two different services component assembly methods: gray box and black box assembly. In general, the study of the service component assembly technology research services component assembly mechanism is based on the service component model, including the source code level assembly and component object-based service interoperability level assembly operation. According to the degree of openness, assembling service components can be classified into three categories: the white box assembly technology, the gray box assembly technology, and the black box assembly technology.

- White box assembly: The white box, which has visibility to all the implementation details of the reuse of service components, is visible. Using the white box assembly method, developers understand the service component; the service component is modified as needed; and then the service component assembly is created. From the service component reuse perspective, the presence of the white box assembly can only be temporary and partial; one can freely modify the software, but it does not allow for reusable service components with a true sense of the product. This limitation restricts the flexible reuse and the completeness of performance.

- Black box assembly: This method does not require the implementation details of the service member. Also, the service member does not need to understand configuration. Application developers assemble reusable service components to obtain the implementation of the system. Developers need to understand the external interface of the service member, without understanding the internal implementation of the service component assembly in the best way.
- Gray box assembly: Between "black box" and "white box," the gray box assembly is the hot spot of service technology. In general, the gray box service members are not allowed to modify the source code directly, but provide a service component behavior that can be modified to extend the language or programming interface. Currently, the research gray box assembly method focuses on methodological framework-based linker-methods and veneers based on respect. The gray box assembly method is able to achieve the flexibility of the service component assembly and is not too complicated.

The JTang service component development environment supports the black box and gray box assembly methods in two ways. The former service members on the proposed preassembled components with a consistent service description specification package, and component assembly may understand the external interface black box service components through the specification and thus be assembled; while the latter uses the intrusive thoughts assembler to achieve a service component assembly at the source code level. This approach does not require modifying the source code and is not limited to a specific programming language, which allows it to achieve a better level of service components assembly code.

10.3.3 Service Component Library

The service component library service system supports rapid development and deployment of a service member management tool, which contains a series of highly multiplexed service member capabilities. By reusing the service component library, service members can quickly customize, develop, and build business applications, which greatly improve the level of software reuse, and improve the development efficiency of the services of the system. Existing large general service components provide applications for a variety of management systems, which are used more commonly in faceted classification management. It can greatly improve retrieval efficiency, but can also help users understand complex service members and target areas. However, with the complexity of the business services component reuse member extending from the base service component, retrieving the appropriate service components from a traditional library service component becomes particularly difficult. Therefore, the design becomes increasingly important based on a high degree of automation within the semantic service component library. JTang service component library management tools use semantic technology to service members. It supports not only an increase in the basic components of semantic information in the service, but also the service member's functional, behavioral, and semantic annotation fields. After the service members are fully semantic, a high precision and recall rate of retrieval are expected.

JTang service component library management tools are an important part of the JTang service component development environment, which provides a service member registration, classification, search functions, and user access control capabilities, support for distributed database management, and application service components. Users can easily access these through the web service component library, registration, retrieval service member, audit, etc. To support the rapid development of the service system, users can register service components through Eclipse plug-ins, download and deploy the service member to a current workspace, and make a service component assembly.

10.4 JTang Distributed File Storage Service

Computer technology has undergone considerable change through decades of development. The mainstream of applications is to compute into pan-computing applications, especially in service-oriented information. This change requires the computer to maintain a CPU as the center stage in memory, to enter an I/O issue, in a particular storage system as the center stage. In this environment, how to efficiently store huge amounts of data has become a hot topic for current computer application services. For this purpose, the need for a large-capacity and high-speed distributed storage system came into being. Distributed storage systems, the basic service content stored on multiple machines, use a small storage space on multiple machines to form a unified huge storage space.

The JTang distributed file storage service provides distributed mass storage files and supports large-scale concurrent access. With a file server-based service content stored on multiple machines, it allows for the use of multiple machines on a small storage space to form a unified huge storage space.

It is optimized for file access, allowing a file to be accessed and distributed across multiple machines, so that there can be access to a file at the same time, and allowing distribution to multiple machines to improve file access performance. By supporting distributed storage and load-balancing technology, JTang distributed file server storage systems can achieve optimal performance. It also provides users with a unified view and is stored independently of the underlying storage structure, so the user can manipulate files on the server as the operation of the local copy.

10.4.1 Architecture

JTang distributed file storage services architecture can be divided into three main components: the main server (master server), file block storage server (from the server/slave server), and client.

- Master server

  The master server primarily takes responsiblity for metadata management. Metadata includes the name space mapping file to the file data blocks and data blocks to the file server from the map or the like. In the system, there is one and only one master server. The main function of the primary server includes:

  - Request listeners: Includes the event listener requests from the client and the server. Client events include namespace to create, delete, create files, write, read, delete, and rename the file list to information, access to resources, lock, release, and so on. From the server-side, events include heart rate information, file data block information, error messages, and so on.
  - Request processing: Mainly responsible for handling the request and the results returned from listening for the event.
  - Metadata management: Metadata here mainly refers to the name space and file data files to mapped data blocks to block file mapping from the server.
  - Name space management: The system uses the directory structure on the way to the tree namespace management.
  - File management: Includes the basic operations on files, which are create, append write, delete, and rename.
  - File data block management: The main block is creating a new file, copy, remove invalid and orphaned files, recovery block, and file blocks.
  - Server load balancing: Due to a large number of file blocks written, loading balance will result in the deletion of each file block from the uneven distribution between servers, so there is a need for file blocks from the server load-balancing operations.
  - Lease management: The client has a lease management, including lease acquisition and release; if the client's lease expires, this should be recycled.
  - Heartbeat: Reporting periodically from the server load through own heartbeat information to the master server.
- Server side

  Server side is responsible for managing the file blocks I/O operations. Based on the master server command, file data blocks can create, delete, and copy operations. The server functions include:

  - Management block information: There may be thousands of data in block from the server; at any time there may be any one of a block of data to operate, so to ensure these blocks go to the centralized management, one uses a high data block information storage structure.

- Read and write data blocks: A client will frequently read and write operations to the data block from the server. Data block read and write operations are performed for the flow. Write data blocks performed during the backup operation should block the operation.

- Transfer data block: Data block transfer operations between servers are very frequent. When the backup operation writes data blocks, data blocks are created from data transmission between the server blocks. The same operation is also performed for the current operation.

- Sending a heartbeat message to the master server: The master server determines whether a heartbeat message from the server is working properly.

- Deal with the main server command information: The system is running, the server will notify the primary backup files from the server block, and then delete or perform a migration operation.

- Report to the master server file information block: Because of file blocks from the server, changes will occur. The main server regularly reports such information to the master server as the latest piece of information.

- Processing customer requests: System interaction is ultimately controlled by the client and the server from the interaction, such as read and write operations of data blocks. So you want to build an interface from the client and server interaction.

- Client
The client provides documentation for the application end user interface, including the creation of the document, append, read, and delete operations. It is the primary server for sending a command from the server to provide services. Client features include:

  - Directory management: Including the new directory, renaming the directories, and deleting the directories.

  - Document management: Including basic file operations, such as uploading files, appending files, renaming files, deleting files, and downloading files.

  - Data streams: When a client uploads to the local file system, creates a file system to the output stream. When the client downloads the files onto the local system, creates a system to read from the input stream.

  - Resource lock operation: A major resource lock and release resource to get the lock.

10.4.2 File Data Block Storage Management Mechanism

When storing file data blocks, you need to ensure the reliability and data integrity, while the block by copying files is to prevent accidental loss of data. For deleted files, these are files of data blocks for garbage releases of the corresponding storage space.

1. File block data check

Because the components of the system may contain hundreds of thousands of units from the server disk, disk corruption frequently occurs in the case of reading and writing data, resulting in the destruction of the integrity of the data. Therefore, discovering each of the corrupted data from the server will provide a check and a way through the data. Although it is possible to recover from the other by a backup file on the server data block, a file comparison operation is clearly unrealistic. Based on the above considerations, the server must be verified by the integrity of the file and block data. Each 64-KB data system generates a 32-bit checksum and stores it to a local file.

When a client or other data reads data from the server, they will first be verified to be read to ensure that no data will be returned damaged. Once an error occurs during verification, the error message is returned to the requesting client, and it is reported to the main server. After the requesting client receives an error message, it will be copied to another file to read the data block and block the main server from recopying the file. When a new generation of file blocks occurs, it will then inform the damaged files from the server to delete the block.

In the spare time of the server, one can create a new master file server backup block. Because these pieces are rarely accessed files, they will probably be damaged if the primary data server is not aware of it; therefore, scanning from the server and verifying the operation of file blocks can help to further ensure data integrity.

2. Copy of file block

The main server has a single copy of the management in which the thread exists, the thread maintains a queue of file block information that needs to be copied, which is stored in the queue. Cloning manage threads simultaneously manage multiple copies of threads; the number of copies of threads can be configured by the configuration file. A thread will be sent a copy of the management task (to be cloned file block) under each copy of the copy task execution file blocks.

A copy of the queue is a priority queue, the master server based on multiple factors to assess the priority of file blocks and to determine the priority of those files that will be a copied block. Among them, the factors are evaluated, including the file block, the remaining number of copies, if the file block has a client waiting to read and write, and if the file block damaged several copies of the file block in the past period that need to be read and written.

Users can configure the weight of each of the above factors and, according to their weights, set a copy management priority thread to calculate each file block. Generally, only one copy of the file's remaining blocks is assigned the highest weight, and the client would wait for additional writing file blocks.

Copying the files into the queue blocks can also remove them as a monitoring thread. The reason could be that the file blocks are located from the server back to normal, so there is no need to continue to copy resources and waste systems. For a copy of the failure of file blocks to be generated, manage threads will reduce its priority waiting to allow later scheduling to try again.

When a file is deleted, the operating system will immediately record it in the log file. However, the system does not immediately delete the file, but the file will be renamed through a special mark. These files in the system will be marked with a special regular scan; if the file has exceeded a preset period (such as 24 h, you can set this up in the configuration file), the system will actually delete the file. In this period, the file can still be accessed via the special file name; if you want to restore the file, you simply need to change the file name.

The system in the scanning process will block those orphaned files (files that do not belong to any file block) for recycling and delete their information. A report to the master server file information block from the server will have its own heartbeat information, while the main server will move those files back to the isolated pieces of information and will be the last block to delete these files from the disk on the server.

A garbage collection mechanism to ensure the consistency of the file has a very important role. In large-scale distributed file systems, a wide variety of hardware failure may frequently occur. For example, when you create a file block from the server and it suddenly fails, resulting in only part of the file block being written, the master server does not record the document information; when you delete a file block, it may also lead to a network failure, which will not receive the news from the server, like a hardware failure, as this would lead to inconsistent data throughout the system. By using the garbage collection mechanism, data consistency problems can be solved. A garbage collection system is a relatively idle thread that only runs as needed; in addition, the file system provides a delay file delete function that ensures that in the case of an accidental deletion you can still be able to ensure a fast recovery time.

10.4.3 Multifile Replication Management

Management strategy can copy multiple files to improve the availability and reliability of the system. Copies of documents pose a problem of management. Copy management can be divided into specific forms for the selection and creation and deletion of files and also provide a copy of the maintenance performed. When some data access is peaked (the existing number of copies cannot meet these visits), it is necessary to create a new copy to share the load. Selecting the appropriate strategy to create a copy helps to further improve the availability and performance of the system. This method creates a copy that takes the physical characteristics of the system load nodes, storage space, network status, a copy of the files size, and other factors into account. At the same time, it is necessary to remove some copies from the system; these copies are often of low utilization or long idle time and should be deleted as appropriate. These copies are conducive to the effective use of system space.

Copies of documents relate to the operation of the main selection and generation of copies. Redundant files can improve storage reliability. The relatively high frequency of downloading files can be made redundant, and load-balancing functionality can be achieved through multiple copies. Distributed storage load conditions are mainly controlled by disk space, and CPU utilization network usage. To improve the success rate and access to establish the efficiency of a copy, one should try to select a high-performance node to place a copy of the data.

10.4.4 File Transmission Based on Cache

The file upload and download rate is an important indicator of the decision of the distributed file storage service, and a multithreading and buffer block file transfer-based approach can effectively enhance file upload and download speeds.

- Dynamic buffer management

To improve the efficiency of file storage, the file is received with the data in this buffer. When the buffer is reached, the thread will be in a unified buffer. The data are written to disk. It is important when writing disk thread extraction blocks from the buffer to choose the best one in the full block.

Dynamic expansion of the buffer algorithm generates a default size and number of data blocks in the transmission task; these two values in the file transfer process will change dynamically based on network speed and disk access speed. Each block of data is generated by default. When it is not allocated in memory, a thread is needed to write data. When there is no thread in this block for reading and writing, the data block can be used to mount on the buffer, thereby reducing memory overhead that can create a data block, and improve memory usage.

There are two threads that buffer operations: a writing thread (idle buffer to write data blocks) and a reading thread (when the buffer block buffer is full, it writes the data to disk space; it is also called a disk write thread). Although at the same time there may be multiple threads to write data to a write buffer, one can ensure that only one thread writes to the file.

10.5 JTang Enterprise Service Bus

The ESB is a core component of computing service technologies to provide reliable messaging, service access, protocol conversion, data format conversion, content-based routing, and other functions. It is important to build a service-oriented architecture-based infrastructure for distributed software systems. JTang's distributed ESB provides the foundation for enterprise communications platform integration. Supporting components, which as the service hot deployment, can be configured with an easy-to-deploy, high-stability, and high-reliability service.

10.5.1 Architecture

JTangSynergy contains ESB general features and components, such as communications, interactive services, integration, quality of service, security, service levels, message processing, management and self-government services, modeling, intelligent infrastructure, etc. In addition, it provides the integration of many useful business modeling components, such as the rules engines and workflow engines. When building ESB-based services to facilitate development and maintenance, JTangSynergy uses a distributed architecture and uses the event mechanism to manage and monitor the environment. The architecture is shown in Figure 10.2.

The JTang distributed ESB can be divided into a container, service components, and a custom assembly services set with three major components. JTangSynergy includes several containers (synergy container (SC)), consumers, and service providers in the form of the container components interact. Each container runs on a different Java virtual machine, and you can install any number of components. The main function of the container assembly includes the local management functions, the routing of messages among components (i.e., the service selection), service consumers, and providers, so that the decoupling can be achieved. The underlying messaging between components works through JTangMQ (JTang messaging middleware application server). Meanwhile, SC registration information will also collect information and push the local information to the registry container and to the different components of the container so they can communicate. The SC also contains all the components, making it the ideal management tool for unified management of all components.

10.5.2 Massage Exchange Based on Content Router

In the distributed ESB environment, service providers and components can be deployed on the ESB, which is equipped with a container for any network node, and can interact in the form of a message. The message must be packaged into a formal specification and provide message exchanges through the routing function of the container to complete the transfer between consumers and providers.

The ESB exchanges messages as the core functionality for deployment. It provides reliable interaction mechanisms. The traditional message exchange method commonly uses remote procedure call technology to reduce the complexity of system development. This

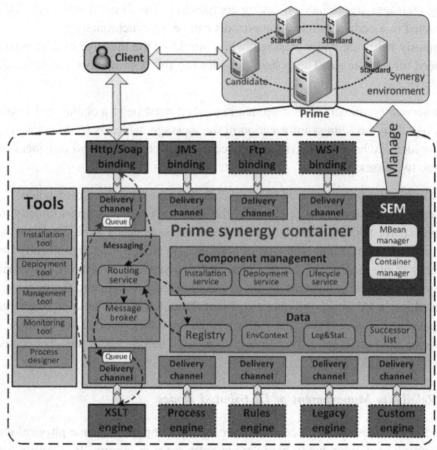

Figure 10.2
JTangSynergy architecture.

technology supports synchronous calls and message exchanges. They work between both sides of the call interface, which are tightly coupled. Currently, a popular message exchange method is to use a message-oriented middleware, which can support synchronous/asynchronous transmission and event-driven architecture news while providing message persistence features.

Message exchange determines the performance of the main factors of a distributed ESB, which uses a simple message-oriented middleware technology that provides a greater impact to the whole system. Two sides exchanging messages are in the same node in a distributed environment. Message-passing performance and the JTang distributed ESB work through a content-based routing message exchange method, which provides a very good fit to solve this problem.

Deploying messages are exchanged among components. The JTang distributed ESB must be constructed in a certain format. Components can be set synchronously or asynchronously when sending a message, while providing the message exchange patterns and the need for persistence. The system provides the ability to receive a message queue for each service.

When the service consumer sends a service request, it must be in a container for routing messages based on the address information in the message, which is set to determine the service provider. Exchange of messages between service consumers and providers can be divided into two cases.

When two components are involved in the exchange of messages in a distributed environment, the message is not required by the JMS servers, but is saved directly to the target service corresponding message queue. If the message needs to be persistent, it is saved to the file system. Using this type of optimization strategy can significantly improve the efficiency of the message exchange. When the two services involved in the exchange of messages are located in different nodes in a distributed environment, the message is encapsulated into a JMS message object and sent through the JMS server to the target service named JMS queue. When the JMS message consumers receive the message, the message is saved to the target service message queue. The process of message persistence is achieved by the JMS server.

10.5.3 Reliability Management of Distributed Nodes

Distributed ESB nodes tend to access their services running on the same physical machine, which may run at any time due to hardware or software stop failures. It therefore becomes important how to ensure that, in the case of a node failure, other nodes are still able to correctly run. After restarting the failed node synchronization, it has to ensure its information is correct, which will reduce the loss of function in the enterprise information system. With the reliability and maintenance methods, the management is good for solving this problem.

- Agent framework

In a distributed computing environment containing nodes for synchronization and remote management, agent nodes work with statistical information to monitor components and service information issues among a broad framework with the use of proxies.

Agent framework uses dynamic proxy technology, the advantage of which is a flexible structure that can facilitate the use of multiple transport protocols and is able to take full advantage of the computing power of the client part of the inspection. In addition, the complex dynamic proxy can adapt to the component environment. When a container

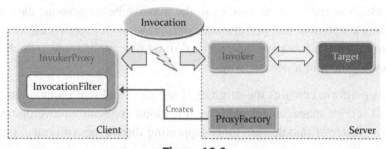

Figure 10.3
Agent framework.

cannot get another component implementation class, dynamic agency will still be able to work properly and ensure the completion of the basic functions.

Agent framework primarily includes the client and server as two key parts.

Client side is responsible for monitoring the receiver for the results of remote call requests and to ensure calls were returned. The server is mainly composed of Invoker and ProxyFactory, as shown in Figure 10.3.

Invoker is responsible for monitoring and handling remote requests to receive and make calls through the Java reflection mechanism, and the results are serialized back to the client.

* ProxyFactory is responsible for the building client agent.
* The client is responsible for calling the serialization and is responsible for checking the reasonableness of the call. Client contains InvokerProxy and InvocationFilter components.
* InvokerProxy is responsible for packaging Invocation and serialized transmitting to a remote server via different transport protocols.
* InvocationFilter is responsible for Invocation. Before being transmitted to the server, the client calls to check the validity.

10.6 JTang-Plus

In recent years, the rapid development in Internet, mobile Internet, and Internet of Things are requiring networks to transform into a software development platform. To address the challenges from the cloud computing and big data management, JTang-plus has been developed by research teams in Zhejiang University based on JTang architecture.

The JTang-plus platform faces the requirements in a variety of novel network applications for cloud services. It provides personalized services, such as application-aware applications, which intend to break hurdles in the massive heterogeneous data process, complex systems adaptation, and performance optimization. It supports all kinds of computing-intensive, data-intensive, and network-intensive applications, which satisfy application development in a flexible way.

The JTang-plus platform contains the original JTang parts and will include three new parts: the cloud service management platform, the cloud application development platform, and a cluster of middleware tools supporting three types of typical network applications.

10.7 Summary

The JTang middleware platform is a system that supports application development in an agile and flexible way in different industrial sectors. This chapter describes the research background and architecture of the platform. It basically outlined the platform into four components and then focused on the JTang service development environment, JTang distributes file storage services, and JTang distributed ESB. Finally, it showed the future direction of the JTang middleware platform.

Index

Note: Page numbers followed by "f" and "t" indicate figures and tables respectively.